A FEARFUL JOY

A FEARFUL JOY

A Novel by JOYCE CARY

GREENWOOD PRESS, PUBLISHERS
WESTPORT, CONNECTICUT

The Library of Congress has catalogued this publication as follows:

Library of Congress Cataloging in Publication Data

Cary, Joyce, 1888-1957.
A fearful joy, a novel.

I. Title.
PZ3.C25884Fe7 [PR6005.A77] 823'.9'12 73-428
ISBN 0-8371-6777-9

Originally published in 1949
by Harper & Brothers, New York

Reprinted with the permission
of Harper & Row, Publishers, Inc.

First Greenwood Reprinting 1973

Library of Congress Catalogue Card Number 73-428

ISBN 0-8371-6777-9

Printed in the United States of America

To DAVID AND RACHEL CECIL

A FEARFUL JOY

1

EVERYBODY agreed with Mrs. Baskett that her baby was a most remarkable child. They delighted to hear how, exploring the cellar, she ate coal to see how it tasted; how, investigating matches, she set the nursery curtains on fire and nearly burnt down the house. They admired the child's power of uproarious laughter at nothing at all; her shouts of rage, her egotism, her greed; and they went away and said that Tabitha Baskett was after all a very ordinary child, and rather a plain one. They shook their heads over the future of a plain girl with a mother so ill and feeble, a father so erratic.

Dr. Baskett was in fact ruining a good practice by two great errors: he was a little before his time in treatment, and a little behind it in conduct. He loved a convivial evening and a broad story, not improved for the prim by a classical quotation. For the new suburban proprieties all latin was Latin, and anything mysterious was immoral. Baskett, too, like other old Whigs, combined radical politics with a hearty contempt for modern innovation. He was the last doctor in the county to visit outlying patients on horseback; and when he stopped for a quart on the way, the round-barreled roan hitched to the fence would confirm to old ladies the story that he drank. And for old ladies, to say that a man drinks means that he drinks too much. Thus when he refused them the purges they loved, when he declared that all purges were the invention of the devil to poison the human system, they said to themselves that the man was a sot whose brains were destroyed by drink. It was obvious to them that a system without frequent purging is in the same unhealthy state as a house with stopped-up drains; and all the advertisements supported them in this act of scientific imagination.

Dr. Baskett grew poorer and poorer, and at last, after his wife's death, did take to drink. Luckily his eldest son Harry, at twenty-six, was then qualified and able to enter the practice. And young Harry, sobered from childhood by his father's whims, was thoroughly up to date, neither behind nor before. He purged freely, but with the latest irritants, not too new nor too stale, and set up a brougham, which, at a patient's door, raised the self-respect of the whole street. Old Baskett, now over sixty, laughed at Harry and despised him a little as a plodder, a time-server; but the boy was only wanting in imagination, and perhaps on this account was a good son as well as a successful family doctor. He might even have made a fortune, after Frood Green, in 1888, acquired a railway station and became a suburb; but he prevented this by marrying an extravagant wife.

Like many good serious young men who never flirt, he was caught by the first determined young woman who wanted him, and at twenty-eight was already the slave of a house. Also he had killed his father. For the young wife could not stand old Baskett, and managed very quickly to provoke a conflict, in which, of course, she was victorious. The old man, clinging to the dignity of the beaten, made no complaint to Harry, who was bewildered by the whole affair, but withdrew to lodgings, which finished him off in six months.

At this time Tabitha was fourteen, a small thin girl with large, too prominent eyes, a thick mouth, a snub nose, and a heavy clubbed pigtail of brown hair. And she was still remarkable for nothing but a certain violence of ordinariness. Her reports were slightly worse than other moderately stupid girls of her age; she was a little more deeply in love with the music master and the head girl; she was more untidy, more critical, more contemptuous of boys than any of her equals, and more apt to break into uncontrollable giggles in church or at Sunday school.

Her longing for a bicycle, which had then the charm of novelty as well as danger and impropriety, was especially violent, so that envy of a rich and spoilt friend who had one, and who, stealing away upon its saddle from parents and teachers, actually made a practice of visiting London alone, where she had a horrible adventure with a sinister old man in an omnibus, kept her awake at night. When her father, dying of sclerosis of the liver, gave her fifteen pounds to buy a bicycle, and insisted that it should be procured at once, and actually brought to his room for presentation, she could not express her gratitude. She kissed the old man so eagerly that he waved her away, disliking the soft childish lips. He did not much care for children, and he had shown no great kindness for his plain daughter, conceived, probably by accident, in his middle age. What he had always loved was doing what he liked and thwarting cocksure persons who tried, as he put it, to shut up the world in their little tin boxes.

He said to Tabitha, therefore, "I made 'em bring the contraption here, so that I could be sure you'd get it. For if I'd only left you the money in my will, I'll bet you wouldn't have seen a wheel for another five years. Harry and his madam don't believe in bicycles for young misses. Most dangerous and improper. So now go and learn to ride, and if you break your nose or anything more serious, they can blame Papa. It won't worry me after next week."

And by this single act of imagination, or what to Harry and Edith seemed a piece of wanton spite, he secured Tabitha's affection, which he did not want, so entirely that for the first time in her life she prayed with real ardor, imploring, therefore, a real god to give the old man life. And when he died she was in such distress and wept so angrily and noisily in church that Edith Baskett had to take her into the porch and give her a lecture on the proper control of feelings. "It is very selfish of you, Tibby, to give way like this; we are all feeling the same sorrow, but we don't give way. We have more respect for where we are, and more consideration for poor Harry, who really loved his father."

These words, implying truly that Tabitha had not much loved her father, increased the child's misery by an access of remorse, in sobs which, rising from some mysterious depth, exploded under her flimsy ribs with a force which sent the tears hopping from her chin, and her pigtail shifting on her back in convulsions which, by some peculiar sympathy, disintegrated even her dress, so that, in spite of new mourning and a new hat, she appeared not only a wretched little girl with pale cheeks and a red nose, but a shabby and neglected one. Moved by affection for Harry, Tabitha did try to check these outbursts, but with little success, until Harry himself, going home in the brougham, took her upon his knees and urged her to remember that her father was in a happier place than earth and that Christians should not grieve for the dead but only for their own loss. And these words, less by their meaning than by the fact that Harry spoke them, and that they recalled a whole dominion of religious sensations, did give her some relief.

2

TABITHA, although at almost continual war with Harry, was devoted to him because she knew that he was good. She respected the integrity which never tried to catch her affection with bribes, or was moved by her tears. In revenge she hated to weep on account of Harry's reproaches, and being touchy and proud like most children, only a thought more so, she did actually attempt by doing a little serious work at school to avoid further scenes.

As for her religious education, though she furiously resented sermons out of church from an elder brother in a frock coat, her young nerves were so agitated by words like love, truth, goodness, Jesus (not Christ), that even in the routine of Sunday church she would be moved by feelings of penitence and resolutions to be a good noble creature. Indeed, after her father's death, coming just before her fifteenth year, with its sudden concentration of private emotion, she suffered a change of nature. In the struggle with her own spasms from below, she took a loathing for giggles and anything that verged on emotional indulgence, such as love, the latest fashions, face powder, romantic novels. All these she described as silly. And now, grasping for the first time in her life an idea of conduct, she entered with fervor, characteristically a little too much fervor, upon its realization. She became a good deal of a prig, a prude. She went to church on saints' days. At seventeen, as a prefect, she made war upon the silly and the weak. She even denounced bicycles, discovering how wide a door they opened to vicious curiosity and evil freedoms. She was a heroine to mistresses, but little girls did not adore her. She was too formidable, too severe; and though her full height was but five foot two, much larger girls, moving out of her way as she walked across the playground, had the illusion that she could look down on them.

Tabitha had already decided to earn her own living. She was, that is, like her father, a little in advance of her time. But she had strong reasons in Harry's poverty while he was struggling to pull together the relics of his father's practice, and in her hatred of his wife Edith.

Edith—handsome, sensual, rather blowsy, fond of bright colors and rich food, critical, like a woman much loved, of her husband—was exactly the kind of woman to be detested by a young girl full of new ideas and disturbed sensibilities. Tabitha disliked even her beauty, her superiority, as an acknowledged belle of Frood Green, a leader of fashion. "Why must she go to Oxford Street and waste poor Harry's money just to show off?" She could not bear even the sound of Edith's silk petticoats or the scent of her powder.

For six months Tabitha was firmly resolved to be a missionary in China, preferably among the most primitive heathen. But this ambition was suddenly destroyed by the arrival of a missionary to stay at the Cedars, for though he was a hero he was also very severe on the modern girl. The sight of a girl on a bicycle caused him horror and misery, and Edith's cigarettes nearly drove him from the house.

Tabitha, in spite of her austere views on female conduct, instantly detested anyone who should dare to criticize her sex or attempt to deprive them of any of the new liberties. She retorted upon the visitor that she herself rode a bicycle, and why not?

He replied with asperity that bicycles were unsuitable for ladies on grounds that he would rather not particularize to a young girl. Tabitha became very red and burst out, "But what do you mean?—What a perfectly horrible mind you must have." Edith and Harry exclaimed, the parson raised his brows and pursed up his lips, and the girl, rising from the chair, cried, "No, I won't apologize," and instantly left the room. She also gave up the intention of joining a mission, and instead determined to be a pianist. Her music had always been good. Now she began to practice six hours a day, and to everyone's surprise maintained this rule of life for more than a year. She was growing up, and therefore becoming more touchy in the matter of consistency. The idea of the Napoleonic soul which plans its career and carries it out with iron will and unshaken nerve had risen upon her fancy, with all its powerful attraction for energetic minds. She toiled so hard at the piano that Edith was driven nearly mad and Harry was concerned for the child's health.

She herself was often seized with restlessness, with a strange horror for the piano and even for her own beloved room. It was in such a fit one day that, leaning her nose and forehead on the window and gazing at, but not seeing, the spring blossom in the front garden below, she cried out, startling herself, "Oh—oh—oh, if only something would happen!"

3

AT THIS very moment, as on every day during the last week, a young man, smartly, even loudly, dressed in a pepper-and-salt suit with a high collar, a blue bow tie, and a gray bowler tilted over the right brow, came round the corner and raised his eyes, blue like the bow, to Tabitha's window. At the same time he vigorously twirled his shiny yellow cane in his right hand, while with his left, neatly gloved in pearl gray, he gave two upward strokes to the ends of his golden mustache.

Tabitha, though she had seen the young man before, was immensely startled by his apparition now, and especially by his glance. True, he passed at his usual time, half-past nine, but she had not, or believed she had not, noticed the time.

She flew back to her piano, and fell once more to her scales, saying while she executed them with her usual impatience, "Horrible man, if he thinks I went to look at him, he's very much mistaken. And what a fearful cad. I'm not surprised that he was barred at the club."

The young man, called Bonser, has in fact been blackballed from the tennis club on account of various faults. He is a stranger, he has debts; and though he declares that he is only temporarily out of funds, till some law case is decided which will give him a large inheritance, he is for some reason, perhaps because of his personal beauty, not believed.

Tabitha, having met the young man at a subscription dance, and danced with him, since he proves a good dancer, three times, has given little thought to him since. She is too busy with music, so important for her life's work. And now she dismisses him again in a series of brilliant exercises for her left and weakest hand, until two days later he accosts her in High Street.

He takes off his hat with the flourish, so despised by the local young men, and cries, "Miss Baskett, what luck."

"I beg your pardon"—with a very cool glance.

"Thank you for not cutting me."

"I wasn't really noticing."

"You know that people have been tipped off to give me the freezer."

"I hadn't heard—I'm so busy."

"Oh, I knew it wouldn't worry you. Do you know, Miss Baskett, you are about the only person in Frood Green who isn't shocked because I don't go to an office every day?"

"But that's absurd—"

"Isn't it?" He turns to walk beside Tabitha. "But, of course, it's a bit provincial down here—suburban, very middle class, very Frood Green, one might say."

"I like Frood Green, it's a very nice place."

"Of course it is, you live here. What a pleasure, Miss Baskett, to meet a woman of the world."

"What do you mean by that, Mr. Bonser? I've never been out of England in my life, except once, to Boulogne."

"Excuse me if I seem a bit uppish, Miss Baskett, but I've had it rather on my mind. I mean you're not sniffy, you're not stand-offish, you aren't small-minded, you're not—well, not Frood Green." They have reached the middle of High Street, and Tabitha, slightly embarrassed, turns toward the grocers'. "I have to go in here."

"Oh, I say, but Miss Baskett, we must meet. Do you ever go on the common—do you know that little wood?"

"You know I couldn't do that."

"I beg your pardon, what a shocking suggestion."

This, however, is a false move. The girl turns red. "Not because it's shocking, but because I'm too busy." And she goes into the shop.

She is much irritated against Bonser. "What nonsense about women of the world," she thinks; "and what an awful necktie."

4 AND she might have detested Bonser if one morning Edith had not said to her at breakfast, "That young man Bonser seems very fond of staring into your window; and just when you've stopped practicing."

Tabitha feels that her brother, though still eating, has transferred his attention from eggs and bacon to her. Though his jaws continue to chew, the upper part of his face is full of watchful anxiety. And this irritates her.

"Do you mean I look out for him?" she asks angrily.

"No, dear, of course not. But you are a friend, aren't you? You and he are always walking up and down High Street together."

"Never—that is once—and that was only—" Tabitha hesitates, then plunges. "Why shouldn't I talk to a friend in High Street?"

"So he is a friend—well, I'm surprised. That common fellow."

Tabitha turns scarlet. "He may be common, but at least he's not petty—he's not Frood Green!" And she stalks with dignity from the room.

Harry at once seeks her out. "My dear Tibby, of course I know there's nothing really between you and this chap Bonser, but I think you ought to know that he's rather a doubtful character." He uses his best bedside manner with this young sister.

"But what's he done, Harry?"

"Well, for one thing, how does he live? He does nothing; he borrows money even from girls. The fact is, Tibby, he's a dangerous man."

"Dangerous? Oh, Harry, what nonsense. What on earth do you mean?"

"My dear Tib, I've no time to argue; take my word for it, the man is a bad hat, a swindler or worse. I must run—"

"Dangerous!" Tabitha thinks. "But Harry is completely under Edith's thumb, and she is Frood Green from the horrid coarse hair on her head to the horrid soles of her crooked feet."

The next morning, as Bonser passes the front gate of the Cedars, Tabitha wheels her bicycle out of the back. She looks at Bonser as he flourishes his hat with peculiar intensity. She is studying him under the aspect of dangerous.

"Which way are you going?" he asks.

"To town."

He turns round promptly to walk with her. She stops suddenly. "Mr. Bonser, why do you stare at my window?"

"Because if it wasn't for you I should want to cut my throat."

"Oh, what nonsense, you've no right—"

"Honest to God, Miss Baskett. And if you were in my position, cut all round, blackballed—"

"But I never did anything."

"You were kind; you treated me like a human being."

Tabitha is now wheeling her bicycle toward the town. She wants to get away from the windows of the Cedars, and also to hear Bonser. She is resolved to treat him like a human being.

"But what *is* your position?"

And Bonser tells her an extraordinary story: that he is illegitimate, the son of a nobleman of the highest rank and a countess, who, leaving her husband for her lover, took her maid's name and gave it to her son.

"But, Mr. Bonser—" The girl stares at him. "What a very *queer* story."

"Truth is stranger than fiction, Miss Baskett, and it's a terrible story for me. Do you know what it is to be despised, to be called a—excuse the word—bastard?"

"But no one would do such a thing."

"They think it, you are thinking it, and yet you are so good, so brave. I know how much you risk even by speaking to me—your whole social position."

"But really, Mr. Bonser, that's absurd; you mustn't get such ideas. Perhaps the tennis club did treat you rather badly; they're rather snobby."

"No, you don't understand, how could you?—You have friends."

Tabitha is moved almost to tears by the man's despair. She begs him to rise above prejudice, to ignore the meanness of the world. And ten minutes later, under the trees by the cemetery, he is assuring her that she is the only girl he ever loved or could love. His life, his soul, his hope. He kisses her hand, her cheek; and when she starts away from him, he blames himself and cries, "But I forget, I have no right to speak of love to any decent girl."

Tabitha is thus obliged to moderate her indignation, and to reassure the man. "But of course you have the right." She is then kissed again, with more apologies, and goes to her shopping in a state of such confusion and excitement that she orders rice instead of sugar and herrings instead of kippers. She scarcely knows where she is. She thinks, "I don't believe a single word; and he can't really love me—it's *absolute* nonsense!"

But two days later she is standing, on a wet evening, under the archway of the Isolation Hospital, a lonely spot only to be reached by bicycle. She is full of guilt and panic. She thinks, "This is the last time; this can't go on." But Bonser is kissing her, and she says to herself with amazement, "Yes, he really does love me!"

And now her life becomes fantastic, dream-like, and also wildly exciting. She refuses to meet Bonser again; and the very next day she is meeting him in the zoological museum, a small collection left to the town by a former mayor. Here, among stuffed badgers and molting owls, in a smell of mothballs and decayed mummies, he proposes marriage. He seizes her in his arms and cries that he can't wait, he loves her too much. For her he will risk all. They will be married secretly and slip away.

"But why must everything be so secret?"

"No one must even see us together." And he explains that his enemies are always on the watch. They have a court order against him, procured by fraud, and if they catch him they may even put him in jail. "I can't afford a scandal just before my case comes on."

Tabitha tries to fix her mind on this extraordinary situation. Her lips open to ask questions, but Bonser's mouth is at once pressing upon them; her nose is full of dust so that she wants to sneeze; a stuffed Russian bear which towers on her left is tottering as if to fall; and she is terrified that Bonser, on the other side of the narrow corner, will push her through a glass case full of varnished fish; her heart is beating like a mill, her knees are trembling, and when her mind says, "But it must be nonsense, it's simply a most awful lot of lies," all the rest of her is not only indifferent to the criticism, but is irritated by it.

However, she does not say yes. She is prevented by a mysterious inability to form the word. And when Bonser repeats his proposal next day, in a secluded part of the graveyard, she says severely, "Have you told me the whole truth, Dick? Are you sure you aren't hiding anything?"

"Of course I am; and if I told you who my father was you'd understand. It's a—well, call it a political question."

"You don't mean he's royalty."

"What are you laughing at?"

In fact, Tabitha is trying not to laugh. Her whole body is filled with laughter which is not so much incredulous as astonished. She is enjoying this new yarn as a child enjoys a transformation scene at the pantomime. But she is alarmed by the man's indignant glance. "Oh, I'm not laughing at you; how could I?"

"Do you disbelieve my word?"

"Good gracious, no."

But Bonser is offended. He produces documents, a letter from a lawyer, headed Re Bonser Estate, and beginning, "Your claim to the settlement of one hundred thousand pounds (£100,000) is quite complete and all legal except for the one document which we mentioned in our last. But the Spanish nurse has now been traced."

Another is a newspaper cutting: "Bonser Case. The Claimant's Strong Position." Another cutting, purporting to be from a gossip column, refers to "Mr. Richard Bonser, related by, it is said, the closest ties with a very exalted personage indeed."

Tabitha is now overwhelmed with remorse.

"You do forgive me, Dick."

And after a suitable interval, while she confesses her folly and meanness, he forgives her. Delight returns to her with double force. Yes, she will marry him in a registry office; only she will have to tell Harry. Very well, she will not tell Harry till after the ceremony, but she must tell him before she goes away. She won't run away. "That would be mean."

In her own room, with calmer pulses, she asks herself in astonishment, "Do I love him, do I even like him very much? Of course, he is very good-looking. His eyes and hair are much too beautiful for a man; but his character—that's the important thing!" She murmurs at night to the dark, "But it's absolute madness. How can I run off with a man?"

Yet she knows perfectly well that, whatever Bonser is, she is going to run off with him. She can no more withdraw from that adventure than a young boy who has climbed up a high springboard can refuse to dive. And she says to herself with elation, "Yes, it must be love; I'm *fearfully* in love."

5

FIVE days later she is sitting in a double bedroom at a certain rather shabby hotel in Bloomsbury. She has left a note for Harry, but she has not given him an address; and though she wears a ring and is entered in the hotel book as Mrs. Richard Bonser, she is not yet married. The plan, to be married on the way to the hotel, has been upset, so Bonser explains, by some hitch at the registry office. Bonser has now gone to put it right and Tabitha waits for him with a feeling of terror and elation, like that of someone who for the first time jumps out of a balloon with a parachute. She thinks, "But how wicked it all is, how cruel to poor Harry. What will he think when he reads my note?" and she feels no remorse whatever. There is no room for it in the density of her other sensations.

Bonser darts in. He is wearing a new gray suit, even louder than usual, and carries a gray bowler. This suit, and the man's eyes, hair, skin, mustache, figure, manner, gestures, appear so miraculously beautiful, that is to say interesting, to Tabitha that she can't look at anything else. Bonser is in a temper. He tosses his beautiful hat on the bed and cries, "Damn those fools, they say we'll have to wait."

"Darling, do take care of your new hat." The prudent schoolgirl picks up the hat with a gesture which is also a caress. She loves the hat.

"Isn't it a curse, and all because some fool spelt my name wrong. What a good thing we registered as Mr. and Mrs.—we needn't change anything."

Tabitha now begins to take notice. "You mean we can't be married this morning?"

"Not till tomorrow morning."

"But, Dick, what an awful nuisance—I'll have to move."

"That's what I was talking about. How lucky it was that you registered as Mrs. So we needn't move."

"But, Dick, how can I stay, if we're not married? There's not even two beds."

"Well, Tibby, you're as good as married! Come, darling, you're not going to be silly and Frood Green about a little thing like this, are you?"

But Tabitha has been well brought up. It is only after dinner, with champagne, after Bonser has shown that she can't get another room in their hotel, nor anywhere else so late at night, that she yields, and then so coldly, so doubtfully, that the man is much offended. "Dash it all, Tibby, you're not very helpful. Perhaps you've changed your mind. Perhaps you'd like to call it off."

"No, Dick, you know we can't, not now."

"That's what I'm telling you, so cheer up, for God's sake." His air is that of one who bears patiently with female whims. He greets her in the morning with a pinch which makes her cry out, and cries, "Tender little wifie, she's feeling better now."

But Tabitha is still ungrateful. She does not respond to this caress, and as soon as breakfast is over she asks, "When are we going to the registry office?"

"Oh, any time this morning. And that reminds me, can you lend me a few quid? I forgot my checkbook. A tenner would do—it's for the fees."

"But, Dick, I haven't any money, only a few shillings."

"That's all right, you can borrow some. I know a man who'll give you all you want, on what's coming to you."

"What's coming to me?"

"The thousand quid a year you're getting when you come of age."

"But I don't get anything a year. Papa left me five hundred when I'm twenty-one, but nothing more."

"Dammitall, you told me—"

"I never said anything about an income; you asked me about a legacy and I said I would have one from Papa."

Bonser flies into a rage. "I might have guessed it, mightn't I? What a bloody fool to believe anything in Frood Green. Well, I've been nicely diddled, haven't I?"

"So that's why you wanted to run away with me? Do you love me at all, Dick?"

"I like that—after the way you chased me! Who was so keen to get off with who? Tell me that."

"Oh, what a lie, a horrible lie; no gentleman would say such a thing."

"Very well, if you're going to insult me as well, but please to notice that it's not you who's risked his whole future!" And he walks out.

Tabitha is surprised by these words, and especially Bonser's abrupt departure. She feels that there may be other aspects of the quarrel. When after an hour Bonser has not returned, she begins to have a sensation of guilt. She asks herself if perhaps she has not been cold, unkind. An hour later she is ready to weep. After five hours, having eaten neither lunch nor tea, she is thinking, "It's all my own fault. I deserve everything. Yes, I'll kill myself."

At seven o'clock, just when she is wondering if a jump from the fourth story onto a stone pavement will be certainly fatal, Bonser marches in.

Tabitha, from the other end of the room, gazes at him with apprehension, not daring to utter a word. He has in fact a grave, an intimidating air. He says, "I didn't mean to come back, Tibby. Not after the way you've treated me. It's not only that you gave no sign of any real affection; not only that you misled me about the financial position —the money doesn't matter a damn; but that you practically called me no gentleman."

Tabitha throws herself into his arms. "Oh, Dick."

"Ah, I thought perhaps you hadn't realized what you were saying."

"I am a beast, a complete beast."

"Well, if you say so."

Gradually he relents. He allows her to kiss him, to get on his knee, but he does not respond until she is suitably convinced of her guilt.

As for Tabitha, she is eager to show gratitude, tenderness, and, above all, submissiveness. For has she not humiliated and insulted the charmer? And when he consents to have her, she is completely his, body and soul. She feels his goodness, in making concession. To reward him, she is even ingeniously amorous. She shows the perversity of the innocent, of nature itself: eager for the simplest, the most guileless pleasure; and Bonser, delighted, cries, "Why, the little devil!"

Afterwards he reminds her that she mentioned a few shillings in her purse. She is delighted to find that she has nearly a pound, and Bonser shows her where for a pound it is possible to get a good dinner for two, and even a bottle of wine.

Both are in high spirits. Tabitha knows she is loved, Bonser is highly satisfied with his bride. And he assures her that they will be married as soon as he can raise the fees. "I'm sorry we can't do it tomorrow, but of course I didn't expect to be so short."

This hint of his disappointment, renewing Tabitha's guilt, makes her cry, "Oh, Dick, it's not so important, is it, so long as we really know we love each other?"

"That's it, Pops." He kisses her with warm appreciation. "Why, I wouldn't mind if we waited a month, so long as I've got you. For you really are a nice little piece."

6

TABITHA is now so happy that she does not venture to spoil that pleasure by speaking of marriage. Two months later she is still unmarried, but possibly even happier. For she is more at ease. She understands Bonser. She is not alarmed when he swears, or, on the other hand, when he drinks a little too much and becomes boisterous. And as she manages him, encourages him, she says to herself with wonder, "What a child I was only three months ago. I'd no idea what life was like."

She has one big anxiety. Bonser has found only a temporary post in a partnership with a friend. The two have co-operated in a bullion deal, the sale of a gold block to a farmer who, knowing something of economics, has a deep distrust of banks. This transaction has yielded a large profit. But now the partnership is dissolved and the money spent.

Bonser, as Tabitha has discovered, is a free spender. As he says himself, "I've always been generous with money. It's in the blood, I suppose. Money is dirt to a real nob; he just can't take it seriously." But for the moment he cannot pay his hotel bill. Luckily, after a few days' anxiety, he has a letter from his uncle, the Duke of E., asking him to bring Tabitha and to stay a week at Horton Towers. He shows this to the manager, asks that a room shall be retained against his return, deposits one trunk in the baggage room, pays his bill with a check, and leaves with Tabitha, one other trunk, and their light luggage, in a cab.

But to Tabitha's surprise he changes on the way from Euston to Waterloo, and takes tickets for Brighton, where he finds rooms in a back-street lodging house.

"But, Dick, I thought we were going to stay with your uncle."

Bonser grins at her. "A change of plan, Popsy; we're stopping here for a day or two. For the air. That's what you wanted—" and he pats her cheek—"a change of air." He is in his gayest mood, with a gaiety that overflows in affection. He draws her on his knee and sings, "The duck, the duckling. I like 'em little. They're quicker." And experience has taught her not to spoil the occasion with tactless inquiries.

The evening is delightful, and on the next morning he takes her early on the promenade to enjoy what he calls the ozone.

It is September. The sun is warm on the cheek, but the wind is cool. The sky is clear, and the sea is reflecting its pale blue in millions of blue sparkles which, for some reason, seem particularly appropriate to the noise of its waves splashing freshly against the iron legs of the pier.

Tabitha feels a little drunk with sensations which flow equally from sky, sea, the touch of Bonser's arm which supports her hand. She thinks, "How nice it is here. Really, there's something in the seaside. What a good appetite I'm getting. How excited Dick was last night; how he adores me—of course he had had a good deal of whisky."

She is pleased that this piece of intuition does not trouble her, but only causes her to be aware of her new womanly wisdom. And that also exhilarates her. There is something between the air, the sea, and herself, some happy correspondence of vibrations, which turns everything into rapture.

Bonser is also in high spirits, but with the same exuberance of the day before. He throws out his chest, and his feet seem to spring. He presses Tabitha's hand under his arm. "You know, Pops, we did that rather well; it was what you call neat."

One of Tabitha's important discoveries about husbands is that they enjoy admiration. She sees that Dick is asking for a compliment, but she is perplexed. She smiles at him and says, "Yes, Dick?"

"I mean, the little operation yesterday; not so dusty for hubby. There we were and here we are, in the pink."

"You mean the journey? But I was wondering—"

Bonser laughs heartily and gives her a pinch. "Oh, the Pops! And by the way, we've got a new name—we're Mr. and Mrs. Bilton."

"A new name? But why on earth—?"

"Because there's a 'B' in both."

And all at once Tabitha understands the affair. "Are we running away from that hotel bill?"

"Well, we couldn't pay it, could we?"

"And your uncle, did he really ask you?"

Bonser gives a shout of laughter. He stops to laugh. "That was a good one."

"Is he your uncle?"

"Have sense, kid, grow up a bit. Here, what's wrong with you? We're all right. That's what I'm telling you."

Tabitha drops his arm. "Do you mean it's all just cheating?"

Bonser whistles and cocks his hat and looks at a tall powerful young woman on the opposite side of the promenade. "Fine piece, that. By God, what a front. I bet she's fourteen stone. I like 'em big."

"I can't stay with you if you cheat."

"All right." He whistles.

Tabitha is amazed by the effect of her threat; that is, by its no effect. Her temper flies out. "What a brute you are! I always knew it."

"What a brain you are! I noticed it right away."

Tabitha hurries back to her lodging and packs. She thinks, "Yes, a perfect brute"; and this makes her still more wretched. She wants to weep. It seems as if these words wound herself more than Bonser.

Suddenly Bonser appears with his hat at the back of his head, and says gaily, "You needn't go if you don't like. I will."

"You might take your hat off."

He takes his hat off and puts it on again at a still more rakish angle. "By-by, clever girl."

He packs his carefully folded clothes in a bag and drops it out of the back window into a flower bed. He then goes into the garden and walks out by the back gate where a cab is standing. Tabitha sees him open the cab door, gets a glimpse of a large female arm and a broad rosy face—the girl from the promenade. The arm grabs the bag, Bonser gets in and shuts the door, and the cab drives away. Tabitha thinks, "So he's arranged with her; he's got another woman already!" But she does not feel surprise or wretchedness. She feels so many different things that they amount to nothing.

Half an hour later the landlord comes in with a policeman. He is apologetic to Tabitha, but there is a question from London about an hotel bill. "Where is Mr. Bilton, and is that his right name?"

When Tabitha confesses that the name is Bonser, that she doesn't know where Mr. Bonser is, and that she has no money, the landlord loses his manners. He becomes abusive. The policeman, on the other hand, is, if anything, more considerate. He apologizes for troubling the lady, while he searches drawers and opens the trunk. It contains old bricks wrapped in newspaper.

Tabitha is taken to the police station, examined, and asked if she has any relations. She answers no. She shudders at the thought of being exposed in all her folly before Harry and Edith. But the policeman has already extracted Harry's address from her bag. Challenged, she admits that Dr. Baskett is a relation, in fact her brother. Harry is wired for and comes down by the next train.

7 TABITHA, at the police station, awaits him with desperation. She thinks, "Oh well, I can always kill myself." She can barely bring herself to look at her brother. But Harry, though he appears more careworn than she remembers, is calm, urbane. He greets her with affection and asks no questions. He pays the lodging house bill; and when at last, seated in the train for home, he says, "Well, and how are you?" she sees that she is not even going to be reproached.

"Oh, Harry, I've been such a fool. But do you understand? It wasn't all my fault."

"Bonser made a fool of you, I understand that, as he has a good many other girls. But you might have written; we've been rather anxious. After getting no news in three months."

"Three months—so it is!" Tabitha is astonished by the passage of time and her own want of consideration. "But I really had meant to write as soon as I was married."

"So you aren't married?"

"He kept on putting it off."

"That's one good thing, anyhow."

Tabitha is amazed by this judgment in the sober Harry. The world expands round her. It seems that her story is not so extraordinary or shocking as she had thought. She kisses Harry and says, "Oh, Harry, how good you are. But weren't you rather surprised—at me, I mean?"

"I'm not a family doctor for nothing." He smiles wisely at her affectionate gaze. He is aware of his wisdom, his patience.

And Tabitha is now delighted to be going home. She feels already the peace of its familiar things, saying, "Here is truth, here is security."

She is astonished, therefore, to meet a dog in the hall, who yaps at her, and to find that it is already an old inhabitant. In her room there is a sewing machine, an ironing board, and an immense new clothes basket full of washing. Her drawers, too, are full of baby clothes. Edith, it seems, is pregnant, and her sister Clara has come to stay in the little back room, so that Tabitha must have the iron and the baskets.

This Clara—plain, shy, an ugly version of Edith, who has already found her place in life as a family slave, called upon in all emergencies but never thanked, a dull creature despised even by maids—even she seems more at home than Tabitha. She effaces herself, but she knows where things are, she belongs to the new routine, the new Cedars. She is busy about Edith all day long. And Edith herself shows the most startling change. She has a new face as well as a new figure, and even character. Her nose is bigger, her cheeks more sallow. She is even more untidy. And her chief virtue, her good temper, is short. She snaps at Harry when he complains that the meals are late. She feels apparently that pregnancy entitles her to be rude as well as a little more lazy and extravagant.

On the other hand, she is much more frank with Tabitha. She will say to Clara, "Go along, Clarrie, we don't want you," and talk to Tabitha with surprising coarseness about men, about Harry's modest prurience. "He never says anything, he just pulls me about; he might be a parson."

She condescends to Harry from a new height, and Tabitha recoils from her. She does not value the new intimacy with Edith. It only increases her feeling that the Cedars has somehow grown not only smaller but stuffier and more squalid. It confirms her determination to escape from it into a career.

8

AND she practices all that winter as never before. She gets up even before breakfast to sit in a cold room, with red pinched nose, and a shawl over her shoulders, to repeat a hundred times her exercises for the left hand. How she hates these exercises for the left hand. That is why she practices them so hard. She is austerely determined to punish herself for her folly.

She wonders every day at that folly, already receding into the past. "How could I do such things? What a little fool I was. How lucky I was to escape so easily! At least I've learnt my lesson!"

After three months her music professor, who polishes her at half a guinea a time, begins to talk of bringing her out at a concert in the next year—a small concert, to give her experience of playing in public, but still, a concert. And Harry agrees to pay fifty guineas in advance for this debut.

But one afternoon, less than a fortnight after this contract is signed, as Tabitha walks quickly across the common, frowning and preoccupied, a man starts from behind a bush directly into her path. Bonser!

She stops as if struck, and gazes speechless. She cannot believe her own eyes. It is as though some legend, some mythical hero, has come to life before her as a middle-sized man, with regular, almost too regular, features, a beautiful complexion, blue-gray eyes, a neat gray suit, and elaborate boots. Her first thought is, "He's not nearly as tall as I remembered, and his chin is too long." But then she feels a strong indignation.

Bonser sweeps his hat off like some actor in a Pinero play, and cries, "Why, Pops, you look quite white. Did I give you a shock?"

"I'm afraid I can't wait." She begins to walk past. He jumps in her way.

"Damn it all, this is too much from you, Pops."

"Too much." She turns upon him, flaming. "After your lies. After deserting me like that. Owing money to a lodging house keeper."

"My God, what about me? I come back and find you've given the show away and done a bolt. I was nearly jugged myself, and all because you couldn't trust me for a single day."

"Lies, lies. Do you really think me such a fool?"

A look of despair comes into the man's face. "That's all I get for trying to give you a good time, chucking away my money. Well, I've been a fool, haven't I? And yet I can't believe it yet. I've been saying to myself all the time, 'She'll come back to me, I know my Tib, the truest little wife in England.' "

"I'm *not* your wife; and what about that woman?"

"What woman?"

"In the cab when you went away—the woman from the promenade."

"What cab? There was a chap in the cab—an old friend who promised me a job. Oh yes, I believe his wife *was* there, too."

"No, Dick. It's *no* good. I'm not so silly." And she rushes past him. But for fifty yards she hears his sad voice at her shoulder, blaming himself for his love. And as she darts toward the Cedars he calls after her, "For God's sake, Pops, don't break my heart! Tomorrow, the same place."

"The liar, the wicked liar." Tabitha rushes to her piano as if to escape. "And what awful cheek, to think I'd believe him. It *was* a woman in the cab."

But even as she calls up the vision of the cab her mind wavers.

Can she swear to the woman from the promenade? Already the whole story of the elopement begins to lose firmness. It is as though a calm and broad pool of reflections, bright and sharp-edged, had been stirred by a light breeze. All is there still—the colors, the brightness—but all in motion, changing its shapes and importance, melting at the edges. Fraud looks like imprudence, and recklessness like a proof of love.

"Oh!" She strikes a double chord with all her force. "If only I could know."

She hits so many wrong notes that she runs from the piano to open the window. "How stuffy it is here." The secure peaceful Cedars seems like a trap.

Even her bedroom, her refuge, feels mean and cold; and all night she tosses between dozes and nightmares. Her head aches and her back itches, she has a mysterious pain which is everywhere and nowhere.

"Oh," she cries, thumping her pillow in fury, "*why* did I ever see the man?" And then instantly she feels that if she had never met Bonser her life would be inconceivably flat and stupid.

But she gets up with a firm resolution. "I know he lied to me before"; and she goes firmly to her practice.

As the time of the rendezvous approaches, she says amid a cascade of notes, "Never, never again!"

But she is tense, and, as it were, full of Bonser. She feels him waiting for her, she feels him say, "I trusted you, Pops. I loved you."

She jumps up. "This is silly. I've got to do *some*thing. I've got to put an end to it, once for all."

9

TEN minutes later she is in Bonser's arms.

"So you'll come," he cries. "Saved, saved."

"Certainly not." Tabitha springs away. "Never! What do you mean by saved?"

"You've saved my life. I was just saying, 'All right, if Pops has deserted me, I'll go to the devil, there's nothing else.' "

"But, Dick, how can you say I deserted you?"

Bonser makes a gesture of despair. "You'll never understand."

"What don't I understand?"

"That I'm really a domestic kind of chap. I'm not ambitious, Pops. I wouldn't be Prime Minister if they asked me on their knees. Oh, I know I've been a bit reckless. But think what my life's been like, all alone with nobody to care for me. That's why I made such a dash for you; I knew that what I wanted was the influence of a good woman."

"Influence! And you didn't even marry me."

He takes her hand. "Marry you! If only I could, this minute."

Tabitha's trembling increases. "But, Dick, you haven't even a job; you only think of betting."

"There you go again, thinking the worst. Of course I couldn't marry without a job. And I've got one, practically."

"Oh, Dick, a real job? But that would make all the difference."

"It does; let me show you." He takes Tabitha's arm and sits her down beside him on a bank of grass. "Look at this—a land agency." He hands her a newspaper cutting. "Watling Estate. Agents wanted."

"But that's wonderful." To Tabitha the very word land implies security and respectability. "And you've really got it?"

"I haven't closed yet. But I went and saw the committee, and everything was even better than I thought. First-class accountants simply swarming in for the posts."

"But, Dick, why on earth—?"

"I wasn't going to move a step until you approved. How did I know you wouldn't think land agency a bit *infra dig.*?"

"But what nonsense. I've been longing for you to have a job." And remembering her influence, Tabitha says firmly, "That's what you've wanted all the time: a settled job."

"Well, if you say so."

"Oh dear, I only hope you're not too late."

"I'll apply at once. The only thing is—I have to make a deposit, evidence of good faith and so on. Of course all the really sound companies ask for deposits, guarantees."

"Yes, of course; but, Dick, how much is it?"

"Only fifty quid—much less than I expected. The trouble is I just don't happen to have it. I wonder—how would brother Harry feel if I put it to him? It wouldn't cost him anything in the end, and it would get you settled."

"Oh no, not Harry; he wouldn't understand."

"No, I suppose not. Well, damn it all, it looks as if I haven't a hope, doesn't it?"

"Oh, Dick, if only you'd have patience. Let me think. There must be some way of managing it when it's so important. I've only got about six pounds in the post office, but I have a ring with pearls in it, and a bracelet, yes, and my fur coat. I'm sure I could get money for them."

"You mustn't give up your things for me."

"But, Dick, don't you see that they don't matter a straw in comparison with getting you a job. We must have a sense of proportion."

"You're the boss, Pops; and I suppose you could try a popshop. That way you wouldn't lose 'em. You'd get 'em all out again as soon as the round ones begin to roll along the pavement."

"And there's my gold chain, too; but, Dick, you do really mean to work, to make the best of this chance? You do see how *wrong* it would be to fall back into the old way, wasting yourself, wasting our happiness."

"Do you think I'm such a fool?"

"Darling, I'm not doubting you."

"I often wonder, Pops, if you really love me as much as I love you."

"Oh I do, I do; it's only I so long for us to be happy."

"But we always have been happy, Pops. We're so exactly suited to each other." He slips an arm around her waist and touches her knee. But she recoils in horror, pushing down her skirt. "No, no, please, it would be wrong. This is different."

He frowns, and she tries to explain. "I mean—now that we're really getting married and starting properly."

"That's all right, Pops." He kisses her languidly. "You're the boss from now on; and perhaps you're right to stand off a bit. I'm not one to quarrel—it's not in my character." He makes a royal gesture, but he is still frowning.

"I must go, I must fly, or they'll suspect something. And they mustn't know yet. They mightn't understand. Oh, Dick, you do believe I love you?" She embraces him anxiously.

"That's all right, Tibbykins."

"You do understand why we mustn't—till we're married? Afterwards, of course, I'll—I like it as much as you do. Truly. Because then I really know you love me."

"No doubt about that, Popkins. We've had some wonderful times. It's something to do with the angles, I suppose."

"Oh heavens, there's four striking. Good-by, my darling, till tomorrow."

10

As SHE flies across the common it occurs to her for a moment that Bonser's ideas of love are more practical than her own, but this does not offend her. Far from it. She is interested; she thinks with excitement, "How strange it is, how wonderful that he should love me so much; how lucky that I should have this power over him.

He gave way at once when I explained. Yes, he's good, good at bottom, so gentle; and now that he has this chance—oh, he mustn't lose this chance. His whole life depends on it—our whole lives."

She is horrified by the notion of robbing Harry, but the very horror increases the need for her to do this bold act, to risk her conscience, her very soul. And she prays with fervor, "Forgive us our trespasses, as we forgive them—"

Harry's safe in which her pearls are kept is in his bedroom and the key in his dressing table. Next morning, while the lazy Edith is at breakfast and the housemaid on the attic floor, she darts into Harry's bedroom and takes the key from the dressing table drawer. She is trembling with fright, but she says, "It's for Dick, to save him." She jumps and turns pale as Harry comes in from the passage.

"Hullo." He kisses her good morning. "What do you want?"

"I wanted—to say good morning."

Both know that this is a lie. They gaze at each other; then Harry, reflecting no doubt that young girls are very odd creatures, pats her shoulder and says, "You look pulled down; I'll give you a tonic."

He walks on. Tabitha rushes to her room. She is almost in tears of dismay. "But what can I do? I must write and explain. He'll understand when I'm married and Dick is making an income. He'll be glad then."

That afternoon, as she steps into the hall with her suitcase and stands listening for any step, any movement, her eyes fall on Harry's second-best top hat, his winter hat, hanging on the stand; and its humble pose, so calm, so unsuspecting of treachery, its nap, worn by gales and snow, strike remorse into her heart. She stoops hastily, as she goes past, and kisses it. Then she runs desperately through the garden alley to the back lane. Bonser's cab is waiting. She dives into it. She is full of the solemnity of the moment; tragic for Harry, for herself, for Bonser.

But the cab jolts forward and causes her to fall on Bonser's knee; and all at once she is laughing. Bonser is laughing.

"But, Dick, we mustn't laugh. It's really a fearful thing. What will Harry think of me? He won't realize that it's all quite different. What are you doing? No, no, someone might see."

"Damn it, Pops, you usen't to be such an icicle."

"Wait, please; it's only till tomorrow, till we're married."

She struggles and implores, but suddenly perceives that the man is furious. Then she remembers that all her influence depends on his affection, and the very thought makes her more feeble in defense.

"Oh please, please, Dick darling, you're *killing* me—" She is tearful in her desperation.

But afterwards, while Bonser is lighting a cigar, she hastens to smile. "And when are you to see the company?"

"What company? Oh, the Watling people! As soon as we've raised the wind."

She puts her arms round him. "Dick, you're not offended with me?"

"You're wonderful, Pops. It's almost better when you fight back. Yes, give me a Christian every time." And he cocks his hat at her with such a look of triumphant impudence that she can't help forgiving him. She thinks, "The job, that's the *really* important thing."

Her chain, bracelet, and furs bring only thirty-seven pounds, but Bonser explains that the company will take a reduced deposit from him because he is a gentleman. "They want real gentlemen for this job, not gents—it needs style."

"Where is the company? Oughtn't you to go and see them at once?"

"I saw 'em yesterday; they're in no hurry. What I thought was I'll send 'em a check later on. What about a little celebration, Pops?"

"But what exactly is your work?"

"Now, Pops, don't worry. We've done enough for one day."

However, after the celebration, at a suitable moment after midnight when the man is fairly drunk, he consents to tell her that the Watling Company has been formed by a group of public-spirited persons to recover the Watling estates. "You've heard of old Lord Watling, who died last year and left two million pounds to a daughter?"

"No, I didn't."

"Well, he did. But the fact is the girl isn't the heir. Old Watling lived a double life and had a son who ought to get the rhino. But he can't afford to fight the case himself, you know what the law is. It's one of the biggest swindles in the country. So he's formed a company to get the estate for him, and when there's a share-out I stand to win about ten thousand pounds."

"But, Dick, what a *queer* story. Can it be true?"

"Oh, you Frood Greens. It's a fact, my Pops, a proved fact. It was in *The Times*."

"Really, in *The Times*!" Tabitha's doubts are calmed.

"Absolutely, I saw it myself. Watling kept a butcher's shop under a false name. And he had a wife at the shop. The question is, did he marry her first? Well, we can prove he did, we've got the certificate."

"Can't you just show it to the judge?"

Bonser laughs and pinches her chin. "As if the lawyers would allow a thing like that before they'd had their cut out of the oodles. Well, I'm not blaming 'em; they've got to live. But we've got to live too; it's human nature."

11 BONSER'S work, as he explains, is to sell shares in the Watling Company at half a crown each, on which his commission is sixpence. The shares are printed on small but impressive forms, promising to pay a hundred-per-cent profit on the conclusion of the Watling case, and Bonser offers nine for a pound. On his first day, after calling on all the widows in the local directory, he makes seven pounds, which he spends at once on a new hat, new shoes, an investment in the Manchester Handicap, and a little party to celebrate the organization of the local branch.

Tabitha cannot hide her delight. "I knew you could do it, Dick; you could do anything you liked." And she agrees fondly to the celebration.

And Bonser continues with great enthusiasm for a fortnight. Indeed, in the last two days he makes more than all before. "A good idea of mine," he says. "The colonels. They're the chaps with a sense of justice; one old boy wanted to get questions asked in Parliament."

Pointing out that he now has a steady income of a thousand a year and can afford a flutter, he puts all his gains on a horse which never starts. This accident, however, does not seem to depress him; he comes home in good humor, puts Tabitha on his knee, and jogs her up and down. "This is the way the farmers ride, the farmers ride."

"But, Dick, it's rather serious; we haven't paid the bill here."

"What's that matter? Six quid! Do you realize I've lost a thousand pounds? That's what I stood to win on the double."

"How lucky this seems such a good place to sell shares."

"Oh, damn the shares; why should I wear myself out for those sharks? Half a crown a time; it doesn't pay for shoes."

"But, Dick darling, at least it's a start, and everyone has to start at the bottom."

"Who sold you that one?"

"Where else can you start?"

"At the top, and that's where you've got to start, too, if you want to get anywhere. Give me a bit of capital, and I'll show you."

"But, Dick, that's just it; if we saved a little more, only a pound a week, that would be fifty pounds in a year."

"My God, hark at her. You women are all the same. A lot of Delilahs. All your game is getting a man tied up and making him grind his guts out for you."

"But, Dick, you promised—"

"Nag, nag, nag!" And suddenly Tabitha finds herself on the floor.

"How can I help it?" The girl's high temper explodes in rage. "If I didn't tell you, you'd never do anything. And how can we go on like this? It's impossible."

Luckily there is a tap on the door. The landlady wants to know if they are going to knock the house down, and Bonser, in his indignation at having to endure cheap lodgings and what he calls hags, forgets his rage against Tabitha.

"My God, I've half a mind to give her a month's notice."

"But we owe her two weeks' board."

"Well, she won't get it, that's one good thing. I've got an idea about that! Did you ever notice that fire escape?" He laughs, and suddenly he is full of good humor again. He is even surprised to see Tabitha's thoughtful air. "Hullo, what's wrong with you, Pops? Look at me—I'm not worrying."

"You've no right to treat me like that."

"A thousand pounds; and it was practically in my pocket." He strolls about the room for a long time with a smile, saying, "A thousand pounds." He pays no attention to Tabitha's frowns; he does not even notice them. It is no good frowning. Indeed, she is obliged to use all her influence to prevent his going out to drink their last pound.

12

Two months later they are in a small Midland town. Their lodgings are of the worst, in a dismal back street. It is May, but the only blossom to be seen is in a funeral wreath at a greengrocer's. Every day it rains. Tabitha, as she carries a heavy shopping bag through the crowded market, continually bumps into other women with bags and mackintoshes. The mackintoshes, the road, the houses, the very sky are all in different shades of mud color. The women frown; their hats drip, their noses are red; even the prettiest seem repulsive and also pitiable. Tabitha runs full tilt into another young woman coming out of the greengrocer's. They stare at each other with amazement, as if they had not before, that morning, noticed another creature. This is quite true. The woman is probably thinking of cabbages. Tabitha is deeply concerned with Bonser. They give each other a glance, which in a woman means, "What a pathetic object, I pity her. How unhappy she must be," and having annihilated each other twice over with scorn and with pity, brush past and continue on their way with the same frowning and worried air.

Tabitha, however, is as unaware of worry as she is of the wet, the ugliness of existence. She has long ceased to ask herself if she is happy. She has no time, no leisure. She is always occupied with some new extremely urgent problem. At the moment, for instance, she is faced with a new and most unexpected development in Bonser, who, that morning, after a week of good temper and some profitable sales, has refused to get up, or even to eat his breakfast. Tabitha, especially at these latter symptoms, has been much alarmed. "But, Dick, are you ill?"

"Yes, I've got leprosy. Go away."

But Tabitha, as a doctor's daughter, does not like jokes about health.

"Perhaps it's the flu. Do you feel a kind of heaviness in your head and pains in your joints?"

"No, in the neck."

She looks at him and wonders if perhaps he is sulking. But on the whole she rejects this diagnosis. He has never sulked before. "Do you think it's a sore throat coming on? Shall I make you a gargle?"

He has answered only with a groan. And Tabitha, as she fights her way through the shops and feels the water squelching in her shoes, asks herself what is wrong with the man. It must be flu. In that case, of course, she must expect pneumonia. Or can he be offended with her? "But I've been rather sweet, I think; yes, even when he waked me up that time. And I'm sure he thought I enjoyed it. And he's been eating rather well. Besides, he's never been ill."

She returns in perplexity and finds Bonser half dressed. "Oh, Dick, are you feeling better?"

"No, worse."

"I knew you ought to stay in bed."

"I'm going to get tight; I'm going to get as blind as David's sow."

"But why, Dick? You were so happy yesterday."

"Is that any reason why I should be happy today?"

"What is wrong with you, Dick, if you're not ill and not cross? Are you cross?"

"You'll find me outside the Red Lion at closing time; bring a wheelbarrow." And he walks out.

Tabitha is now quite panic-stricken. She asks herself if the man has gone mad. After some anxious reflection she goes to the Red Lion and sees Bonser at the bar drinking a double whisky. He appears so sunk in misery that she can scarcely recognize him.

13

SUDDENLY two large heavy men come to the bar and begin to talk in loud voices of some wonderful coup. It appears that they are bookmakers, who have had a good day. They laugh and slap at each other.

Tabitha gazes at them with immense disgust, when she feels a prod in the waist. Bonser, transformed, is murmuring in her ear, "See those two old legs? Cunningest old welshers for a hundred miles round; a Yorkshire flea couldn't bite 'em in ten jumps. Bet you I spoof 'em on the Watling lay."

Tabitha, thinking him crazy with drink, presses back his arm and whispers, "But it's so late."

Bonser shakes off her hand and goes up to the bar. "Good evening, sirs." He nods to the bookies. "Want a good thing? No, not a winner this time. It's something that can't fall down. Hear about the late Lord Watling? Well, look at this." He shows a cutting. "Death of the Marquis of Watling. Certain Eccentricities. No, it's not what you think; he had his girls of course. Two of 'em. That's where the trouble started which is going to land somebody a couple of million quid. I'm not joking. It's all in the paper—Watling Estate."

The bookies grin at each other, and Tabitha trembles for Bonser; but he says, "You don't believe it, do you? Of course you don't. It takes a clever chap to know the truth when he sees it. Now look here, this Lord Watling had a home in Eaton Square and a butcher's shop, where he used to call himself Smith, down in Bermondsey. How do we know it was the same man? Because there's an underground passage all the way. We've found it. Of course it's an old one. Been there hundreds of years. Made by the monks to get at their girls that they kept locked up in a nunnery down over the river—convenient for drowning 'em if they gave any trouble."

The bookies look more serious and nod at each other as if to say, "We know about monks, this sounds more the thing."

Bonser now brings out more cuttings, typewritten extracts said to be from the memoirs of Lord Watling, and urges the bookies to apply to the Lord Chancellor for further particulars of the case; or if they want to see the underground passage they should write to the Lord Mayor.

"The Lord Mayor," says one of the bookies with a doubtful glance.

"Well, Mansion House, you know," says Bonser as if impatient with a provincial who does not know how things are done. "Drains Department—it comes under drains. And you'll have to get a permit and pay something on the stamp."

"The stamp?"

"Yes, the stamp. One of those black ones, for permits. Have you never had a permit?"

"Go on, Bill," says the fatter bookie to the doubter, "you've seen a shilling stamp before!"

"Ah, permit stamp."

"That's it."

Both the bookies, somewhat ashamed of their doubts, apply for a pound's worth of shares. Tabitha is in a kind of fever. She does not know whether to be more furious with Bonser for this last invention or astonished by his impudence. She gazes at him, their eyes meet, and he gives her a sudden wink. She is seized with an irresistible desire to laugh, and goes hastily out into the street.

14

She is in misery. She says to herself, "But he's hopeless; it's not only that he lies and cheats, he's—" But she can't put a word to this madness of Bonser's. And then again the recollection of his calm face and astounding impudence starts up before her and she is overwhelmed with laughter. She laughs till, between her misery and this strange delight, she has a pain, a cramp, and painful tears are forced to her eyes.

Bonser struts out and takes her arm. "Hullo, old girl. That was a good one; it made you laugh, what?"

"But, Dick, why did you?" And she begins to laugh again, but frowns and tries to control herself. "It was absolutely mad, that passage; you know there isn't one."

"Of course not. But what a tale! And I just thought of it that minute." He cocks his hat and swaggers like a conqueror. "I swear to God, Tibs, that minute. And did you see their faces? Well, I nearly laughed myself." He gives a short crow of laughter. "You saw 'em swallowing it. Two of the smartest old bastards in England. The fact is, Tibs, I could sell a milestone to the Bank of England."

"Yes, but suppose they found out. It's such an obvious lie."

"But that's the whole point. The bigger the better. And I'll tell you why." Bonser presses her arm in joyful pride of the artist. "If you tell a real whopper, a real hairy one, people think, 'He wouldn't dare tell one that size if it wasn't true.' See, it's what you call a flycatcher. Not that it doesn't work on flats, too. But flats don't need working. They just come and lick your hand and say, 'Take everything, old chap. That's all I've got, and you can come back for more.' A whopper is wasted on a flat. But those two chaps are fly—nobody flier. And that's why I gave 'em the extra stuff about the passage. And the monks. Did you see how they took in about the monks? That was the bit that got 'em. It always does. It's a flycatcher. Always play the monks for dirty work—well, everyone knows what they were. Monks or parsons. It gives you the right touch, a bit of human nature. Well, I think we've earned a little celebration." He turns toward another pub.

"No, please, Dick."

"Yes, thank you."

"Don't you see how you're wasting yourself?"

"Do you think it was easy to sell Watling paper to that brace of crocodiles?"

He goes into the bar and drinks. His expression is gloomy. He says nothing. At closing time, swaying down the street, he cries to the houses, "She thinks he's no good."

"But, Dick, I didn't say—"

"Why, of course I'm wasted. I ought to be in Par-lia-ment, spoofing the bloody world."

"If you'd only stick to something."

"What chaance do you think I had, chucked out of a knocking shop into a goddam office at fourteen."

"But I thought you were at the university."

"The office was at the university. It was a college office, and if you're going to call me a liar every time I open my bloody mouth—"

"Dick, it's so late, we ought to be in bed."

"Go on, poot the poor mug to bed and go through his pockets. Cleean him out body and soul and sell the old skin for Sunday knickers."

He stops and addresses her with an oratorical wave of the arm. "You don't appreciate me, Topsy; you think I'm a flat fish. But you're wroong. My guts are made of tripe; my liver and lights are real cat's meat; I've got egg in my egg; my bottom doesn't hang on a gas bracket; I don't wear my face to hide my back hair."

Suddenly he smiles broadly, sadly, and knocks his hat over his eyes. He repeats the last phrase to himself with relish and says, "That's a good one." He has sung himself into a good temper. He puts his arm round Tabitha's shoulder. "Go on, take the juggins home and walk on him."

Mourning his wasted gifts with an eloquence which gives him great pleasure, he lets her undress him and put him to bed. He creeps into her arms, and sighing, "Go on, Pops, do me in the dags, break my heart," he goes to sleep on her breast, and snores like an elephant.

Tabitha does not move. She is facing a great, a surprising discovery. "It's simply no good expecting Dick to be reasonable. He's got no sense. I could argue till I was black in the face, but he wouldn't listen."

15

THE amazement passes into a deep sadness. It seems to her that she is filled with a sadness and a wisdom so heavy, so profound, that life can hold no more surprises for her. "There's something lacking in him, he's like a child. I must be patient, infinitely tactful."

As a beginning in maternal patience, she lies quite still, saying, "I shan't sleep a wink, but I mustn't wake him or he'll have a bad head tomorrow and be fit for nothing."

But she wakes at half-past ten in the morning to find Bonser drowsily embracing her and to hear him sigh, "Oh, my stony-hearted wife, my little bit of ruin."

She says with a soft tactful air, "You know, Dick darling, we ought to have paid the bill before we spent all the money yesterday."

Bonser receives this hint with great good humor. "That's all right, Mam, don't you worry. Here, let me show you a new one."

"But, Dick, it's getting late."

"No hurry, bless you."

And getting up at his leisure, he wanders smiling round the room. "Do you know who I'm going to touch?"

"You have all those addresses."

"Oh, I'm sick of colonels; I'm going to take another cut off those two sorcerers at the Red Lion."

"No, Dick, please—" She jumps out of bed to implore him. "After those stories you told them it would really be insane."

"There you go again. And next minute you're telling me I don't work hard enough. What is a man to do?"

"Dick, I know you're clever, but you don't need to—"

"You watch, that's all. I've just thought of a real Catch-em-alivo." He smiles with rich anticipation. "I'll milk those two snakes like a dairy pump; come along and see them part."

He insists on taking Tabitha into the bar where the bookies are at their usual place in conversation with a dark young man who looks like a prizefighter. But before Bonser can even greet his visitors, this man jumps up and says to him, "What's this about Watling shares? I'm the only agent here. Where's your credentials?"

Bonser indignantly refuses his credentials on the ground that no gentleman could cast doubt on another's bona fides. The man knocks his hat off, there is a shout, "All out there," and Tabitha finds herself pushed back through the swing door into the street, together with two old charwomen and an excited youth in a bowler, by a very large fat potman. And while, staggered by this sudden event, she is trying to disentangle herself from the two women, she sees the same door fly open, Bonser's hat go sailing through the air, and Bonser himself skating across the pavement on his ear with all his limbs wildly beating space. But before she can even cry out he has somersaulted to his feet and is vanishing round the next corner at a speed which makes his legs seem like a blur.

She has barely time to pick up the hat and retreat toward the lodgings before two policemen come running.

16

TABITHA, left almost penniless, hears nothing for three days. Then she gets a wire from a seaside place on the south coast, Heathland. "Come at once. Promising prospects."

She has to pawn her best dress for a railway fare, and to creep away from the lodging without paying the bill. Thus for the first time she is herself obliged to bilk the landlady. Her self-respect is deeply offended, and she is furious with Bonser.

"I've been too weak with him. He thinks he can do what he likes and I'll still be nice to him. But I'll show him he's wrong. After all, it's just because he does love me so terribly that I *can* be firm. And it's not really unkind. It's the only hope for us both."

And her first words to Bonser, who, in a new hat and a new necktie, meets her at the station, are an ultimatum. "I'm sorry, Dick, but we can't go on like this."

He beams upon her. "That's what I think, Poppet."

"Was that man right about the Watling Company? Were your shares forged?"

"I don't know; I got 'em in a pub."

"And you just lied to me."

Bonser's good humor is not disturbed. "It's what you call an open question, isn't it?"

"I suppose I was stupid to believe you. But it's the last time. Unless you get a proper job, a real job, we'll have to part."

"Absolutely, Poppet; a proper settled job of work, it's the only way."

"I'm glad you see that at last—"

"And I've got it, Pops; that's why I sent for you. A real regular job. Through a friend of mine."

Tabitha is suspicious. "What kind of job?"

"It's a tea shop, to play the piano."

"But can you play it?"

"No, of course not; but you can. Soon as I heard of it, I thought of you, Pops. And you can begin this very day. At four o'clock."

"But, Dick, I couldn't—"

"Just as you like, but I don't know what you came for if you don't mean to help. It's a big chance, too. It's only this chap Manklow's influence got it for us; it won't be open tomorrow."

"But, Dick—"

"Only don't try any more spoof about me lying down on the work. It's not me who's being kept."

"That's really *wicked*."

"Or, as you say, we can part."

"Don't think I didn't mean it."

"Certainly not. Nice weather we're having—"

Tabitha keeps silence and dignity. And at four o'clock she is playing the piano in the Kumfy Tea Rooms. Her duties are to play at lunch, tea, and supper, for five shillings a day and her meals.

"A fine opening, Mrs. Bonser. I know a girl who started this way and ended in the Albert Hall."

This is Bonser's friend Manklow. He is a square-shouldered, sandy-haired man with a broad pink face and gold spectacles. His large forehead is deeply wrinkled, but his wide mouth carries usually a rueful grin, as if amused by its own grief. Bonser, it seems, has known him for years, and he has come to Heathland to sponge upon him. But Manklow is out of a job, and as poor as himself. He has been able only to give room to Bonser in a humble attic in the old town; and now, on Tabitha's coming, moves his bed into a kind of cupboard under its eaves.

Tabitha, who has taken a strong dislike to Manklow, chiefly because he bites his nails and stares at her when he talks to Bonser, objects to this arrangement. But Bonser answers her carelessly, "Well, we're using his room; and why not, a rat like that."

And Manklow can't be snubbed. He is indeed most attentive to

Tabitha. His hands caress the air about her, his grin is only just short of an insult. He hints to her that she is too good for Dick Bonser. "This is no life for a girl like you, Tib."

Tabitha, hating to be called Tib, answers severely, "Thank you, Mr. Manklow, I don't mind my life."

"No, but your chance may come. Yes—" gazing at Tabitha with a professional inquiry—"I wouldn't wonder if you weren't coming in; there's signs."

"Coming in?"

"Your style. Piquant. Of course I couldn't bet on it, but the Jersey Lilys have had a long run. I like the Venus de Meelos myself, they're more healthy; but in a rotten age like this I shouldn't be surprised if the choirboy faces come in, the herring-gutted monkey type."

"Do you mean that I'm like a monkey?"

The man suddenly grins enormously, showing rows of large white teeth, and says, "It might be an asset; well, anything can. I knew a girl got married to five thousand a year because she had a wooden leg."

And becoming grave again, he directs his spectacles thoughtfully aside. "I shouldn't have minded being a woman myself; there's an opening there." Manklow's mind dwells much on openings. "They're all round us, Tibby; don't talk to me about the hard world, it's soft, soppy. All you want is to watch where it cracks up next, and get your hook in quick."

Manklow himself has failed in half a dozen jobs—as a schoolmaster, where he was turned out after some scandal about the accounts, and in a publishing firm, where again he has speculated. Lately, he has been sacked from a local newspaper for offering to suppress certain names in his report of a case. The suggestion is that he asked for payment to suppress the names, and that he has used blackmail in other cases. But he denies the whole story. Manklow's dream is to start a paper of his own, any kind of paper. "Look at the opening. All these board schools teaching kids to read. That's the big thing, Tib, nowadays, education. The country's rotten with it. Now's the time to get in." He points out that new papers are coming out every month. "Look at *Answers*, and all these new evening rags. It's a disease, and it's going to get worse. Well, we're getting new schools, aren't we? I shouldn't mind betting we'll be a republic in ten years." He is much disgusted that he cannot find any rich man to finance a paper for him. "A real live paper, with a kick in each leg and a bite in every tooth. I've written all round, but nobody believes me. I wrote to that old bag-belly Sturge at the Heath, but he cuts me in the street. Rotten with money. Well, I suppose he can't help it. Everything goes rotten in a rotten age."

17 HE POINTS out Sturge to Tabitha on the promenade as he comes out of his hotel, the Heath, on the seafront.

Heathland is one of those smaller seaside places, with a bad beach, rocky bathing, no theater, a short parade, which are therefore very fashionable with all persons who hate a mob. Its few boarding houses and bad hotels are crowded out every year with judges, generals, successful doctors, even a few West End actors; and always many amateurs of art. At one time there were art classes at Heathland every year, attended by a princess and two brigadiers. And in the summer season there is always an art shop from London, where one may see the newest productions.

In such a place, distinguished annual visitors walk like owners, and Sturge, as each morning he takes his walk along the promenade, seems to occupy most of the pavement. He is a middle-sized man in the early fifties, with large pale eyes. He is all pale, with pale graying hair, a large white face, deeply wrinkled, a large white nose. He wears a pale-gray suit, very loosely cut from some very light silky cloth, and a white silk tie with a large pearl pin. His hat is a panama of the finest straw. And as he strolls with slow important tread beside his handsome notable wife, who carries her sunshade as an officer in a ceremonial march carries his sword, he is always surrounded by a little group of friends, whom Manklow describes as his bugs, fleas, moths, and beetles.

One is Jobson, who always walks beside him on the other side from Mrs. Sturge and who listens to his conversation with an air of jovial admiration, like some rustic at a conjurer's. One is a tall yellow-faced woman in fluttering draperies who is seen usually when Mrs. Sturge is away. And there are always two or three young people attending on this court: young writers, a painter who is exhibiting at the art shop impressionist landscapes which Manklow calls copy-cat French stuff.

Tabitha, who has learnt water-color painting at school, in the Birket Foster style, agrees with Manklow that these pictures are a "try on—any kid could paint better than that with a cow's tail."

"There's no drawing at all."

"All the same, it's a good bet; I shouldn't wonder if it didn't catch on."

"It couldn't catch on, rubbish like that."

"Well, the old stuff has had a long run." And reflecting deeply, he says, "It might be worth trying; as you say, you don't need to know anything."

But Tabitha is indignant both with the pictures and those who admire them. She knows from *Punch* and Harry what æsthetes are: affected creatures, moral degenerates, enemies of all that is British.

One trick of Sturge's offends her deeply. Every now and then he will stop and, making a window of his thumb and forefingers, gaze at the beach and the sea. One or two of the party will at once copy him with little exclamations of pleasure or sudden queries, "Would it be better perhaps to leave out that boat, and abolish the fat woman with the little girl?"

"Just showing off," Tabitha says. And Manklow, staring at the rich man and his friends with his frigid eyes, like green tea, will comment, "That's the æsthetic pose—they're æsthetic all through, that lot. Look at the old boy, dripping with money and muggery. Did you ever see his magazine, the *Symbolist*? Came out last year; it only ran to three numbers. But he'd got the idea all right—a bit of dirt wrapped up in hand-made paper."

"Dirt?"

"Why, Tib, that's what I'm telling you; ten years ago a publisher couldn't publish damn. He had to put two stars. And now they're printing Zola. It's the biggest opening in the century; there's been nothing like it since before the French Revolution." He deeply reflects with a faraway gaze. "And that one started in the same way, with dirty books. Rousseau and Voltaire and the rest of 'em. Well, we've asked for it. What a joke if old bag-belly Sturge gets his throat cut, after all the stuff he printed about culture and knocking off the censor."

"Why did his paper fail?"

"Good God! How could the old jelly know how to run a paper—he couldn't push a pram downhill! Now if he had the sense to take advice—"

Manklow has plans for all kinds of papers, including an æsthetic quarterly. He has even tried to tempt Sturge with the drawings of someone called Dobey, a young London artist, hitherto unpublished. Manklow has got drawings from Dobey under promise to have them published, and meanwhile he makes crude tracings of them, which he offers for sale in the saloon bars.

Tabitha, busy for most of the day, weary at night, and going out only for a morning walk with one of the men, does not see the drawings, till one morning she finds them lying on the table in the main attic. Then she is revolted.

"But, Mr. Manklow, what horrible things."

He smiles at her with his sad friendly confidence. "I know; they all look putrid, don't they? That's what I mean. Dobey has got a real idea there—something new, and naughty as well. People will lap it up, and the critics will foam at the mouth."

And Tabitha looks at the man in horror. She feels such repulsion that she can't stay in the room with him.

18

SHE is the more resolved upon getting rid of Manklow because of her happiness with the new, kindly Dick. Never has she been so happy. It is not that the man is more amorous. As she tells herself, like an old wife, "All that is not really important." It is his true friendliness, his respectfulness, his regard for her as a person. He runs after her to wrap her up from the wind, he is deeply disturbed to find that she has a headache. And though he takes her wages, he always confers with her on their disposal. He agrees that at least half a crown shall go into the money box. And though it is understood that she shall budget for at least one bottle of whisky, at three and sixpence, he always kisses her when she does so, and says, "Ah, the little housekeeper."

So that when that Friday night she hands over her thirty shillings and leans on Bonser's strong supporting arm, she begins at once, "Do you really like Mr. Manklow, Dick?"

"Good God no—that low cad! I just don't think of him at all."

"Don't you feel it would be nicer without him? Now that we're more settled."

"Yes, but the tout is useful, and we don't need to pay him anything. A kick up the ass is good enough for a dirty swine like that; and to do him justice, he never tries it on with me. Now just you run and wash your teeth while I see a dear old friend in the Goat about the state of his health."

"Don't forget the whisky."

"No, that's an idea. Thank you, Pops, I won't forget the whisky. I'll make a note of it. Thank you, sweetie."

And when he comes in, having had a sample of the whisky, he puts her on his knee and begins to pinch her black and blue. This is a sign of his highest regard, and Tabitha says at once, "Oh, Dick, I simply can't bear that man any more; we simply must have a place of our own."

"The Pops, the whisky winner, the prop of the house. She speaks, and all obey."

"And, Dick darling, do you realize that if we only had another pound a week we could have a real home?"

Bonser, growing fond, does not permit himself to be annoyed by this suggestion, but merely gives a rather crueler pinch. And when Tabitha cries out, says in a languishing tone, "How he loves his Pops."

But waking up in the morning he catches the words, apparently at the end of a long speech, "Only two or three rooms—but a real place of our own."

Bonser, after satisfaction, is affectionate. A certain lazy good nature in the man infuses him with kindly feelings. He squeezes Tabitha and says, "A nice little home for a nice little spoofer."

"And then we could be really married."

"Married?" He is growing sleepy again. "What's the hurry?—All you girls are mad to get married. I don't think so much of marriage; making a business of a pleasure."

"But, Dick, you promised—"

"Well, don't nag me just now, don't spoil it all."

"But, Dick, we can't go on forever like this."

"All right, don't; you can always take a holiday with brother Harry."

"How can I ask Harry for help until we're married?"

"Just do it, that's the way to do things. Do 'em."

"Dick, you know it *might* be necessary."

"What for? You can always say you're married. I don't mind; I'll back you up."

"Well, but—suppose we had a family."

Tabitha has put out this remark in a casual tone, as if offering a pure hypothesis. But Bonser is at once fully awake. "What's this?" He sits up in bed. "What d'you mean?"

"Oh, I'm not sure yet—but—"

"And didn't I tell you to look out for yourself? Well, it's your own funeral."

He jumps out of bed and dresses with indignant speed. "My God, telling a chap like that, when I was feeling so happy."

Tabitha, sitting up in bed, stares at him. "But, Dick, aren't you glad?"

"Glad?"

His tone is such that Manklow, thrusting his head out of his cubbyhole, quickly draws it in again.

Tabitha gets slowly out of bed and puts on her dressing gown. She has a surprised expression.

"But, Dick, don't you really want me to have a baby, our own baby?"

Bonser suddenly walks up to her and thrusts his nose almost into her face. "Nag, nag! If you think you've got me nailed with this baby—"

"I don't think anything. I only know this baby is yours, too, and you've got to do something about it." Tabitha is very angry.

"Got to?"

"Yes, got to. Really, Dick—" and her tone implores him to be less childish—"it's quite time you faced the facts."

"What facts?"

"That you're just playing at life. I don't want to nag you, Dick, but you simply will not realize that you can't just dodge out of everything."

At this moment Tabitha feels in the middle of her face a dull painful shock, and finds herself lying on her back in the midst of darkness, illuminated by an explosion of brilliant comets. The comets go out, and she protests in wondering tones, "Dick." When at last by a strong effort she sits up she is just in time to see Bonser, with bag and coat, in the act of disappearing through the door, which bangs behind him. Tabitha cries out in her surprise, "But this is beyond everything. I'm not going to stand it."

Blood is spouting from her nose. She gets up and goes to wash her face, which is painful and, what is worse, swollen and ugly. When she looks in the glass she sees before her the evidence of a disaster. Her eyes are closing fast and the pain of her nose seems to be spreading through her whole body. She sits down in a chair, holding a wet handkerchief to her nose, and reflects, "At least I know what he is now—a complete brute and cad. I see that he never loved me at all. I never want to see him again. Yes, that's one good thing. I'm cured of Dick Bonser."

But at once sobs take hold of her, tears burst from her eyes, and she exclaims, "Oh how I hate him, how I lo-oathe him."

19

SUDDENLY she jumps up, dresses in frantic haste, thrusts some cotton wool into her nostrils to stop the bleeding, and hurries into the street. "No, I won't stand it; I'll teach him! Yes, I'll jump into the river—no, under a train. Yes, a train." And she is solaced by the idea of this violent bloody end, a revengeful end. She greets it eagerly as it approaches.

She darts wildly across the streets, careless of traffic. Car men shout at her; a cabby, swearing, pulls up his horse, but not before the shaft glances against her shoulder and spins her into the gutter.

Several bystanders run to pick her up, and support her into a shop, a draper's shop. Tabitha, dizzy with a blow on her head, mutters, "No, no, no," in a faint voice. She doesn't want brandy, she doesn't want that consolation. She wants to kill. Meanwhile her eyes dwell vaguely on an extraordinary object in the glass opposite her chair: a young woman with blackened eyes and swollen nose, covered with mud and blood, who is making extraordinary faces. But what especially seizes her attention is the woman's hat, a large flowered hat which has been knocked sideways and smashed, so that every flower hangs broken and crooked. It is, in short, an utterly dissipated hat; and the contrast of its dissipation and the woman's miserable grimaces is for some reason extremely comical.

Tabitha, as she gradually recovers her senses, begins to be aware of this ridiculous aspect of misery; and then perceiving that this woebegone creature, with blackening eyes, swollen nose plugged with bloodstained cotton wool, torn and muddy clothes and ridiculous hat, is herself, suddenly breaks into laughter.

The young men look alarmed, and call, "Hi, hurry up with that brandy." The draper's assistant, a thin young woman in black, takes Tabitha's hand and slaps it.

"But I'm not—it's not hysterics—" Tabitha gasps. "It's because—it's so—funny. Everything happening all at once—"

The brandy is at her lips. She tries to refuse it, but drinks out of politeness to the young man who has brought it. "Oh thank you—it's awfully good of you." But immense waves of laughter seize her. She is again the schoolgirl who, when she giggled, giggled a little more wildly than the rest of the class. She is carried away, borne off upon this strong laughter, dissolving her will, her anger. With tears in her eyes she tries to explain, "But I'm not—it's not—it's only—so funny."

They put her in the cab, and the cabby, grumbling but relieved that no policeman has appeared, drives her back to her room and helps her upstairs to the attic. Manklow, poring over his drawings at the table, gets up with a grin of astonishment, and Tabitha, seeing him, begins to laugh again.

" 'Igh strikes," the cabman explains briefly. "Young lady 'ad a fall." He deposits Tabitha on the bed and disappears with alacrity.

Tabitha, laughing, protests to Manklow, "But it's not—I'm not—it's only—everything—everything at once."

Manklow brings out the whisky, and again Tabitha drinks. He sits down beside her and puts an arm round her. "Now tell me about it."

And, laughing, she tells him. "First, Dick hit me; and he's gone—left me. And then I was going to throw myself in front of a train, but I fell down and—look at me. Aren't I a picture?"

"Poor Tib—and you say Dick's gone?"

"Yes, and I'm glad. I hate him."

Manklow consoles her. "You know, Tib, I couldn't make out how you stood that cad. To treat you like that, in your condition, too. Yes, I know; I couldn't help hearing. Not only a swine, but a fool, too. Chucking away a girl like you." His voice rises with contempt. "Simply a fool."

"Oh, I hate him, I never want to see him again."

"You're quite right, you could do better for yourself than that any day of the week."

Tabitha perceives the man's new elation, but pays no attention to it. The laughter has left her weak, exhausted, but warm. There is a warmth in her, a mild warmth like that of a convalescent whose temperature is sub-normal, but whose blood is running free. And this animal warmth is highly genial. She appreciates Manklow's arm; she is grateful for his deft, almost feminine handling, while he pulls off her muddy frock, takes off her shoes, sponges her face, washes her hands, and tucks her up under a quilt.

"I'll see the café people and get you off for today."

"But I don't want to go back there."

"I shouldn't throw up the job right away."

She thinks lazily, "He wants the money"; but she is neither surprised nor indignant. She is amused, and the amusement itself is not cynical. It is warm, lazy, uncritical. She smiles to think that the detestable Manklow should rely upon her to support him. "And with two black eyes! I wonder what the café people will think."

But Manklow arranges everything. Within twenty-four hours Tabitha is back on the platform, thumping the piano. Only certain ferns in pots have been arranged to hide her, and she keeps her back turned on the tables. She is not now amused by her situation. Her head aches, she feels sick, and no words can express her loathing of the tinkling cheap piano and the cheap tunes she is playing for the hundredth time. The warmth of that big laugh is no longer a pervasive luxury; it is a more concentrated heat in her breast. She does not want to kill herself; on the contrary, she can't imagine how she came to form such an intention, for, as she says, "Dick was not worth it." But she is impatient, she is full of that restless sensation which is life looking for a purpose.

Manklow is still charming to her; and to her surprise, he is also most discreet. He has moved out of his cubbyhole to a lodging next door. He has never been so respectful, and he does not ask for her money, so that she is actually paying her way at the lodgings.

Tabitha is grateful to him, and even glad of his company. For she is shy of the street, with her bruised face; and since she has never been a reader, she welcomes Manklow's amusing talk.

He is anxious about her face, and sends her to a chemist; he is delighted that her nose is not broken, and insists on her buying some ointment. "But my face doesn't matter," Tabitha says. "What matters is what I'm going to do next. I simply can't go home."

"Get your face right," Manklow says with his grin, "and we'll see."

"But what will we see? Of course, if I could get a better job—"

"Yes, you must get a better job."

A week later, when her nose has recovered its shape, and a slight darkening about the eyes, as Manklow points out, only increases their brightness, Tabitha is coming down from her dais after her luncheon performance when she sees two men get up from a table and stand in her way—Manklow and Sturge's friend, Jobson.

Manklow presents Jobson, who shakes hands with her in an impressive manner and thanks her for her beautiful music. "But I hear you are a real musician, Mrs. Bonser. You oughtn't to be playing in a café—"

Tabitha admits that she detests her work in the café, and Jobson asks her if she would agree to play to some friends of his at the hotel. "Really musical people who will appreciate your art."

"But I'm not really very good, Mr. Jobson—I was only learning."

Jobson, however, is enthusiastic. He declares that great artists are never satisfied with themselves, but that, of course, allowances will be made for Tabitha's lack of practice. Manklow says gravely, "Of course you must go, Tibby—it's your big chance!" And Tabitha sees that indeed she can't refuse.

Manklow takes her to a second-hand dress shop where he insists on a frock which seems to Tabitha much too tight in the hips and much too low off the shoulders. "That's the style, Tib; give them all you've got, and your figure is one of your big assets. Regular Dresden. Pocket Venus. Go in and win. We're off."

And in fact Tabitha, to her own surprise, has a great success. Jobson's friends applaud loudly; Sturge is especially kind. She has, he says, gazing at her intensely with his pale eyes, "a remarkable talent." He insists that she shall accept five guineas for her concert, and repeat it next week. Meanwhile he will be honored if she will use the piano in his sitting room, for practice.

20 Jobson asks her to dinner, and Tabitha finds herself at once a member of the little group which surrounds the rich amateur, which flatters him and chatters about the arts. All defer to her with particular respect. What does Mrs. Bonser think about the influence of Constable on Delacroix?

"I'm sure it was good."

"How right that is," Sturge says. "Yes, it was a good, a liberating influence."

Tabitha sees her first Beardsley drawings, greatly admired by the whole party. She says cautiously, "Aren't they *queer*?"

"The exact word," says Sturge. "It's the queerness—she has caught the very nuance."

Tabitha is astonished by the ease of her triumph. She is moved by the generous kindness of her new friends. She has never met people who wish so much to give pleasure, especially Sturge. "Really," Tabitha thinks of her benefactor, "he's a perfect dear. And what luck for me that he is so keen on art and helping artists. If he gives me a real start, I shall be eternally grateful; I ought to be."

Mrs. Sturge is away, and Sturge takes her walking on the furthest part of the front, which is almost deserted. He talks to her in his soft mild voice, about art and its enemies.

"Prudery, British prudery, that is the enemy," he murmurs. "Look how they treat their artists." And he speaks of the conventionality of everybody and everything in England. "People hate everything that's new and important simply because it is important, because it threatens to wake them up and make them think or feel—really think and really feel." And bending a little toward Tabitha, projecting his large white nose, which seems, in a certain aggressiveness, to contradict the soft voice, he says, "I can say that to you, Mrs. Bonser, but not to Mrs. Sturge. She wouldn't understand." He smiles like a conspirator, and Tabitha says, "Mrs. Sturge looked very nice; and I'm sure she's very good."

"Of course, of course, the best of women—but she doesn't understand art, Mrs. Bonser; she is not an artist." And after a moment's pause, he begins to praise Tabitha's music. He has never been so moved. Tabitha has a great gift. "I can't tell you, Mrs. Bonser, what your friendship has meant to me: a new life, a new courage; I have indeed been born again."

Tabitha is astonished. She wants to laugh. But Sturge is talking, not like a lover but like a philosopher, and this makes her ashamed of her impulse to laugh. "You don't understand how life dies out of a man, Mrs. Bonser; how it drains away until in a few years he is simply a dead thing. Millions die like that, on their feet. You only have to look round railway carriages or omnibuses to see them—walking corpses. And they don't even know how it has happened. A man does not know even that he is dead until by some accident, some spiritual experience, he is revived, and can compare his new state with his former one. Yes, life, life—" and here the greedy nose which makes Sturge for the moment resemble a white bloodhound on the scent, prods forward—"how precious it is, how mysterious in its sources. Beauty, love, art. But after all, Mrs. Bonser—" and the nose approaches nearer to her cheek—"should we be surprised? Life is experience, it is personal in its very essence, it is feeling, it is the true joy which arises from the sensation—"

"I see what you mean," Tabitha says. "People in love do feel rather excited and lively."

"Yes, yes, you understand, I knew you would understand; it is a rebirth, a resurrection."

One evening the new *Yellow Book* is handed round, and Sturge shows Tabitha a Beardsley drawing of a girl in a garden. "Beautiful—marvelous."

"She's certainly rather—" Tabitha stops. She has found it safer not to be too explicit.

"You do not recognize yourself?"

"Me?"

"You are a living Beardsley, Mrs. Bonser."

And all the group exclaim that she is a living Beardsley. "Quite beautiful—"

Tabitha begins to laugh, but seeing in Sturge's eyes a sad reproachful look, she grows serious again. And when she describes this scene to Manklow, he says with mild disgust, "It's what I said, didn't I? You're the new style—well, take my tip and make your hay quick, before some of those artists think up another funny one."

21

ONE afternoon, Sturge, handing Tabitha down the rocks and holding her hand rather longer than usual in the operation, says, "You have been a wonderful friend to me, Mrs. Bonser; is there nothing I can do for you in some slight return?"

"Oh, but you have done a great deal; it has been awfully good of you to let me practice, and to engage me to play."

"Nothing, nothing; a duty." And half an hour later he is repeating his offer. "Suppose you were in any kind of difficulty, Mrs. Bonser, you must not hesitate to call upon me. I beg you most earnestly."

When he repeats a similar remark for the third time, Tabitha sees that Sturge has more than the common motive of friendship. She thinks, "He's heard something, the place is full of gossip." But she feels a revulsion against Sturge. She says to herself, "It is kind of him, he is a wonderfully kind man"; but she does not like it, that he should know her secret. Her feeling is that the secret ought to be between the despicable Bonser and herself. She complains of the cold wind and goes home.

On the next afternoon she manages to avoid Sturge. She slips in to her practicing by a back door, and excuses herself from playing in the evening. And she is just about to say her prayers, as usual, before getting into bed, when there is a knock on the door, and Jobson walks in.

"Excuse me, Mrs. Bonser, but it's rather urgent. I have to go to town tomorrow, and I'll be away some days."

Tabitha has already thrown on her dressing gown. She answers coldly. "If you really can't wait till tomorrow," and takes a seat on an upright chair.

Jobson is neither embarrassed, nor, like Manklow, evasive and tactful. He goes to the point. His friend Sturge, he says, is very fond of her and very worried about her, because he happens to know her situation; that she has been deserted, that she's in the family way, and that she hasn't any money. Mr. Sturge can't bear to think of anyone so dear to him, so talented and so charming in such a position, and he has a plan to help her.

"But why doesn't he tell me all this himself?" Tabitha asks, highly offended with Jobson's breezy manner.

"Because you never let him. You've been dodging away. And another thing, because he's shy. Fred Sturge is a great man, Mrs. Bonser—I've been his friend for twenty years and proud of it—but he's a shy man. I don't suppose he's ever told you what he feels about you. All I can say is, he feels a lot; don't make any mistake about that. Yes, Mrs. Bonser, this is a big chance for you."

"What do you mean by chance?"

"Fred's idea is this. To be quite frank, it was my idea and he jumped at it. You go over to France, to a nice quiet flat where I know the woman very well, get over your little misfortune—we'll have the best medical advice; and then—well, then you'll have the ball at your feet. Fred would do anything for you, Mrs. B."

"But all this will cost a lot of money."

Jobson makes a gesture. "Fred will be only too glad, and so will I."

The man suddenly bursts out with a kind of jovial candor. "Really and truly. Because it's what Fred needs, a nice little girl of his own, where he can get away from his damned family."

Tabitha suddenly understands Jobson's plan, and jumps up. "I think you're perfectly disgusting, Mr. Jobson; and Mr. Sturge is worse. At least you dared to come yourself and make what you call your proposition."

John has also got up. He is much surprised but also indignant. "You don't mean to say you were that chap's wife—"

"Go away at once, please."

"I was told that you were just touring round with him and bilking landladies. I'm sorry, Mrs. Bonser, if I made a mistake, but I certainly understood that you would be open to an offer."

"Please go—"

"Certainly." Jobson goes out, and Tabitha packs. She is determined to leave Heathland by the earliest train. She cannot sleep for rage, and in the morning, when Manklow comes in, she gives him a glance which is meant to annihilate. But Manklow is grave, and indignant.

"So you turned him down."

Tabitha puts on her hat in silence. Her fingers are shaking with anger.

"Dick owed me four pounds, by the way; I don't know if you would like to pay it."

"I suppose you suggested that wonderful plan to Mr. Jobson. How much was he going to pay you if I accepted?"

"I was doing you a good turn, Tib; best chance you ever had to get your hook in. Why, that old rabbit would have done anything for you—anything. And I shouldn't wonder if he was impotent to boot."

Tabitha picks up her bag and carries it to the door. It is heavy and pulls her light figure sideways. Manklow tries to take it from her, but she resists him. She cannot bear to let him serve her. But he keeps his hand on it, supporting some of the weight, and speaks to her with the tone of a moral preceptor, "Your trouble, Tib, is you don't see things straight. It's a rotten world, but that's no reason for getting huffed when someone throws you a lifebuoy. I did think Dick had taught you something with that slap."

"You would."

"You couldn't let me have two quid on account? I've been to a certain expense, you know."

He follows her down the street, while she seeks frantically for a cab. "Ten bob for Jobson's drinks and getting my boots mended to go into the Heath after him. As for me being a pimp," he says with mournful reproach, "who was I pimping for? You ought to go down on your knees and thank me."

At last Tabitha reaches the cab. Manklow takes the bag as she opens the door, and retains it to give his last instructions. "You think you're a victim, Tib, but what did you go with Dickie for? It wasn't for religious exercise exactly, Tib, was it? You didn't do it on your knees. You're another of the sisters who want it both ways, Tib: all the fun of the fair, a halo to go to bed in, and choirs of angels to open the dance."

Tabitha says with dignity, "Please give me my bag—unless you mean to steal it."

"And don't forget you owe me four pounds—four pounds three and two pence."

As she drives away, Tabitha sits very upright. She thinks, "How right Dick was; a low horrid cad. As if I enjoyed being with Dick."

They have reached the station. A porter seizes the bag. Tabitha has not yet decided where she is going, but suddenly she is overwhelmed with a desire for home, for Harry—so good, so wise, so understanding. She says to the man, "London," and buys her ticket.

She thinks, as the train rushes her away from the disgusting Heathland, "I needn't tell him anything. I'll just stay for a little until I can get work—any kind of work—perhaps teaching; there must be something."

22

When at the Cedars she enters the hall, always dark, and runs against a perambulator, her first impression is simply that she has somehow come into the wrong house. But at once she notices that what is changed is merely the position of the hatstand, to accommodate the pram, and of the chest to take the place of the hatstand.

"Hullo!"

She turns to see Harry, who stands, with his little bag in one hand, his hat in the other, at the door.

"Oh, Harry, it's me."

"So I see."

She notices at once that Harry is annoyed about something. She flies to him and throws her arms round his neck. "Oh, Harry, you can't believe how lovely it is to be back."

"Ah!"

"You haven't been too worried about me."

"No, we didn't expect to hear anything this time."

"Harry dear, I know I've been an *awful* nuisance, but really if you knew—"

"I'm afraid I can't wait now."

And it appears that Harry is not good any more. He does not want to understand, even to listen. He is indeed most strangely changed. He is always in a hurry. He rushes, shouts. There is an influenza epidemic, and he is awaiting three confinements. He worries at breakfast about patients, about the brougham which has a bad horse, and about bills. It appears that the baby has been very expensive, and that Edith, after producing the baby, has indulged herself in a complete trousseau of new frocks.

And Edith is even more disastrously changed than Harry. She greets Tabitha with the words, "So you've turned up again—like a bad penny. What did you do with the key of the safe?" And after that she scarcely speaks. But not only has her good nature disappeared, so have her looks. She has a third new face and figure; she is fat and red; her cheeks have filled up, but her nose is still large and it has also acquired a reddish flush on the wings. She has coarsened beyond belief, so that Tabitha thinks with wonder, "How can Harry love such a common vulgar woman?"

The baby is a boy, and when Harry complains that his breakfast is cold or that lunch is not ready, Edith says with calm indignation, "Well, you've got your boy." Harry then makes an angry despairing face and hurries away to his work.

Tabitha is shocked to see how old and worn Harry appears. She thinks, "That woman will worry him to death." But she does not offer her sympathy to Harry because she feels his unreasonable anger against herself.

She looks back upon her fearful and extraordinary experiences of the last five months, and thinks with indignation, "He's no interest in what happened to me; and, after all, I admitted I'd been a nuisance."

She is aloof from these uncomprehending unkind people. She lets it be understood that she will soon go, as soon as she can get a concert engagement. She comforts herself with that grand dignity necessary in a dependent. And she practices eight hours a day with the moral devotion of one aggrieved.

But one day when she has been sick after breakfast, and is lying down afterwards with a headache, Edith brings Harry to her, and when he has examined her, he says in his weary voice, which seems to be exhausted by his worries, "Do you realize your condition?"

"I tell you, I'm going away at once."

"And what then? Who's to pay for you?"

"Me, of course."

Edith, meeting her as she goes haughtily to practice, says, "I know what I should do—jump downstairs or take a pink pill."

And the same day there appears on Tabitha's bedroom mantelpiece a box of pink pills. Tabitha can hardly believe her eyes. "As if I was a bad woman, to do such a thing."

It is the slight upon her morals which enrages her. She snatches up the pills and runs to Harry in the surgery. "Edith gave me these."

Harry accepts the box and throws it into a drawer. "Have you taken any?"

"Of course not. Harry, you didn't know Edith was going to give me the pills?"

The man walks to the door as if in disgust, but turns at the door and says, "Edith was acting for the best—she was thinking of your good, as well as mine. You have no right to take that tone about Edith."

"So you did know?"

"I think we'd better drop the subject—I see you are determined to be unreasonable."

"Unreasonable." Tabitha breathes the word aloud. It expresses her astonishment and despair. "Because I won't do a crime."

"Don't talk such nonsense." He goes out and bangs the door.

Tabitha, who has still a few pounds left from her musical evenings at Heathland, leaves the same afternoon for a lodging in Pimlico. She has decided that she cannot wait to be a concert pianist. She will teach, even play in a tea shop, rather than stay any longer as an unwelcome guest at the Cedars.

And Manklow, pushing about the saloons of Heathland with his bad tracings of Dobey's masterpieces, receives, about ten days later, a note, enclosing a postal order for ten shillings. "Dear Mr. Manklow, this is only an installment, all I can afford just now. I hope you are well. I am staying here for the present till I can get a job. Yours most sincerely, Tabitha."

Manklow thinks, "She's learnt sense." But he finds a young woman whom he scarcely recognizes—very thin, rather feverish—who receives him with a cry of, "What a surprise, Mr. Manklow."

"Didn't you expect me?" he asks, offended by this parade.

"I'm so glad you've come."

"And brother wasn't so pleased?"

"Oh, my brother was very nice—it was my sister-in-law who made trouble. You wouldn't believe it, Mr. Manklow." And she tells the story, giving to Edith all Harry's remarks. "And, you know, she sets up to be a most *respectable religious* kind of person."

"Of course she does, it's her job. But look here, Tib—"

"It's just what you said at Heathland, people like that only think of themselves, and what they call their position."

"They'd better, but, Tib—"

"Oh, how rotten it all is." And the girl, flushed with indignation, continues to abuse respectable people for a long time. "And it's not only," she says, "that the British people are the most narrow-minded in the world, but the biggest Philistines." She understands now how right Mr. Sturge was. "No one in England cares for the arts. Look how they treated Whistler, and how they ban the impressionists. As for music, they don't even want teachers. The agents simply laugh at you if you ask for a post."

Manklow, fidgeting, groaning, snatches at the name of Sturge. "That's our ticket, Tib, all the time, Sturge—"

"Above all, it's the awful hypocrisy."

"Look here, what are you after, Tib? Are you going to see Sturge or shall I get on to the business man?"

"Who is the business man?"

"Jobson."

"I rather hate Mr. Jobson. Do you know, Mr. Manklow—Roger, that woman even took a moral tone about it. I believe she was proud of herself."

"Yes, yes; well, it's a bit late. What time will you be in tomorrow?"

"Oh, I'll be in all the morning. I've really nothing to do. But I mustn't waste your time."

"You're not wasting my time, Tib; at least I don't think so. Good night, say your prayers."

"Oh, I've given all that up."

And the next day he brings Jobson. There is a conference which is surprisingly short, amicable, explicit in detail and yet vague in general support.

Tabitha is to have an immediate advance to enable her to go to Paris, and study music, for at least nine months. Jobson will find her a lodging there with a friend who, as he says, knows the ropes. At the end of her training, she will return to a lodging, also to be provided by Jobson, on Sturge's behalf, in some suitable quiet street in Mayfair, where a piano will not be objected to. She can then look for an engagement.

"And of course I shall pay Mr. Sturge back."

"Of course you will." Jobson is heartily in agreement. "Of course you will, Mrs. Bonser. He has, as you know, the highest opinion of your talents; he will be delighted to see you making the best use of them."

The party then adjourns to supper in a neighboring restaurant, where Manklow, to the surprise and discomfiture of Tabitha, gets solemnly drunk and, repeatedly leaning toward her across the table, toasts her in the words, "Here's to the talents, both of 'em."

She is relieved when Jobson, with sudden brutality, remarks, "You don't look too well, Mr. Manklow; I think that you need fresh air," and breaks up the party.

Jobson in fact is highly irritated against Manklow. "What d'you mean?" he growls. "With your funny jokes you might have bust up the deal."

But Manklow is moved by an equal wrath. He answers sharply, "She's been going on like that for two days, putting on an act. It's silly, Jobson. What right has she to play the fool? And she owes me three pounds ten."

"That's all right, we're looking after you. And as for what you call nonsense, that's just feelings. I don't set up to be an expert in women, Mr. Manklow, but I do know that much; they've got feelings. You leave Tibby to me."

Jobson indeed is most solicitous. He conducts Tabitha to Paris, and assures himself of her comfort. He agrees even to hiring a grand piano and a teacher, though, as he says, an upright piano would have done. But he is anxious to please Tabitha, because, as he says, she has been so reasonable.

He receives only one shock, when it appears that she is determined to have her baby.

"But what," Sturge asks, "did she go to Paris for?"

"Goodness knows," Jobson answers. "Does anyone ever know why girls do anything? They don't know themselves. But don't worry, old man; I'll see that she gets well looked after. It's largely a question of after care; the stays. And there's one thing, the kid will make her safe."

"Safe?"

"Yes; with a kid she's bound to come to hand. Bound to."

And this expectation is perfectly justified. At the end of six months Tabitha has her baby, a son; and after that there is no more talk of concert engagements, except as a distant prospect. Instead, it is established that she shall come home and live in a lodging provided by Sturge, while she looks about her.

The flat is ready; and, by another excellent plan of Jobson's, it has been obtained, by paying a fine to the sitting tenant, immediately above Jobson's own flat in West Street, near the park. "You can go in there when you're supposed to be seeing me," Jobson says; "and besides, I can keep an eye on the bit in case she tries any games. Not that you've anything to be afraid of there." And as the two men wait for Tabitha on the appointed afternoon, he encourages Sturge. "She's good stuff, that kid. Why, look at her having that baby. The fact is, Fred, she's been brought up all right; she's a bit of a lady, and that's always the best buy in the end. More expensive at the start, but more reliable all round. It's character you've got to go for in a case like this, character all the time."

23

Sturge, at fifty-three, is a man whose life has been utterly respectable. He has always been well off, with a good business in wholesale groceries; he has married well, and has two daughters. All would be well with him if he had not acquired, from another rich amateur, instead of golf, a taste for art.

Mrs. Sturge has been taught to like art; but unluckily she has been faithful to her early tastes, while Sturge has moved on from Rossetti and Ruskin to Swinburne and Whistler, to the impressionists. So that Mrs. Sturge has come to despise a taste so unreliable, that runs after every new fashion in art. As for Beardsley, his latest craze, she finds him disgusting. She asks very reasonably how art that shows evil people, whose every line breathes the corruption of vice, can be good art. "How can it be good," she asks her husband, "if it teaches evil?"

And Sturge cannot explain. He can answer only that her views are old-fashioned, an argument that fills her large sane mind with contempt.

The two daughters have been brought up in the same contempt, so that Sturge's interests can find no sympathy in his own family. And this, by natural consequence, has driven him to extremes. The lust for what he calls discoveries, that is, new unappreciated artists, is the first motive of his life. It takes the place for him of racing, collecting, gambling, hunting, big-game shooting; he would perish of boredom without it. But, of course, as his passion has increased, he has found it more unpopular at home. He has been glad, for the last ten years, to use Jobson's flat for the entertainment of his more ragged or drunken discoveries.

Jobson, an early friend of Sturge, detested by Mrs. Sturge for his vulgarity and bad influence, is of course delighted to lend his flat to encourage all the artistic schemes, and now the passion for Tabitha. "Well, old boy," he has said, "if you like her, why not take her? I'm pretty sure she's to be had. Put her in a flat."

Sturge has smiled sadly and shaken his head. "Not for me, Jobson, I'm not the man."

"Then you ought to be; it's just what you need."

"Put her in a flat." The idea haunts Sturge like a vision of impossible delight, an enterprise too exciting, too dangerous. But Jobson laughs at his terrors; he mentions highly respected city men who keep mistresses—he himself has kept one woman or another from the age of eighteen. He never lets go of his scheme. And now, by means that he scarcely understands, Sturge is committed to the adventure of his life. He is to possess this beauty, this living work of art, who is not only entrancing to his senses, but delights him with her sympathy and admiration.

But he visibly trembles while the minutes drag, and the girl does not come. He turns to Jobson and says with relief, "She won't come now, she's changed her mind."

Jobson shakes his head. "She can't do that."

Sturge takes an agitated turn in the room. "I suppose not. It's a cruel thing, Wally."

"Cruel. Not a bit of it. You're doing her a damned good turn. So long as you're firm. Keep her straight, Bunny. She's young, but she's had some big knocks. Don't rush things, that's all. Give her time to get used to the idea. After all, you're sitting pretty. She's got to toe the line sooner or later. She knows who pays the piper."

24

SUDDENLY there is a loud ring at the bell. The new maid, a smart young woman with experience in the profession, goes to the door; Sturge turns quite green, Jobson slightly pink. And a strange young woman, a girl with French clothes, a new poise of the head, a different shape of face, a new walk, even a new figure, sails in, followed by a Scotswoman, tall and bony as a wardress, with a young baby in her arms.

This new Tabitha, carrying her nose very high, does not even say how do you do to Sturge. She simply asks in a cold, a new and imperious voice, "Which is the nursery, please?"

Jobson hastens to show her the nursery. She disappears into it with the nurse and is not seen again.

Jobson, after a long delay, perceiving that this is the end of the episode, says to Sturge, who, with a slightly better color, is sitting hunched up in a chair, "So that's all right."

"All right?"

"Well, there she is, landed. Go in and win." He goes out, leaving Sturge, in extreme agony, to hear the distant cries of the baby and the sharp comments of the Scotswoman.

He departs stealthily, fearful of being noticed.

But the next morning, no sooner has he entered his office than he is handed a note: "Dear Fred, the water was quite cold last night for baby's bath. Will you please see about it at once? Tabitha Bonser."

And he spends most of the next week interviewing plumbers, seeking patent towel rails.

His proposal, very timidly offered, to buy her some frocks, which he thinks would suit her delicate style better than the French models, is badly received. And Tabitha is indignant because he sends her a bracelet.

When after some weeks she consents to accept a new frock, only to save the French ones, she puts it on so badly that he is obliged to appeal to the maid.

As for entertainment, she is rarely to be seen when he visits the flat. Sturge has looked forward to showing off this new artistic treasure, his Beardsley girl. He has planned little parties for her in quiet good restaurants, at which old comrades, like Griller, the English scholar, or Dewpark, the critic, will meet his friend, the charming young widow, Mrs. Bonser, and afterwards spend the evening at her flat. But on each occasion, when all is arranged, Tabitha defaults because the baby has some small ailment. When Sturge ventures to reproach her, she answers fiercely, "How can I go out when Johnny is so ill?"

And Jobson, full of anxiety for his friend, says to him, "My dear boy, it's always the same with these bits when they get a bastard; either they hate it or worship it. But it's a danger. If she finds she can play you up, she'd do it on purpose. You've got to show her where she gets off."

25

STURGE is still meditating this advice when one evening, coming to the flat, and insinuating himself through the door with his usual deference, he hears a sound of men's voices. And entering the sitting room, he finds Tabitha in the most lively conversation with three men—Manklow, a very youthful and spotty boy with an immense bush of black hair, and a tall languid man, with a singularly long face.

"Oh, Fred." Tabitha jumps up in excitement. "Here's Mr. Manklow come back; isn't it nice? And this is Mr. Dobey, who does the most wonderful drawings, and Mr. Hodsell, who writes novels. Look, isn't this good of Mr. Dobey?" She shows a drawing in a portfolio.

Sturge, still confused, and therefore pompous, looks at a drawing entitled "Onan among the Rocks" and says, "Yes, yes."

"I suppose you're shocked," says Tabitha tartly. "It's not quite so *respectable* as Beardsley, is it?"

"Very interesting."

And Manklow, who has not troubled to take the cigarette out of his mouth, remarks, "That's it; Tib has it, Mr. Sturge. Dobey goes one better. Take my advice and freeze onto him, or Mr. Wrinch will get in first."

Wrinch is a Quaker, a banker, renowned like Sturge for his encouragement of young artists, but usually about ten years behind the van.

"Wrinch," says Sturge coldly, "is a millionaire; he has money to throw away."

"Oh, Fred," Tabitha cries, "but you wouldn't let Mr. Wrinch beat you. Here's Mr. Manklow says he will go to Mr. Wrinch if you don't have him."

"What we need in this country," Hodsell says in his high indignant voice, "is something with real distinction, cachet. Something without the stodginess of the *Yellow Book,* less timid, and remembering your *Symbolist*—"

Sturge answers that he does not propose to repeat an experiment so expensive and so troublesome.

"What you wanted there, Mr. Sturge," Manklow says, "was a good editor, someone with experience of the public demand."

"Yes, Fred. And do you know Mr. Manklow is free? He's resigned his job in Glasgow. You could have him for editor, and publish Mr. Dobey. And Mr. Hodsell has a novel he could let us have too, a novel that has been refused by all the publishers—the *respectable* publishers." No words can express Tabitha's scorn when she utters the word respectable.

"Most interesting." Sturge, attacked by mysterious feelings, strange commotions which are not wholly pique or quite jealousy, grows more and more pompous. "What is the novel about?"

"It's about a clergyman who runs away with a nun. It shows up the whole of religion, what wicked hypocrisy it is."

Manklow supports her. He points out that, on account of the new education, the masses are turning against the Church. "And it hasn't a real answer. In fact, since Darwin, it's been asking for the knock-out."

"But Darwin—ah—was a good Christian himself."

"So am I." Manklow is amused. "So are we all, I hope; I'm only pointing out which way the wind is blowing. And I do strongly agree with Tib, that—"

Sturge, attacked on all sides, defends himself with obstinacy. But the young men do not go home till midnight, at which time he also, due in Kensington, is obliged to go.

And the next day, at tea time, there again he finds Manklow, Dobey, and two other young writers, all most enthusiastic for a new paper to destroy convention, respectability, pull down the Church and abolish the Academy.

Sturge is accustomed to this violence among his young friends, full of scorn for everything established and admired, for all current reputations, for Kipling, Rhodes, Tennyson, for the imperial idea. They detest the whole structure of the old society; and because that structure has been large and comprehensive, the attack is comprehensive. They hate not only the view of art as a function of the community, in which the Academy, like the Church, is an organized body, charged to keep up certain standards of production for the communal taste, but its whole moral position. Because the generation before has set up duty and public service, the family and the state as ideals, they despise them all, and proclaim self-expression, self-realization, art for the sake of beauty, the virtue of egotism. Sturge finds it exaggerated, crude, and he does not take it very seriously. He has seen too many revolutions of opinion: Ruskin, worshiped like a prophet, and then denounced like a fraud; the rise and fall of the philosophic radicals. But he is alarmed by its powerful effect on Tabitha. He has never seen her so animated, so beautiful. And when, her cheeks glowing, her eyes flashing, she denounces marriage as a crime against love whose soul is freedom, he feels such pangs of admiration, mixed with terror at the consciousness of her anger against himself, that his very bowels seem to dissolve.

"But *why*, Fred, *why*?" she cries at him one night. "*Why* can't you see that it's a *duty* to protest against all this rottenness?"

He dreads now those week ends when he may stay with Tabitha at night, for apart from the growing embarrassment of being put to sleep in the dressing room, which he feels to be, as Jobson says, an imposition and a humiliation, he is now exposed to a continual attack on the subject of the paper.

"But *why* don't you want to publish, Fred? What's your *reason*? Have you any *reason*?"

And he can't avoid these nights. For Tabitha, who has for the first three months appeared quite indifferent to his visits, now presses him to come, no doubt because she can also bring Manklow to worry him, and afterward worry him herself. On every day when Mrs. Sturge goes to the country, and he is permitted to stay with Jobson, she sends for him. "Look," she says one evening, showing him a small new magazine. "I've been keeping it to show you, it's really quite well done, and it only cost five hundred pounds to publish."

Tabitha, who a year before would have balked at one pound for a hat, now scorns five hundred.

Sturge, who has had a detestable evening with Manklow's friends, ventures to be annoyed. "My dear Bertie, five hundred wouldn't be the end of it. There are more pleasant ways of spending money, and I have thrown away a good deal already without much return."

Tabitha stares at him with her nose in the air, and answers, "Do you mean *me*?"

"No, no, no. On that symbolist review. Come, dearest, let's hear no more about starting papers. I'm tired of the subject."

"That means you're tired of me. Don't argue, please. What else can it mean?" And she insists on a quarrel.

But Sturge, remembering Jobson's advice, grows indignant. Suddenly he turns to the door. "I'm sorry, I have to go."

"I thought you were staying tonight."

Her surprise increases his firmness. "I've changed my mind." Trembling with rage and alarm, he goes to his club. "No, I'm not going to stand any more, it's ridiculous."

26

He is much gratified by the success of this move. He receives a note from Tabitha on Monday morning, at his office, asking him to come to dinner at the flat because she has a good dinner for him. And she adds in a postscript, "Or after dinner. But you *must* come. It's not about the magazine. I'm sorry I nagged you about the wretched thing."

Sturge, in triumph, writes that he will try to come after dinner. Like a conqueror he is magnanimous; but not weak. He goes, but he goes late, entering with a graceful dignity, of which he is visibly conscious, after so many humiliations. He is slightly put about to find Tabitha pacing the floor in a dressing gown. She stands like a tragedy queen until he has shut the door behind him, and ejaculates then, with peculiar sharpness of emphasis, "Mr. Jobson says I treat you badly, and you're tired of it."

Already Sturge is alarmed. He feels that his strong action is not producing the results he expected. He answers that he has no complaint, no complaint at all.

But Tabitha frowns at him with an overwhelming contempt. "I'm not going to have Mr. Jobson say I'm a grabber. It's not true. I quite understand that you've paid for me; I just thought you would take what you wanted when you wanted it." And she adds, with warm disgust, "I hope you don't think I'm a *respectable* person."

Sturge, revolted by this crudity, cries out that she has misunderstood his feelings, that Jobson has no right to interfere; but Tabitha has walked off into her room, and half an hour later, the unfortunate man hears her call for him. In his agony of delicacy he cannot decide whether to stay away and exasperate a situation already painful, or to obey and create a new situation even more painful. He curses the hour when he took Jobson's advice. He thinks, "Perhaps I have been weak, perhaps the girl has taken advantage of me, but I can't change myself, and this is a horrible position. The worst is that the girl does not even realize what she is destroying, that our whole relations must be brutalized. She is too young, too crude, she doesn't know what she's doing."

He hears Tabitha's voice again, imperious and irritated. And because the man is undecided, he obeys with a gesture of despair the more reckless will.

He finds the room in complete darkness so that he has to grope his way among furniture, under a drumfire of warnings. "Don't knock the table down, it's rather fragile. Mind my clock." The man is sweating in terror of even greater humiliation, for no one could feel less potent. But Tabitha's modesty, it appears, is no less formal than her view of what is required. She receives him with an energetic initiative which is, for the moment, even more terrifying than her ultimatum. As she exclaims, "I'll never speak to Mr. Jobson again," it seems to the poor wretch that he is simply an instrument of revenge. But when he cries out, she says in a tolerant surprised tone, like a clumsy absent-minded nurse recalled to herself by a child's protest, "I'm sorry, I didn't mean to hurt you."

This speech, even in the midst of his agony, produces a strange tremor in the man's soul. It strikes deep into some mysterious nerve, which is still vibrating when, exhausted, ravished, suspended between a heavenly bliss and a hellish self-disgust, he drags himself to breakfast next morning.

Tabitha has been up for an hour. He hears her high rapid voice exhorting, commanding, in the nursery, the kitchen; she comes in at last and asks him if he wants another egg.

And seeing her not only unembarrassed, but more friendly than she has ever been; seeing that for her, in short, the night has not been a brutal disgrace, but a transaction necessary to clear the moral air, he begins to revive. And now that nerve is singing like a discovery of a new relation, a relation quite different from the old, and far richer. His soul, so crushed and bruised, expands in the foretaste of enormous, incredible joys, in the love, in the sympathy of this entrancing creature. He gets up suddenly and kisses Tabitha. "You are the dearest child, Bertie."

"That's all right." Tabitha appears slightly surprised by the embrace. "More coffee?"

She sits down to pour out his coffee, and gazes at him with a thoughtful expression while he drinks it. Then suddenly she utters a deep heart-rending sigh.

"Darling, you're tired." He is full of solicitude.

"No." But again an immense sigh.

"What is it? Johnny all right?"

"Oh yes. I was just thinking—but I mustn't say, must I?"

"What about?"

"Why do you so hate Mr. Manklow, Fred?"

"I can remember when you disliked him."

"Oh, I know he's a little—what shall I say? But you can't deny that he's an exceptional man. So clever and brave. He's never afraid to say what he thinks about the Queen. He sees the rottenness of everything. And he wants to do something about it. He doesn't just sit and twiddle his thumbs."

Sturge is silent. He feels suddenly an extreme bitterness. It is so violent that it startles him. He has never felt like this before. He says at last, "Manklow seems to be here very often."

"Well—" The word is thrown out so sharply that Sturge jumps. But he is still more angry.

"As you have just admitted, the man is a cad on the make. Do you think he ought to have so much encouragement?"

"Has Jobson been reporting on me?" This in a quiet soft voice, as if asking for information.

"My dear, how can you believe—?"

Tabitha bounces up in a flame. "Don't be stupid, Fred; your spying is too clumsy." She darts into her bedroom and shuts the door.

Sturge, alarmed as well as angry, goes to her door and finds it locked. And he perceives that to knock would be a humiliation. He has no recourse but to go away.

27 JOBSON now reveals all his anxiety. For a long time, he says, he has been worried about the course of things at the flat. "It's like this, Bunny, she thinks she can do what she likes with you. And when a woman does that, you know, she doesn't stop anywhere. If you go on with that little fireship, you're done for, absolutely finished. The fact is, this is a tricky position for a man of your age. I've seen several chaps absolutely ragged and hagged to death by kids like this, kids who get the bit in their teeth, and haven't the sense to care what happens to anybody or anything. Get rid of the bitch now. I'm sorry you ever met her, I'm sorry I ever suggested her. Fact is, I thought her being more or less of a lady was a recommendation. But in this kind of show, the best are often the worst, and the worst the best."

Then he proposes to find Sturge a good simple girl, out of a shop or an office, and he points out how easily and well he has managed his own young woman of the moment, a girl called Madge Moon, who works in an insurance office. "Three quid a week and no extras, and she's never given me a day's trouble. 'Cause why? She knows that if she did, it would be the finish. Discipline, Bunny, that's the secret—especially with skirts. 'Cause why? They haven't any principles. They're just a bundle of jumps. Give 'em an inch and they'll make a hell."

"I see that very well," Sturge says, sweating in his despair. "Yes, hell. So unreasonable, so untrustworthy. She has no idea of an obligation. No, she must go—this is the end."

"That's it. And now you're out, you can stay out. It's her own doing. Send her a couple of tenners, if you like, and pay the bills and put the flat in the agent's book. That's the best of these arrangements, they leave you so free."

"Yes, indeed, she's behaved very badly, disgracefully."

Sturge returns to his office and writes to Tabitha an eight-page letter, containing a dignified explanation, a qualified apology, and the hint that reconciliation on suitable terms might not be impossible.

When no reply comes within the week, he begins to lose weight, his clothes hang upon him; even his wife, between two important meetings, notices his misery and asks if he is ill.

"No, my dear; it must be the weather."

"You need a holiday; you see too much of that man Jobson. I suppose he's been making you sit up late with him, and drink too much."

Sturge is too broken to defend even his old friend. Besides, he is embittered against Jobson, who has brought all this wretchedness, this indignity upon him. "Why couldn't he leave me alone?" he thinks. "Why must he think I needed a mistress at all? I was quite happy when he began this stupid scheme." And when Jobson accosts him in the street with his sympathetic expression, he looks sourly upon him.

Jobson is most concerned to see the man's yellow hanging cheeks and miserable expression. "Cheer up, old man, the worst's over."

"I don't see that I have any responsibility toward her. I did my best."

"What you want is a change, Bunny; let's run over to Paris for a week or two."

Sturge eagerly embraces this proposal. "Yes, yes, a good idea. Why should I stay?"

It is arranged on the spot, and Jobson, patting his old friend's shoulder, apologizes again for introducing him to Tabitha. "But you won't see her again; if she's not gone when we get back, I'll push her out myself." And he walks off.

Sturge says to himself, "He thinks I've been too weak all along, but it's not weakness at all. I have certain feelings, that's all; I'm not a brute. However, it's over now, I'm quite determined on that. In fact, if I went back now, after all that's happened, I should deserve every kind of disaster." He sees Tabitha's scorn, he imagines her cruelty, he sees himself utterly ruined, a byword, a social castaway. And at once such a longing rises in him, such an acute torturing desire, that he is quite staggered. Sweat breaks out on his face and head. He thinks, "But this is fearful, revolting; that girl will be my ruin."

As he walks slowly along the pavement, hardly knowing where he is, he perceives the meaning of Jobson's anxiety, the new depths of horror that open beneath him. And this horror also draws him on, makes his head swim, seems to whisper in his nerves, "Jump, get it over; now's your chance to escape."

Escape from what? He does not know. Perhaps only from making a decision. And the next afternoon, pale, quivering in every limb, he is seated in a hansom which is carrying him at full speed to West Street. He is painfully aware, like most mad people, that he is mad. He quite comprehends his humiliation, his danger; and his self-contempt is a large part of his pleasure. He is in the state of the worshiper who throws dust on his head and asks to be trampled on.

The thought that Tabitha may have left the flat is now horrifying to him. He rushes upstairs, and finding her in the act of mending stockings, utters a cry, bursts into tears, falls on his knees and kisses her hand.

Tabitha, much surprised, and rather put out, says, "My dear Fred, mind my needle. Why didn't you say you were coming?"

But when she understands that Sturge has come with a full and complete acknowledgment of his bad conduct, and is ready to promise that Jobson will never visit the flat again, she gradually forgives him. She is indeed more kind than he could have expected. She kisses him on the forehead, the first time she has ever kissed him; she makes him promise to stay; she notices his drawn cheeks and advises him to take Parrish's Food; she speaks with reproachful sympathy of his habit of catching cold and sniffling, compares this tendency with the baby's delicacy in the same part, and suggests buying him a chest protector. She gives him terrifying pleasure, but with such good-natured indulgence, that he is drowned in love. He accuses himself now of his jealous folly, and says, "You are my life, Bertie."

"Yes, Fred," she murmurs, "I worry about you a lot. And you'll be sure to get that protector. If it's scratchy, I'll line it with cambric."

"My dearest soul."

"But what I've always thought, Fred, is that you need some distraction; a man ought to have something to *do*."

"The business takes up a great deal of time."

"That's nothing, you *have* to go to business; no, what you really want—but, oh dear, I promised not to, didn't I—?"

There is a long silence. Then, as if from Sturge's very entrails, a hoarse voice murmurs, "You mean the paper?"

"You see, Fred, it's for your own sake, it would be so good for you. Take your mind off business matters."

"I'll—I'll think of it."

"As for the expense, suppose Mr. Wrinch took a half share and you were joint editor with Mr. Manklow."

Sturge does not answer this. Even as the driven sheep, he balks.

It is nearly a fortnight before Professor Griller is able to announce to literary London that Fred Sturge is going to found a new review; and six months before it has a name. But after much argument, somebody suggests that Mrs. Bonser should be applied to, and the result is decisive. She chooses *The Bankside*, which is Manklow's favorite, and Sturge at once perceives that this is the best.

28 IT WAS in these six months that Tabitha began to make a reputation and learn the art of a hostess; and that Sturge, as slave, came into his own. For since Tabitha has mastered him, she can accept his most critical hints.

"My dear Bertie," he will say, "excuse me, but I noticed that you were talking to Lady Millwall about Johnny, and she certainly left rather early—she didn't meet Dobey at all."

"She remembered an engagement."

"Have you noticed that mothers, as a whole, don't take much interest in one another's children?"

"I see; you think she was bored?"

Another day, unlacing Tabitha's stays, a privilege allowed to his servitude, he murmurs, "Griller didn't seem to sparkle at dinner tonight. I'm afraid he went away in a compressed mood; he will say something spiteful."

"Was that my fault?"

"Oh no, my darling; but, of course, if someone had mentioned the French symbolists."

"There now, I knew there was something; why didn't you write it down for me? I simply must keep Griller happy. And write down that Mr. Dewpark is deaf in the left ear, and knew Thackeray."

Now, too, Tabitha does not merely submit to new frocks bought for her; she comes to Sturge and says, "Will this do?" She asks him before a party, "Am I all right?" And if he corrects her for wearing too much jewelry or too many frills, she answers with tranquil scorn, "You know, Fred, it's a wonder you don't want to choose my chemmies and petties."

"My sweet, now you mention it, it might be no harm. Though those things are not seen, they make a difference. A well-dressed woman should feel well dressed all through, and the feeling is most important to her carriage, her tournure."

As for wine and cooking, Sturge takes charge, and spends a great deal of money as well as taste. After three months, Mrs. Bonser's parties in West Street are not merely successful but talked about.

Though probably all the guests tell each other that Tabitha has a past, and is rather too friendly with Sturge, they also boast of her invitations.

For several other ladies, perhaps cleverer and more beautiful, but certainly much more blown upon, have in the last ten years established the same kind of salon. There has been a change, a subterranean disturbance in the foundations of society. Some long slow process of movement, of tension, has suddenly produced large cracks, especially between the old queen's set at Windsor and the prince's set at Marlborough House. That spring of new wealth, of South African gold, whose fertilizing stream has produced such a varied and fantastic growth, of buccaneers in politics, idealists of Empire, adventurers in art, in science, has also split society, causing merchants to grow richer than dukes, and to give entertainments which are less tedious.

For a duke, the poorest of his rank, is still a moral power, which sets limits to the freedom even of princes, so that they naturally prefer for hosts new men, climbers who utterly depend on their good will. And this will is for distraction. It is boredom that has broken the immense fortress of the old Christian society. It is because of boredom that the younger set fly from Windsor and that there are two ruling groups in England: the old, exclusive, high-principled clique dying of age, of lack of imagination; the new, selfish, often vulgar, but full of life. It adores novelty, and is easily penetrated by anyone who can give amusement.

Mrs. Bonser and her like, artists, writers, actors, playwrights, are novelties much in request, and so Tabitha finds among her circle, as well as under-secretaries, peers, rich men who are patrons of art, and smart young men and women.

The latter indeed do not much please her. She finds them frivolous as they find her still a little provincial, a little too earnest. She is too fond of advertising her review. She will have long mysterious conversations with the scruffy Manklow about their contributors. She is heard to say, "If B. comes, I'll speak to him." And the other replies across the room, "You'd better—F. won't do anything."

And such exchanges irritate even those who know that B. is Sturge's new discovery Boole, and F. is Sturge. They find them arrogant. They exclude. They pretend to a special importance. And this is Tabitha's own feeling. To her, the problem of Boole is very important. For Sturge has commissioned from him a sonnet sequence of twelve pages, and cut in proportion Manklow's political section.

Tabitha detests Boole. When she hears his high voice addressing Sturge, she frowns with a disgust which at once abolishes the hostess and brings out in the girl's face an expression which recalls the impatient young girl.

She is furious to see her man's subservience before Boole. The very shape of Sturge's back, of his soft white neck, bent down and sideways as he listens to the poet, expresses his deference; his twitching fingers locked behind his coattails are eloquent of his excited joy in having this genius for a friend.

Boole is a flimsy little creature of doubtful age, perhaps in his middle thirties, with a long neck and large bald head, and a thin virgin beard. His face is thin and long, but spoilt by an ugly red nose. He has charming manners, but so exaggerated that Tabitha can barely be polite to him. It enrages her, in some very deep part of her nerves, to see him with this same manner, which seems to her so affected, charm others; to see him at dinner, where he sits between Miss Pullen on his left with pale yellow draperies, and a countess on his right, Lady Chadworth, in full evening dress, making a conquest of them both. Lady Chadworth is the wife of a minister and daughter of a most formidable duchess, who would be horrified to see her in such company. For this very reason, she is flushed with the delight of her adventure, and bends her beautiful smile toward Boole as if to an oracle of grace.

"But she is a donkey," Tabitha thinks angrily. "I'm sure she doesn't really understand a word he says. And why should he be so dirty, so rude?"

Meanwhile, Boole, delighted with himself and the party, already rather drunk, not only with champagne but ladies, who always go to his head, is explaining to them why vice must be allowed, even encouraged. "What is vice," he asks, "and what is virtue? Are they not forms only—and can we be sure that the forms are not a prison, a chain upon the soul?" And turning his eyes first to Miss Pullen and then to the countess, he appeals softly to them, "Have you not known the liberation of vice, of indulgence? They call me a decadent, but what is that but one who breaks rules? Yes, this is a time of decadence, which is also a fertilization. When the flowers wither, the seeds are scattered on the wind. It is a time of exploration, when blackguards and outcasts who have become impossible to civilization—people like me—are driven out into the wilds to find a new Klondyke and build new cities. Heaven and hell are mapped. And Wells has sunk his borings into the lower middle class. There are Cook's tours to the very realms of love. I mean the true, wild, and miraculous habitations of Eros himself. Yes, all is open, to the bottom of the soul, the nerves. There are no limits any more, no custom houses, no morals, no shame. For shame itself is a pair of blinkers; the true decadent has no modesty. He is become as a child; he embraces the innocent perversities of nature herself."

The ladies are delighted with Boole, and the countess asks him to tea. And after dinner, he reads, in a still higher voice, for champagne always elevates his pitch, a long love poem which is about a broken Pierrot and a cruel Columbine. He reads very badly, dropping his voice at every full stop; and whenever he wishes to be impressive, he stretches out his neck and winds it about in an extraordinary manner. Professor Griller smiles his little malicious grin; he is annoyed to lose the center of the stage. Dewpark, an old man who cultivates new poets, so long as they can be labeled with an old label, and who finds in Boole a new Ronsard with a dash of Villon, looks deeply concerned, but glares now and then at his cigar to make sure that it is burning straight. The countess gets up cautiously, and still with an ecstatic expression, steals from the room. She is going to a party in the real world. She has achieved her aim, which was to catch Boole for tea, and startle her friends with this wild creature.

"There," Tabitha says to herself, "she only came for Boole, and because he's queer. She doesn't care a penny for things that really matter." And she feels still more indignant with Boole for attracting irresponsible countesses.

29

THE company breaks up at midnight, with cries of gratitude; they yawn only on the stairs. Even Miss Pullen finds Boole a bore. Tabitha, as always, is in her bedroom almost before the door has closed on the last guest. She tears off her clothes still in a manner which shocks Sturge, who does not like to see the beautiful materials insulted.

He, now free of the whole domain, like any pet dog, strolls from bedroom to the devastated sitting room and back again. "What a wonderful evening—another triumph for you, my darling." He carefully praises Tabitha for all successes.

"Except for Boole," Tabitha cries, shaking down her hair. "Why will he get drunk and talk so much—and such nonsense about decadence? It's so dull, and we aren't decadent—it's *Punch* that is decadent."

Sturge is smiling at her vehemence as she sits at the dressing table. He takes a long strand of her hair which he loves to touch, and gently presses it, as if fearful of hurting its strands.

"Yes, an historic evening. Do you realize that, Bertie? I know Miss Pullen keeps a diary for one."

But Tabitha has never had much imagination. She takes her hair from Sturge as a punishment, for being polite to the poet, and says, "You never meant to print twelve pages of Boole's sonnets?"

"My dear, I'm delighted to have them."

"But you can't—there's no room. I told him tonight they were crowded out."

"But, my darling, excuse me, that's not true."

Tabitha turns round and stares at her slave in haughty amazement. She sees that an extraordinary spasm has seized him. His face is very red, his mouth hangs open; he gazes at her with an expression of terror and defiance.

"Don't be silly, Fred, we must refuse somebody."

"But, Bertie, no; you can't really mean that you prefer Manklow to Boole. No one with any real discrimination—"

"Do you mean I've no taste?"

"N-no; it's only that in this matter I really must ask you, my precious—"

"If my taste is as good as yours, what are you complaining of?"

"But you have no taste at all. No-o, excuse me. I'm afraid so. How could you? Be reasonable, my dearest. Think of your education. You are completely ignorant of the fundamentals, prejudiced, Manklowed—"

Tabitha feels all the irritation of one who is bitten by a sheep. She bursts out in fury, "Manklow is worth ten of your miserable Booles. At least he sees that rottenness is rotten. And I won't have him cut."

At this ultimatum, Sturge becomes mad with desperation. His face grows scarlet. His voice rises to an hysterical bleat. "But it's abominable, I won't bear it. It's beyond everything— You've no right— Excuse me, but I must go; I can't— And if you think it's funny—"

In fact, Tabitha, glaring with scorn upon this extraordinary display of terror and rage, has been taken by a sudden impulse to giggle. She represses this undignified tic, so out of place at this important crisis of her power, but she has not been quite successful. Her young muscles are not entirely under control and defeat her will; her broad lips twitch at the corners.

"No, I see it's no good talking to you." Sturge is shaking all over; tears stand in his eyes. "You can't understand anything; you have no heart, no mind. Excuse me—I am a fool."

And now Tabitha is carried away by laughter. She cannot prevent the vast force of laughter which overwhelms at once the remnant of her manners and her dignity, her self-respect. She falls back on the bed, laughing helplessly. "But, Fred, you don't realize how funny you look!"

"Yes, I am a fool, but excuse me—I must go now. I beg your pardon for—" Sturge blunders toward the door.

Tabitha springs off the bed and runs after him. She is still laughing. "But, Bunny, really, what a fuss! And you're not really going—you mustn't—" and this is the first time she has called him Bunny.

"No, it's too cruel, excuse me—"

"Oh, Bunny—" she catches at his coattails—"don't be so stu-pid; come to bed."

"No, I won't come to bed. I absolutely refuse to—come to bed." His voice trembles at a last outrage. He brushes off her hand and disappears through the front door. He has gone.

Tabitha, in her nightdress, says, "Oh, well, if he's going to be so silly," and she goes back to her room, full of amusement. "Really, what a great baby; but who would have dreamt he would go on like that!" And her amusement, like that of a nurse in a child's naughtiness, is full of surprise and even pleasure in such a display of character in a child. "Fancy," she thinks, as she squats on the bed, "making all that fuss about an old poem. Well, of course, I know I don't understand Boole, but really, how absurd!"

The next day, feeling a little surprised that Sturge sends no message, no flowers, no apology, she writes him a note. "Don't forget the party for the artists. Dobey is coming"; and in a postscript, she writes, "I know I am stupid about poetry; why not give Boole a page at the end—or two pages?"

But there is still no sign from Sturge. And Manklow, calling for news, is gravely irritated. "You've got no sense, Tib; you always overdo it."

"But you asked me to get rid of Boole."

"Your first job is to manage the old tripe."

"I don't manage people"—in a tone expressing her disgust for this piece of vulgarity.

"That's what I'm complaining of. And here we go on footling about while other people catch the market. There's two new quarterlies this month."

"But what can we do if Boole is so bad?"

"Tell him you love Boole." And seeing Tabitha's indignant glance, he gives an impatient sigh. "Look here, Tib, what do we know? It's all so rotten that it may be good, in a rotten way. What I mean is, in a rotten time like this you need a few rotten ideas to keep the whole thing loose. And everything's going to smash anyhow. All right, if you don't, I will. I've got some sense of responsibility toward a chance like this, if you haven't."

Manklow then writes to Sturge expressing his admiration for Boole, and Sturge, after a week's delay, which Tabitha calls sulks, but is really recuperation for his nerves, returns one afternoon to the flat.

He consents, with a slightly dignified air, to be kissed, to be put in the best chair before the fire, and to have laid before him the new poems that have come in.

"I kept everything for you, Bunny; but these top ones are the ones I thought rather better."

Sturge takes up the top one, reads a few lines, makes a face and drops it on the floor with an expression which causes Tabitha to smile. He stares haughtily at her. She says quickly, "Oh, I know my taste is bad. Yes, Bunny, I'm sure you're right."

Tabitha is indifferent to his judgment, and neither does she value taste. She does not indeed respect Sturge for standing up to her on such a foolish point; she only regards him as someone who requires humoring. But even with her best efforts, weeks pass before the man is reassured, before the deep complicated suspicion of that distrustful soul can believe that it is not being played with.

30

BUT since Sturge has this strange obstinacy of character, since he has to be humored, he is once more a power. And West Street becomes more like an office than a love nest. The chairs are heaped with contributions, the tables with proofs. Excited young men look in at all hours to know what has happened to their essays, their drawings, or to persuade Tabitha to buy their new stories, and they are difficult to get rid of. They argue, they almost weep, sometimes they try to charm. And the old established authors are still more troublesome.

"Look at this from Dewpark!" Sturge exclaims. "He expects me to print ten thousand words on Matthew Arnold."

"Then let me deal with him, Bunny. He's coming to the weekly dinner, isn't he? I'll tell him we're keeping it for a special number."

"I wish you would. Dewpark likes you; make love to him a little."

And Tabitha does not smile at this request from a jealous lover. As a responsible partner, she takes his orders, and pursues the great work of liberation.

The first number of *The Bankside*, advertised for the autumn of 1897, is brought out, by immense efforts, in the spring of '98. It achieves a great success. It is, in fact, very like all the other little magazines of the time. It has the same critical essays, solemn stories, constructed on French models, and erotic-mannered drawings; the same note of æsthetic adventure and pagan license. It catches the public which has already approved this note.

Boole's poem has not appeared, for Boole, taking Tabitha's rejection seriously, has not finished it. Luckily he has forgotten his own reason for not completing the work, has given Sturge vague excuses, and is now once more lost in drink. But Tabitha, since she need not blame herself for the disappearance, can rejoice at it. It has removed a dangerous influence. She has enough anxieties without fending off Boole's enormous manuscripts.

She is at work on the second number; she is faced by the terrible problem of all editors who reach a second number—to make it better than the first. And in this ambition, it succeeds only by spending more money. In fact, it was from this time that the editors began to discover a fundamental trait of little reviews: that it is necessary to spend rather more money on each successive number in order to keep the same circulation. Readers, that is, are never satisfied. So that after six numbers, Sturge's losses have trebled, and the paper has no more readers.

The sixth number, three times more expensive than the first, sells, perhaps on account of the war in South Africa, rather less than half. Sturge cries out for the sixth time, but with more reason, that he can't go on, he will be ruined.

To Tabitha the war is simply a part of the government plot to crush every good impulse of humanity and ruin *The Bankside*. She complains to Jobson that if the sales fall off any more, Sturge may really give up the paper. "And really it's the last hope."

She has been much too busy to remember her hatred of Jobson, and she cannot do without him in the management of Sturge. He comforts her as usual. "Don't you worry, girlie. There's plenty of money. You go on with the good work, and I'll shake him down."

Jobson has once more adopted Tabitha. Unable to explain to himself exactly why Sturge, though completely subjugated, has not gone to ruin, but instead, though slightly more rickety, even debauched in appearance, has found the energy at last to gratify his ambition, he takes the whole credit. "Didn't I say he wanted to be dug out?" And he boasts everywhere of his prescience in picking for his friend so well brought up a mistress. "Give me a lady every time; she's got a conscience, even in bed!"

He quite disagrees with Manklow, who, irritated by a recent piece of diplomacy in which Tabitha has juggled away an article likely to offend Griller, declares that she is getting to be a two-faced tart.

"I call it a pretty sight," he says, "to see girlie finding her feet."

"She needn't put them right on people's faces; it's not sense. Suppose I walk out? They're bust." There is no annoyance in Manklow's tone, only indignant regret that people can be so foolish, in such a bad world, as to throw away their advantages.

"And all this stuff about freedom, it's silly."

"It doesn't do any harm to us, and it does her good."

"No one has any right to be silly on a paper, even this silly paper—it's too dangerous."

He is annoyed with Tabitha, on ideal grounds. And when, as often, late in the evening, she throws herself exhausted in a chair and cries, "Really, I'm too utterly worn out," he assumes at once an ironical expression. But Tabitha rarely notices expressions. She sighs deeply. "I don't mind Wally Jobson bringing up Madge Moon just after breakfast in the middle of my letters and asking me to keep her happy because she's feeling low—after all, Madge is a dear—but I do find it *rather* superfluous of Dobey to take that Joliffe girl into the bedroom after tea, and let her burn holes all over the new quilt; apparently she smokes *all* the time. One has to bear with Dobey, though he is such a moon-calf; but why the Joliffe creature? It's not as though she does anything for us."

"Poor Tib, we know you're wonderful."

Tabitha is surprised. She looks at Manklow with a puzzled frown and says at last, "I'm sorry about that article, but we do need Griller; he's got a lot of influence."

"Well, say so, then; say we're on the make."

"But we aren't."

"Yes, we are; and why not? It's as likely to be right as anything else—more so!"

"You don't really believe that, Roger?"

"There you go again; you think no one's got any principles because you've none yourself, and that's a major error."

Tabitha looks at the man with a sympathetic smile. Is he not assistant editor of *The Bankside*? But she does not notice what he is saying. She is preoccupied with a hundred more important matters: bills, Johnny's cough, a crack in the ceiling, a stain on her newest frock; and again she sighs. "It's too much." Her voice is full of the luxurious pleasure of a young woman who is thoroughly busy.

31

MADGE MOON is a large plump girl of twenty-five or six with a loud voice, who is generally acknowledged to have a heart of gold. She loves everyone, as well as beer and noise, and all the younger men on *The Bankside* are devoted to her. Tabitha has welcomed her therefore to West Street as a true bohemian and free-liver, and agrees with the general opinion that she is a great dear, a good soul, all that a free spirit should be. But when Madge, losing her job, begins to come to West Street almost every day, sprawling over the sofa and spilling whiskies and soda on the chairs, Tabitha more and more finds herself in the nursery.

This large cool room is secluded at the end of the flat, and, under a good nurse, it is kept in very good order. It has, in fact, that special character which belongs to all nurseries, stamped upon them by the private will and special problem of all mothers and nurses, conservative by need. Its white walls, its floor covered with well-washed oilcloth, its plain scrubbed table and hard chairs, all seem to say, "Here is order, cleanliness, and discipline."

When Tabitha, half a dozen times a day, shuts the nursery door, she has the sense of shutting out confusion and entering into a place under government. Everything here goes by the clock, a small American clock ticking loudly on the mantelpiece, and this is a great satisfaction to Tabitha. For it allays one of the great anxieties in her busy and irregular life: lest Johnny should be neglected or allowed to run wild, or to have too much excitement. For the fragile child, who is always catching colds, asthma, bronchitis, has very early shown a disposition to adventure. As soon as he has begun crawling, he has set himself to break bounds. If a door is left open, even for a moment, he will dart out at once and make for some forbidden dangerous spot like the kitchen or the back stairs. His whole idea seems to be to escape from wherever he is placed, in security, to somewhere else, preferably new and dangerous. Already before he can walk or speak, whenever he hears someone approaching, he will move near the door, and as soon as it is opened a fraction, squeeze himself through and scuttle away—a trick that becomes really dangerous when he begins to walk. For tottering on his stick-like legs, which seem as white and brittle as sticks of celery, he will fall down every moment. Tabitha, chasing him, as he totters toward the stairs, can't help laughing, and yet she is frightened and angry. "John, John, stop, come back." She catches up the child at the very edge of the stairs and holds him while he kicks. He throws up his arms, stretches out his body like a sack, and tries to slip out of her hands.

But when she brings him to the nursery and shuts the doors, he appears at once reconciled to be a prisoner again, and begins to play with a cheerfulness which, as Tabitha knows, is perhaps only another trick to remove suspicion and to escape.

And this character has grown worse, or at least more dangerous. At four John is still a thin, sickly looking child, apt to catch cold, but full of mischief and rebellion. He invents a new trick every day, so that

Tabitha is amazed by his inventive cunning in ill doing. "How can he be so bad? Really, he does it on purpose." And she is tortured by the thought, "Is it Dick coming out in him, Dick's selfishness and Dick's frightful lying?"

The nurse does not console her by relating numerous stories of other children's wickedness. Like most nurses, she seems to delight in telling how little so and so, such a darling to look at, stabbed her in the face with her own scissors; and how this other, a perfect angel with grownups, tortured a little brother into the grave. In nurse's view, all children are capable of anything, at any time. And Tabitha thinks, "But John may be worse; and he mayn't get over it."

32

THUS she never comes to the nursery without a special apprehension, and her first question is always, "Has John been good?"

So, driven from the sitting room one afternoon just before tea by the agonized boredom of keeping a sympathetic face while Dobey relates to her and to Madge the long complicated story of how some horrid soldier has insulted him, she finds the nurse wearing a severe expression, and John one of special cheerfulness. He runs to her at once and seizes her skirts, and kisses the air in an upward direction. But Tabitha, an experienced mother of twenty-three, is not to be deceived. She looks anxiously at nurse. "What is it today, nurse?"

"Dragging, mam, worse than ever. I had to carry him half the way."

Johnny, prevented from running off into all the shrubberies of the park, has lately invented the new method of lingering behind, or dragging.

And both women look anxiously at the small boy as at a dangerous small animal. Tabitha says in her severest tone, "Now, John, you know what I said would happen if you went on being a nuisance to nurse."

John, having turned to the basin, is swimming the soap dish in it. There can be seen in his expression not only the obstinacy but the cunning of a four-year-old who joins the intelligence of a small boy to the complete egotism of a baby.

"Answer me, John." Tabitha takes him by the arm. "You hear what I said; do you want to be smacked?"

John adds the sponge bowl to the soap dish, and keeps silence. Tabitha turns pink, wrinkles appear between her brows; and in the young face there appears suddenly the shadow, the hint of an old woman, an old woman, as it is said, of character; that is, one who has acquired from her battles a strong will and decided opinions, rather than resignation.

"Do you hear, John? Answer me at once."

The two women exchange a glance; both are aware of the supreme quality of the crisis. For a slap is the last resort. After the slap, there is nothing. A slap is the old guard, and if it fail, the battle is lost; anarchy must come.

Tabitha's glance is really an appeal to the nurse for support, for some brilliant decision which will save the last terrible risk. But at such moments the supreme commander is always alone. The nurse's expression says clearly, "You've threatened that slap before, and now you must do it; the consequence is not my responsibility."

"Very well, John." Tabitha takes the child's arm and draws him away from the basin.

"For the last time, John."

But he says not a word. Tabitha, quite infuriated with this obstinacy which is, she perceives, pure wickedness, an evil will enjoying itself, puts him across her knee and gives him two hard slaps.

There is a pause, and awful silence. Is John going to win? Tabitha holds her breath. But suddenly a loud cry is heard, a protesting wail. Tabitha's face clears, she smiles with relief; and hastens to take John on her knee. "Now, darling, it was your own fault."

"I'm sorry, Mum," the boy howls.

"You see what happens if you're naughty." But she kisses him, a weakness which causes the nurse to turn away with a look meaning, "Oh, these mothers."

"Yes—Mummy."

"And now if you're really good again—are you good?"

"Oh yes-ss, Mummy, I'm good."

"You shall have a chocky."

Two minutes later, John, with the virtuous expression of one reconciled, purged of sin, and renewed by grace, is eating chocolate. But he remembers, now and then, to embrace Tabitha, to assure her that he is good again, and to assure himself that this powerful person is once more well inclined toward him. The powerful person, full of gratitude to those mysterious forces, which have secured her victory, returns the kisses with warmth. For the gratitude, seeking expression, naturally finds part of its object in John.

Afterwards nurse congratulates the commander-in-chief. "That was just what he needed, mum; it was in the nick."

"Yes, I thought the time had come; it would be easy to spoil Johnny."

33 But no sooner is John turned away from this dangerous inspiration of dragging than he breaks out in a new rebellion, and a more serious one. He refuses one evening to say his prayers.

Tabitha for a long time has been much concerned with the problem of John's prayers. Already, just after his third birthday, the nurse has remarked that Master John doesn't say prayers yet. Tabitha has answered, on the spur of the moment, that he is perhaps a little young; but the nurse has plainly disagreed with that view, and Tabitha has remembered that her own prayers began before her memory of them. She is startled by a feeling of guilt toward John, and this feeling has not been removed by the argument that since there is no god, and the Church is nothing but a conspiracy to keep power for bishops, it would be wrong to let Johnny pray.

It seems to her that by not teaching John to pray she may be depriving him of something important; she is taking a fearful risk, that is, not of offending some god, who is a ridiculous old legend in a book, but of causing a permanent injury to John.

She has already put the question of religion to several people: to Sturge, who is, to her surprise, Church of England, and contemptuous only of Mrs. Grundy; to Dobey, who, however, shocks her by his regard for the pope; and once to the local vicar, met in Miss Pullen's drawing room, "How soon, vicar, ought children to begin their prayers?"

The vicar, a shrewd old gentleman, accustomed to smart women, discreetly asks Tabitha about her own church. "Oh, I'm afraid I haven't got one, I'm not religious myself. But I rather feel that children ought to have *some* religion. If they didn't they might be missing something they need."

"I perfectly agree."

"I mean for their own happiness, as children."

"Or even as men."

But this, it seems, is going too far. The lady gives a little smile and says, "Perhaps," in a tone which asks what good prayer can be to a grown person. And she prompts the vicar, "Would you suggest the Lord's Prayer and Gentle Jesus? I started with them, and I know I enjoyed them very much."

"You couldn't do better."

And Tabitha goes home resolute that John shall say his prayers. There is of course a battle. But tact and bribery, without a slap, win the day for the administration. In six weeks John even demands to say his prayers. He values prayers as an activity, a part of the day's achievement.

And then one evening, such is the perversity of children, perhaps seeing Tabitha too eager to get him to bed, he creeps, at prayer time, under the bed, and declares that he will not say prayers. Tabitha, who has a large party in the sitting room, is highly irritated. "Come out at once, John."

"He's been very bad all day, mum," the nurse declares. "Just trying it on."

"Then I shouldn't give him his biscuit; not unless he comes out at once and says he's sorry and says his prayers."

There is a pause. But no sound from below the bed.

"Johnny doesn't think," the nurse says, "what happens to little boys who don't say their prayers."

"Wicked, naughty little boys."

"God will punish them," nurse says.

Again there is a pause. But no response from the hard-hearted John. His breathing is loudly defiant.

"And they won't have any more stories," Tabitha says, but without much hope. "They won't hear about the three bears."

This is another silence, in which it can be noticed that John has ceased to breathe. The two women look at each other across the bed, and nurse says, "Or Jack the Giant Killer."

"Or Jack and the Beanstalk. Never, never again."

There is a movement beneath the bed, and John's tow head appears below the edge of the quilt. "I don't *want* Jack in the Beanstalk."

"Or Red Riding Hood," nurse says.

The boy stands up and says with indignation, "I don't *want* Red Riding Hood."

The nurse and Tabitha exchange another glance. Some intimation passes, noticed at once by the child who looks suspiciously from one to the other. And he repeats loudly like a general refusing all terms, "I don't want Red Riding Hood."

A Metternich of less experience than Tabitha might have supposed that the negotiations were at an end. Instead, with a cheerful air she sits down on the bed, as usual when about to hear the child's prayers, and holds out her arms. "Very well, you shall choose."

John, with the air of one who has obtained an honorable peace, at once climbs into her lap and says his prayers, followed immediately by the urgent cry, "Puss in Boots, Puss in Boots."

He has heard this story at least a hundred times, but he is still young enough to enjoy the same thrill over and over again.

34 AND Tabitha, going from her bright austere kingdom to the sitting room, where the very sunlight slanting across the tobacco smoke seems to have a different quality, sophisticated, matured, coarsened, turns upon her guests a smile of welcome which is really a smile of triumph, of a conqueror who has defeated insidious evil.

At such moments, refreshed, as it were, with nursery victories, and the consciousness of having done the right thing in that difficult sphere, she is all the more eager to do the right thing also in *The Bankside* sphere of revolt and artistic enterprise. She is more than usually sympathetic with the lugubrious Dobey; with the melancholy Hodsell, whose novel about a priest who falls in love with a whore is giving him such trouble; and with Madge Moon, who, as usual about this time in the evening, is firmly drunk and very blasphemous. Madge is distressed about her young brother in the army, and curses the war, the Boers, imperialism, the government, and also the men who have not gone to fight. This makes her very quarrelsome. She insults Hodsell, and looking at the gangling Dobey, who, like many heretics, is a keen theologian, she cries, "Don't talk to me about God; if there is a God, why doesn't he stop the bloody war?"

Dobey, getting up and falling down again, growing still more excited than he is drunk, and very much more confused, begins to explain the problem of evil.

And Tabitha, smiling still, is obliged to murmur, "Not so loud. Yes, how interesting. I see, it's all a question of—"

She exchanges the smile for a very serious expression, such as she always uses for Dobey whether he is talking theology or love. He is a boy who, on account of his foolish and erratic nature, needs to be taken very seriously.

The war is going badly. The buccaneers of new adventurous politics have found to their surprise that the army has not been adventurous in ideas. There are defeats; and volunteers have been called for. Thousands of clerks rush joyfully from their offices to join this adventure, to become heroes at a stroke; and as they ride through the streets on the way to embarkation, it can be seen that life has become for them dignified and significant. They are risking their lives for an idea, for a love, for glory and honor. And although the paper, to everyone's surprise, continues a small sale to its special public, making only a small loss, the contributors have a sense of difference and so of brotherhood. As the year goes on, West Street becomes more and more like a committee room of rebels; but outlawed rebels, exiles. They don't belong to the war world. And as they tend to spend whole days at West Street, they become more pervasive. They invade even the nursery.

Tabitha is indignant, coming in late one night, to find Jobson and Dobey and Madge smoking there. She asks why they are not comfortable in the sitting room.

"We like it here, girlie," Jobson says. "It's liberty hall, and away from the Grillers and your countesses. And the kid's an attraction, too, don't you forget it. Look at this."

This is a drawing of two naked men and a woman in a landscape of trees. It is certainly clever, but Tabitha is already convinced of John's brilliance. She therefore glances carelessly at the drawing and says, "I suppose all children draw rather amusingly; but really, you know, Wally, you oughtn't to smoke in the nursery. It upsets nurse. One simply must have rules in a nursery."

And a few days later, finding Madge Moon romping with the child, tickling him till he rolls on the floor in shrieks of laughter, she suddenly loses her temper. "Get up, Johnny, don't be so silly."

He pays no attention. Tabitha picks him up, shakes him. Madge cries, "How can you! What harm is he doing?"

"I'm sorry, but he mustn't get so excited."

"Why don't you say straight out you don't want me coming here?"

Tabitha ignores the woman, but this excites her still more. "Oh, you don't want to talk to me—too much class, I suppose. Why, who are you, I'd like to know!" And she repeats all the usual gossip of the group: that Tabitha is a sly bitch who tells the tale to everybody; a snob who sucks up to the parsons, and kicks up her heels for a living—a nasty double-faced hypocrite!

Since Tabitha in her amazed fury is still silent, she is growing more violent, when she hears Jobson's voice and rushes out to claim his support.

Luckily he takes Tabitha's side. His judgment is based not so much on a sense of justice as the view that Madge is getting above herself. "It's time that silly sheep had a knock; she needs a good setback every three months." And Madge is banished from West Street.

But she finds a good deal of sympathy. From this time there are two parties in West Street: those who admire Tabitha as a clever little woman, maintaining a difficult position with much diplomatic skill; and those who despise her for the same reason.

Jobson and Manklow belong to the former party. "Funny," says Jobson, "how these fillies run true to type. Here's our little girlie setting out to make her by-blow into a bishop, whether he likes it or not." To which Manklow answers in his reflective manner that this was natural; it was only another example of the swing of the pendulum.

And both men, with something of the curiosity of zoologists studying the antics of that strange animal, a woman, watch Tabitha's maneuvers, first to cut the nursery off from the flat, and then to hire the local curate as John's tutor. She is successful in the second, after a short struggle, because Sturge is ready to pay. But in the first she has to fight a long battle, lasting many months.

For the younger *Bankside* party, led by Dobey, see in her purpose not only a slight on its manners but a hateful treachery to moral principles.

It is only by luck and very strong pressure on Sturge that she achieves her end, when the tenant of the next flat dies, and she manages to get two of his rooms for a new nursery, with a separate entrance at the end of a passage.

35

TABITHA herself, during all these months, goes about with a deep resentment. The words snob and double-faced have given her wounds that refuse to heal. She feels their brutal injustice all the more because she cannot defend herself. "It's no good telling creatures like Madge or a silly young man like Dobey or bachelors like Wally, Roger, Manklow, what it means to be responsible for a child."

So far from her noticing any inconsistency in her own conduct, it seems to her absolutely necessary. "*The Bankside* people are one thing, and what's good for Johnny is another."

In her disappointment and indignation, she grows a little more arbitrary. She makes it plain that the new nursery is not for visitors. She removes one of Dobey's best drawings, of Jezebel among the Dogs, a gift to John, from the nursery wall. She says to herself bitterly, "Let them talk."

About this time, people say that Tabitha is looking older. In fact, she is only acquiring an older expression. She has lost that naïve air of a young girl looking out upon the world and is beginning to wear that aspect which is called mature, which seems to say, "People don't understand. It's no good expecting it. One must simply do one's best without it."

And when John—six at the end of that year, already a small boy with pockets in his breeches, charming, friendly—begins suddenly to tell the most astonishing lies, she has no hesitation, after a conference with the curate, in sending him to church with the nurse. Remembering, too, that Harry's boy is about the same age, and that, with such a good father, he is probably a good boy, she writes to Harry. She says how sorry she is to be divided from him, asks after Edith and the children, and adds, "My Johnny is very precocious, but rather mischievous. I wish he had some companions of his own age."

Tabitha has never dared to visit the Cedars, and her letters have received the coldest and shortest of answers. It is plain that she is not to be encouraged. She is not so much surprised as disappointed when her letter is not answered.

But at once she forms new schemes. She reflects, "It's probably Edith is the trouble"; and she remembers Edith has a favorite shop in Oxford Street. She inquires, and hears that Mrs. Baskett is still a customer. A few days later, as if by chance, she finds herself face to face with her, among the heaps of cheap hats and gaudy trimmings.

The two women stare at each other, as if to say, "Who is that? I used to know somebody like that." Then they recognize each other.

Edith looks fifty. She has a thin yellow face, from which the black eyes protrude, and the nose juts to an absurd size. Her body, on the other hand, is thick and clumsy. And the bright frilled dress makes it seem thicker.

Tabitha looks at her dress. She thinks, "Some Oxford Street sale, a bargain." And she is astonished, for she has thought of Edith as a woman who dressed well.

"How is Harry?" she asks. And the pronouncing of the name aloud moves her strongly, not only toward Harry but Edith, toward everything that has belonged to the old peaceful and secure life at home.

"You'd better ask him, he doesn't tell me." Edith's voice is cold. Her eyes rove over Tabitha from hat to shoes.

"And the practice?"

"I suppose it's doing well—Harry is never at home and doesn't even remember the children's birthdays. Are you still with the Sturge person?"

"Oh yes."

"We know about him. One of Harry's patients is a friend of a man who writes in that magazine."

Tabitha answers nothing to this.

Edith says with a malignant glance, "I'm sorry for you, you know. But it's no good saying that sort of thing doesn't pay in the end, you couldn't change now, could you? We're all too old to change."

"I suppose so." Tabitha wants to laugh, but also she is disturbed by the other woman's look of indignation.

"We never meet," she murmurs. "It's a pity. Do you and Harry still go to Sancombe for holidays?" Then seeing Edith's expression, she adds, "But I suppose it wouldn't do."

"I shouldn't mind, but Harry might." She speaks with bitterness as if her indifference to Tabitha's bad character was also Harry's fault, as if he had worn out her morals as well as her patience. She asks abruptly, "Is that hat the latest from Paris?"

"It's fairly new."

"I call it silly; and when the French are being so nasty."

Suddenly the two women stare at each other as if through glass, then suddenly touch their hands together and separate.

"She hates me," Tabitha thinks. "She's got narrower and meaner and more unforgiving; she'd kill me if she could."

She has let down her guard and received a blow. Her heart beats quickly as she goes through the crowded streets. She thinks, "They all hate me—all the Harrys and Ediths; they'd all like to see me in the gutter."

Panic touches her. She rushes home to the flat as if to assure herself that Johnny is still in his nursery, and still loves her, as his mother, without a second thought about her position in the world.

She takes him sweets, toys, and he throws his arms round her neck. But this love, which gives her so much delight, increases her panic. "What is going to happen to him in a world full of Harrys and Ediths?"

And Manklow himself is surprised by the energy with which Tabitha throws herself into the reorganization of *The Bankside* for a triumphant and scandalous edition after the war. She is indeed more bitter than ever against the morality of the time. "It's the meanness, the hypocrisy, the smallness."

The old queen is dead, and even Sturge is ready to believe that great changes are coming. The immense moral power of the widow, like the sky of a late summer—rich, heavy, which seems golden because it is full of old dust—has not been perceived till it has gone.

36 THIS new and bolder number of *The Bankside,* a special number prepared for the new age of revolution, is published in the June of 1901, when the war, though not over, is plainly won. It is a ruinous failure. Few buy it; no one pays any attention to it.

For though, as everyone has expected, there is a powerful reaction against everything Victorian, everything prewar, it has taken not a moral, but a political form. And what is new about it is not so much its theory as its practice. It is more violent, more extreme.

Peace is opening, like every peace, with civilian war, because civilians want the glory of warriors. The new century starts with battlecries as of savages. And the new party tribesmen, who conceive politics in terms of primitive war, have the contempt of savages for those civilized relics which they find on the ground. For them, mid-Victorian art and literature are grotesque heaps of rubble, remarkable only for their size and the clumsiness of their proportions; that of Pater, Wilde, Beardsley, and the *Yellow Book,* are like the torn rags of a marionette show abandoned in the mud of some ruined fair ground.

"It's politics or nothing," Manklow declares; and he wants to buy a novel by Wells. But Sturge will not hear of Wells, whose prose gives him physical distress. And he says, "We are not a political review."

"We'll be no review at all unless we get readers."

But Sturge is not to be moved. At sixty-one, he is growing difficult to move in any direction; he has formed too many attachments.

It is now Tabitha who saves the paper. For when Sturge declares that in any case his losses, due to the peace and the fall of prices, make it impossible for him to throw away more thousands on *The Bankside,* she hits upon the great scheme of a partnership with Wrinch. "I believe he'd love to take a share—he's always wanted a paper. And he's a millionaire, like all these Quaker bankers."

"Wrinch? It's no good asking Wrinch; he's very strait-laced."

In fact, the banker proves difficult. He wants a veto on contributions. He objects to Dobey. It is only by Tabitha's impetuosity in visiting him at his office that he is persuaded to come to West Street and to look over the proofs of the next number.

He is a very tall thin man, with the manners of a professor, which indeed he could have been had he not inherited a bank. He wanders about the room, gazes vaguely and with slight alarm at Tabitha through his large spectacles, and murmurs, "But why does Dobey insist on the blood, and what does he mean by representing success as Judas?"

Tabitha has put on her smartest frock for duty. The importance of the occasion gives her a becoming color and brightness of eye. It adds also a certain importunity to her attack.

"Oh, but Mr. Wrinch, it's from the Bible; you remember that place where Judas hanged himself—he fell down and burst asunder."

Wrinch, gazing at Tabitha with the expression of a horse alarmed by some bright unfamiliar object, murmurs, "More blood," and then he continues, "I hardly understand—"

"The vampire of youth," Sturge explains.

"Of course." Wrinch raises his brows and examines the conception with extreme suspicion.

"Oh, I know, Mr. Wrinch," Tabitha says breathlessly, "that Mr. Dobey is difficult, but don't you think—" she appeals to Wrinch as to a connoisseur—"that is perhaps because he is original?"

Tabitha has made this point a hundred times to critics, and to patrons like Wrinch. She has picked it up she knows not where, and has never examined it very closely. Probably she does not understand it. But she knows its efficiency, especially in the magic word original, and uses it with confidence. She is delighted to see, by a slight relaxation of Wrinch's forehead, that it has worked again. "He is certainly original."

"And, after all," Tabitha murmurs, using another well-tried movement of attack, "genius has its own laws."

"Yes, yes, indeed," says the other.

"It must be free, don't you think, Mr. Wrinch?"

And Sturge chimes in on this other magic word, "It requires freedom."

"Oh, certainly." The man's protestant soul can almost be seen embracing, in this alien ground, a solid doctrine of the faith.

And from this moment it takes barely twenty minutes for him to be won over. He is assured that in supporting Dobey, however repulsive to himself, he is serving the cause of freedom and providence. He is at least trying to do the right thing, in this difficult world. He makes only one condition, that Boole shall be rejected. "You must forgive me, but Boole is quite certainly blasphemous and obscene. In my experience he has been the worst of influences."

Sturge is outraged. "Perhaps the most important poet of our time."

But at this moment, when the negotiations between the two idealists are about to end in deadlock, the practical Tabitha remarks cheerfully that the problem of Boole need not be solved unless Boole should reappear. And this reminder is decisive. Wrinch takes a three-eighths share in the paper, with the only other stipulation that his name shall not be printed. He is a modest patron, and besides, he does not wish to offend stricter and narrower members of his connection by revealing his taste for modern art and letters.

37

For this diplomatic success, Tabitha receives much honor. She feels indeed that a great victory has been won. She begins eagerly to work for the new number; that is, upon her endless task of conciliation and encouragement. And it is actually ready for the printers when one afternoon, coming home from the science museum with John, she finds the flat full of excited persons, not only Sturge, but Dewpark, Jobson, Miss Pullen, three other ladies in their fifties, a doctor and a nurse.

She can scarcely recognize Sturge. His cheeks are pink, his eyes are bright, he treads on tiptoe with a muscular spring.

"What is it?"

"Boole"—with a look of triumph.

"Oh, the upholsterer."

"Boole, Boole. You remember Boole, the poet?"

Tabitha is startled. She feels for a moment a certain shock. She cries, "But how wonderful. Where did you put him?"

"I put him in the nursery. He was very excited. Wally thinks we ought to lock the door."

A sound is heard like wind sighing on a wire. Sturge hastens away, and Tabitha, following him to the nursery, sees sitting up in Johnny's bed a little wizened old man with a thin gray beard and a long blue nose. He is wearing Sturge's pajamas of blue silk, which makes his sallow cheeks seem jaundiced, and he is talking to Jobson and Johnny, in his usual soft mild voice.

"Yes, I have been drunk, I have been drunk beyond dreams; I have lived in the uttermost realms of the drunken."

Johnny is amazed and delighted by this extraordinary event. He has never before seen anyone like Boole. He stares at the poet with round eyes and a smile of excitement; then, unable to express his energy of joy by word of mouth, jumps into the air and slowly turns right round.

"For, as you see," Boole is explaining with that gentle sincerity which has always brought conviction, "it was necessary for me to be drunk; it was even my duty. For to know the resurrection of the spirit, the body must perish with the beasts—to breed the rose, one must become as an ordure."

"What is an ordure?" John interjects.

"It is me, my child; the wretch you see before you." But at this moment, perceiving Tabitha, and at once comprehending her feelings, he murmurs, "But I must go, I trespass—"

He begins to get out of bed. The doctor, Sturge, and even the Scots nurse at once surround him and restrain him. They explain that he is ill; he can't go out or he will die. They drive out the audience. The nurse explains, "You excite him too much." She is a children's nurse, but she wears a uniform and feels herself to belong to the official medical class. She thrusts John from his own room with an abrupt hand and a glance in the opposite direction toward the doctor who is asking her to have a prescription made up.

Boole, he says, must have complete rest. He is in the first stages of delirium tremens complicated by pneumonia.

John is put to bed in the drawing room. But he returns to the nursery by himself, at some early hour, and is found in the middle of a long conversation with Boole about a recent murder case. The two, it seems, have taken to each other. Boole is fond of all children and loves to talk to them, and Johnny finds Boole's stories of Soho, of fights and murders, even more delightful than Dobey's fairy tales.

Tabitha goes to Sturge. "Why did you put Boole in the nursery?"

"Because it was necessary to keep him away from his friends; in the nursery, fortunately, we can give him the quiet and seclusion he needs—we can watch him."

"And what about Johnny?"

"But that is another advantage. Boole is devoted to your Johnny."

And Sturge is astonished when Tabitha exclaims that she will not have Johnny sacrificed for Boole, that Boole is very bad for Johnny.

"Bad for Johnny to have a man like Boole for his friend? Do you realize that Boole's friendship is a privilege for which many distinguished persons would give their eyes? Boole loves children; he has written poems to them. Suppose he were to write a poem for your Johnny."

But Tabitha answers by demanding a time limit for Boole's stay in the nursery. Sturge is shocked, and becomes, as usual in a quarrel with Tabitha, sulky and aloof.

Jobson, called in by both parties, urges that Johnny should be sent to school—a boarding school.

"At seven!" Tabitha cries. "And with his chest!"

But it appears that Sturge, offended in himself and, above all, shocked by Tabitha's smallness of mind in refusing to a genius the refuge so important to his very life, is not going to give way.

"Very well," Tabitha says to him. "Johnny must go to school. And if he is miserable there, or if he dies of pneumonia, I suppose you'll be quite satisfied."

"That's not fair, Bertie."

But to Tabitha it seems a moderate statement of her wrongs. And as less than a month later she is looking from the window of a South Eastern train on orchards and hopfields, she feels her bitterness even more deeply. "Boole's little finger is more to Bunny than Johnny's whole body; and as for me, I count for nothing at all. After six years. And goodness knows I've tried to make him happy."

38

SHE is filled with self-righteousness. Her grievance increases every time she looks at John, who, in a new school coat and knickerbockers, is sitting opposite her with a scared and angry face. His whole pose, his drooping hands in the too-long sleeves, to allow for growth, his languid feet in new boots, are those of a victim asking, "Why, why?"

He has asked why. "Why must I go to school?" And Tabitha has given the usual answer. "To learn things; to be with other boys." But these answers have not answered even her own question. Why?

An enormous why. Why should Johnny suffer because his mother has been deceived, because Sturge is obstinate and crazy about his Boole? Why can there never be any security, even for a small boy's nursery?

She sees the boy's terror, which has made him, for once, sit still. She aches with pity for him and anger against the world that has made him suffer. But she does not take him into her lap to console him. She knows that if she does so, he will say, "Don't take me to school, I can't bear it," and they will both weep.

It is her duty to be cruel to him, to withdraw herself from him. She thinks, "He must grow away from me. I must wish it."

The school, Halliton House, is one recommended by Jobson, who has taken the advice of an agent. It is a large old villa with a fine garden, close to the village. Its playing field is half a mile away, but it keeps a play yard for morning exercise. This yard, between the side of the house and the road, is as hideous as most school yards, with a cinder floor and a fence of wire mesh eight feet high all round to keep balls in and strangers out.

As Tabitha's cab drives up to the school, the first thing she sees is this cage, in which three small boys, wearing a uniform like John's, stand silent, ten yards apart, with their fingers hooked into the wire, gazing outwards.

Tabitha looks upon this cage with horror. As she enters the boys' gate, passing close to the prisoners, as she sees their eyes fixed upon her with exactly that look of new-caged animals, young deer or small monkeys, observing in silent imploring terror the visitors to their zoo, she feels, "But what am I doing? It's cruel, wicked. I can't."

But already the matron, a cheerful young woman in a coat and skirt, is advancing from the school door. Tabitha, hesitating on one foot, is too late to escape. The machine, whose power she has invoked, has already gathered her up.

"How do you do, Mrs. Bonser. And this is—?"

"Johnny."

"Of course. Perhaps Johnny would like to stay here?" She opens the cage door and presents Johnny to the three other new boys.

Johnny, finding himself in the cage, turns and flies to catch Tabitha's arm. "You're not leaving me, Mummy." He is in a panic.

But Tabitha finds herself supporting the matron. She has passed already, by some process that she has no time to examine, to the side of the machine. She reassures Johnny, "It's only for a little, and you can have a nice game with the other new boys."

"No, I hate them." He wrings his fingers. "I hate this place; I want to go home."

But now a master appears. He is a cheerful young man, with a fair military mustache and a rather loud tweed suit. He has just arrived, and still has a fashionable bonhomie. "Come on, boys," he cries. And he smiles at Tabitha, including her in the conspiracy. "Let's have a kick about."

A small football is brought out from the house and the young man executes some brilliant kicks. "Come on, lads." He takes one of the boys, a lanky child, by the ear, and says, "Go on, bust it."

The boy kicks the ball, grins, and runs after it. It appears that he has played before. He becomes suddenly noisy and confident, and takes charge of the game. The young master retires with a glance at Tabitha which is almost a wink.

Tabitha, talking to masters and headmaster with an effusion which is used also by the others and which admits and covers a crisis, suddenly catches her breath and loses her thread. Her throat swells. She wants to cry. Her whole soul protests against the cruelty of leaving a child of seven among a pack of strangers in this unhomely barrack. But the matron says with tremendous gaiety and charm, "Now about aperients, Mrs. Bonser." And Tabitha hastens to answer with an eager responsiveness, "Oh, the usual, I think."

39

WHAT Tabitha dreads above all is the moment of parting. How shall she explain to Johnny that now she must leave him, that she has sold him to the enemy? "He will cry, and that will give him a bad start." But when her cab arrives and she goes with the headmaster, a tall, bald, heavy man dressed like a farmer, to say good-by, Johnny is shouting in the court among a dozen others; he yells among the loudest. When he is called he glances hastily round and then rushes after the ball. He is not going to interrupt his game. It appears that he has established a certain authority over the lanky boy so much detested by Tabitha; he charges him joyfully and bellows, "Get out of my way, you." The master has to fetch him to say good-by. He is brought up panting, dirty, his hair on end, cinders on his nose, and a wild intoxication in his eyes. He has never before had such a debauch of noise and victory.

"Say good-by to your mother, Johnny."

Johnny puts up his face, his eyes still upon the game, and says, "Goo'-by. Kick it, you f-o-o-l." The headmaster and Tabitha laugh. She kisses the dirty hot cheek, gets into the cab, and drives away. Her face springs out of shape, she presses her hand to her cheek to keep herself from weeping. But she finds herself compelled to smile at some vast disappointment which has made not only her anxiety but her very life absurd and superfluous. "I might have expected it. It's all so new and exciting for him—and really what a good thing."

But she is depressed, and West Street seems to her intolerable. The sacred nursery is full of Boole's visitors; Madge Moon sprawls in the sitting room; Dobey and Hodsell, arguing about the nature of sin, make her head ache. She cannot take the faintest interest in the new number of *The Bankside*, called, even by Sturge, her number; and when Wrinch comes to consult with her, she has difficulty in affecting the interest that his deference requires.

And now again she writes to the Cedars, this time to Edith. She sends the news that she has taken Johnny to a good school where he will be well taught. "It is rather chancy, but if Johnny is to be confirmed, he will need the proper lessons. And I think children ought to be confirmed—it's a pity for them to be too different."

She waits anxiously for an answer. She hopes even for a word of approval. But she receives only a note from Edith suggesting tea in a West End café.

They meet. Tabitha exerts her charm. She is humble, affectionate. She listens to Edith's complaints of Harry's selfishness and her children's virtues. She even admires the women's frocks. At last she reminds Edith of her proposal that they should go for a holiday together.

Edith hesitates, then suddenly agrees. The tea, an expensive one, has made her reckless.

When Tabitha tells Sturge that she is going away for a fortnight's holiday with a friend, he is surprised and angry. "A very awkward time," he complains. For in the excitement of his enterprise he has gradually ceased to need so much that other excitement of the lover. He has become less a slave and more a husband. Tabitha is no longer the only important concern of his life.

"I'll stay if you really need me," Tabitha answers. But she speaks coldly, from pride. She feels that she has discharged all obligations to Sturge, and that his indifference to John's fate is unforgivable.

"I suppose if you want to go, you will go," he says in a peevish tone.

And this air of grievance also irritates her. "He needn't be so cross—he has his Boole."

40

EDITH, at Paddington, is like someone better than a friend: a relation who shares old family sympathies. Tabitha kisses her warmly and insists on buying the tickets—first-class tickets. "Let's be comfortable."

"Yes, for a change," says Edith. "I could do with a change all round."

"Oh, so could I. Oh, heavens, yes."

And the two women, as they settle into their carriage, have for a moment the same expression of impatient longing.

"A change," Tabitha thinks. And it seems to her that she couldn't have lived another hour in West Street, in that atmosphere which seems to her now so oppressive, as if the very air of the flat were stale and thick with strange æsthetic anxieties, Jobson's suspicions, Manklow's greedy ambition, Boole's fevered dreams.

And Edith, full of the same nervous disgust, talking of her

grievances against Harry and the children, forgets her anger against Tabitha.

She is pleased, too, when Tabitha admires Sancombe, a small place with a very fine beach, and approves the Beach Hotel. She is an old visitor and regards herself in some measure as responsible for the beauty of the one and the comfort of the other, which, however, astonishes Tabitha by its shabby squalor.

Edith at once meets old friends, a Colonel Quare and his wife, and immediately makes new ones, a lawyer called Prince with a daughter of twenty. The lawyer, the colonel, the colonel's wife, are eager with welcome; for all have come for a change. And in their faces, printed, as it were, like the large red letters of a newspaper poster upon the common type of their daily lives, cautious, reserved, is the advertisement of their plans and of their needs. They want a change; they want to talk, to let themselves go.

At once it is agreed that Edith, Tabitha, the Quares, and the Princes shall share a table. It is a lively table, for everyone talks, smiles; everyone has the animation which perhaps has belonged to them ten years before; perhaps never. Edith rallies the men in the style of Frood Green in the late 'seventies, when she was its belle. Mrs. Quare chatters about her ambitions and her two children so like a schoolgirl that it appears incongruous for her to have children. She has longed, she says, to be an artist; she is disappointed in her children, who are so stodgy, so dull. "The girl is nice-looking, but really so stupid; the boy is clever but so uninterested." Miss Prince, the lawyer's daughter, pretty but uncouth and vaguely aware of her uncouthness, grows excited, wriggles and cries, "Oh yes," "Oh no," with an eager desire to be part of the conversation.

And these new friendships develop, in this air of holiday, with great speed. On the next morning, Edith disappears with the lawyer. He is teaching her to putt. The colonel takes Miss Prince to hunt for shells; Mrs. Quare and Tabitha, congratulating themselves on the absence of men, have a long talk about Mrs. Quare's children.

And Tabitha, full of sympathy, of interest, cries, "But how wonderful!" "How extraordinary!" "Yes, children are *queer.*"

She, who has liked company so much, now delights, for a change, to be alone. When Mrs. Quare is writing letters, she goes walking by the sea, and gazing at an endless prospect of small green waves, under a calm pale sky, she says to herself with delight, "What bliss to be alone for once. What peace. I'd forgotten what peace was like. Oh, I could live here forever."

In the evening, while Edith is learning billiards from the lawyer, she listens to the colonel's stories of tiger shooting and is entranced by his various escapes. She wonders how Mrs. Quare could bear the anxiety of bringing up young children in India. "Children are difficult enough in England."

They even talk politics. Colonel Quare takes an individual line. The South African war, he says, though forced upon the country, was a misfortune. The empire is a great responsibility. "I'm not afraid of a liberal victory," he says boldly; "the country needs waking up."

"But that's just what I think," Tabitha exclaims in a tone of gratified surprise. "We're asleep. Oh it's awful how asleep!" And she is glad to talk politics with this delightful colonel, while Edith flirts with her lawyer and hangs upon herself even more gaudy blouses.

A friend of the Quares now arrives, a young man called Burne, dark and plain, but with an expression so humorous and lively that it is impossible not to like him. While the Quares talk to Tabitha at breakfast, she catches Burne's eye, full of laughter. She does not know what amuses him, but she smiles.

Next day he comes down early and finds her alone in the hall. He laughs and says, "I admire the way you put up with old Quare."

"But he's very nice, don't you think?"

"Kindness apart, isn't it amazing that people can go on saying the same thing over and over again?"

He appeals to Tabitha as one member of the great world to another. In fact he is on leave from large railway works in Egypt. He has moved in official society. "What a pleasure to meet someone here who's not quite dead. How those poor women gape at your tailor-mades." He laughs loudly. "I say, do you bathe?"

"But I adore bathing—simply adore it."

And since Edith is still playing golf every day, they go bathing together. Burne proves to be an expert diver. He gives Tabitha lessons in the swallow dive.

Afterwards they stroll together among the dunes, and Burne, rejoicing in a practiced listener, talks. He points out that the South African war, though forced upon the country, was, contrary to the usual opinion, a disaster. The empire, regarded by Britain as an achievement, is really a heavy responsibility. Reforms are needed, a new vision. He is all for the liberals. "Why not pensions for the old; even women's votes?" And he cries, "Why not try 'em, anyhow? Take a chance. We can't do much harm by a change."

He has, in fact, the usual notions of a young man of his time. He is tired of the old government, the old ideas, and he wants new ones. Tabitha has heard all his schemes and many more, and they seem to her very tame. She has heard Manklow abolish monarchy, property, marriage, and even the human race. She knows the conservative case as deployed by old Dewpark, not as a plan to keep the rich wealthy, the poor in subjection, but as a philosophy of life. She hears the old man, so poor himself, say in his gruff voice, "We're lucky that the thing works at all. The miracle is that there's any peace or decency or what we call civilization anywhere in the world. For God's sake don't rock the boat, the sea is damn deep; and if there is one kind of progress I do believe in, it is sharks', and they go fast." But she says to herself with indignation, "People like the Quares and Burne are worth ten Manklows or Dewparks or Booles; they believe in something positive, they help one."

And she is enthusiastic for all Burne's schemes. She is sure, she says, that they will make an enormous difference to the country. "And goodness knows, we need it."

The Quares have now accepted the young couple as a young couple. When they meet them, they smile with a particular significance. Tabitha says, "They think we like to be alone."

Burne is silent. Suddenly he exclaims, "Do you realize what you've meant to me here?" He declares she is the nicest, prettiest, most intelligent girl he has ever met, and the pluckiest. For how unlucky to lose her husband so young. He discloses his prospects. His father is an engineer, very well off, and he is an only son. Has he a chance?

And this proposal, so unexpected, does not seem startling in Sancombe, in the free blowing air, the bright deep sky. It is even appropriate to a place so unsophisticated, so different from West Street. Tabitha is moved so much that she cries, "Oh, but Mr. Burne—"

The young man fears a no. He exclaims, "Don't throw me down at once. I know I've been too quick; but the time is so short."

"No, it's not that; it's only—that perhaps you don't know me very well."

"I know all I want to know."

Tabitha escapes in confusion. She is astonished by the young man's goodness. She thinks, "But he really does love me, and he is charming. So honest, so simple. Really it would be amazing luck for me, but of course I should have to tell him—or should I?"

She longs for advice. She thinks even of putting the case to Edith. But at bedtime, when she goes as usual to say good night, she finds her in an irritable mood. The lawyer's wife has arrived, and she has played no billiards that evening. Her pain has come back.

"What pain is that?"

"Oh, I always have a pain."

"Can't Harry do anything?"

"Harry! He never takes any interest in my health."

Tabitha is chilled by this bitterness, but also, looking at her sister-in-law—coarsened and narrowed by life, in pain and frustration—she is frightened. She feels suddenly an immense loneliness and weakness. And going in silence to her room, she says to herself, "No, I shan't tell him. Why? Afterwards, perhaps."

41

YET next morning, as she walks again in that miraculous air, in this place so full of pure thoughts and kind honest people, and sees Burne coming toward her with his solemn trusting countenance a little embarrassed by love, she exclaims, "Mr. Burne—Teddy—I must explain." And she hastily tells the story of her escapade with Bonser, and John's birth. She does not, however, mention Sturge. Burne takes her by the forearm and presses it hard. "But Mrs. Bonser—Tibby—what does all that matter? I love you, I want you." And he implores Tabitha to say yes there and then.

"Oh, but are you sure you realize—?"

"Yes, yes, everything."

"Oh dear, there's Mrs. Quare. I must speak to her about my sister-in-law—she's not very well."

Tabitha hastens to Mrs. Quare and manages to attract her to the party. She has no idea why she has not answered Burne.

And when she is at last alone in the hotel she is shocked by her hesitation. "But of course I shall have him—if he were ten times more—" She examines the quality of Burne, with which, ten times multiplied, she could still be complaisant, and exclaims warmly, "But he's not *really* dull. Heavens, I ought to thank my stars for such a chance."

There are several more letters from West Street, and several periodicals. Much has been coming from West Street every day, but she has not opened any of it. She does not want to think of West Street. There is, for instance, a card from Jobson, which, because it is a card, has twice presented itself to her eyes and annoyed her more at each time of reading. "Nice old games with B. F. very worried. M. playing up about editorial. Can you wire Dobey's latest address and nursery key. Job."

"What on earth does he mean, wire nursery key? Of course Fred is worried—he always is; and Boole was bound to be a nuisance. As for Manklow, I suppose he is trying to stuff *The Bankside* with politics. Naturally."

She tears up the card and, after a little hesitation, all the letters, which she throws into the basket. Then she goes to bed in exultation, feeling like a Napoleon. "Now I can't go back. I've made my decision."

But at once she is attacked by the idea that there may have been something important in the letters. The question rises before her. "What are the nice old games? Why is Fred worried? What is Manklow doing?" What, she asks herself, will happen if he provokes a quarrel with Wrinch, who, though radical in word, is, she feels, far from radical by inclination. And she cannot get rid of these anxieties. If she drives them out of her mind they torture her nerves. She cannot sleep. Her whole body is awake with a tension of anxiety, with the question, "What is wrong in West Street?"

She is now quite sure that something is wrong. The only doubt is, how much and how badly?

She has no peace until, toward the small hours, she resolves, "I'll just run up for the day and see what has happened." And in the morning she gets up very early, writes a note to Burne—"I have to go to town on urgent business. Back next week. Writing—" packs her bag and dressing case, and slips out to the station.

Twenty minutes later she is in the early market train for the junction and the London express. She is confused and astonished at herself. "Really, what a fuss; and it's not fair to poor Teddy Burne. I must write at once."

But her mind, with all the energy of a constitution refreshed by sea air, by a thorough change, instantly throws itself again upon the problems of West Street. "If it's about Boole, I'll suggest publishing him in a book. Yes, I'll say he is too important for a magazine."

She is enraged by the slowness of the country train, stopping at all the stations. It seems to her now that every moment away from West Street is full of danger. And if anything has gone wrong, she will be responsible. " 'M. playing up'—more quarrels, I suppose. Really, men are perfect children!"

And the situation at West Street is both what she expected, in the main lines, and quite different in details. Manklow has demanded political articles, and he has also refused to print Boole. He declares that Boole's period is finished. "The decadents are dead and buried—you can't even smell them; and the new lot are all for politics, new left politics. We can't be too extreme."

But the surprise is that, having been refused money to hire political writers of note, he has resigned.

Boole, on the other hand, is never seen. He has used the remoteness of the nursery as a means of evading all interference. He has made for himself there a fortress heaped with torn papers, empty bottles, where he lives, eats, sleeps, and drinks. And with the cunning of a lifelong fugitive, he slips in and out unheard.

He is not at all disturbed by Manklow's attack. "A good thing," he tells Tabitha, "if I am out of fashion. Now I'll be able to do something good."

But Sturge is outraged. "He can go; Boole's worth all the Manklow's in the world. Manklow's nothing but a time-server."

"My dear, but the *real* point is, can we do without him?" Tabitha is patient but insistent. She thinks, "Fred is getting old, he's much older than I remembered." And indeed everything at West Street seems older, shabbier than she had remembered: the curtains, the paint; Manklow, who has gray hairs; Boole, who is a ruin; Sturge, who is falling in, sagging, who walks like an old man with bent knees, and has already an old worried expression, eyebrows fixed in permanent desperation.

"Heavens!" Tabitha thinks, before she has been three hours in West Street. "What a mercy I came back, or everything would have gone to pieces." She flies to Wrinch, who proves a loyal ally. He will support her policy. He lends her his own brougham in order to pursue Manklow into Bloomsbury.

It is while she enjoys, in this brougham, a few moments for reflection, while she is arranging her arguments for Manklow, that she recollects Burne. "Oh dear, I must write to poor Teddy. I must make up my mind."

But now, to her surprised glance, Sancombe and all its affairs seem to lie in some remote place, remote not only in space, but even in time. She cannot believe that only thirty hours have elapsed since she left it. It is eleven o'clock, the Quares will be walking on the beach; Edith will be putting; Teddy Burne, with the air of a revolutionary statesman, will be laying down the law for a new government to Miss Prince. Tabitha thinks, "Poor Teddy, poor boy."

Tabitha, at twenty-six, is five years younger than Burne; but she thinks of him as a child. "And the dear old colonel; how sweet he was about tigers." She smiles sadly and kindly, as on the inhabitants of some distant island, where gentle and innocent people lead a life of charming simplicity, but cut off almost entirely from anything to be called life—the real world, where things happen, things that are important. "I simply *must* make Roger understand that he can't leave us like this." And in an instant she has again forgotten Sancombe.

42

She is indeed very successful with Manklow. He proves ready for a compromise, without even pinching her arm or stroking her hair. He will spend only two hundred on political articles, and print two new sonnets of Boole's, on the condition that his name appears as editor. Sturge is in despair. He cries to Tabitha, "So you've gone over to the enemy."

Tabitha perceives her cruelty, and yet she has no time even to feel it. The publication party, for the fifteenth number, is due in two days, and Manklow must be there or his resignation will be known. She soothes Sturge with caresses; she thinks, "Poor old man; what a nuisance he is in a difficulty, with his crotchets about art."

In fact Sturge gives way only an hour before the party. Tabitha rings up Manklow and receives his congratulations. She thinks, "Thank God that's something settled!" Her head is aching, her nerves are quivering; she lies down to rest. She is not yet accustomed to the stress of life at West Street. A dozen problems still press upon her. And they do not include the problem of Burne. For she knows already that she will not marry him. She does not know now how she has ever dreamt of marrying anyone so callow. She thinks, "I must wire to him tonight. I can write later, that's easy. But what *am* I going to do about Boole? He simply can't go on in the nursery, especially if Johnny is being difficult."

A first-term report from Halliton Hall has arrived, describing John as idle and troublesome. "He has made friends and appears happy, but he does not show much sense of discipline."

"But what does that *mean*?" she asks herself. "Is Johnny really bad or is the man stupid?" Her head whirls. Her little French clock tinkles seven on its silver bell, and she starts up. "Heavens, I must dress." She feels for her slippers with her toes and rings the bell.

"Who's coming tonight? I suppose there will be trouble with Wrinch about the Dobeys. Come in"—this to the maid. "Oh, Bennet, what am I to wear? I've really nothing, have I, and it's rather an occasion."

And again, two hours later, when she stands before the fire in her drawing room, waiting for the first guest, she presses her hands to her forehead and thinks as she has thought a hundred times before, "Why shouldn't he be bad?—He began all wrong."

Suddenly the door opens and she sees Jobson in a loud tweed suit. He, too, looks changed, incredibly coarse and red.

"Hullo, girlie. You look nice. Fred about?"

"He's dressing."

"That's all right." And approaching Tabitha closely, he mutters, "He's here—in my place. I headed him off."

"Who?"

"B. Didn't you get my letter? Where have you been all this time? What have you been up to? Sent you a card, too."

"But who is it?"

"Bonser—Bonser, girlie, the old original; just out of jug."

Tabitha feels stupefied. She murmurs, "Out of jail?"

"I told you. Six months, for the old Spanish prisoner trick—which seems a bit stale. But don't you worry. I've got him in hand for to-night. The only thing is, what's the policy? Can he make trouble?"

"I haven't seen him for more than seven years."

"Take my tip, girlie, and if he's got anything on you, go to the police. Don't be afraid of the police. There's no better friends in a thing like this. Bless you, they're men of the world."

Tabitha is growing more and more agitated. She says to herself, "No, I mustn't go near him, it would be madness."

Jobson pats her shoulder. "It's all right, I'll send him off."

"No, wait."

"I suppose he is the boy's father?"

"Yes, and besides—"

"Look here, girlie, take time—think it over. Don't make a big mistake."

But Tabitha has reassured herself. "No, I'll see him; he can't do anything. I wouldn't allow it."

Jobson is impressed by this resolute air. He stands aside. "Of course, if you're sure, you know best what he's got in his hand."

But in fact Tabitha has no plan at all. She feels that she is doing something enormously foolish but also necessary.

Jobson's door is ajar, and in the sitting room beyond, Bonser and Boole are sitting at a small table with glasses in front of them.

Bonser's appearance, as he gets up, startles Tabitha so much that for a moment she can only stare at him. He is thin and gray-faced, his blue eyes seem larger and paler. But she thinks. "They're Johnny's eyes."

"Why Tibs, don't you know me?" He takes her by the arm. "Not a day older; pretty as ever." He kisses her. "Nothing like a quiet life."

Tabitha draws back, and suddenly the question forms itself. "Did you get a letter I wrote to you from France? Or weren't you interested?"

"What's this, Pops? When did you write? But of course you had a kid!" Bonser is delighted with himself for this recollection. "How is she? I hope she's got your looks."

"It's a boy; and it's not a baby any more."

"No, of course not. Why, it must be five years—seven—eight. But what'll you drink? Have a chaser—that's what you need!"

"Perhaps I ought to go," Boole says in great perplexity at finding himself present at so delicate a conference. "I could sit on the stairs."

"I've no time," Tabitha says severely. "People are coming."

Bonser pours out a drink of neat whisky and presses it into her hand. "Why, you're as white as a starting gate. Here's to the old days. What times we had, Pops. I'll never forget 'em. You may say we were a couple of damn fools. And you certainly made the spondulicks fly, but I've never held it against you. What did you know? I've often laughed to think of you that first week, opening your eyes on the world. There's a lot to be said for bringing up a girl in the old-fashioned way. If anything can keep a girl straight, it's a good religious training, hell and damnation, and a quiet style of going on. Where are you sending our kid? Why not a convent?"

"He's a boy, Dick, I told you. His name is Richard John."

"A boy! That's funny, it was a girl just now." And looking keenly at Tabitha, he says, "I'm glad it's a boy. Yes, every time. I'd like to see him. Does he go to school yet?"

"Of course he does. He's at a boarding school—he's just begun Latin."

"Quite right. Nothing like the classics for boys. He ought to have brains, our kid; there's a lot of brains in my family."

Tabitha thinks, "He doesn't care a penny for John."

Steps are heard outside on the landing and Tabitha turns. "I'm sorry, but I must go now—people are coming."

"I'll come."

"No, Dick. I can't see you in the flat."

"Why not?" He glances fiercely at her. "You're not going to throw me down all over again?"

"Don't bully me, Dick. That's stupid."

She walks out with dignity and runs upstairs in a fluster. "He'd forgotten I wasn't a silly little girl any more. But how astonished he looked." She begins to laugh, and the laugh threatens to become tearful. "What has happened?" she asks herself. "Am I really disappointed? What on earth did I expect?"

But there is no time for her to discover what has happened to her feelings. Already there are seven guests in the drawing room, and Sturge, whose tie is crooked, gives her a reproachful glance, meaning, "Why did you desert me?" which recalls her to official life.

43

And the practice of years makes her not only self-possessed, but gives her that exhilaration which belongs to skill. The confidence which defied Bonser now examines a field of action. Manklow, with his open-mouthed smile, is receiving the congratulations of Lord Ducat, the great penny newspaper man; Lady Ducat is talking to a little pink-faced man, a millionaire iron master, a new friend of Sturge's, whose name Tabitha can never remember. He is chattering like a jay and turning repeatedly to Griller, who, however, holds himself bowed toward Lady Ducat as if to say, "We understand each other." Dewpark, in a very dirty shirt, stands against the wall scowling at Manklow; Lady Chadworth, in a fine pose, is gazing with delight at a new Pissarro.

Tabitha, who understands this sign of boredom, rescues her and presents Mr. Dobey, "whose new work has shocked all the critics."

She turns then to Dewpark. But Dewpark is in a rage. "Does Fred know what he's doing? Does he really want a revolution? Has he gone mad? Is everything going mad?"

Tabitha smiles and takes the old man's sleeve. "Fred didn't see that political article." She thinks, "Poor old man, he really is old; he's aging even quicker than Fred. The war seems to have made all the old men ten years older, and the young men into boys." In fact, two young soldiers, lately returned from South Africa, are riotously slapping Manklow on the back.

The room is filling. There is a crowd even greater than usual, and everywhere one sees and hears the evidence of an event. Faces are flushed, voices are raised, and their sound is full of that special liveliness with which people to whom all the current products of art and science and fashion are familiar, and therefore somewhat boring, welcome a new sensation.

For Manklow has succeeded in giving even this number of *The Bankside* a political flavor. He has slipped in, under Sturge's very nose, two articles: "The Death of the Dead," with some rude comments on the late queen, and "Socialismus," which has frightened even the radicals; while his review of the 'nineties has enraged every intellectual above the age of forty.

Miss Pullen's long yellow face, as she stands talking to Wrinch, is twisted with vehemence. She has not been so animated for years.

Wrinch himself, propped against the wall, and listening with the deference of an ambassador, has got that abstracted look in his eyes which ambassadors sometimes wear in the midst of their deferences. He has been taken aback by the new Dobeys, which represent the Seven Deadly Sins, under the heads of Rationality, Temperance, Thrift, Modesty, Remorse, Prudence, and Chastity. His eyes, wandering from Miss Pullen, seem to inquire of the air, "Is Dobey really a force for spiritual good?"

Tabitha smiles upon him in passing. "Your Dobeys—really his masterpiece." Her smile calls up a flush to the banker's cheek. She is in full beauty for she knows in her nerves that there has been an achievement. "We've done something this time. I knew Manklow could pull us through."

And seeing Sturge, flushed and damp, his tie still more crooked, she touches his arm. "Congratulations." She feels a moment of tenderness toward the man in his success.

"It's extraordinary!" He looks round with a smile full of confusion. "Ducat says we've made history."

Suddenly the little pink millionaire shoots out of the mass and seizes Sturge's arm. "Come, state banks! You don't want that, Sturge; you can't mean it. What about credit?"

Old Dewpark thrusts his way toward the hero. "Damn it, Sturge, your silly paper is simply anarchism. Abolish the empire. Do you realize what happens when empires are abolished? Have you forgotten your Bacon? Do you want wars, massacres, poverty, misery, all over the world?"

Tabitha smiles upon these critics. She feels the triumph of *The Bankside* like the success of a child, and does not inquire into its nature. Sturge is more critical. He complains to her afterwards. "Those political articles—Manklow altered them in proof—made them much worse."

Tabitha, who knows this very well, who has juggled with the proofs in order to keep peace with her two masters, answers gaily, "But they were a great success—they've made a regular sensation."

"It's not the kind of sensation we want, Bertie. We must be more watchful next time. And, mind you, Manklow is quite wrong about the political feeling of the country. He ought to talk to some of my friends in the government."

And eager to reassure himself, he points out that England is more peaceful and well off than it has ever been. Communism has not raised its head since 1870. The Irish question has been settled by land purchase, giving the land to the peasants. "They don't want trouble. In my view, the key to this century is plain already; scientific progress, giving prosperity to all—and that means peace."

Tabitha, who like a wife has lost the habit of attending to Sturge, answers in a soothing cheerful voice, "Poor Mr. Dewpark, he's very reactionary, and he's jealous of Manklow. Don't you think Manklow ought to have more pay?"

She has chosen the right moment, Sturge agrees. Indeed, in the next week, as he begins to realize the extent of his success, he proposes to give Manklow a bonus as well as a rise.

But Manklow has already had offers from Lord Ducat to edit a new radical evening paper, *The Progressive*, at a salary far beyond Sturge's means. And since this is what Manklow has been aiming at for years, he accepts at once. He is much irritated by the indignation of the *Bankside* clique. "Don't they know they're dead? And why? Because they wouldn't see what was right in front of their eyes." The Banksiders are still more enraged at this judgment. Wrath inspires them to great efforts. "A good riddance," Sturge says. And a new committee is formed with Wrinch, Boole, and Dewpark. More funds are raised for a new and splendid *Bankside* to eclipse the old, and to make Manklow feel his treachery.

Dewpark agrees to be editor, and after six months' great effort and much confusion, the number appears. It is richly produced and much advertised. Dewpark has put his essay on Matthew Arnold between a Boole play and a Dobey drawing. His intention is to give the public a choice of masterpieces, but the effect is confusion. The number is a complete failure, and it is the last of *The Bankside*. Sturge can afford no more losses; Wrinch is shocked by a disaster which seems to show that providence is not behind his venture.

44

AND now it grows dreary at the flat. The old friends come still, but not at the same time. There have been too many quarrels. Failure has left bitterness; Dewpark blames Sturge, and Sturge declares that Griller has worked against him. *The Bankside* is a forbidden subject, and its old supporters agree only in abusing the age. They go away leaving behind them the sense of defeat and superannuation.

Tabitha still finds the days too short, but no longer rewarded. She must entertain, but her guests are sad. And even when she is housekeeping, shopping, she is incessantly preoccupied with John. At twenty-eight she has already anxious wrinkles between her eyebrows.

The boy has a regular bronchitis every winter, and asthma at harvest time. In between he has colds, earaches, and all the childish diseases, one after another, in an acute form. He is one of those delicate boys who are all legs and neck; who drop exhausted into every chair, and yet can't sit still for two minutes; who refuse to do any work, but ask questions from morning till night. His holidays are a long agony, for Tabitha delights in his company, and yet is obliged to find fault with him constantly. Moreover, the boy exasperates Sturge, whose health is beginning to fail. When now he comes to West Street, it is usually to be nursed and cosseted. He has lumbago, indigestion, and each winter a bout of influenza which lasts him almost to spring. He shows suddenly that premature decrepitude that falls on middle-aged men who take powerful stimulants, or keep young mistresses. He has burnt up ten years in five. Above all, he is discouraged. He is deeply wounded by the attacks upon him; by a rude letter from Dewpark; by a caricature of Dobey's showing him as an old vampire sucking the blood of youth, represented by an idealized Dobey.

Especially he is startled by the cruel ingratitude of Manklow when he publishes, in 1904, that series of articles which made his name as a popular humorist: "Darkest London of the Lost Century."

These affect to give an account of expeditions into the jungles of Belgravia and Mayfair and of the wild tribes that live there. There is a description of the Woolly-woollies, who used to explore each other's woolliness every morning and exchange souls every night under the moon. Their chief was called Balfoofoo. And there were the Troglodytes who lived each in his mud hole hatching out small green frogs and murmuring, "Hear them sing. What originality, what music," while the frogs for their part sat and croaked all day, "Our god and our begetter whose name is called Bunsurge."

The picture is clever and malignant. Even Sturge's friends are amused by a description of the Bunsurge trundling through the groves of Hyde Park, turning out his toes and smiling to himself as he says, "I am the great Bunsurge, the begetter of green frogs." They are amused, too, by Manklow's spite, which has never forgiven Sturge for sharing the editorship and forcing Boole upon him. "Poor old Sturge," they say, "Manklow will hunt him into his grave. But he asked for it. A man who actually looks for geniuses is lucky if he only gets himself hated."

Sturge can't behave even with dignity under this attack. Apparently he is sensitive to ridicule. He weeps; he is broken. Tabitha is alarmed for his life. Discovering that she has grown attached to this weak gentle creature, she is impatient with his despair. "You mustn't mind what that horrible man writes; you ought to despise him."

"But perhaps I was wrong about Dobey."

"No, of course you weren't wrong, it was I who was wrong about Manklow. But I always knew he was a beast."

And Boole, astonished, cries, "My dear Sturge, what does it matter what Manklow writes? He has no style. And style is the man. Manklow is nothing, a puff of emptiness, a piece of vacancy."

Boole alone of the *Bankside* clique is still gay and free. He appears indifferent to the fact that his vogue has passed, and is writing a vast book on *The Virtue of the Decadence* from which, in the evenings, he reads to Tabitha long chapters about the Importance of Damnation, the Discovery of Hell, saying cheerfully, "No one will print the stuff, and so I can write exactly what I think."

He has become welcome to Tabitha, for though she laughs at him, he is always ready to run messages for her, to talk about John.

45

BONSER has not come again to the flat. But every now and again he writes to Tabitha, compliments her, asks after John, and demands a small loan. "Just till next week. Or shall I come along to the flat and explain the circumstances?"

This sentence really means, "Pay me by return or I'll come and make a scandal," and so it is understood. Tabitha always pays by return, but without resentment because it is not quite certain that Bonser is blackmailing her. What is not expressed may not be understood even by those who act upon it.

And during that long cold winter while West Street sinks deeper into the special gloom which belongs to deserted shrines, while Boole's book is refused by one publisher after another, and Sturge moans "that nasty fellow Manklow was right; the vulgarians have inherited the earth," how delightful to hear the chink of the letter box and find a letter from Bonser.

"We've got to remember," he writes, "that Johnny is handicapped. I'm not going to say whose fault it is, but it isn't his. We want to put him in a really safe job where no one will ask questions. The army or the Church. Grand games for those with the gift. We'll see how his voice turns out. Also he might be too short. Soldiers and parsons want to be tall or nobody notices them. I suppose you couldn't lend me a couple of yellow boys till next week. Say five to make up the fifty."

"That's the only reason he writes at all," Tabitha tells herself. But she answers at once with extracts from John's last report. "The real trouble seems to be that he won't work. But, of course, as I tell him, he's unusual in one way; being so delicate, he needs a lot of encouragement." So on for six sides. And as she looks at the fat letter and slips a five-pound note between its leaves, she has exactly the sense of one who recovers from a debauch—an amused shame, a dying elation.

And when suddenly Bonser demands twenty pounds, with something like a threat, she writes, "Dear Dick, you mustn't pester," and sends nothing. She is surprised, however, to hear no more. She has expected at least abuse. As the weeks pass she begins to regret her snub. Perhaps it was too severe. Bonser's letters were only an amusement, but how much she misses that amusement. The idea that she will never get any more, that nothing will break the monotony of her existence, becomes intolerable. One day she asks Boole for news of his friend.

Since the rejection of his book Boole has spent most of his time drinking in pubs. He is, in consequence, in miserable health, but also, in consequence, full of ideas for new chapters of the book, which he proposes to enlarge to two volumes. He intends to dedicate the new work to Tabitha, but never writes any of it. And when Tabitha reproaches him for killing himself with drink, he answers, in his usual state of drunken excitement, "To die is to live, to be blind is to see—I am a wretch, dear lady, and so I can adore with a pure heart."

He is delighted to seek Bonser through the pubs, and comes back, after three days, with the news that he is often to be found at the Postboy near Shaftesbury Avenue.

"A great man," he says, "so strong, so good-hearted, and full of faith. Simple, proud. But of course that is natural in a man of such ancient family; I suppose about the oldest in Europe."

"What family is that?"

"The Paleologues." Boole is surprised that Tabitha needs to ask this question; still more surprised to see her laugh. She begs his pardon. "I'm sorry, I don't know why I did that."

"Do you want Dick?"

"Good heavens, no."

But on the very next afternoon she is examining the Postboy from across the street. The bar curtains are high, she cannot look over them, and she is afraid to enter the bar. She thinks, "I should be mad to encourage him—but it is stupid for him to be offended."

On the next day she is in the Postboy saloon with a port at her elbow and a newspaper in front of her face. She is glad of her newspaper when Boole puts his long neck round the door. Fortunately he goes to the public bar.

And it is only on her third visit that she sees Bonser. He comes in at seven, just when she is leaving. He is even shabbier than before, but appears in high spirits, and shows no surprise at the meeting. "Hullo, Pops, how are you? How's Johnny? How's the young chest?"

"His chest is better, and he's had no asthma this winter." Tabitha looks curiously and nervously at Bonser. She is smiling, but her heart beats quickly. "And how are you, Dick? What are you doing?"

"A lot you care."

"Of course I care."

"If you want to know, I've got the biggest idea of my life, to set us all up, set Johnny up. But what of it? A lot you care!"

"Well, Dick, you haven't even told me about it."

"Oh, it's a big thing; you wouldn't understand, you never had any money sense. Look here, Tib, do you realize that there's thousands and thousands of people, millions if you like, who never buy an investment because they don't know how. But what does it mean to you? Nix."

"Of course I want to know, Dick."

"Look here, Pops, put it like this: half the money in England is kept in the old biscuit tin. Why? Because people don't know what to do with it. Well, then, why not give 'em a chance to invest, to buy real shares."

"I see."

"Of course you want something to start with. An office, a few circulars—say a thousand pounds. Come, Tib, what about it?"

"I haven't a thousand pounds, have you?"

"It's not a joke. And if you haven't, your old man has. He's rolling."

"You don't think I'd ask him. No, Dick, I must go. I can't keep the horse waiting."

Bonser runs after her to the door and holds it against her. "Pay it by installments. That's the usual way. A half share for five hundred, a hundred down, and the rest to be called up."

"No, no, Dick; it's impossible."

She is glad to be safe in her cab. But yet she is laughing; her eyes sparkle; her cheeks glow; a mysterious energy pours through her nerves. "It's a good thing I got away or he would have been troublesome. I won't go again, it's too dangerous. And it's not fair to Bunny."

A few days later she gets a letter from Bonser, giving a box number at the paper shop, and enclosing a printed circular, headed "Trustees Mutual Guarantee Association," and in a line beneath, "Established to eliminate gambling on the Stock Exchange. Mutual benefits. Direct dealings. No fees. All profits to the Association."

It contains a long list of shares, beginning with consols and ending in respectable industrial companies, divided into odd lots and offered at fixed sums. Bonser's note explains, "I think this is a good list to start with. No mines, nothing risky. What we have to do is to overcome the public prejudice against stocks and shares, which stands in the way of the prosperity of the Empire. You might show this to your old man; tell him if we get out a list every mail we'll pull in a hundred per cent a year." Underneath are the words, "You owe me twenty jims to make up the monkey."

This surprises Tabitha, who had thought that the latest scheme had been an invention of the moment. But she sends five pounds, and writes about John, who has been keeping goal for the second hockey eleven. "It's worth it to get Dick's nonsense; but I'm not going to be victimized." And after another month she sends another five.

46

HAVING written off her payments to Bonser as doles due to an old sentiment, she is much surprised, one day that autumn, to receive a postal order for thirty shillings, and this note: "Your divvy, beautiful Pops, at twenty per cent, with bonus for foundation members. Pay us a call at the office, and I'll tell you more about our new Life and Fire Insurance Guarantee Funding Bonds. I think you owe me a little celebration for old times' sake." Beneath the signature there are three large crosses, with the names written beneath—Adam, Eve, and Pinch Me.

The address is just off Holborn. Tabitha has no intention of going near Bonser again, but she is puzzled by the address. "He can't have an office, but how does he dare to print it? What is this new trick?"

In that incredulity which is, by itself, a preparation for astonishment, she drives one afternoon to Holborn. And when she finds, on a modern building, among six brass plates, one at the top with the full title of the company, she is more than impressed; she receives that kind of shock of surprise which changes, like the jerk given to a kaleidoscope, the whole pattern of the mind.

For a brass plate cannot be denied. It is a solid object and it has cost money. It sticks in the imagination.

Tabitha, driving home in the cab, has quite new ideas of Bonser. "He really has a business, he really has started; perhaps it was true that he only needed a little capital. And why couldn't it have been true? People *do* need capital."

It seems to her now that she has treated her old lover very badly; she has misjudged him. She remembers his words, "I'm really a domestic chap; all I want is a home and garden and a nice little family," and she says to herself, "Why shouldn't it be true?" and is confronted by the new question, could she ever, if the chance occurred, return to Bonser? Would it not be her duty to do so, for Johnny's sake?

The very notion throws her into a state of confusion. Does she love Dick Bonser? Certainly not. But then, that Dick Bonser who has treated her so badly has apparently never existed; or at least she has misunderstood him. And even that Dick had certain good qualities, even domestic good qualities, strong affections, an easy temper.

After a week, indeed, she finds that these different Dicks are in such a tangle that she can no longer form any clear idea of her old lover.

And when one morning she gets an express note by messenger, "Must see you. Urgent. Very important. Today or tomorrow, Postboy. Half-past six. Don't believe any rumors about me or Company, all will be explained," she decides that she must take the risk of a meeting. She is impatient to see this new successful Bonser, and is sorry that she can't go till next day.

47

FOR on this afternoon, a Wednesday, she is at home, and during the last year, since Manklow's articles, her Wednesdays have gradually become once more large and important occasions. Manklow, perhaps seeking material for new articles on "Darkest London," has returned to the circle, and brought with him a whole set of younger journalists and writers, some merely curious to see his victims, and others to enjoy Tabitha's good food and drinks.

And Sturge, after his first horror at Manklow's impudence in showing his face at West Street, has begun to enjoy his company. He reminds him about old incidents. "Do you remember that first number—how nervous we were about Boole's sonnet to Ganymede? I'm still surprised that there wasn't an uproar."

Manklow, studying the old man, answers with grave satisfaction, "We certainly pushed some Gadarene swine over the edge."

Manklow's pessimism has not become admired, especially as his articles in the Ducat press are full of statements like "The future is with the people," "No one can deny the immense progress that has been achieved. But that is nothing to what is open to us now."

A pessimist who believes in progress, on the grounds that a general decay is perhaps ordained and necessary, seems very deep. Sturge now imagines that he has always had a high opinion of Manklow. For he has passed from the time of despair, while ambition was dying, into resignation, where, like a mystic who has renounced the world, he can once more enjoy visions. He no longer broods over the fire at night, muttering that he were better dead. He reads old *Banksides*; and, pointing out some forgotten article to Tabitha, says, "Manklow again." He raises his brows in surprise. "Those were wonderful days!" And it seems for the first time that the four years of the review, which seemed so anxious, so packed with quarrels, disappointments, losses of money and friends, have been the crown of the man's life. He recalls them as an old Prime Minister, retired and forgotten, lives again in his days of glory and power.

Mrs. Sturge, though younger than her husband, now rarely comes to London. She prefers her garden and local charities. She goes to stay with her married daughter. Her unmarried daughter is in India. Sturge often spends five nights of the week at West Street. Indeed, like an old man, he grows careless of pretense, takes Tabitha to the private view of the Academy, and when he is accosted by a sister, a formidable old woman from the north, presents her without any explanation as "My friend, Mrs. Bonser."

He can't do without Tabitha. For she has seen all the triumph of the *Bankside* period, and can remember the very day on which Manklow proposed it. And he looks forward especially to the Wednesdays, when he can talk to Manklow's young men about the days of old, and claim the glory of discovering their hero. "What drive, what imagination. The Troglodytes, a wonderful idea."

For in reminiscence, seeing the whole story as a story, as a piece of art, he enjoys even the caricature of himself.

"Bunsurge—that's me, you know, and the green frogs. Yes, green frogs. Brilliant, brilliant." He chuckles with delight; and Tabitha, seeing these chuckles, also smiles, but not in pity. She is delighted to see the man happy, and to know that her party is a success. She takes much trouble to attract the right people, people who will listen to Sturge.

On this afternoon she has brought in not only old friends, lately reconciled, like Hodsell, Wrinch, and Dobey, but Lord Ducat. She is especially glad to see Ducat, because she wants to congratulate him on Manklow's "Darkest London," not without hope that Bunsurge may appear in it again; and she has just opened her batteries upon the millionaire, with a certain smile and lift of the chin, meaning,

"You are really a most attractive and interesting man," when the hired butler announces, "Mrs. Richard Bonser."

A few guests, hearing this name, turn toward the door and see a short woman, with a pale oval face, a madonna face, in the doorway. She is wearing a green silk frock, obviously her best, a large feathered hat, in very bad taste, and she carries a gold-topped blue umbrella, so as to show the gold. She has the defiant air of a simple person intruding on what she supposes to be a fashionable party.

As Tabitha steps forward, she makes a little desperate run toward her, stops, stares, screwing up her eyes as if from shortness of sight, and inquires, "Mrs. Bonser?"

"Yes."

"What do you mean calling yourself Mrs. Bonser?"

Tabitha is startled. And before she can think of an answer, the woman screams, "What are you doing with my husband? How dare you?" raises her umbrella, and falls to beating Tabitha over the head with it.

The guests stand horrified. Manklow has already disappeared into the crowd; Ducat makes a vague gesture of reproach. Only Boole has presence of mind. With a loud whoop he hurls himself against the woman and thrusts her out of the room to the stairs, down which they roll together.

The woman picks herself up and disappears with great agility, carrying off even the umbrella. Boole, who is bleeding at the forehead, is carried into Jobson's flat, to avoid alarming the party. "Keep it quiet," Ducat says. "We want to keep it quiet!" And Sturge warmly agrees with him.

Tabitha, with the same impulse, is laughing and exclaiming to the crowd which surrounds her in affectionate eager curiosity. "What an extraordinary thing. No, I'm not hurt, thanks. No, I never heard of her before."

The guests look at each other and do not smile. Conversation is soft but intense. A stranger could tell that something unusual, new, amazing has happened. The very impassiveness of the servants declares, "We do our duty, though the sky should fall."

The party breaks up early. Everyone is eager to tell the story. Ducat goes first; he has no wish to appear in the news.

Sturge and Tabitha, left alone, gaze at each other with doubt and inquiry. Sturge is shaking with nerves.

"Do you know anything of this, of Bonser?"

"I did see him about six months ago; I helped him a little. I didn't want you to be worried."

"My dear Bertie, you should have told me. That woman might

have done you an injury, disfigured you—and Boole was nearly killed."

Boole, in fact, has mild concussion. The doctor orders complete quiet. But the little man sits up all day with a bandage round his bald skull, relating with great excitement the glory of his valiant conduct. "How strange that it should happen to me, and yet not strange. For I was born a man of the renaissance. Violence follows me, events cling to me. Yes, that is why I, who adore women, had to throw a woman downstairs." He is anxious to apologize to the lady. "I owe it not only to the lady, but to the sex."

Sturge and Tabitha are glad to be able to assure him that the lady cannot be found.

"She knows she had better keep out of the way after that kind of proceeding, or she might find herself in jail," Sturge says severely.

The papers, thanks to Lord Ducat's presence at the affray, have printed nothing about it. Tabitha and Sturge have assured themselves that the whole affair will be forgotten in three weeks, when one morning Sturge receives a summons for assault upon Mrs. Richard Bonser. "What nonsense," Tabitha exclaims.

But Sturge is frightened. He goes to his lawyers, who take a dark view. "Your position is very ticklish."

"Surely there is some defense against a piece of lunacy?"

"None that is really effective. Of course we will do what we can."

It is agreed to find Bonser and if possible buy him off. But Bonser has disappeared. A bewildered clerk in the office of the Association is threatened with arrest by angry clients who have paid for shares and received nothing in return.

Mrs. Richard is traced to a small house in Putney, where she is living with two children. She declares that Bonser married her in 1896, that he has been a good kind husband, attentive and fond of gardening. They have been very happy until Bonser's disappearance a fortnight before. She has no money, and she shows part of a letter, taken from a wastepaper basket, dated West Street, and beginning, "My dear Dick, it was nice to see you looking so well. I send some money, all I can manage just now."

She is full of jealous rage, and she is sure there is a conspiracy to steal Bonser from her. She insists on bringing Sturge into court and telling her story: that she went to remonstrate with Tabitha, and that Sturge had her thrown downstairs, so that she is injured internally and has terrible pains. She adds rapidly that Tabitha has no right to the name of Mrs. Bonser, and she is a kept woman, and incited Sturge to commit the assault.

The magistrate checks her, and she loses her case. But she has achieved her object, which is to blacken Tabitha's name, and she does not care if she has damaged Sturge.

48

AND now, to everyone's surprise, Mrs. Sturge brings in a suit for divorce. She has, it seems, known of the liaison for years, but has wanted to avoid a scandal. Now that the scandal is public, she wishes, for her daughters' sakes, to regulate her position. But what is surprising is her rancor against Sturge and Tabitha, an ideal rancor, based not so much on her wrongs as on her hatred of Sturge's taste. Tabitha sees the handsome woman of twelve years ago, now white-haired, but with a still grander, a more majestic dignity, enter the box and, surrounded by the respectful sympathy of the court, pronounce a fantastic tale of Sturge's ruin, by the evil influence of Mrs. Bonser and her depraved friends, such as Dobey and Boole.

A sonnet of Boole's, read by her counsel, has a great effect on the jury, and does Tabitha immense damage. Sturge's counsel of course fights against this irrelevance, but it happens that the liberals have just won the great election of '05, there is a feeling of revolution in the air, and, as in all revolutions, a sudden intensification of moral violence. The neurotics, the cranks of every shade of opinion, believing that the millennium has come, when their special whim will be achieved, are shouting at the tops of their voices that the Empire is Chinese slavery and also a divine trust; the British worker is a serf, and the fountain of wisdom; vaccination is a crime, but science is the hope of the world; marriage is bondage, but divorce is the cancer of the state—notions which renew themselves in a certain kind of brain forever and ever. It is like an earthquake, when sewer pipes tower like steeples and college towers fall down.

Judges and juries, like most respectable people, feel that the country is in danger. They see Mrs. Sturge as a representative of all that is good, vindicating right against a decadent wickedness. The judge, who has not read any book except law books for forty years, prepares a summing up on the corruption of the age, which will, he feels, have a good effect on the public.

He has not noticed that decadence is already out of fashion, and that the age is not corrupt but primitive and crude.

Unluckily, before this important judgment can be given, Sturge, suffering from his usual winter influenza, takes pneumonia and dies in three days. He does not wish to live. He cannot do without Tabitha, nor without his family. He leaves his affairs in very good order. He has made a settlement on Tabitha, in the last week of his life, of a thousand a year, with the contents of the flat; and arranged that the costs of her defense, put forward by her as an independent person, shall be met from the estate.

But the three women of the Sturge family do not mean to let iniquity go unpunished. They bring an action to prove that the settlement was extorted from Sturge. They show that it is illegal for his executors to pay the costs of Tabitha's action. Witnesses swear that Sturge was completely under Tabitha's thumb. And all evidence tells against her. If a mistress is unfaithful, she is plainly selfish; if she is devoted, she is no less plainly dangerous. The case is given against her, on the grounds that Sturge was too ill to know what he was doing when he made the settlement; and she is obliged to meet the costs of both actions.

She escapes bankruptcy only by selling the furniture and lease of the flat and all her jewelry, to produce at last a surplus of nearly six hundred pounds, with which she moves at once to a quiet lodging near Kew Gardens.

But her friends seek her out, chiefly with bad advice. Dobey wants her to spend her six hundred pounds on a trip for both of them to India. He is eager to study Indian religion. Jobson offers to sell her a tea shop, which he wishes to get rid of. Fifteen men, including, to her surprise, Lord Ducat, a celebrated but very old peer, a very young millionaire also with a famous name, and a retired minister, offer her a new establishment. Three, an undergraduate of twenty, a bookmaker, and a retired major-general of seventy, want to marry her.

Hodsell urges her to accept Ducat. "He wants a salon, and he thinks he can get it ready-made by buying you. He buys everything ready-made, but he pays well."

"But I didn't have a salon; it was Bunny who brought his friends."

"You've got the name, that's all that matters, and the old gang will still rally round—it's a habit."

But Tabitha recoils from everything connected with her old life. She hesitates only before a suggestion of Boole's that she shall buy a cottage in the country, where he can live as a guest. "I know a place just big enough for us two and Johnny."

Boole is now in very good health, and neatly dressed. He is staying with the Wrinches in great luxury. "Think," he cries, "our own orchard, a close, a pasture, some fruit trees, perhaps a stream, and beehives under a hedge. Wrinch will pay. He'll be delighted. He wants nothing so much as to pin me down; the poor old man is longing to clip my wings."

"But I don't think Mr. Wrinch would pay for me."

In fact Mr. Wrinch arrives five minutes later to carry Boole away. Now convinced, as usual ten years later, that he has found a true unique genius, he is not going to let him fritter away gifts that are possibly divine in obscure and possibly unsanitary surroundings.

49

TABITHA is glad to be alone, because she desires above everything solitude and peace, time for reflection.

She cannot forget the case, Mrs. Sturge's evidence. She has a terrifying sense of the conflict of life, the hatred and misunderstanding. She thinks in terror, "I must keep it away from Johnny."

But her reflections always turn back to the same point, that she has no plans and that she needs money. She is glad to see Jobson when he calls one day. "You know, Tibs—this tea shop is a fine opening."

He's even smarter than usual. He gazes about the sitting room with a new topper in his hands, looking for some place not too dusty for its support.

"Let me take your hat."

"Thanks, girlie. Really, it's a chance. Snug little room on the second story. Eight tables all curtained off. Four girls working, pretty girls, too—or pretty enough with pink shades."

"But what sort of a shop is it?"

"Oh, you're thinking of the Raspberry Tart case. But they were silly. They let the girls play about on the spot. Nothing on the premises, that's my rule. And it isn't necessary." Jobson leans over to assure her on this point. "Why does a chap come into a place like that? For the talk and the adventure. That's it, the adventure; and it's worth five bob for half an hour and a cup of weak tea every day of the week. All perfectly proper—on the premises—which is all you've got to worry about. A little gold mine."

"But if it's so good, why do you want to get rid of it?"

"Well, girlie, it's my wife. She was upset by that case, and she doesn't discriminate."

"Your wife? But are you married?"

"Last week." Jobson smiles a wide doubtful grin, which seems almost apologetic. "You think I'm off my rocker. But the fact is, girlie, I'm forty-eight, and it's quite time I was settled for my old age. If it's a case of a wife or a nurse, give me a wife every time. She's got a vested interest."

"But who is the lady? Not Madge?"

Jobson looks grave. The grin disappears. "I'm not an ambitious chap, as you know, and marriage is a big risk. Why gamble more than you need? I know the worst of Madge, and it's not too bad."

Tabitha congratulates him, and he answers with the same mixture of resignation and ethical resolution, "Well, it will be our own fault if it doesn't work. In fact, old Madgie is determined to make a go of it. We're to have some kids, and cut the pubs. Everything respectable. And that's why I can't go shares with you in the shop."

Tabitha is divided between rage and amusement. She contemplates Jobson as if from a moral height. But suddenly he looks at her sharply out of his little yellow-colored eyes, and says, "I talk to you straight, girlie, because you've got sense; you made a go of poor old Bun and you want to make a go of the kid. All right; but that takes cash, and none of us is getting younger. We all want to be settled."

These words make Tabitha feel small and cheap. She tells Jobson that she will think about his offer and let him know at the office, "so that Madgie won't suspect you of seeing me."

But Jobson scorns such female pricks. He answers, "That's it, keep Madgie out. She's touchy on the point of respectability; and that's no harm, in Madgie."

Tabitha cannot sleep in the dilemma which, every moment, grows more formidable. She sees very clearly Jobson's point, that for John's future she needs a settled income. Her whole experience has taught her the terrible force of that truth. But when she sits down to accept Jobson's offer, she says to herself, "But really, the place is almost a brothel," and she does not write. She argues till her head aches, and she flies into the gardens to escape from the argument. She says to herself, "But this is weakness; I am simply a coward." And still she walks about, as if by walking and keeping her mind empty she will find by inspiration, by luck, or merely by time, the solution to a problem which she scarcely recognizes to be moral.

It is spring, the trees are budding, the daffodils are out. The birds are in their first rage of passion. They are defending their nests and property rights, fighting with self-sacrificing valor to extend their conquests and the margin of safety for their queens and princesses. Tabitha looks round and says, "How beautiful it is, how peaceful." But she can't enjoy this peace which she imagines, she can't even feel it. She is ravaged by the thought, "At this very moment that tea shop may be going out of my reach."

She flies home to write, but does not write. And now in her frustration and despair she is suddenly seized with an urge to pray, a sensation which afflicts her very muscles. Her legs seem to bend, her body aches to fall, to relax.

"But what nonsense," she says to herself, in shame and wonder. "Even if there were anyone to pray to, he couldn't tell me what to do in a case like this."

And in order not to pray she walks about the room, trembling, stupefied by perplexity. All at once there is a knock at the door, and the landlady's small girl answers, "Doctor Bathgate, he wants you."

Tabitha goes downstairs slowly. She sees in the doorway a high-shouldered bald man in an immense shabby overcoat. Then Harry's voice says, "Hullo, old girl, don't you know me?"

He is much gratified by the affectionate excitement with which Tabitha embraces him, pressing him in her arms and bursting into tears. He does not know that he has become a substitute for God.

"Oh, Harry, how marvelous of you to come now."

He kisses her affectionately. "I got your address from the lawyers." And in a tone full of eager curiosity, "I say, can I come in? Is the coast clear?"

"Of course. Who would be here?"

"Oh, I just thought some of your artist friends." He comes slowly through the door, and stares at Tabitha's shabby little parlor with the uncertain smile of a pioneer exploring strange but dangerous territory.

Tabitha, meanwhile, is studying her brother, not seen for nearly twelve years, with tender loyal excitement. She is startled to find him so much changed, grown fat and bald, with a bulging neck. She notices his shabby unbrushed coat, his yellow teeth, and a whiff of stale tobacco. But these signs of age, of indifference to self, are only more endearing. She thinks, "How good he is; you can see it even in the way he stands."

He smiles upon her with the same naïve curiosity, and says, "And how are you, Tibby? You've changed, yes; you've turned out quite pretty. But of course you haven't had much to worry you."

And he tells her that Edith is dead. He is surprised Tabitha did not know this fact, already a year old. He seems to think that everyone should have heard of his wife's death. "A most tragic thing; cancer of a very strange type. A unique case." A fearful blow for him; and he speaks of his wife as if still at the funeral, in a high voice, full of tears. Then suddenly expression and voice change once more to affectionate interest.

"But I mustn't bore you, must I?" And smiling again with a curious interest, he says, "Yes, I can understand how all those clever men found you so attractive." He laughs with an expression which suddenly makes him seem like an overgrown boy. "My smart little sister. Well, I wouldn't have believed it; you make me feel like an old buffer. But there, you had the pluck to break loose and do what you liked."

Tabitha is astonished. "But, Harry, that's just what I've never done."

Harry does not even hear this protest. He is complaining of his own fate. Probably he has come chiefly for that purpose. "And look at me—what a life!"

"But you've been so successful; you built up the practice from almost nothing."

Harry sits down and seems to fall into himself, to be a bundle of dejected bulging old clothes. "Oh, I've worked, but what for? The truth is, Tibby, I'm in a rut, I'm a back number." And suddenly he asks Tabitha if she would consider housekeeping for him. "Come and keep us alive, Tibby. I know it's a lot to ask of you after your gay life. But things are improving a bit even at Frood Green; we have the moving pictures, and there is a new bus service. At least try it. If you find it too dull you can always say so; I'll understand."

"But, Harry, I should love it. If you knew how I long to be settled. You see, I have to think of John's education, it's so fearfully important for him."

"Johnny, Johnny? Oh, the boy, of course—I'd forgotten. Where is he now?"

"At school; but the holidays start next week."

"Next week." Harry looks blank. "It's where to fit him in."

"Oh, Johnny can fit in anywhere. He could have your old room."

"That's Timothy's."

"Of course." Tabitha is about to say that she's forgotten Harry's eldest, Timothy, but checks herself in time.

"And Ellice has the night nursery with the nurse." But catching Tabitha's eyes fixed upon him in anxious and wondering inquiry, he cries, "Never mind, we'll manage; the great thing is to have you back, Tibby. And when will you come? Why not today? It will be like the old times." He puts his arm around Tabitha's shoulder. In its thick sleeve it appears to be as large and heavy as an elephant's foreleg.

"The dear old days," Tabitha cries, welcoming this weight. "How happy we were."

"We always got on so well," Harry exclaims.

"I won't upset your patients, will I? I suppose everyone read about the case."

"Hang the patients—let 'em talk."

50

And, in fact, Harry, long established as the chief doctor of Frood Green, takes a very careless and peremptory air toward his patients. He abuses them even to their faces; and Tabitha hears him, as he goes into the surgery, shout at some unseen sufferer, "Hullo, Mrs. Jones, there you are again. What you want is a new inside, eh?"

But the patients seem to enjoy it. The telephone which has just been put in rings all day, and Harry, answering it, cursing the weather, cursing his practice, cursing the day he was born, bundles himself into one of his enormous coats and lumbers to his brougham.

"Take me away," he says to Tabitha; "take me out of it!" and Tabitha arranges for a theater and a supper in the West End. "Good egg," Harry cries, using a phrase Tabitha has not heard since her childhood.

But when the day arrives, he is in consternation. "I say, did I arrange it for today? It's my day for the bills."

"You can do the bills tomorrow."

"But Clara is coming in; she always helps with the bills."

"Clara?" Tabitha can recall Clara only with an effort. "You never told me about Clara."

"Oh, she's nobody to matter; you needn't mind Clara."

In fact, he pays no attention to Clara, who, lodging in some obscure spot, comes and goes in the Cedars like a spirit, appearing suddenly in some room, and disappearing with equal celerity and completeness. Clara is now, at forty, strikingly and startlingly ugly, with an immense red nose and eyes like boot buttons, full of the humble circumspection of the slave. She is always busy. She not only does Harry's bills, she takes the little girl Ellice for walks, she shops, she mends. She has developed, however, with the years, an ecstatic manner, which irritates everyone. She beams upon Tabitha, "How lovely to see you again"; she greets Harry with cries of "Poor man, you look quite worn out, you do too much. It's a shame." And Harry complains to Tabitha, "She drives me mad with her chatter."

"I could add up for you."

"I'm afraid Clara would be hurt."

The theater has to be put off, and indeed no day can be found for it. Every hour of Harry's time is allotted. As Clara explains to Tabitha, "Harry is so popular." And opening her little eyes as wide as possible, a trick comical in her as it was impressive in Edith, she exclaims, "He kills himself for his patients. Really, he deserves all we can do to give him a little peace and quiet."

This is aimed at Tabitha, who does not answer because she detests Clara. She complains to Harry, "That woman is always poking about the house; you'd think she was the housekeeper."

"Yes, Clara is a nuisance. I think she expected to be housekeeper, but I couldn't stand her fussing."

"I could give her a hint that she's not wanted."

"No, no, for God's sake be careful. She's very sensitive, she'd come to the surgery and cry, and I'm really too busy. I've got quite enough on my plate. God damn that telephone—I wish the thing had never been invented." He plunges at the telephone and is heard shouting down it, "Yes, but you're all right, you know—there's nothing wrong with you. Before tea, perhaps; but I'm wasting my time and your money."

Not only every moment of Harry's time is preoccupied, but every corner of the house. Tabitha, trying to find a room for John, who is due in two days, discovers enormous obstacles, especially as Timothy has already arrived and seized on the old day nursery for some chemical experiments.

Timothy is a pale thick-set boy who combines the worst features of his mother and aunt. His lips are broad, his nose is long, his eyes are small.

Tabitha takes to the ugly gentle creature. She pities his plainness; and while she does so, a picture of John rises in her mind. She sees his delicate features: the fine-cut aquiline nose; the Byronic mouth, too pretty for a boy's; the coloring like a girl's, alarmingly fair, the color that too often goes with a weak chest. She smiles with dazzling kindness on Timothy, and says, "You must show your cousin John how to make gas."

Timothy reflects for some moments on this suggestion, and then answers, "We might give a lecture together."

"A very good idea. I wish John would learn some chemistry."

"Is he going to sleep in my room?"

"Your father is afraid you'd make too much noise."

But Timothy is so disappointed at this deprivation that Tabitha makes up a bed in his room, at the cost of driving Harry to despair. He glooms all day. He says, "Those boys will kick up hell, and wreck the furniture."

But she hardly notices this protest while she awaits John's arrival. She feels only a little nervousness lest Harry, comparing John with

Timothy, should be jealous. "But Harry," she thinks, "never had any jealousy. It's one of his best qualities."

John, as usual, has given no time for his arrival. He likes to make a dramatic entry. Tabitha, after waiting at the station for an hour to meet a possible train, rushes home to find the boy exploring the house. He is examining Timothy's apparatus.

"Oh, Johnny, why didn't you tell me when you were coming? And what have you done to your nose?"

She gazes at a red and swollen nose with consternation.

"Don't fuss, Mum, it's only boxing."

"But are you sure it's not broken?"

"Oh, Mum, if only you wouldn't fuss." A test tube falls and breaks.

"What are you doing—those belong to poor Timothy."

"It's your fault for fussing."

Tabitha is in a panic. She tries to rebuild the apparatus, but is interrupted by Timothy's entrance.

The boys stare at each other and Tabitha says, "Shake hands with your cousin." The boys then turn their backs. John goes out of the room. Timothy, approaching the table, finds the broken glass and says, blushing, to Tabitha, who apologizes, "It doesn't matter, it doesn't really."

He seems, by his demeanor, to feel guilty toward both Tabitha and John. After a few minutes he disappears into hiding. But two hours later, at tea time, Tabitha, trying to find John, sees first John and then Timothy slink around the corner of the garden shed. Neither boy comes to tea, and after this they are inseparable, or, rather, Timothy follows John wherever he goes, except now and then when John sends Timothy forward to find out if a branch across a stream will bear the weight of a passenger, or if there really is a dog in a certain apple garden. Timothy, it seems, has plenty of courage, even rashness. But he has the bad luck of all honest slow minds. The branch does not break, but he slips and falls into the river; the dog does not bark, but he is chased by a gardener and tears his coat on a fence nail. Finally, on the very last day of the holidays, when Tabitha is congratulating herself that all has gone so well, Timothy is arrested in an empty house, while John, who has broken into the house, manages to escape into a cupboard, where he lies safe.

The policeman, who knows Harry well, takes the boy home. Harry reprimands him, but he is furious with John. He complains to Tabitha, "I haven't time for this sort of thing. You really must keep your boy in order. The fact is that he's right out of hand."

And Clara seizes this good occasion to protest against John's bad influence. He is teaching Ellice bad words, like hell and damn.

Tabitha goes to Harry. "You realize that the creature is trying to drive me out."

"If you women must quarrel—really I've no time." He makes a gesture of despair at the follies of women and goes into the surgery.

Tabitha is frightened. She thinks, "I must be careful; things might become impossible."

She is very gentle and patient for a week. Then one night, finding Harry in front of the fire smoking his pipe, she speaks of education. "How hard-working Timothy is; he's cleverer than John. John specially needs a good education."

Harry takes out his pipe and says, "What about East Street? It's convenient."

East Street is a proprietary day school in Frood Green. It occupies two shabby old houses and employs masters of very doubtful qualifications. It is, however, very cheap.

Tabitha is shocked out of discretion. "But Timothy tells me he's going to Chilton."

"If I can scrape up the money."

"We couldn't send John to East Street and Timothy to Chilton."

Harry bounces up. He is in a temper which is chiefly confusion. Being a kind and fair man, he feels the difficulty of his position even more strongly than Tabitha feels its injustice. He ejaculates, "I'm sorry, but you don't expect me to educate the whole of Frood Green," and goes to bed.

51

TABITHA is even more indignant. She sees the dilemma, but she will not admit the strength of Harry's position. "Why should Timothy," she asks, "have a better chance than John? What an outrage! It's intolerable." She trembles with more than rage; with horror at the meanness of the world.

The next day she writes to Jobson, but the tea shop has been sold, and Jobson has no other posts to offer. Tabitha is seized with panic. She puts on her best morning frock and goes to Griller. The professor, smiling through his mustache, which is, however, trimmed to modern neatness, cries that he longs to be of help. But alas, he is a man without influence. He recommends Dewpark or Manklow.

Dewpark has vanished from his lodging; and when she calls upon Manklow, that prosperous editor, sitting at his enormous desk, he says cheerfully, "My dear Tib, I haven't any jobs for ladies; try Wrinch. He's one of the biggest jobbers in England. Come with me this afternoon, about five. No, six—and dodge the crowd. Or wait, can I do it? What about Griller?"

"He recommended Mr. Dewpark, but I can't find him."

"Ah, Dewpark, Uncle Dewpark. Didn't you know? He's bust! He got the sack. Last I heard he was in a workhouse infirmary. The old donkey didn't even insure. However, if he had, he'd probably have been robbed by some fraud or other."

"But Mr. Dewpark was such a great scholar. He was quite famous."

"The trouble with Uncle, Tib, is that he couldn't keep up to date. Not like Griller, for instance, who gets a finger in new pies every week."

"I always thought Mr. Dewpark was supposed to have better taste and be a better writer. How strange he should be a failure."

"But that's the very reason, Tib. Old Griller has no taste at all. He doesn't really care a farthing for any of the arts, except in theory, of course, and so you see he's free to suck every rising bum. If you'll excuse my modern similes. Whereas Dewpark really loves his Tennyson and his Arnold."

"I think Tennyson is a very great poet."

"So do I, Tib; I was brought up on him, too," and he grins at her fondly for a moment. "How fatal is love, Tib—I mean the genuine article."

Tabitha sees the man's relish of this injustice, of this treachery in fate, but she feels not angry, but confused, as if she has perhaps been born deficient of some necessary comprehension.

And as she walks down Fleet Street in the June sun, she says to herself, wondering, "But why does he laugh?"

The sky, with its pale blue, its firm golden clouds, is like a background for Italian madonnas, serene and passionless; the town below with its dirty buildings, all of different heights and different ugliness, squeezed together as if by some frightful earthquake pressure, the clerks jostling in confusion along the pavements, whose anxious faces seem, like their worn top hats, silver stained by rain, and their dusty bowlers, mere necessities of a livelihood, eyes to see ledgers, ears to hear orders, holes to be fed, cheeks to be shaved, necks to be collared, are like a piece of hell, more graphic, crowded, lively, and packed with feeling than anything by Bosch. And Tabitha, seeing neither, yet feels a panic urgency. She is almost running along the pavement, as if this work which she must have is flying from her at that very moment. She thinks, "Dewpark in a workhouse—how can anyone laugh at that?"

52 As for Wrinch, when she calls that afternoon, she finds a large party already in being. Wrinch, who is brought to see her in the hall, looks at her with his vague withdrawn gaze and utters the suggestion that Professor Griller may have something, perhaps in a publisher's office. Meanwhile, will she have tea? Tabitha refuses tea, and is making her escape, when Boole comes running. He catches her by both hands and utters loud cries. "Dear lady, where have you been? Our light was put out."

He will not hear of her going away. "Of course Wrinch will get you a job; I'll make him. Do you know he is publishing my book on the Decadence, with all the Dobey drawings? A perfectly shocking work." He gives a joyous cackle. "How he hates it—that's why he's so keen on it. Now that the liberal millennium is stale news, it seems that we've come in again."

Tabitha looks with impatient surprise at the excited little man as he draws her toward the stairs. It seems to her that he has changed very rapidly for the worse, become much older, more freakish. It does not strike her that the change is in herself. She thinks, "He's very kind; but really, I've no time for literary nonsense."

And in the large double drawing room, crowded with old masters, on the first floor, she feels still more impatient while Boole brings up to her one young man after another, crying out incomprehensible names. "Mrs. Bonser, Mr. Meoo—he wants to abolish property; Mr. Sniy—the fire-walker," and laughing, he drags up a large shy red-faced youth. "My friend Mr. Tssmoa—he believes in bombs, and he adores you."

In fact, both the last young men utter speeches which seem to congratulate Tabitha on the famous case. It is a recommendation to them that she has quarreled with the law.

Tabitha, now taking more notice of the guests, thinks, "But what a collection! Where does poor Wrinch find such extraordinary people?" She looks with suspicion and distaste at her host, where, with his long melancholy countenance, still marked by the formal discipline of a polite education, he moves among a crowd of ecstatics, yogis, followers of Kropotkin, Bucharin, mystical celtists, Rosicrucians, expressionists, with of course a mixture of rich art tasters and fashionable ladies; in his own words, the new age.

53 And this new age is present to everybody's imagination as something quite clearly divided from the old, not only by the magic figures 00 on the calendar, but by war and the death of the old queen. It is so strongly apprehended that it seems like a change of physical air. People seem to breathe it, and its quality is pure novelty, a looking forward over enormous stretches of virgin territory. The next 00 is more than ninety years away.

Everyone expects newness in art, law, politics, morals; and history itself is renewed from day to day. Enterprising young men, looking for a new field of exploitation, have already discovered the nineties, and Sturge's obituaries, written as always of the dead, with an historical bias, have placed him and his clique as important figures of that epoch. Boole at forty-seven is a living relic of antiquity. When, therefore, he cries to all comers, "Let me introduce you to Mrs. Bonser, the Mrs. Bonser, of *The Bankside, chère amie* of Bunsurge," glances directed at Tabitha are full of approval as well as curiosity. She is soon surrounded by men.

"How do you do, Mrs. Bonser? Did you really know Beardsley?"

"No, I'm afraid I only met him once." Tabitha's voice shows that she does not value Beardsley very highly.

"Mrs. Bonser, excuse me—" An eager youth accosts her. "I've been *so* longing to meet you. I'm engaged on a thesis about the æsthetic movement."

"But was it really a movement?" Tabitha looks with sad inquiry at the enthusiast. "Was it really important?"

"Enormously important. One of our great revolutions, it brought down the Victorian bastille." And delighted by the very idea of this destruction, he draws a picture of heroes going out to war against a tyranny; of Morris routing the money grubbers, Pater and Symons undermining a Philistine morality, Sturge and Boole releasing imprisoned souls from dark oubliettes.

"But Mr. Sturge was a churchman," Tabitha says, "and he greatly admired the old queen."

"Now that is a most interesting point."

But Tabitha has already pretended to recognize an acquaintance and is moving toward the door. She can bear no more of this trifling which exasperates her mood. She is preoccupied still with that confused panic which she has felt so suddenly and powerfully in face of Manklow's grins. It rests with her as a sense of urgency and fear, as if perhaps she has been deceived about the whole nature of things, betrayed by a dream.

She looks round almost with rudeness when, at last near the door, she feels a hand on her arm. "Mrs. Bonser, Mrs. Bonser"—in a shrill voice.

She sees a little pink-cheeked man, at least in his sixties, wearing with his striped morning trousers a very short black jacket, which, like the clothes of most old men, seems to be too big for him.

"But this is delightful, a piece of luck." He seizes Tabitha's hand in his bony claw and jerks it to and fro. "Caught you at last, and just in time. Making your escape, eh? So am I. What a museum. Old Wrinch's parties get madder and madder. Since this new government came in he's been scraping the lunatic asylums. We'll go together."

"I'm so sorry, but—"

"No, you don't know me from Adam, from the Empress of China. Never mind. Why should you? You didn't read my letter either. Gollan, James Gollan."

Tabitha remembers the name as that of a rich iron master, whom Sturge had tried to bring into *The Bankside* committee. And glad that he is not an author or an æsthete, she answers with more politeness, "Of course, you wrote to me about some drawings—yes, by Dobey."

"Dobey, Dobey? No, you asked me to meet some writer. But I'll confess it, Mrs. Bonser, I didn't take to Fred Sturge's nest of singing birds. I went in for roses instead. You must come and see my roses. I can show you something good. A black rose. The first in the world."

"I should like that very much, but just now—"

"Come, no time like the present. And my bus is at the door."

"I ought really—"

At this moment a short thin young woman, very pale, with a high forehead already marked by lines of perplexed anxiety, offers her hand, as hot and almost as dry as her father's, and presents herself. "Mrs. Stone." And goes on with a nervous rush, "Do come. Papa loves to show his new rose; it's such a nice hobby, don't you think, rose growing?"

"They're trying to find something for me to do when I retire," Gollan says, with a snort of laughter. "As if I shan't be able to amuse myself." And taking Tabitha's forearm, he cries, "Ten—five minutes—come. Yes, you'll come."

He urges her toward the door with unexpected force. Tabitha is surprised by this treatment, but before she can resent it she is in the bus, which proves to be a large new Daimler.

"Retire, retire," Gollan cries, as they drive away. "I don't need to retire."

"Oh, Papa," Mrs. Stone cries, "you know what the doctors say."

"Doctors, doctors, they say anything. Pick your doctor and you get your answer."

Tabitha is driven to a large house furnished elaborately in a mixture of styles. In a drawing room upstairs she is shown four roses in a glass vase.

"Grown down in Sussex. That's where I have my roses, all the newest. And look at this, it's going to win all the medals. Gollan Black."

Tabitha admires the rose, which is, to her eyes, red: a very dark red. But she perceives that she must not say so, that among rose growers colors have special names.

"And this, Mrs. Bonser, won the medal last year. Gollan's New Century." He shows another dark red rose, of a slightly different tinge. "We nearly called it Gollan Blue, but we thought we might get it bluer and put it in for the prize as a black."

"Oh, but it is blue," Tabitha cries politely. "Quite blue."

The little man is delighted. "You must come to Hackstraw—and see them growing. Why not now? It's only half an hour. Come and stay—"

Tabitha, surprised by this urgency, makes excuses, escapes at last, and goes home. But Gollan telephones next morning to ask her to lunch. Afterwards he takes her to a matinee.

On the day after, he calls at the Cedars to drive her to a famous rose garden, and to tea at the house in Portland Place. Here she is received by Mrs. Stone, who asks, "You will like to wash," and leads her into a small sitting room. She looks then at Tabitha with alarm. "I believe he has asked you to Hackstraw. I ought to warn you that for some time we have been very anxious about him; he is in very bad health. He has overworked for years; and his blood pressure is quite tremendous; he may fall dead at any moment." And with a glance of desperation, she mutters, "But we don't choose that anyone shall take advantage."

At this, another voice breaks in. "Now, Annie, think what you're saying."

Tabitha, still more surprised than hurt by this unexpected attack, looks round and sees behind her a fat bald man of about fifty, in a tweed suit.

The fat man offers his hand. "Stone is my name. You mustn't listen to my wife; the fact is that she is very anxious about Sir James's state of health."

"It's not that at all; it's the whole situation."

"And what exactly is the situation?" Tabitha asks.

But now it appears that the Stones are in a panic about Gollan, who, since his wife's death two years before, has made offers to three different women. "He proposed to Lady Bingwell only last month, but fortunately she refused to live in the country."

"Of course a woman like that would simply rob him," Mrs. Stone says. "Though I must admit her connections are respectable."

Tabitha, understanding these hints, answers coolly. "You needn't be alarmed. Sir James has made no advances to me."

"He will." Husband and wife speak together with extreme energy.

But at this moment the door flies open and Gollan darts into the room. "What's this—a family council? Never mind them, Mrs. Bonser. They want to bury me already. Come to tea. We'll take it out, I think." He leads Tabitha downstairs, puts her in the car, and calls, "Gunters."

He explains, "Nice people, Mrs. Bonser, but a bit fussy. No man has a better daughter than Ann, or a better son-in-law than Hector, but they're always in a fuss and they want to lock me in a glass case."

"But, Sir James, you yourself say that you ought to retire."

"Retire. So I am retiring as soon as I can. But who's going to do my work? Hector Stone? He thinks he can. He fancies himself as chairman of the Consolidated Lines. But this is dry stuff, dull stuff. Not for a lady. Tell me, do you like sapphires?"

"I like everything nice."

"I know where to get a good sapphire, table cut—a wonderful stone. I'll give it to you."

"No, please, Sir James, you mustn't."

Gollan apologizes. But the next morning he telephones. "I wrote to you, Bertie, just after that case. You don't mind Bertie? Sturge used to call you Bertie."

"Yes, but—"

"You never read the letter, of course; ladies never read letters. But I asked you something in that letter. I said, come and see Hackstraw and see how you like it, the finest drawing rooms in Sussex. I know what I'm asking, Bertie; you could take your pick. I don't mind saying I gave you up when I heard that Ducat was bidding."

"But, Sir James, I'm sure you could find—"

"Don't you believe it—I've tried. Women who can do a job like that are pretty scarce. There's Lady Bingwell, of course, but she's so damned ugly; and Mrs. Fratt, who used to give parties for the White Cross League, but she's a tartar. Besides, I esteem you, Bertie, I admire you. Tell me, what was Ducat's idea—or is that too much to ask?"

"I'm afraid I can't—"

"Quite so; but that wouldn't do at Hackstraw. I wouldn't dream of it. I'm making a firm offer. If you would agree to become my wife, I should consider myself the luckiest man in the world. But perhaps I'm too old, perhaps you think me a damned old nuisance. Very well. No bones broken. Ring off."

Tabitha is glad to be rung off. The proposal has astonished her. She shudders at the idea of Gollan as a husband, his aged skinniness, and his cracking joints.

It does not improve the offer for her that he seems to set a value upon her as an experienced hostess. She is growing accustomed to the idea that she has a special reputation, that her parties in West Street are renowned. She has met Lady Bingwell, of whom it is said that she made her first husband a bishop, and her second a cabinet minister, and she has detested her for a hard rattle of a woman, full of talk and manner, but without any sincerity. Sturge, Tabitha's instructor, has described her as a buffet, complete with marble top and stale sandwiches.

A reputation seen from the inside always appears empty, unfurnished. One cannot live in a shrine. Tabitha has entertained for Sturge, not as a career, but because he has desired it, for the good of the cause.

54

BUT almost at once, as she leaves the telephone and moves through the crowded gloomy little hall, she is seized with a feeling of smallness, and self-contempt which rises spontaneously in one who runs away from a challenge to duty.

She perceives that this match will give her security, a legal position, which is all-important for John's future as well as her own.

She has her shopping to do for the Cedars, and as she walks from grocer's to butcher's, among a crowd of women whose summer frocks, for some reason, make them seem not gay but rather more preoccupied and totally unaware of summer, she repeats to herself in agitation, "What if he is old and queer, and simply wants somebody to show off his new house—I should be wicked to refuse. I've no right to put silly feelings first."

It seems, however, that these silly feelings, romantic feelings, still linger, at thirty-three, in her breast, for she argues with herself for two days before she writes Gollan a dignified letter, apologizing for her abruptness at the telephone.

And within an hour the Daimler appears at the startled and curious Cedars to take Tabitha to town.

Gollan is excited. "Come, don't say you don't love me. Of course you don't—why should you? But you're a clever girl. I saw how you handled things at old Fred Sturge's, and you're the girl I want."

Tabitha speaks of John, and he cries, "I know, I know; apple of your eye. Why, of course, John's welcome. I like boys."

But the answer that there is no question of love has already decided Tabitha. It is with the sense of performing a moral act that she says firmly, "If you're quite sure, Sir James."

"James, James. Of course I'm quite sure." He presses her hand. "Bless you, I know what I want." He stops the car at the jeweler's, and Tabitha is engaged.

She is at first surprised, then angry and contemptuous, when the engagement is announced, to see Clara and Harry's disapproval.

Clara, with a smirk, says, "I suppose Sir James isn't as old as he looks."

"Sixty-four, Clara; you can see it in *Who's Who*."

And Harry says, with a perplexed and suspicious air, "You don't really care for that old stick, Tibby, do you? Of course, I suppose he's rich."

"You ought to be glad that I'm marrying someone who is rich and can give Johnny a proper education."

"Yes, I suppose I oughtn't to be surprised. You've changed, naturally."

"Thank goodness I've changed. I hope I'm not quite so silly and selfish as I used to be."

And it is with some austere firmness that she sets out to do her duty by Gollan.

The papers, having elaborated the engagement, are already hinting that Sir James Gollan will retire with his bride.

The Stones, who, once alarmed and now impressed by Tabitha's powers of seduction, have hastened, on the very day of the engagement, to make their peace, take the same tone. "I'm sure you'll agree, Mrs. Bonser, that the important thing, for us all, is Sir James's health. We must persuade him to retire, to give up all these directorships."

And Tabitha, perceiving that this is the offer of a family compact, warmly agrees that Sir James must retire. The three, discussing this necessary project, draw together in common respect.

Tabitha, at her next morning with Gollan, says to him, "I suppose, James, you will retire before the wedding? That would be the best time."

"Yes, yes, whenever you like, anything you like, my dear—I'm yours to dispose of. Yes, I'll retire. I'm retiring as fast as I can."

Hector Stone, in fact, that fat man, so sedate, so benevolent, has shown demonic energy in using this chance of getting rid of his father-in-law. Directors are already telephoning, reporters call, new combinations are forming in half a dozen companies, to put him in the old man's place. Two factories open a subscription for an address and presentation to Sir James Gollan on his retirement.

"See how they run to push me out," he says to Tabitha in his nervous and yet impersonal manner, which tells so little of his real feelings. "Rattle out the old bones. But never mind. I'd be a fool to go back on them. Hector is a schemer, but we mustn't mind that. Now if I minded and went back on him, then he'd have caught me, wouldn't he? I'd be as big a fool as he is. And we want all our time to ourselves, don't we, Bertie?"

And he shops every day. He has a passion for shopping. He is buying carpets, china, pictures, curtains, and for everything he must have Tabitha's opinion. "Do you like that, Bertie?"

"Whatever you like, James."

"No, no, it's for you to choose. It's for your house. I want Hackstraw to please you."

Tabitha returns home every day so exhausted by decisions always difficult to her uncertain taste that she can only creep to bed.

The wedding, after all, is a relief, a gateway to peace. It is true that Harry, still moved by high moral displeasure, attends it in his second-best frock coat—a shabby one, with a large pink spot of acid on the lapel; but at the breakfast he drinks much champagne and becomes elevated. He looks down upon his fate with indignation and wonder, and catching Tabitha on the stairs at her going away, forces her into a corner. "And we haven't even had our talk yet. Oh, I know it's not your fault. I let myself get pushed about. I've got in a rut here, Tibs. I've no time even to do my job properly. Damn the patients; they push you down and keep you down, and then they wonder that you're behind the times."

The double line of guests is waiting all down the stairs; Gollan is at the hall door, but Harry spreads himself out like a wall, and his voice rises. "And now this! It's a shame, Tibby; you ought to have given us another chance—me, and yourself, too."

Brother and sister look at each other with mutual disapproval. Tabitha gives him a hasty kiss, but as she goes downstairs and enters the car she has a sad and forgiving expression. She feels like the prophet who has no honor in his own country, because it does not perceive that he has grown to be a prophet. She does not wave from the window as the car rolls away.

The old man takes her hand and gives his thin-lipped smile, showing rows of china teeth. "Hey, now we're off; now we're all right."

And these words are answered by Tabitha, still wounded by the condescending eyes of Frood Green, with an impulsive agreement. For now she feels, with immense force, how right she has been; how wrong, how narrow, Harry and the sentimentalists of Frood Green. She is penetrated with the sense of the goodness which belongs to a legal and acknowledged situation. She is a wife, with rights and duties. She presses Gollan's hand and answers his smile with a maternal kindness. "You're not too tired, James?"

"Tired, me? I'm never tired."

But she vetoes the theater, designed for that evening. James is too tired. He must go early to bed.

"If you say so, Bertie." He is obedient to his darling. "Just as you like—"

55

THE couple are to stay in London that night, and go on to Paris the next day. But the next morning, when Tabitha wakes, and looks at the other bed, she finds it empty. The waiter pushing in the breakfast table brings a note. Gollan, so he writes, has had a telephone call from the architect carrying out certain improvements at Hackstraw, and he has run down to tell the fool what to do. "I'm afraid we'll have to put off the trip till tomorrow, but I had to be sure that Hackstraw would be ready for you."

He telephones at lunchtime to assure her that the work is going well; at dinnertime to beg her to join him. "We're held up by a lot of damned idjits; it may take a week to get settled, and I can't do without you for a week, Bertie."

Tabitha, a little surprised, excuses the man on account of his nervous condition, his premature age. She goes down to Sussex and finds him extremely excited, in a fury with architects, garden designers, decorators, navvies and electricians, directing them all at once, fussing over them.

The house, except for one magnificent bedroom, and the little dressing room next door, where Gollan sleeps on a servant's iron bed, is under reconstruction.

"It was to be a surprise for you, my dear, but the fools have got it all wrong. If I hadn't come down they'd have been muddling till Christmas."

Everything, it seems, is for her. Tabitha, indeed, cannot make out whether Gollan has gone to such trouble to secure her because he wants a hostess suitable to his new toy at Hackstraw, his new hobby of playing the county magnate, or whether he has dangled Hackstraw in front of her as a bait to her supposed passion for entertaining. He is like a man who delights in some new possession, not only because it is beautiful, but because it is rare, and who pays a double homage in designing for it a magnificent case. He showers presents upon her; but all—frocks, jewels, furniture—are also to glorify Hackstraw. They are essential to her as the mistress of Hackstraw.

He tells her this frequently, for though Tabitha is surprised and even regretful that he demands so little of her, he does expect her company. He chats to her all day; and at any time of night he is capable of rushing into her bedroom with some odd piece of information, some proposal for a new extravagance. He sleeps, apparently, very little; and seeing him out in all weathers, she remembers her duty to take care of him. She protests against his long hours. These protests have no effect, and it is with a certain pique that on one chilly afternoon, seeing him in the garden, without a coat, directing some new enormous excavation, she goes to him and points out severely that it is now tea time, that he has been on his feet since luncheon, and is getting wet.

He apologizes profusely. "I'm sorry, my dear. I'm an old noosance, aren't I? But what can I do? Someone's got to keep 'em moving."

"But you must give yourself *some* rest."

Gollan gazes at her with a vague expression, as if he has not heard, and says, "Just look at this; they aren't going to put in the fountain because the cable hasn't come for the pump."

"If it isn't there, they must wait." And taking him by the arm she says with the gentle but inflexible voice of the woman in command, "Now come into tea—it's waiting."

But Gollan does not move. "Dash me, there's miles of it in London. What are telephones and motors for? Most of these folks are living in the Middle Ages."

"Do you realize that it's past five?"

"Just one moment—" and suddenly he is gone. She does not see him again till dinner, which is very late. She reproaches him and again he gazes at her, or rather past her, with an absent-minded stare. "I'm sorry, Bertie. What an old noosance I am. But there you are—it's all for you."

Tabitha looks at him suspiciously. It strikes her all at once that this little polite man is playing a polite game with her. She exclaims suddenly, "I believe you do it on purpose, James."

"All for you, my dear; all for you, Bertie." For a moment his pale washed-out eyes are looking into hers, but with such a peculiar expression that she cannot read them. "All for you, Bertie. Bless me, I'd forgotten about—" and he rushes away to the telephone. Dinner waits another half hour for him.

Tabitha, in spite of her irritation, perceives that she has been naïve. "He's very obstinate—what did I expect in a man like that, who has made a big fortune out of nothing?"

And when Gollan comes at last, full of apologies, she looks at him with respect as well as irritation. She thinks, "Yes, I've been silly. You can see what a will he has; he's just been teaching me."

And in the thought she feels unexpectedly, with all her annoyance, a certain comfort. It is as though she has had a new reassurance. She feels a relaxation as into a new peace. She feels for the first time in her life the meaning of the words "to belong." For the sense has not been with her since her childhood.

56

BUT this very discovery of Gollan's active power, his lively will, makes her more anxious about the first meeting between John and his stepfather. In June, when the boy has his mid-term holiday, she arranges for him to spend it at Hackstraw; thinking, "In a week end he can't make too bad an impression."

But while she waits for him at the local station, with her new car, she can hardly stand still with nerves. "Thank goodness," she thinks, "that he's got over that craze for boxing. Please God he will behave better than he did with Harry."

The train comes in and John hurls himself out of the carriage into Tabitha's arms, but at once seizes her hand and drags her toward the exit. "Come, Mum. Oh please don't *dawdle*!" And he cries, "Will I have a horse, and a gym? You remember Grove at school. He has a gym, a private gym."

Tabitha has never seen the boy so excited; the calm buccaneer of last holidays has changed into an enthusiast.

"But, Johnny, you won't ask for things?"

The boy stares fiercely at her, his cheeks flush pink, and he cries, "Oh God, if you're going to be silly."

And in the car he draws himself into a corner, making himself small, leans his cheek on the window frame, and remains silent.

"A great boy of twelve," Tabitha says, warm with indignation. "And now you sulk like a baby. I'd be ashamed." The boy makes a jerk of his shoulder which expresses contempt beyond words.

And Tabitha says to herself, "Of course, he'll behave as badly as possible, simply because it's so important for him not to." And at the same time she notices the beauty of the boy's skin, marvelously fresh and fine, his long lashes, as he stares sulkily at the flying hedges, his hair, his pouting lips. And the delight of this beauty is like another more acute pain. Her whole soul protests against a lot which will betray that innocence and beauty into some mean unhappy fate.

"If you're rude to Sir James, I'll never forgive you."

"Oh God, can't she let me alone?"

But they pass through the gates at the lodge, and at once the boy forgets his rage. He sits up and gazes out of the window, and, catching sight of the big square house in red brick and stone chimneys, a Queen Anne house which resembles something out of a giant's toy box, he shouts, "There's masses of room. Besides, I must have it."

He turns, and presses up against her. "Oh Mummy, Mummy darling, what's he like? Is he awful? Is he mean like Uncle Harry? What I'd really like is a motor."

"Don't shout, Johnny; and don't worry your stepfather too much. Remember he's not very strong, and he's not used to being worried by small boys."

Johnny hears this with a blank stare which does not comprehend anything. The car stops. He darts into the house and carries out his own exploration. It is he who, at last, finds Tabitha in order to tell her the wonders of her own bathroom, her own looking glasses. He tells her that the electricity is made by an engine in its own engine house, that there are three cars in the garage, a work bench full of tools, and a pit.

He is hanging upon her arm as they walk through the back or garden hall, when Gollan comes in from his routine morning visit to the roses. He wears his garden hat, a straw shaped like a tyrol felt.

The boy turns and says loudly, "Is that him? I say, he *is* old."

"Don't, John; not so loud."

But Gollan, whose senses are exceedingly sharp, turns quickly and exclaims, "What's this? Who's old? Hullo, Johnny. I was just coming to meet you. You're the boxer, aren't you? How's the nose? I'll box you." Adopting a strange crouching attitude he jerks around the boy, flourishing his fists, and twisting his head from side to side. He wants perhaps to show how young he is.

The boy's gaze is now full of disdain. He plainly thinks this queer old man is also an old fool. Tabitha attempts to break an embarrassing scene by asking when the new electric lamps will be ready.

But Gollan cries, "The old two-handed style, Johnny, like Mendoza." He pulls out a cigarette case. "Have a smoke?"

John stares at him. "I don't smoke."

And Tabitha protests. "James, he's not thirteen."

"I smoked at his age, and it didn't do me any harm. Well, Johnny, what next? Seen my new engine? You know all about engines, don't you? Come and tell me what's wrong with this one."

John slowly shakes his head. He stares suspiciously at Gollan. He knows that he is being offered a bribe, a toy.

"It's always the same with these oil engines; the jets get blocked," Gollan explains.

For a moment the suspicion and pride struggle with curiosity in John's expression. But his eyes brighten. He is still too much of a child to maintain self-respect. "What are jets?"

"Jets, if you ask me, are a blinking bally noosance. But come and look, old man. We'll get the mechanic to take the thing apart."

The two males vanish down the passage, and Johnny's voice comes back explaining that he also has an engine, a model locomotive. Gollan joins in on a note little less shrill and animated.

Tabitha sighs in her relief. She feels that she has turned a dangerous crisis. And she is grateful to Gollan. She thinks, "At last the boy will have something like a father to take an interest in him."

In fact, for the rest of the three days she scarcely sees John except at meals. He spends all his time with Gollan in the engine house or in the garage, or even at the blacksmith's in the village. The blacksmith is also the chief motor mechanic for the district.

And all day the two talk engines, apparently on equal terms. Yet it seems to Tabitha that Johnny is the more serious. For Gollan is perpetually staring at John, laughing, glancing at Tabitha to make her notice something comic or something intelligent in the boy, and uttering those cries, making those faces with which old people, especially those unaccustomed to children, are wont to express the mysterious excitement that children cause in them.

"I suppose it is an event for him," Tabitha thinks. But she begins to grow fond of Gollan in her delight at this unexpected friendship. She supports him warmly when one day he declares that John must go to church.

Gollan, having bought Hackstraw, and become a squire, has ascertained that part of a squire's function is to go to church.

"But we don't have to go to church," John objects.

"It's different now," Tabitha explains. "In the country everyone goes to church."

"Church in the morning, engines in the afternoon," Gollan says; "that's the schedule."

John makes no further protest. And at the family gathering in the family pew, partly because it is a family pew, Tabitha finds herself enjoying the service.

"Hallowed be thy name." As she utters these words she feels a deep regret that there is no God to receive the thanks of those who have been blessed with peace and love.

57

GOLLAN's affection for John does not diminish when the boy goes back to school.

He dodges into Tabitha's room that night to exclaim, "I'll miss your Johnny; he's got brains, that boy."

And again with another dodge round the door, "Why didn't that lump of a Hector give me a grandson?" He disappears as suddenly as he came. "Yes, nice chap." He hops in again with his tie in one hand and his collar in the other. "He'll make a good engineer."

"But, James, all children love engines; they're just big toys to them."

But Gollan, like John, seldom listens to argument. He answers with enthusiasm, "Of course they are; they love engines. I loved engines. I made my first out of an old paint tin. You should have seen Johnny at those cylinders. He'll be an engineer, a real engineer, that boy. But you want to sleep. I'm an old noosance."

Gollan vanishes, but reappears again at three o'clock in the morning, when, wakened by a cough, Tabitha starts up and sees the old man in his nightshirt standing in the middle of the floor with his night light glimmering in his hand.

"I didn't wake you, did I? You were awake, weren't you? No, you weren't awake. I'm an old—"

"Yes, truly, I wasn't asleep."

"I was thinking, we'll put Johnny's shop next the dairy; but really he'd be better in a works, a real works. Nothing like an engineering shop for teaching a boy about the world."

"But, James, Johnny's only twelve and a half."

"I was in the shops at eleven; can't begin too young."

Tabitha does not take this seriously. She is pleased to find that Gollan and John are in correspondence, and when, as a result, workmen arrive at Hackstraw to turn a stable into an engineering shop, she admires it. "How like James—he doesn't waste a minute. And what it is to be rich! Now he and Johnny have a nice playroom."

In fact, when John comes home for that Christmas he spends most of his time in this shop, where Gollan, teaching him to use lathe and drill, tells stories of his own apprenticeship, fifty years before. Already new machinery is ordered, there is a project for making John an engine of his own.

And the boy has not been back at school for a week before Tabitha hears for the first time talk of a motor-repair shop in the village.

Whether the factory at Hackstraw, the whole industrial development of this quiet parish, began with Gollan's friendship for his stepson and John's workshop, or whether, which is much more likely, Gollan was a man who never could retire, who never could give up that experimenting and planning on which his fortune had been built, so that John's playshop simply touched off an explosive force which would have exploded in any case, is a matter for argument; but in fact the project of the repair shop grew after less than a month into the first plan for an engine factory, a small experimental factory, in Hackstraw village. And before the next Easter, Gollan, even in John's absence, was spending long hours at the bench with an engineer called Robinson, engaged to design the factory.

The gardens, completed and admired in their finished state by the whole county, are now despised by Gollan himself. He is bored with them.

Tabitha hears no more of black roses. Instead, she is waked in the small hours with the news that Robb Robinson has just had another good idea for— And she grows used, as she moves through the house, to seeing this person silently rise from a chair, or, more often, steal out of her way. When Gollan brings him to meals, which happens more and more frequently, he glares at her with rude shyness, and she is glad that she is not expected to take part in a conversation entirely concerned with valves, turbulence, compression, and ignition.

Gollan now prefers Robb Robinson's company to that of fellow magistrates. He says of him, "Robb's a great man, and don't you forget it. Why, some of his ideas are simply revolutionary." But to Tabitha he is a burden. He has no small-talk at all, and appears to scorn news, books, local events, plays and local people, all women, and all the arts. He is tall and pale, perhaps thirty-three or four years old, with black hair already turning gray, and he walks about always with the preoccupied and desperate expression seen only in young priests who mean to reform the whole nation, or mechanics who carry in their breast pockets, ready to be pulled out at any moment, the blueprint of some invention which, they assure you, is revolutionary. So Robinson has informed Tabitha that his new engine will "revolutionize" the petrol engine, and that flying machines will revolutionize the world. Revolutionary, revolutionize, are great words with Gollan and Robb, when they want to express high appreciation. Politically, both are strong conservatives.

Robb's dream is to build an airplane. He has spent much of his working life in France, with the millionaire Lebrun, who in 1906 broke his neck with an experimental plane of his own design, just in time to escape bankruptcy.

But Gollan's interest in planes is careless. He has been brought up on engines, and his feelings are only moved by ideas included under the word engine. He is absorbed in the plans for a new motor engine, planned by Robb and himself, and already under test in its third model.

58

WITHIN six months of her marriage Tabitha is used to finding her house full, not of the county, for whose entertainment she has been so carefully equipped, but of engineers and racing motorists, enthusiasts who draw designs on her table linen with flat pencils, sit up half the night with Gollan in the workshop, and leave oil on her cushions.

The little factory building near Hackstraw Halt station has now stretched itself, mysteriously, into two acres of footings and a small wood of scaffold poles. Tabitha on her duty visits to the sick, her calls at the vicarage, notices that large works are in progress, but she says nothing of this to Gollan, because he has said nothing of it to her. Tabitha's impulsiveness is now balanced by a married experience that advises her not to raise questions to which Gollan has not offered an answer.

When the Stones, making a rare and unexpected call, ask her about the Hackstraw building, she answers with the reasonable and confident air of the good wife who knows and approves her husband's activity, "James has made a few workshops; and really, I think it's a very good thing. He enjoys them so much."

The Stones look at her in pity. Does she realize that this factory is to cost half a million? And Annie wails, "You didn't know; he's told nobody—that's what looks so bad."

"A mad scheme," Hector says. "Competition in the motor trade is already acute. After all, the class of person who can afford a motor car is very limited."

"I don't know why they have them at all," Annie cries. "Horrid things, frightening our horses. No one really wants them except young men and these inventors. Oh, why do people allow inventors?"

"H'ss, Annie; that's absurd. You don't want Germany and America to get ahead of us, do you? No, my argument is simply that your father has neither the health nor the capital for such a scheme. And where is he now? He said he would be here if we came."

"I'm afraid he was called away."

"Disappeared," Annie wails. "He always does that when he's got mixed up in some mad plan. He just disappears. What can one do with people when they get old and queer? Why must they be so childish? First it was women—"

"H'ss, Annie. What we wanted to say, Tabitha, is that this factory must stop. In any case he can't get the money to complete it. I believe his wage bill is now over twenty thousand a year."

Tabitha is suddenly alarmed. For a moment the picture of her security, of Gollan himself, the competent, the masterful, disappears like a serene landscape seen from a train when the train runs into a tunnel. And she sees only the reflection in the window pane, of fellow passengers, of John and herself, enclosed in a small illuminated fate, whirled helplessly, dumbly forward.

Annie Stone's words have a sudden meaning. "Mad scheme—it used to be women." In an instant, what has seemed like enterprise, decision in Gollan, takes on the look of crazy speculation and the obstinacy of an old madman.

She sees ruin coming upon Hackstraw, and John thrown once more upon the world, perhaps on Harry's charity. She can barely wait for Gollan to sit down to dinner that evening before she attacks him. And the attack is abrupt, defiant.

"Hector says you want to build a real factory at the Halt."

"It's like this, Bertie. I've got an idea to assemble this new engine on a sort of moving bench—each engine is wheeled along a rail."

"But, James, you know you were supposed to retire."

"What's my factory got to do with Hector? He never made anything in his life."

"He says we can't afford it, either."

Gollan looks at her and says, "That reminds me, I must write to Johnny about Robb's new model; it flew fifty feet."

Tabitha, in her fright, suddenly grows angry. "You don't mind what I say; I really don't know why I bother to say anything."

"My dear Bertie—" Gollan seems much affected by this complaint—"you're everything to me; I take your advice before anybody."

But in that very week, the first week of June, 1908, she sees tents in Pickles' meadow, and learns that hundreds of building laborers are to camp there. The factory is starting up into walls, and two tall chimneys grow so fast that in a month they top the woods of the park, so that Tabitha can see them from her bedroom windows.

Gollan says not a word about these new larger developments. He is, as usual, affectionate, bland. But Tabitha is enraged and humiliated by this calm defiance. She could not respond if she would.

59

And now a battle begins which is unacknowledged and almost without action. It is a conflict, that is, entirely of will and feeling. Tabitha gives no sympathy, and when Gollan comes to her at night with his stories, his little outbursts of confidence, she listens in silence and answers only with politeness, "I see," or, "I understand."

This course is very effective. It appears now that she who seems to have given the man so little has in fact given him something essential. He appeals to her, "Come, Bertie, what have I done?" He explodes in rage against the Stones. "I suppose Hector has been telling you that I don't know my own business!"

Gollan now wears a pestered, anxious air. He does not visit her room at night, and avoids her in daytime. He begins to take his luncheon at the works, eating bread and cheese with the men.

"So be it," Tabitha says to herself. But one day she has a call from the village doctor, Bain, an old Scotsman in whom Gollan has much faith, saying, "Bain always admits that doctors don't know anything. He's an honest chap, Bain."

Bain is blunt with Tabitha. "I don't like Sir James's look at all, your leddyship. He's off his form, he's worried."

"Of course he is; but not so worried as I am about this new factory. It's the wildest scheme."

"It's a deeficult position, cairtainly." The doctor's long pale face, deeply creased, wears an expression of contemplative interest. For the moment Tabitha is reminded of Manklow's grin. "It's a deelemma, your leddyship, which is not uncommon with patients of Sir James's strong character. But cairtainly family worries are bad for him. He's vairy fond of you, your leddyship."

"But do you expect me to encourage him in all his wild schemes?"

"Oh, he's set his heart on these new works."

What Tabitha resents is the unfairness of the pressure. "He's just like John when he doesn't get exactly what he wants, and makes himself ill. It's just blackmail."

When Gollan, every day more visibly wretched, looks at Tabitha with despair, she assumes her coolest expression. The door is still shut between their rooms, and Gollan even begins to spend nights at the factory.

But just when the deadlock appears insoluble, John comes home and at once falls in love with the new factory. He declares that he will be an engineer, and that he must start at once. He demands in Gollan's very tones, shrill and positive, why should he go back to school.

"My dear Johnny, you have to have a proper education."

"But James left school at thirteen."

"You can't even be an engineer without mathematics."

And Gollan, at the other end of the table, says to the air, "You don't want maths for engineering; you can hire an expert. I had two university chaps on my staff before I was twenty-five."

Tabitha is too angry to reply. It is only now that she feels the depth of her determination that John shall have a good education. She will fight for that to the end. When she is once more alone with Gollan, she attacks him furiously. "You have no right to encourage John to be silly. You know he's no sense at that age."

Gollan, with his sad humble air, mutters, "I'm sorry, Bertie, but I'm fond of Johnny, he's a fine chap, and I'd be sorry if he was spoilt. What do you want to make him learn all that stuff for—latin and algebra?"

"You don't understand." But she checks herself for fear of uttering some rudeness. She had been about to say that Gollan, having no education, cannot understand what education is.

Besides, she does not want to argue on the subject without better preparation. She can't, for instance, explain what latin and algebra are good for. She is only convinced that they are necessary to achieve a good education, that is, one which produces a certain kind of man.

The notion of this perfect man is not very clear in her mind, but often, when she speaks of education, she sees the picture of her father, driven from home, in his lonely old age, to a back-street lodging. Tabitha had never seen her father drunk, or heard him talk nonsense. For her, who has seen him only in the dignity of resignation, he remains the wisest and noblest of men, secure in his own soul against every misfortune.

Perhaps it is because of this picture, and because her father quoted sometimes from the latin grammar, and because he had a 'varsity degree, that she is determined to give John the same wisdom, the same security; but she is not accustomed to analyze her motives. When she says that she wants John to have a good education and to go to a public school, she is uttering a conviction deeper than logic.

But for this very reason, she is frightened by Gollan's obstinacy. She does not know how far he will go in opposing her. She feels how alien he is from her in all his ideas. He is, in essence, a man of a different class. His mind has unfamiliar simplifications, and also unknown depths. Often, when she thinks him stupid and shallow, he will utter a phrase or give a look which startles her with the idea of a profound cunning, the complexity of a peasant who knows every turn of a conflict between wills. Even his humble despair, in face of her anger, seems a piece of cunning.

"I wish I could please you, Bertie. What have I done?"

"You never do anything to please me. And now you want to ruin John as well as Hackstraw."

Husband and wife look at each other. Gollan's little eyes, which resemble those of a boar, seem to grow redder, as if some rage, slow and hot, were inflaming his blood. Then, to Tabitha's surprise, he says, "He's your son, your job," and walks off.

But Tabitha is suddenly full of gratitude and remorse. The immensity of her relief generates a proportionate kindness. At dressing time she takes occasion to open Gollan's door and say to him, "How did things go today at the new works?"

Gollan, staring at her, gives a visible jump, a rheumatic jerk of the shoulders. His expression passes from suspicious melancholy, the downcast sullenness of an old dog, through lively inquiry, to affectionate eagerness. "My dear Bertie, my dearest, very well, very nicely. You must come and see—"

"It looks very large."

"Why yes, my dear, my love—that's the idea. We have to build big to cut overheads. You see—" And he follows her into her room, pouring out details of floor space, output. "And it's quite a new layout, revolutionary. We're putting everything on rails. We're going to bring the work to the men instead of the men to the work; each job on its own truck."

At midnight, dressed in his extraordinary nightshirt and carpet slippers, in which he seems like a small boy prematurely aged in face but much retarded in self-control, he is still describing to Tabitha the immense market that awaits his new engine.

"The cheap car is coming, and it will run to thousands."

"I'm sure your engine will be a great success."

"Of course it will be; it can't help it. But I'll show you tomorrow."

At a suitable moment, when he is saying good night for the third time, she murmurs, "By the way, I think I'll get a tutor for John in the Easter holidays; he really must pass his exam for Chilton."

There is only a moment's pause before Gollan answers, "Yes, you know about these things; you know what to do."

The peace is founded on the principle, each to his job. And being established, it is more cordial, much more affectionate than before. It is as though each, in doing battle and suffering terror, has learnt to set a higher value on affectionate offices. Tabitha takes occasion to say how clever Robb Robinson is. She visits the new factory and admires it. Gollan snatches a holiday of three days to take her to Paris and buy her a thousand pounds' worth of frocks.

When Hector Stone, coming to one of the Hackstraw dinners that winter, speaks again to Tabitha about the dangerous enterprise of the new works, she answers cheerfully that there is no danger. They are bound to succeed. "James has built a good many factories, and has never had a failure."

She speaks with such confidence that Stone can only gaze and tell himself, "The cunning old rascal has got round her."

But he is wrong. There is no tacit agreement between the parties. Tabitha does not know why or how she has recovered her faith in Gollan. It is simply there.

60

IN THIS victory, in the thought, "John is to have a proper tutor and to go to Chilton, to Oxford," and in the new sense of confidence in Gollan's business powers, Tabitha feels an extraordinary gaiety. At the time of her marriage, she had looked older than her age, staid, worn by experience; now she seems ten years younger, naïve in her exuberance and her new frocks. And like a young girl, she has great energy of conviction. She assures Gollan that his new factory will make millions; she criticizes the vicar's sermons; she subscribes to the liberal club in the village. In the quarrel between the liberal government and the Lords she is highly indignant with the Lords for their stupidity and obstruction; in the campaign for women's votes, she approves, not violence, but what she calls strong measures. When Gollan is surprised to hear that she has been sitting on the platform behind a radical candidate, she cries, "But I am a radical; I always was. We are a radical family," and she tells him that he is old-fashioned. But he laughs at her; he does not take women's politics seriously. And he is charmed with this livelier Tabitha in her new clothes, who comes to his new factory, praises everything, and even pores over blueprints.

To Tabitha the blueprints are even more incomprehensible than the poems, long forgotten, of Boole, but she finds that the comment, "I *see*, but how *neat*!" is adequate. She gives half an hour a day to factory visits, and the workmen's canteen, and at least half an hour a week to Robb Robinson, while he tries his model planes in the park. And when she cries, "But, Mr. Robinson, it must have gone fifty yards; how marvelous!" she does not only mean to please, she is truly delighted by his success.

Everyone is full of enthusiasm for flying, which is described, even in *The Times*, as a revolutionary development. The Wrights' experiments in America, Santos-Dumont's in France, have caught the imagination of the world, and every small boy is designing planes. Schoolrooms flutter with ingenious cutouts, and every second professional engineer is designing a model.

Robb Robinson has now eight, which he and two solemn assistants in Hackstraw park fly for hours. There are monoplanes, biplanes, planes like a children's dart, a triplane like a box kite, even a quadriplane, meant to pack into a small space.

Tabitha admires them all, but especially, because it is Robb's favorite, the triplane, a machine of great power and steadiness. She is astonished at Gollan's coolness and skepticism in face of Robb's experiments. "The truth is," she thinks, "he's getting old; he's no imagination. He goes on developing new ideas in engineering because he has always done so, but he can't see, he can't feel how wonderful it is to fly."

Gollan's faith is in the Zeppelin. But he enjoys Tabitha's enthusiasm for the plane, and allows Robb several hundred pounds for his experiments. "It's worth it," he says, "to keep the man happy. Robb's a treasure, a wonder—don't talk to me about microscopes, he can see what goes on inside a cylinder head by instinct."

61

TABITHA has asked the agency for a thoroughly good tutor, and offered a large fee, and the agents have recommended Mr. Sloop, scholar of St. Mark's, who fortunately will be free in April. This conjunction of scholarship, St. Mark's, a most distinguished college and a high fee, has given Tabitha high hopes. And what is strange, her faith is not weakened but actually strengthened by Mr. Sloop's failure. He is indeed a charming young man, with the most graceful manners. He is very confident; he seems to know everything, and he plays the piano almost as well as Tabitha herself. He talks housekeeping, liberal politics, and village responsibilities with Tabitha, engineering with Gollan, farming with the steward, filing with the secretary, roses with the gardener, wine with the butler.

But he spends most of his time with Robb Robinson, testing a new man-carrying plane in the park. In fact, like everyone else, except Gollan himself, he is mad about planes. And when one day Tabitha, slightly surprised to find him, in lesson hours, watching the new Gollan Robb model being towed behind a car, asks him how John is getting on, he answers, still gazing at the plane, "I can't say he's wildly interested, Lady Gollan, but I doubt if I should be, in his place, with such a fine career open to me here, a really practical job of work."

"But he must go to the university first."

Mr. Sloop, withdrawing his eyes reluctantly from the plane, soaring at the end of its rope, passes his long hand through his long fair hair, and sighs. "I wonder, Lady Gollan, if 'varsity education gives one anything of value."

Tabitha, full of that earnestness which the very word education inspires in her, looks at the young man with astonishment. She has never before met a young scholar in his second year enjoying a natural reaction from books. She exclaims warmly, "But, Mr. Sloop, you can't deny that men from the university are much more—"

"Please, please, don't say cultured, Lady Gollan." Sloop shudders.

"And why not, if it's true? Is it the fashion to say you don't like culture?"

"That is possible. You mean that I am too civilized?"

"Perhaps too conceited."

"I quite see what you mean."

And even in her anger Tabitha admires the young man's candor; apparently he is proof against her rudeness.

"And you can't blame Oxford for that."

"The responsibility would be very difficult to place; my poor parents made great sacrifices for my education. I should not like to say that they had made a mistake. Shall we say that tradition, convention—?" And warming to the subject which in fact he has prepared for the next debate at the St. Mark's literary society on the proposition "This Ancient Society of Clerks of St. Mark's considers that humanity should be abolished," he points out that all civilization tends to destruction. Women are now going in for education, and educated women refuse to bear children. "Thus civilization will destroy itself; though I fear it will last my time."

Tabitha is glad to see the last of Mr. Sloop, who, for his part, pays her an affectionate farewell, and writes afterwards two long letters telling her that he hopes their friendship, so valuable to him, will never cease. "It was so delightful to escape for once from my monastic cell and meet real people, and especially yourself. It is said, I believe, that to meet a certain great lady was a liberal education; I can certainly say that it may correct and even cure an academic one."

Tabitha, who does not recognize herself, through Sloop's innocent eyes, as a great lady, is merely irritated by this conquest. She says to herself, "It's wicked that young men like that, with so many advantages, should attack Oxford." She thinks of Sloop as a traitor, and is furious to discover that he has established a great ascendancy over John.

"If he spoils John's chances I'll never forgive him."

In fact, John is heartbroken for his friend Sloop, and writes to him frequently. The two exchange ideas for a new kind of airplane with immensely wide corrugated wings.

John fails at the Chilton entrance, and Tabitha spends a night in tears. But she receives a friendly letter from Sloop. "If you really want John to go to a public school, I can get him into Bradley. They'll take him on his bowling. How much I miss Hackstraw, and all your goodness. Do ask me again."

Tabitha wires, and John is accepted for Bradley. But she does not forgive Sloop. He has committed for her a crime against the spirit of good education. Above all, he has raised up new unnecessary dangers and difficulties in a world already perplexed for all mothers. "He's the worst possible influence for John. Why do children always take to people who will do them most harm?"

But John, after a first term at Bradley, has utterly forgotten Sloop. His reports are bad, except for football; but he scorns them. He is too much interested in school, which he displays before his mother with the pride of an explorer as a strange new world, unknown to women.

It gradually appears, by casual remarks, that this new world of school is dominated by a hero called Fox, captain of house football.

Fox, it seems, is a giant, with an extraordinary amount of hair on his chest, a stern ruler of the team who beat three forwards for slacking, and a Christian; that is to say, his language is very bad, and he detests the Church, but he regards Christ as an example.

And John's new love for football has a strong religious bias. For when Tabitha compliments him on getting into the house second fifteen, he answers with a serious air, "I don't really like half, but Fox says he can't get anyone else who's willing to be killed."

"Killed, John?" Tabitha is alarmed.

"Everyone gets killed at fly-half." John speaks with mournful relish. "The real trouble is that we're too light in the scrum." And he explains that Browns, that is to say, his house, having been cock house at football for three years running, is very likely to be beaten next winter, for it has lost its heaviest players.

"It's only fair," Tabitha suggests, "that some other house should have a turn."

John looks sadly at his mother, as an old statesman looks at the abstract dreamer. He frowns and says gently, "You don't understand, Mummy. Browns stands for something; it has a tradition. It's the only house in Bradley that really has any sort of guts or decency; it's the only place where a worker is respected. Why, if Fox had gone to Trotters, he would have been kicked out of his skin, just for being a worker. And if I'd gone to Philpots, I would have been absolutely ruined in body and soul."

"Oh, John—"

"It's a fact, Mummy. Philpots is a sink."

"But, Johnny, isn't it very bad that boys should be sent to Philpots? Oughtn't something to be done to make it better?"

"You couldn't make it better. But you don't understand."

"But, Johnny, that's why I'm asking. Because I want to understand."

Whereupon the boy makes a face, and suddenly changes the subject. One day Tabitha, affectionately eager to share John's interests, has been snubbed three times within an hour, and she exclaims, "But, Johnny, why don't you want to tell me things? One would think we weren't even friends."

The boy's eyebrows go up; he looks at his mother with an expression of perplexity, and suddenly he ceases to talk about school. When Tabitha, puzzled by his strange mood, asks him with her usual impulsiveness, "What is wrong?" he answers impatiently, "Nothing, I'm all right."

And in fact he does not himself know why that word "friends" has caused so mysterious a revulsion in his spirit, and why he can no longer chatter to his mother, why he even avoids her.

A few days later he is hidden in a dark corner of the old library, a room never used by Gollan, who reads only technical books, or Tabitha, who rarely opens any book, when a gardener puts his head in at the open window and shouts, "Quick, quick, plane coming."

The boy jumps up as if touched by a pin. All about him the house is alive, as if waked from some trance. Windows are thrown up, there are shrill cries on upper landings, a footman, in a most indecorously loud tone, is calling from the back corridor across the hall. Someone is flying down the stairs with a great rustle of skirts.

The handle of the library door rattles, and John hears his mother's voice. At once he falls back into his chair; before he has even reflected, he is in an attitude of indifference.

Tabitha darts into the room. "John, come quick, a plane."

"Must I?"

But secretly eager, he allows himself to be brought out of the house into the December sunlight, already darkening, and finds a crowd gathered, staring over the roof. They point suddenly. Tabitha catches John's arm. A young maid gives a peculiar squeak, something between a scream and a laugh. A large biplane has suddenly appeared seemingly close above the chimney pots. No one, except a few mechanics, has yet seen a plane in flight. John, staring with high raised brows, is even more astonished than he has expected, and in quite a different manner. He has forgotten himself in wonder.

"But it's not a bit like a bird," he thinks; "it's more like a train."

In fact, what is astonishing is that the thing, flying low, is visibly a large and heavy machine, which is proceeding through the invisible air with both the smoothness of a train and also an immense noise. For a moment it appears incredible and causes in John that confusion which is perhaps the permanent state of lunatics: a feeling as if the very structure of the brain itself has become unsubstantial so that none of its opinions can be relied on.

Gollan's voice squeaks in his ear, "See that—see that—a biplane—with a passenger. Must be Farman."

The plane roars past and diminishes into the distance. It seems to travel with the slowness of a wagon, heavy, solid; but in a minute it has disappeared beyond the wood. The watchers break into excited talk; two young maids are giggling; Gollan, crimson, with staring eyes, stutters, "What about that, Johnny? What about it?" Gollan has seen the light.

But John does not perceive that this is a crisis for Gollan. He does not know that old people can have crises of faith. And he recoils from an enthusiasm which invites him to feel another's emotion. He assumes a lofty air, and remarks, no doubt in the manner of Fox, "But why all the fuss?—I suppose the papers started it," and strolls off, with his hands in his pockets.

And when he sees how deeply he has offended both Gollan and his mother by this coolness, he is ashamed and also irritated with them for causing the shame. He says to himself, "Really, they've no right; Hackstraw is getting impossible."

62 AND now he delights in school because it is not Hackstraw; it is his own dominion, precious to him because his mother and Gollan have no part in it. Their very interest in him obliges him to fly into a secret world, in order to have a world at all. So that he finds a pleasure, a power, even in their mistakes. When Fox leaves Bradley, and Tabitha condoles with him on losing a friend, he does not tell her how much he is bored by the very idea of Fox, that he has now much more exciting friends. He is now in the Upper Fifth, which Fox never reached, and he has discovered a new universe of experience, a new relation, in the form master, a celebrated character called Toad, with a passion for history.

It seems to John, who, like Tabitha in character as well as face, has a somewhat headstrong nature, and who has never before been aware of an intellectual passion, that Toad is a wonderful person. He calls him Toad because it is necessary to feel an amused condescension toward this fascinating teacher in order not to be caught in the bonds of admiration.

To Tabitha he speaks of Toad with derision, as a ridiculous and ugly old man in shapeless trousers and a snuffy coat. For the real Toad whom he admires is an important part of his private life. He is also a valuable armory; for it is from Toad that he gets some of the best ammunition with which he defends himself from Hackstraw, by a vigorous offensive.

"You're coming this afternoon, aren't you, John?" Tabitha says to him one afternoon in the spring of 1912. Her voice is full of excitement, anxiety, her eyes are both commanding and imploring. What she is asking him to do is to come and see the trials of the first full-sized plane from the Robinson factory, the Gollan Robb.

But because she is excited, and her excitement is something that belongs to Hackstraw, to the old stale world of home, he answers, "Why, Mother, what's happening?"

"My *dear* Johnny, the trials."

"Well, I've got rather a lot of work."

"Oh, John, you promised. Aren't you excited? How can you not be excited?"

He allows her to bring him a hat and to lead him into the park. He is no longer rude and gruff like Fox, but serious like the head of the house, Truby. And as he walks beside her he says gravely and a little impatiently, like a master instructing a stupid pupil, "After all, flying makes no real difference."

"No difference? But people will be able to go anywhere—to America, India, Australia—in a few days!"

"It won't make any difference to civilization, Mother, except perhaps for the worse."

"Oh, John, you can't say flying isn't progress."

This is the word that John wants. He has just learnt to criticize the idea of progress. He says in his Truby manner, "And what exactly do you mean by progress?"

"Why, John, you know there's progress. Look at our railways and motors."

"Do you call them progressive because they move? Do you realize, Mother, that probably the most civilized time in history was the Roman empire, under the Antonines?"

"Oh, John, you and your Romans; they hadn't even drains or anæsthetics."

"They had peace. The truth is, you don't know what you mean by civilization."

"That sounds so arrogant, John; you mustn't be arrogant, it offends people. I daresay Mr. Toad despises stupid people, but it doesn't matter for him in a school."

"What has Toad got to do with it? Why do you always worry about me?"

"I must worry when you are so rude."

And again the war breaks out which neither can understand; and not understanding, cannot control. The boy frowns. "But it's so unnecessary." He walks away.

For the rest of that day he does not speak to Tabitha. He simply cannot do so. And when he comes to say good night, because he resents the necessity, he asks with a severe air, as if reproaching her, "Why don't you want me to know my father?"

The effect is even more violent than he has expected. His mother turns scarlet; and he, too, alarmed, sympathetic, feeling that he has hurt her, becomes very red.

"Your father? But I don't even know where he is."

"Isn't he the R. B. Bonser who writes to the *Automobilist* about tires?"

"It can't be."

"Yes, Mother, it is. I asked about him, and one of the boy's fathers knows him quite well in the city. He's in some rubber company."

"You haven't seen him, John?"

"No, but I wondered if I ought to."

"Why should you? He's never taken the least interest in you. He's a bad man, John, thoroughly bad."

"I know you didn't get on, of course."

"He *is* bad, John; a liar, a cheat—" Tabitha is imploring the boy to believe her. "You can't *believe* how bad he is."

"Very well, Mother, but don't *worry*." He kisses her solemnly, like one who forgives an injury; and on that same night, perhaps simply to justify this attitude, he writes a long letter to Bonser.

However, having written it, and established his grievance against Tabitha, he does not post it. For, after all, his father is also a parent, and may turn out to be curious and troublesome.

63

It is not till three weeks later, at school, in the summer term, that he recollects this letter. He is watching the cricket one afternoon, from a rug under the trees, with his friend Truby, and among hundreds of boys in pink and white blazers, he is wearing a suit. He has just been made a prefect, and at Bradley, prefects are entitled to take tea in certain tea shops, and therefore to wear suits in the afternoons. John, since his promotion, has often worn suits even on match afternoons. And now, feeling something sharp press on his ribs, he puts his hand in his pocket and finds the letter. He is too idle, too happy, to be surprised; he gazes at it with a smile.

It is a hot afternoon, when the air seems thickened with heat as if gently cooking in the sun. To lie in the shade, which is, if not very cool, at least green, and to watch the cricketers where they seem, in their glittering flannels, actually to flicker in hot vapor, seems to John a specially luxurious pleasure.

He and Truby have been talking about their future. From neighboring rugs come schoolboy exclamations about the match, about some new airplane record, sudden outcries, jokes, threats, which make the two prefects aware of their difference, their responsible age. The feeling of difference is even perceptible in Truby's voice, while he murmurs, "I'm rather sorry now I didn't go into the navy. That's what my people wanted when I was a kid, but I was rather against it then." He selects a new piece of grass to chew. "But if there is a war the navy will get most of the fun."

"I suppose it will be over almost at once; modern explosives are simply terrific. These dreadnoughts, they say, will sink each other at the first broadside."

"Yes, battleships are out of date. Wars get shorter and shorter. The last real war, I mean the German and French war, only lasted six weeks, at least till Sedan, and that was really the end."

"There probably won't be any more big wars, except perhaps in the Balkans."

"But the Slavs have never been civilized; they didn't come under Rome."

"Neither did the Germans. Oh, good shot."

Both boys give three or four claps, and then fall back on their rug. Truby, a plump, energetic youth, says, "All the same, I'd have liked to see what it was like—"

John has dropped his letter and is lying on his side with his cheek in his hand, and his straw hat over his nose. He feels immensely languid, careless, and it seems to him that life, taken not too seriously, is infinitely pleasant. The very sound of the players' bats, ringing across the hard ground with startling loudness, increases his sense of privileged repose. It is as though these things—the hot sun, the cool shade, even the exhausting energy of the cricketers—have been designed to give him this sense of happy peaceful emancipation. He is aware that two young fags on the next rug who are pretending to hit each other with bats are carrying on their warfare partly to catch his eye. He takes great care not to look their way.

It is tea time. The players suddenly move together at a special easy stroll, toward the pavilion. Truby says lazily, "Shall we have it at the tucker or down High Street?" and John answers, "I meant to go downtown, but really, it's too far." He gets up and carefully dusts his knees; then notices the letter and picks it up. But it stays in his hand, and on the way to tea as he passes a pillar box, he raises his hand with the gesture of a captain of fate, and shoots it resolutely through the slot.

Yet he is astonished, like any child who pulls the trigger of a gun, to see if it will really go off, and deafens itself with the explosion, when five days later he is called to the housemaster's study, and sees before him a square-shouldered man with a ginger mustache, a man who at once catches the eye by his florid good looks and does not altogether repel liking by his bursting self-satisfaction. For it seems to say to all the world, not so much admire me, as rejoice with me. So that the boy at once begins to smile. Bonser is addressing the master on the value of a classical education. "I was at Eton myself, but I know there are other places."

John stares at the man's clothes, the loudest and tightest suit of gray, the strangest shoes of gray and white suede that he has ever seen. He cannot even decide that the man is a bounder; he is too unusual, like a foreigner in some native style.

Bonser turns and seizes John by both hands. "So here he is! Johnny—at last! I'd have known you anywhere." And looking at the master, he wags his head. "A well-bred 'un, eh?"

"But have we met before?" John asks.

"Met before? But I'm your father, Johnny. I danced you on my knee, I brought you up all through the most important years. Your dear mother always took my advice. It was me who arranged all this for you"—with a gesture which seems to indicate all Bradley. And turning to the housemaster, he exclaims, "Nothing like a public school education, sir; it made England what it is. I swore my son should have it, if I starved to get it for him. But come on, old man, what about a little drive, and tea somewhere? You'll let him out for the afternoon?"

John, between confusion and wonder, is led to the drive, where an immense open two-seater Bentley, in sky blue and silver, stands blocking the gateway.

"Not a bad little runabout," Bonser says. "It will do a hundred, but that's not really good enough if you want to move."

And as they whirl along the narrow dusty roads, he leans back, steering with two fingers, and talks about his cars, which are all unique, his clothes, made by a tailor who, otherwise, makes only for royalty, and his shoes, which cost ten pounds a pair. "What I say is, the best is always the best. I'm not really a rich man, Johnny, not as Rothschilds go. I live very quietly. I suppose I'll have to get a real place of some sort, but just now I'm camping out in Jermyn Street. Just a bachelor flat. Glad to see you any time; we'll have a chop at the Ritz. It's not very select, I know, but it's convenient, and they know me there; I use it a good deal for entertaining—one must entertain in my job."

His job, it seems, is promoting and directing rubber companies. "I don't claim to be infallible, Johnny, but I do know something about the markets. For instance, on the rise last week I raked in a nice little bit—about four thousand. Not bad for a week. But it's not a thing that comes to everybody. It's a kind of sixth sense, an intuition. My grandmother had second sight, which may have something to do with it. Scotswoman, very old family—"

"What was her name?"

"Scott. In fact, I believe she was related to the chap that wrote the *Lady of Shalott*. And that reminds me, don't forget to remember me to your dear mother."

"Yes, of course."

"And dear old Jimmy Gollan. I hear he's in trouble with the banks over his airplane gamble. If Jimmy wants a spot of capital at any time, I believe I could lay my hands on it. I'm in a little syndicate that might take an interest. Don't say anything directly, of course, just mention that the Bilman rubber group has its eye on airplane development generally."

And after a large tea, at which he drinks whisky, he drives John back again at the same pace, tips him a sovereign, and is not seen again for four months. Moreover, he does not leave the address in Jermyn Street.

64

JOHN is left with suspended judgment. He has no standard by which to judge this man. He feels only an excitement, a sense as if his experience has been suddenly enlarged by an event, which ought to be comic but can't altogether be laughed away. For at least a fortnight Toad and his exposition of classical antiquity seem equally faded. The boy is continually remembering Bonser. "But how could that fearful bounder be my father? How could Mother have had anything to do with such a cad?"

And when in the next holidays he sees his mother on Sunday morning in her black Sunday dress, with a pearl cross at her neck, new white gloves on her diminutive rather short hands, grasping a vellum-covered prayer book, a little frown, meaning probably that she is expecting to suffer from a bad lesson, or bad hymns, a raised chin, bright anxious eyes, a kind of enthusiastic primness, contriving as usual to seem at once extremely neat and highly electric, he laughs with wonder. "How could she stand him, even his clothes?"

He is charming to her, he sympathizes warmly with her usual Sunday wrath against the Church, which does not know how to manage its own business. "Why do they have such lessons? Think of that lesson on Easter Sunday, about murdering people just out of spite! It isn't even Christian; and it gives all these atheists such a good chance of saying the whole thing is just nonsense." But this time he says nothing about Bonser. It is because he can keep that meeting to himself that he can feel his independence, and is able to endure, with good nature, the growing excitement at Hackstraw, so unbalanced, so undignified.

Toad, quoting Tacitus, "they told of prodigies, cyclones, *extraordinary birds*, monsters," and adding with a sudden explosion of silent laughter, "See papers," has put the airplane in its place as a popular toy.

John, like Truby, like Toad, loathes a craze; and since Blériot's flight over the Channel airplanes have rapidly become a craze. Already the art of flight has passed from the co-operative to the competitive stage. The era of races, of record-breaking, has started.

Everywhere rich men, connoisseurs of innovation and inventiveness, are offering prizes. Harmsworth of the *Daily Mail* has paid Paulhan ten thousand pounds for his winning flight from London to Manchester; Ducat, having for the moment laid aside the patronage of art, and especially the post-impressionists, offers fifteen thousand for a flight across Europe, with three stops.

And these plane races have proved even more exciting than the first motor races of twenty years before. Scores of planes, in every size and form, are being built to compete in some adventure of glory.

The Gollan Robb is already entered for the Ducat prize. Robb's crew are working often all night. Already there are stories of spies, stolen blueprints. Hangars are guarded, watchmen patrol.

There is an atmosphere of devotion and competition, in which everyone is a little mad. The famous gardens, in the charge of their experts, are still kept up, but on the magnificent lawns, right in front of the drawing room, there is an immense marquee, set up partly to house, and partly to hide, the race model.

It is about this tent that the whole life of the surrounding country now turns. It is like a shrine; and at each entrance sentries stand to keep out unauthorized persons, untouchables, forbidden to approach the god. There is, in fact, always a small crowd of such persons—visitors to the servants, tradesmen from the village—standing about the gates of the yard, and gazing at the tent. And privileged persons, engineers, Gollan himself, Tabitha, are going in and out all day, as if to offer up prayer.

Probably there is prayer, as an essence, as an appeal, as well as admiration of power, of beauty, in all these worshipers of a machine, which, they feel, is much more than an idol, because it has potency of its own.

But when John meets his mother going toward the tent with that same preoccupied look which she has worn on the way to church, and she calls to him, "Oh, John, are you going to see it? They've just put on the top canvas," he is now able to answer, "I should love to!"

The sentry at the door, lifting the flap for them, smiles gaily, like a priest of the occult, who seems to say, "We're all in the secret."

And John, looking up at the special race model, a high narrow triplane, can allow himself to admire.

"It's certainly big enough."

"It's the biggest in the world."

In fact the plane nearly touches the convex shoulders of the tent.

With its three layers of sails, it seems as tall as a three-storied house; much too large for its fragile woodwork and long delicate struts. And the August sun shining through the canvas makes the whole complex figure seem even less substantial. The wires are like rays, the struts like columns of motes, the upper wings like a dazzle of sparks as seen through a horizontal refraction in the air. The thing is less like a solid construction than a problem in geometry worked out in a medium neither completely physical nor quite imaginary.

"But it looks rather flimsy for its size."

"You're quite wrong," Tabitha cries; "it's very strong."

And Gollan, who has suddenly appeared, looking in his white dungarees, stiff as new sails, and much too large for him, like a marmoset imprisoned in a barrel, cries, "It's the toughest there is; that's the idea." He turns his wrinkled face quickly from one to the other, and the sun behind his large pink ears makes him seem still more like some pet monkey, full of the nervous erratic impulses of a half-wild animal. And suddenly he darts away among his wires. He has come to find John's presence insupportable. For he perceives quite well that the boy is determined not to be enthusiastic, and it is enthusiasm that he demands. For him, planes, and especially the Gollan Robb, are a revelation, and those who cannot worship must be mean small souls.

Gollan perhaps is all the more fierce in his devotion to Robinson's plane because he is uneasy about the race. No worshiper is more violent in defense of his faith than when there is reason to doubt it. It is the ages of enlightenment that are the ages of persecution.

65

It has been arranged that Gollan shall go to the field early for the final test of the engine, and Tabitha follows at leisure. But after all he wakes her up at half-past six, apologizes, and so obviously wants her to come with him that she volunteers.

He needs encouragement. "We're going to win by hours," he tells her; "by a thousand miles." And she knows that her role is to assure him that there's no doubt of it. The Gollan Robb is the finest plane in the world. "We've proved its speed in the trials."

"Never mind the trials, it can do better than that; we put twenty miles an hour on it last night with the new propeller."

They reach the airdrome at eight, while the autumn mist, already chilly and smelling of winter, lies in the ditches about the vast rough field without runways. In spite of the early hour, there are already many visitors: groups of serious-looking men, experts, mechanics, from distant parts, or even pilots, who walk slowly from one plane to another in deep discussion on the merits of different designs, and a large sprinkling of amateurs, men and women who have found a hobby in aviation, and like nothing so much as to be on familiar terms with mechanics and engineers. These last may be distinguished not only by dress, for most of them are rich and inclined to be smart, but by a different, a more solemn gravity. They resemble indeed those pious laymen who at a religious ceremony look so much more ecstatic than the clergy.

The planes, which have all arrived on the day before, eight in number, are still in the hangars or hidden under temporary shelters of tarpaulin, from which one hears now and then the roar of an engine being tested.

Near the row of hangars and close to a hedge there is a coffee stall, probably designed for the mechanics, but already surrounded by fashionable ladies and important-looking men drinking hot coffee.

Tabitha, seeing that Gollan, who feels every draft, is shivering, takes him at once to this stall.

Large cars are now driving into the ground, bringing a new kind of visitor: journalists, business men. The Secretary for War has arrived with two generals; Lord Ducat himself, in his celebrated sombrero, is making a majestic progress with a staff of more than a dozen editors and directors.

Tabitha, who is anxious that he shall give due credit to Gollan's inventive brilliance, is speaking to him, when a smiling rosy face and scented mustache is interposed between them.

"Hullo, Pops. Prettier than ever! By God, you don't look seventeen. What do you think, Sir James? Ah, you did a smart job there. You knew a good thing when you saw it. Trust you, if I may say so."

And seeing Gollan's sharp look of inquiry, he seizes his hand. "Bonser. You've heard of me, Dick Bonser, of Bilman Rubber. Well, sir, what about the race; who's going to win?"

"The race? We're going to win—can't help it."

"So I heard; and I wanted to see you about a proposition." He takes Gollan's arm and walks him to one side.

Tabitha has been aware all this time of John at her elbow. He has arrived with Bonser, and now he begins to explain that he has a day's holiday from school. "Father asked for me especially; he wanted to meet you and Jim."

"I don't know how you can bear him—even to look at!"

And the boy, smiling like a man of the world, answers, "Of course he's rather a bounder, but then he's also rather fun. Oh, I can understand that you wouldn't appreciate him. You're so completely different in character. He's rather a pirate, and you're so much the other way," and he goes on talking gravely and sensibly, to avoid the crisis. He points out that it is natural for mothers to be conventional, because they are bound to be nervous. "You're always afraid I'm going to catch cold, or be run over, or fall under bad influences."

"But, John, there *are* bad influences, you know there are, and this man is the worst kind. Don't you see he's being nice to you for his own purposes?"

"Oh no, Mother, you're wrong there. He wouldn't bother. That's his great charm. He doesn't bother about anything except enjoying life; and what a driver. If you could see his two-seater—it's as big as a train. He let me drive it last week."

"You're much too young to drive a car."

"He didn't think so. He offered to give me one of my own, one like his. Of course I don't suppose he really meant it."

"He wouldn't mind if you were killed."

The anger of the voice makes the boy raise his eyebrows. His smile becomes vague; his eyes wander.

"You don't really think you ought to have a car?" Tabitha stares at him with a frown.

"Well, it would be very nice. But I quite see you wouldn't like it. Hullo—" He steps aside to accost the designer, who, in flying kit, is drinking his coffee at the counter and listening with abstracted eyes, and the blank expression of a sleepwalker or inventor, to a famous statesman's comments on the flying machine as an instrument of war.

Both turn as John speaks, and relax, smile. Tabitha, watching him, thinks, "He's more sure of himself. He's even imitating Dick, but perhaps it is only because he knows I'm looking. Why is he so impossible? Why does he always want to do the opposite of what I ask? What have I done wrong?"

She feels such fear for the boy, such hatred of Bonser, that she cannot reason. She says, "I *must* make him understand." But what John is to understand is not clear to her. "I never say what I mean. I must tell him how important it is to—"

But she cannot grasp this important thing that she wishes for John, so much more keenly since the reappearance of Bonser. When words like wisdom, goodness, sincerity, nobility come into her mind, they at once begin to assume different shapes, vague or even absurd; moreover, they call up before her mind the picture of somebody like a spiritual Hector Stone, and she cannot admit that she wants to make of John an important magisterial person. Yet she cannot detect in the compound the element that she needs to defend the boy against such as Bonser: security in the spirit. And recoiling once more from the vision of a pundit in a frock coat, she says to herself in despair, "Now he wants a car; what madness."

"How do, Lady Gollan?"

By a reaction which is almost mechanical she smiles and utters the appropriate answers. "Why, Lady Chadworth! How long it is! And Roger—how nice. I see you've been writing about us."

And Manklow, who has grown not fatter but more solid, as if importance had changed his very flesh into a firmer substance, whose bald pink head has somehow given him a look of integrity and benevolence, bows. "Don't thank me, Tib, it's a matter of business. You are news, quite big news." He straightens his back and produces his comment, probably prepared for the day, "Nothing like flying to make the time fly."

"Perfectly marvelous; you wonderful people make me ashamed." Lady Chadworth at forty is now collecting flying men and inventors. She wants to be introduced to Robb Robinson. So does a keen young general.

"So I hear you've got the winner, Lady Gollan."

"Of course, General."

"The trouble with your triplane is that it would be too big a mark in the air."

"But it's so safe, so steady—that's the whole idea."

"How do you do, Lady Gollan? A great occasion. I suppose you'll win, or James wouldn't be in it. What a nose for success. All the same, you know, the future is with the Zeppelin."

A great engineer interjects, "Seventy per cent of power in the heavier-than-air machine is wasted in keeping it up."

And a fashionable voice behind says loudly, "Actually the flying craze is nearly over—it's been run to death, like diabolo."

Cars and carriages are now arriving in a stream, as for the Derby. And they bring similar parties. The crowd is changing character for the third time. As the engineers and the amateurs of novelty have been diluted by business men, politicians, journalists, and students of affairs, so now the latter are outnumbered by a race crowd, consisting as usual of the very smart and the very low; fashionable duchesses rub shoulders with betting touts, and both have the same interest—a gamble.

The race is due to start. Stewards herd the strolling groups from the field toward the spaces between the hangars. Bookies begin to call the odds along the fence. And as at a country race meeting, important people, privileged to stroll on the course, are named by the watchers: famous pilots, a member of the Jockey Club, the Minister of Transport, with a large cigar and a peculiar John Bull hat, a popular Field Marshal.

Some of the pilots are not only heroes of the air but of the drawing rooms. They are rich young men who have taken up flying when they might have chosen instead to explore Everest or Greenland, or to go tiger shooting. Princesses ask them to dinner, and debutantes beg for their photographs.

The first machine, a biplane, takes off, bumping across the short grass. Its narrow wheels leave the ground, descend again, and bump violently. One is seen to be buckled. The crowd utters cries; a woman near Tabitha cries out, "The whole thing is wrong."

The plane has risen again two or three feet. It shaves the hedge by a few inches, and begins slowly to rise. A long sigh comes from the crowd, then at once laughter, a chatter of excitement. The next plane takes off suddenly at an alarmingly steep angle. The crowd claps, and voices say, "He'll win."

The third, already in position, refuses to start. Mechanics and backers gather round it, disputing. The stewards call for the next, which is the Gollan Robb, and John, Bonser, and Gollan run to the hangar to assist in pushing it forward. Robb is the pilot.

The appearance of the plane causes a louder burst of talk. Many of the crowd have seen it before, and its triple wings have caused argument between those who have proved that the biplane is the best possible design, and those who put their faith in Gollan's enterprise and Robb's genius.

The engine starts with a roar, delightful to Gollan, who smiles about him. The plane rushes across the field and turns a somersault over the distant hedge. Its tail jumps up, and the whole structure gradually collapses sideways. Police and stewards are seen running, but the crowd follows close. Tabitha is hemmed in and pushed off her feet. She is trying not to weep; and finding herself pressed against John, she cries angrily, "Where are the police?"

"He's not killed."

And Tabitha, struggling with the crowd, says, "It's all my fault."

66

DURING that morning Halt shares fall so quickly that when the news of the crash has been printed in the evening papers they become unsalable. The banks send down their agent to Hackstraw to take charge of all the Gollan affairs and to live in the house—a man in possession. It appears that Gollan has already pledged everything. A meeting of creditors is announced to decide if anything can be saved from the wreck.

Gollan is not to be seen. He declares that he can't stand those jackals. His excuse is that he wants to be near Robb's bedside in London, to protect him from the surgeons.

Tabitha does not complain of this desertion. She carries an air of concentration, and is ready every moment with decisions. She gives preliminary notice to the servants; and when the committee of creditors arrives at the end of that week, she receives it with a grace which irritates the more moral like Hector Stone, and excites admiration in the more sympathetic.

In fact, her dignity is that of preoccupation; she has too many urgent problems on her mind to think of herself or her misfortune.

The delegates, consisting of two bankers, four lawyers, three stock-brokers, an accountant, and a famous engineer, are entertained to a magnificent and stately luncheon, where they are charming to their hostess, and afterwards, sitting in private, decide to sell Hackstraw, with all its contents, to put the works under new management appointed by the creditors, to end airplane building, and discharge the research staff.

They are polite, but they behave like masters, and also with an air of ethical superiority. They are wise and careful men with good investments. They have inherited fortunes and added to them by directorships, management, handling the wealth created by such as Gollan. They have never gambled on a plane race. Already, as Tabitha and John, in Gollan's absence, conduct them to their cars, they have dismissed the agony of Hackstraw from their minds as a judgment. They are discussing with the wisdom, the weight of their importance, the great subject of important men at that time, the danger of war.

"If the Austrians move—"

"If they don't, they'll be done for. Slav nationalism is out to break up the empire."

"Nationalism; that's the trouble everywhere."

"All the same, the Germans! What ability, what industry, what discipline, what progress. I was amazed. But one must see the danger."

"I don't agree with you. This war scare is based on a complete misunderstanding of the German situation, indeed of the world situation. The interlocking of trade has already made wars impossible. That, I may say, is Ballin's view; he told me so himself. War would ruin us all equally."

"Quite so; but then this naval race."

"And the Slavs."

"Certainly there are dangerous currents."

And having thoroughly perplexed themselves, believing at once that war is inevitable and impossible, they make their important way to the cars. Their black overcoats and tall hats, mostly rather out of fashion, seem to be the only solid and dependable objects in sight. The park, the great trees, the house itself, with its twenty windows in front, appear like the bright canvas and gauze of a transformation scene, which is caused to appear at one moment and disappear at the next, at word of command by some stage manager in a tall hat.

John, full of indignation with them and sympathy with Tabitha, takes her arm. "Thank God they've gone. I think the engineer was the worst. He told me the moving-bench system had always been a failure; it destroys craftsmanship."

"Perhaps he's right; he's a very distinguished man."

67

It is on the tip of the boy's tongue, continuing his instruction of Tabitha, to ask her what she means by a distinguished man, and to point out how dangerously conventional are her ideas of distinction. But he refrains from mere lassitude. Now that the committee has gone, that its decision is known, there is a sense of emptiness and insignificance in the house that extends even to the feelings of those who remain in it. The very servants have a perfunctory air; they know that they are merely filling out their time.

The marquee has been taken from the lawn but no one tries to fill in the holes that it has left.

When Gollan arrives that evening, his first question is about the lawn. "It's a disgrace. What is everyone thinking of?"

"But, James, I thought it was better for the men to help in taking away the marquee; it was costing five pounds a day in rent."

"Damn the tent; we want to make the place look decent, or people will say we're broke. They're saying it now, trust 'em. Yes, they'd like to get me down; they've been counting me out for the last two years."

He is in an aggressive temper with these mysterious enemies who, he assures Tabitha, have been plotting to ruin him. "That fellow Hector has always wanted to write me off." And he exclaims suddenly, "That plane; they knew it was a winner, and so they cut the wires."

The engineers, reporting on the Gollan Robb, have declared that its failure has been due to lack of power, and too small a rudder, but

Gollan has already invented a plot to cut the steering wires. In fact, to his mind, the whole world is full of his enemies who want to destroy him by one move or another.

He is very angry when he hears that Tabitha has given the servants notice. "You'll ruin us, Bertie."

"But have we any money?"

"Money—that's not the trouble; I can always get money." And he exclaims with a new impatience, "You leave all that to me, and get yourself some new frocks. Yes, yes, you've got to look expensive, you've got to show 'em."

"But, James—"

"Now, now—" he makes a gesture as if pushing her out of his way—"you do what I say, it's important. Never mind about the money; just do what I ask."

He is no longer ceremonious. He gives abrupt orders even to Tabitha; he loses his temper and quacks, "Just leave it to me, just do what I say!" When he catches sight of John he makes a face of disgust and waves his hand as if to clear his path of lumber.

And everyone is set to work to remove all traces of the tent, to restore the drives, and within the house to polish and renovate. "We'll show 'em," he says, with that threatening air which has suddenly appeared, even in his gestures.

"I've got a friend coming," he says to Tabitha. "Put on your sparklers."

"For luncheon, James?"

"Yes, yes, now, Bertie; never mind all these rules. The more rules you break, the better; it shows 'em you mean business."

And Tabitha, feeling at once foolish and therefore virtuous, puts on a diamond necklace and earrings to receive a shabby little man called Eckstein, with a worn ivory face and white hair, who comes two hours early for luncheon, and at once begins to run about looking at things. He wants to see the pictures; he is in ecstasy over the furniture, the carpets, the gardens, the roses. His little narrow face, at once so full of worldly cunning and a naïve eager curiosity, wears a perpetual smile, as if to say, "How delightful everything is—how pleasant is life."

He looks at the works and admires them, declares that the moving bench is a stroke of genius—"At least for its advertisement value. We shall write that up, Sir James; you must get it photographed"—and returns again next day with two friends. These are Hackett, a tall bald man with singularly pale eyes, and a certain Gilman, who looks like a prizefighter and talks broad cockney.

These two also go over the works, while Eckstein plays the piano, very badly but with much feeling, to Tabitha; and afterwards Gollan drives them all back to town.

But when he reappears next day, it is only to bring Tabitha a bouquet from Eckstein, and to assure her that she has made a good impression. "He liked you, Bertie—you knocked him; and he's no fool either. He could be a gentleman if he liked—but he didn't care. He'd rather enjoy life."

And when she asks about his plans, he says impatiently, "It's all right, you needn't be afraid."

"But I'm not afraid, James; I only want to know."

He tells her then, carelessly and abruptly, as if putting off a troublesome child, that there is to be a new company called the Hackstraw Halt Engines, to take over the assets of the old, and that he is to have control. "That was the real question—who was to be the boss. But they gave way. I knew I could fix it."

"Do you trust those people, James?"

"Trust 'em? No—a lot of crooks. Now, don't get up on your high horse—it's all right. I've got my eye on 'em, and we understand each other." And then again, looking angrily at Tabitha, as if she were obstructing him, "Why, of course they're crooks; but who else would do the job? Crooks have their uses, Bertie, when you know how to use 'em. They're always good for a gamble, because they've nothing to lose." And he grumbles that Tabitha has worn an old frock for the lunch party. "I told you to get some new frocks. Yes, it's important."

At night he calls upon her to complain that she does not give enough parties. He is a new Gollan, rougher, more impatient; or perhaps the old Gollan of twenty or thirty years before, who has fought his way out of poverty and harried his first wife to death: a driving and ambitious will resurrected by the pique of a failure, as an old neuritis is inflamed by a cold wind. He has even a new voice, rasping and dangerous, and shouts at servants. And when Tabitha remonstrates he says to her, "Do 'em good; a lazy lot; you spoil 'em," and one sees in his irritation a real grudge against these dependents, who, as he thinks, take life easy.

He hardly speaks to John, who, for his part, avoids his stepfather as a traveler in the jungle might avoid a savage wild animal, which could in one moment reduce the most superior dignity, wisdom, and grace to pulp.

But one night after dinner he snaps at him, "You want to go to Oxford?"

"I hadn't really decided. Of course I was entered for this scholarship at St. Mark's."

"Never mind that—you don't need charity; put your name down."

And he proposes to Tabitha to fix the boy's allowance at a thousand a year. When she declares that this is too much, he is offended, and cries, "Too much? Do you think I can't afford it? If the boy goes to Oxford, he wants to do it properly—cut a dash, make 'em jump."

John, of course, now sets to work very hard to take a scholarship; and since he has plenty of brains, and at Bradley a good classical coach, he achieves at the end of six months an exhibition.

Gollan, when he sees the boy's name in *The Times*, and understands that he has won distinction, congratulates him in these terms. "So you've beat 'em; that's the style," and he gives him a small fast tourer. "There you are, that'll show 'em at Oxford; that'll cut 'em down." And he speaks in the same tone as when he declares "Old Billy Kaiser! We'll make his hair curl; we'll trim his mustache up without barber's glue!" The Germans to him are only a special kind of competitor, of enemy, in a world which has tried to ruin him, James Gollan.

68

PEOPLE who said afterwards that it was the armament manufacturers, including Gollan, who made the Kaiser war were of course writing history backwards, and history does not go backwards. The armament manufacturers made war much less than the poets; and it is doubtful if wars need making, any more than the weather. There are always winds of opinion, clouds of imagination, changes of local and national temperature; and electricity is everywhere, lighting lamps and setting fire to steeples. Others, Gollan's admirers, who claimed that he was one of the few big men in the country who foretold the war, were equally deceived.

He was not before the war a big man in the proper sense of the word, and every intelligent person in Europe had foretold the war for twenty-five years. What they did not foresee was the time of its outbreak, its nature, and what they were to do about it. They imagined that peace might last their time; they conceived a war like the last great European war of 1870, which did not cause much more disturbance of private lives in Europe, outside battle areas, than a boom and a slump. As for doing anything about it, if they called for armaments they were accused of provoking it, and if they approached the Germans for an agreement they were snubbed.

It was Gollan's special feat of intuition, that of a very simple man without enough political education to weigh secondary causes, to perceive that the war must come soon, and that it would need mechanical transport. This was why he founded the Gollan Truck Company, Gollan Axles, and Bluetail Bearings.

These, unlike the Hackstraw Engines, were at first private companies, with capital raised in doubtful quarters at high interest. But they enabled Gollan to approach Brighthouses, the great steel firm making armor plate and naval guns; and, later in that year, to become a director.

The financial structure supporting this new group of Gollan companies was probably ramshackle. The more respectable and conservative firms in the city shook their heads at it from the beginning; but Gollan himself was making a large income even before the war, and, by the very fact of his success, causing the conservative financiers to lose prestige.

And this prestige had been sinking for a good many years. That is to say, what had been conservative twenty years before was now considered stick-in-the-mud. The new moneyed power which had replaced the old landed power was not truly conservative at all. It kept up nothing. It had no social theory or standards of its own. It was merely competitive, and had to be so.

Gollan's profits were always a mystery; but he found the money for very large expenses. Hackstraw was now always full of guests, and this was the time of the famous garden parties, to which hundreds of guests were brought by special train; parties where large Gollan shareholders, financiers of every status from the private banker to the company promoter who had just escaped jail, fashionable duchesses and cabinet ministers, were brought together in hopes of mutual advantage; parties in fact which everyone voted dull, vulgar, mixed, but to which everyone went, for the food, the gardens, to see celebrated persons, to get tips for investment, and to talk about for six months afterwards.

And Gollan, having commanded Tabitha to find some new attraction—a band specially brought from Hungary; a diving display—would appear very late, in a tweed suit; and, shaking hands in his impatient careless manner with the nearest persons, would say, "You like this sort of thing? My wife's party. It suits you, does it? I haven't time, I'm too busy."

He says of Tabitha, to whom these events mean simply immense work and anxiety, "She is in her element, ain't she! Well, all you ladies love a party."

He presents John as, "My wife's son. He's a great man for parties. He's amusing himself at Oxford—baccarat and poker and all the fun of the fair. That's the place for spending money!"

And it is hard to say whether the tweed suit, the abrupt tone, and even the crudity of speech, new in the last year, are the arrogance of one who is really contemptuous of others, who is truly a vulgar soul, or an attitude meant to hide the profound boredom of an old man with everybody but one or two intimates, and everything but his private schemes and ambitions.

69

THE guests, new people, who for the most part know neither Tabitha nor any of her local friends, gaze at her as at a showpiece. They see that she is dressed rather too smartly and always too tightly, even for the fashion of that time, so that her small compact form seems to be stiffened within its silk sheath; and perceiving the tense formal manner, a complex of anxiety and preoccupation, and being themselves socially uneasy, being anxious to prove that they themselves, with their new fortunes, are not deceived by Hackstraw's social pretensions, say to each other, "Another of these new rich, trying to climb into society. Why do they do it, working like a black to make themselves ridiculous?"

And studying her without pity or gratitude, they agree that she is obviously a vulgar fool; her very dress, her diamonds, betray her ignorance.

"And tough, too," somebody says.

"Oh, she's an old hand. Gollan took her on for the job. That type of professional hostess is made of brass. All the same, she hasn't caught any royalties yet; they draw the line somewhere."

Tabitha is perfectly aware of this contempt, which blandly examines her, from the eyes of the women, even while they shake hands with her, and utter cries of congratulation upon the weather, the scene, upon her marvelous party. And she offers to them that complete indifference which has given her, at forty, the look of the successful adventuress, the air of the woman who says, "Take me or leave me; why or what should I care?" and with that indifference has the alarming air of an armored weapon. People condescend with Tabitha, but they do not provoke her. She is like one of those metals which are hardened for polish only by thousands of light blows—which if they did not grow hard would be beaten down and broken, and while they grow smooth and impenetrable, also become hot.

And it seems to Tabitha herself, at these great parties, that not only her body is compressed to indecency in the sheath of hard silk, which, gripping her hips and thighs far below the knee, almost prevents her from walking, but her feelings. She is full of impatience, of a kind of positive agonizing boredom which, unable to escape, seethes in her breast, like some acid liquid boiling in a brittle retort. At every moment, even of crisis, when she has to decide quickly what shall be done about this or that, she is pursued by the sense of futility. "But what am I doing? What is the good of it all? I'm forty already; soon I shall be an old woman."

She wonders at the graceful nonchalance of the young men and girls who lounge so cheerfully through a world of parties; and when she thinks, "At least there is John; and I have got him to Oxford in spite of everybody," she is filled again with a new sense of helplessness. For it seems to her that John is surrounded by immense dangers, and that she cannot save him from any of them. He will take no advice from her; indeed, she can be sure that he will go directly against her advice. She has offered her experienced taste to help him in furnishing his rooms, and he has promptly hung them with hideous curtains of the brightest orange, and still more hideous pictures from a new school of artists, who, as she says, think to be original simply by despising the great names of Monet, Renoir, and Degas. He goes driving with Bonser, and entertains actresses. He gambles and drinks. She suspects that he keeps a woman. And she says to herself in angry despair, "It's not as though he were an ordinary boy. He could do anything; he could have a great career."

70

TABITHA has been astonished by John's success, which she has foretold from his childhood. She is still like the young bride who carries her baby for months, and knows that she will delight in it, but when it is born looks upon it with amazement and exclaims to herself, "But what a miracle," and at once she is full of terror at the idea of all the dangers that threaten this minute fragile helpless creature. And women who have never had children seem to her both pathetic in their ignorance of the world and lucky in their peace of mind.

When John, after a great deal of hard work, carefully dissembled, scrapes a first in classics, her delight brings at once the fear, "But now he will think that he doesn't need to work—he never takes anything seriously."

John laughs at her. "What are you worrying about now, Mother? You can't do without worry; if it isn't bills, it's the war."

"You don't want a war, do you, John?"

"No; but I think Jim's right. I don't see how we can avoid war. Tirpitz couldn't stop building ships, or his precious followers would sack him; and if Germany goes on building, we'll have to fight. And really, you know, war would clear the air."

His voice expresses his annoyance at this oppressive anxiety, which prevents him from enjoying himself. He is greedy for the new pleasures which every day offer themselves to him. He has been traveling and gambling abroad. He sees the road races at Milan, and takes the fancy to be a racing motorist. He demands a road racer of his own.

"Road racing is fearfully dangerous," Tabitha says; and this rash objection is enough to fix his resolve. He asks Gollan's advice, and Gollan, with that condescension which he now shows to the young man, the air of one who indulges a spoilt puppy with lump sugar, orders him a special road racer from the Hackstraw works, with a Hackstraw engine.

This car, an enormous two-seater, at once becomes the delight of John's life and the misery of Tabitha's. And it is John's peculiar pleasure to inflict the misery. He loves to drive his mother at sixty miles an hour along dangerous roads, to see her pale and tense, to know that she is in terror. He is like the lover who tortures his sweetheart because he is tired of kindness, because his love demands a new kind of gratification.

He succeeds, toward the end of that year, in winning a race at Brooklands. And Gollan is pleased with the advertisement for his engine. He forms at once a plan to beat the hour record, and enters the car next year, with a new engine, for the road tests at Leipzig. He picks German trials on purpose, saying, "It's quite time we showed the Fritzes what we can do."

John warmly agrees with this suggestion. He is interested in German philosophy; he wants to learn German, and he is attracted by this energetic people whose ambition and whose inventive energy alarms the world almost as much as Napoleon's a hundred years before.

In late June, therefore, after the end of term, he sets out for Southampton with two mechanics and with Gollan, who proposes to see the machine embarked.

Tabitha, as usual nervous when John is in the car, and therefore restless, spends the morning with the housekeeper in a critical survey of stores.

At eleven a footman brings a wire. "Slight accident to car. Come to Brent hospital. Jim."

Tabitha arrives, after a long slow journey, at a small cottage hospital. Gollan receives her on the steps. His right arm is in a sling, but his injury is only a large bruise. John has a fractured skull and a broken arm, a compound fracture of the right leg and possible damage to the spine. He has been unconscious ever since the accident, and it is doubtful if he will live. But Gollan has sent for a specialist and is full of confidence, the optimism of a busy man who does not want to be worried by anxiety. "Johnny's young—he enjoys life. He'll want to get well—that's better than any of your doctors."

But Tabitha, with white face and enormous eyes, answers only, "I knew it would happen."

"My dear Bertie, how could you know?"

"Because we had no business to give him such a car. We knew it was too big for his strength."

"Believe me, Bertie, we were crawling—under twenty. Johnny's not such a bad driver—always careful at crossings. It was the other bus that ran into us. A damned young fool, going at fifty, and didn't even sound his horn."

"It's what I say: boys oughtn't to have cars."

"They've got to start some time. John is twenty." Gollan is impatient.

"I don't know why road racing was ever allowed."

"My dear Bertie, these road races have already put fifty miles an hour on the speed of cars."

"But who wants to go so fast? What is the good?"

Gollan makes a face as if to say, "It's no good talking to the woman. She'll never understand."

The specialist arrives from town at five. He is at once hopeful and depressing. He says cheerfully that he has seen such cases recover with proper nursing; he is plainly doubtful of the nursing at this hospital; he is against moving the patient because any shaking may do fatal damage.

The boy is unconscious for three weeks. One day when the local doctor has paid his visit, he remarks to Tabitha, "So we've got this war."

Tabitha, who has not looked at a paper for three weeks, answers, "What—in Ireland?"

"No, Germany has invaded Belgium."

"Yes. My son said it would happen."

"It will soon be over, thank goodness. The Belgian forts are impregnable."

71 A WEEK later it seems that Paris must fall; but Tabitha is full of happiness because John has opened his eyes and recognized her. She reflects, "The war will be over before he is strong enough to fight; he is saved from the war."

But this reflection is followed at once by the thought, "How selfish that is; how wicked I am."

She is glad when the patient can be moved to Hackstraw, where the whole of one wing has already been turned into a hospital, because, as she says, "I ought to be doing something to help."

And she throws herself into the work with a desperate energy. She is glad to tire herself. Her work, in fact, is an offering, an expiation. It is an appeal to some unknown power. "Don't punish me; I am trying to make reparation."

After the first six months of war, and the long deadlock on the Somme, there is already a deep anxiety and also simplicity. People do not hide their feelings, and speak of their fears and doubts. The churches are crowded, and Tabitha finds that others as well as herself are pursued by guilt. Young soldiers denounce the egotism of the civilized world, and declare that everything must be changed.

Tabitha, coming from morning service with the absorbed air of one who has had a new and a powerful experience, is met by John as he struggles on two sticks along the terrace. He grins at her. "A good sermon?"

"Yes; it was about sin and egotism."

"I know; the war is a punishment."

Tabitha gazes at him with parted lips, as if about to speak. She has a sense of revelation. Words like love, sin, guilt, have come suddenly alive to her, and the world makes sense. She can't imagine why she has been blind and deaf before; that after three years of church-going and a thousand sermons, she has only just perceived that all love is from God, that to use the word love, and mean it, is to believe in God.

And so, too, it seems plain to her that to deny love, to be selfish, cruel, is to bring punishment. Has not the war come upon the world because of man's selfishness and self-seeking? It is so obvious to her that she can only marvel that the whole world does not see it and fall on its knees to ask forgiveness. She says to John at last with a note of urgency, "Don't you think it is terrible enough?"

But before he can speak she moves away. She is afraid of some retort which she will not be able to answer, and which therefore may do harm, not to her, because her faith is beyond argument, but to John himself. She thinks, "He's only a boy still, and cleverness is everything to him. He's not old enough to understand *real* things."

And John, looking at her, says to himself, "Her Sunday look again. Who'd have thought Mother would get religion."

But while Tabitha, to John's irritation, has become attentive to sermons, Gollan stops going even to the Hackstraw pew on Sunday mornings. War has simplified life for him as well as others. Like a powerful light thrown from the wings of a stage, which abolishes a mass of detail, and reveals the characters in black and white, it has given him his chief significance. As some society women who have seemed merely experts in passing the time are now discovered to be responsible souls; as trivial creatures, popular and entertaining, are revealed as monsters of spite and meanness; as the ambitious grab and the unscrupulous rob with a new barefaced openness, so the natural organizers, the born drivers and bosses, appear as if by word of command. Every village, every street, discovers that so and so, who seemed like everyone else, is the natural and obvious person to call a meeting, to form a policy, to be obeyed.

Gollan, among dozens of manufacturers, is not only perceived to be a leader, but knows himself to be such. And being such a character, he gives himself wholly to the work. He has no time for anything else. He declares that the vicar, with his extra communion services, attracting workers from the factory, is a danger, and has no real sense of emergency. He is highly impatient when, before breakfast, he misses Tabitha from her room. For him the cause of the war is nothing in human nature or the state of the world; it is a criminal attempt, long prepared, by Germany to dominate Europe and destroy Britain; and as for egotism, he cries out every day, "What we want is leaders. Give me a man who can take responsibility." He himself has been made a production chief under the Ministry of Supply, which he abuses continually; but the Hackstraw factories now spread over half the park, and nine great chimneys smoke day and night beyond the wood. The old workshops in the yard are given to research, and there is unlimited money for experiments. As Gollan says frequently, with warm satisfaction, "The war is a curse, but it has done one good thing: it's given our inventors a chance. It's pushed forward car design by about ten years, and planes by twenty—not to speak of surgery. Wonderful what the surgeons are doing. Well, look at Johnny."

72 IN FACT John has profited by the very rapid development of surgery due to the concentrated practice of the war. Though he cannot walk without irons, he is promised a complete cure.

At Easter, 1915, he is back at St. Mark's, reading philosophy, much interested especially in Bergson, who is still the reigning novelty. And now he has gone so far away from Tabitha that she does not even try to share his interests. She comes as a visitor from another world, and John receives her in the same mode. The whims of her female brain, her new religious fancies, are so remote that they do not trouble him. When she is surprised that he has not heard the latest war news, he answers with the very air of Sloop, which has once enraged her, "Perhaps you're right; one does get a bit detached."

But plainly he thinks this detachment an excellent thing; and Tabitha does not criticize it. She thinks, "No doubt it is the proper thing at Oxford."

For with John's friends—a major of twenty-two, who has lost an arm, a scholar who has been gassed, a blind man who is writing a thesis on the two Napoleons, an American, two undergraduates in hospital blue—she feels equally at a loss. They are charming to her, entertain her in their rooms, take her up the river; but she is always aware of that special politeness, that patient courtesy shown to an intruder. While one makes polite conversation with her, she hears among the others fragments of private talk, much more exciting and important to them, about essays and lectures, about the necessity of change, the nature of the eternal creativity.

And John, at every moment, will turn from her, to interject, with a quite different tone of voice, with the indignation of serious concern, some objection or suggestion.

But in this new relation, from which something has been lost, something exciting, barbarous, they no longer quarrel. They have established a formal kindness. John, as he conducts his mother through the square of the schools, limping slowly by her side toward Broad Street, where Gollan is to meet her, invents conversation which may please.

"How nice of you to come when you're so busy; you quite livened us up."

"But I love coming, and your friends are so nice. I suppose the Major is the cleverest, he looks the cleverest."

"It doesn't go altogether by looks. He's more keen than clever, you mustn't take him too seriously on Bergson," and he gives a little discourse, simplified for mothers, on Bergson's theory of time.

Tabitha looks at him with an attentive air, and thinks, "He really is brilliant, and if he hasn't quite got Dick's features, he looks much more distinguished. Oh, how right I was to insist on Oxford; he's happy and he's safe."

"Have you heard a word, Mother?"

"Oh yes; you were saying something about the Major?"

"Never mind." He smiles at her without the least pique, from his new detachment, his new exciting elevation of thought. "Why should you care about a lot of queer notions?"

And when they reach the car, Gollan snorts, "Talking philosophy, you two. Atoms, atoms, that's the stuff. Atoms and electricity. Of course I'm not against the Church, the Church has got its own job. But it's all electricity, really; pushing the atoms round. Come on, Bertie, we've got to be at Cowley in five minutes."

Tabitha gets into the back seat next the typist, and Gollan shouts his good-bys, "Don't work too hard, Johnny. Have a good time." And as they roll away, he says to Tabitha, "You might have a look at that report." Tabitha feels that she is once more swallowed up by the world at war, full of suffering and despair. What she calls the real world. She thinks, as she opens the report, "John is not in the real world at all"; and her thankfulness and her guilt increase. She opens the report. Her escape is in work, which grows every day. For though she is not Gollan's official secretary, she is indispensable to him. He leaves to her all his private letters and most of the official reports, saying, "Tell me if there's anything in 'em."

It is no good for her to protest that she does not understand the technical points; he answers, "All right, get Robb to explain. But don't ask Smyth; he'll put me up against the wall—and I've no time." Smyth is the official secretary: an important and conscientious man, despised by Gollan because he is a civil servant. "They put him in to keep an eye on me—don't tell him anything, the black beetle."

73

THE black beetle, or fly, is Gollan's name for all government clerks, in their black coats and bowlers. "Buzzing about the larder and turning good meat into maggots." He is at perpetual war with the government, the civil service—especially his own department. But he has an immense reputation built up by the Ministry themselves to reassure the public. The papers describe how he works ten or twelve hours a day, wearing out relays of secretaries. Manklow, in the Ducat Press, has made him a symbol of "victory at the bench." His name, like Kitchener's, is one of those selected by a private committee of the cabinet and turned into magic which gives faith. It is also for this reason that he is encouraged to travel like a potentate. His fleet of enormous cars, full of politicians, experts, and county magnates, whirls across England, leaving everywhere the legend "That's Gollan on the job." And everywhere there are rising new factories, if not sited by him, designed in his name, of which many will not be ready for production within five years. But this again is held for a virtue, because it reminds everyone of his saying, "The tenth year will be the clincher." Such utterances make people laugh, and in the laughter, for some reason, a desperate confidence is born. Even Gollan's age has become a merit in him, because it carries with it the idea of wisdom and makes a greater miracle of his energy.

His obstinacy, his refusal to take advice, are terrifying to his staff, which expects every day some enormous disaster, some scandal which will ruin the department. But when colleagues write furious letters, Tabitha or one of the secretaries intercepts them and gives only a polite paraphrase. For if Gollan does by chance hear a word of criticism or abuse, he is so much upset that he does his work in even more summary fashion. He cries, "My God, do they think I'm enjoying myself? Do they think I like working myself to death?" And it is obvious that he really believes himself to be oppressed, that he does not notice his own enjoyment; he is immersed in it like a salmon in a freshet, which struggles and no doubt protests, but still must drive on.

Deeply offended by some chance word in a political speech, he keeps Tabitha awake half the night to complain, "The old men who made the war! What old men? The Kaiser is a boy—the boy who never grew up. It was boys who shot the Archduke; it is a lot of boys who started the Irish rebellion. As if I wanted war. Look at the stuff we're turning out; it's a disgrace."

Tabitha is not given to panic, and this has won her a reputation for usefulness even among the secretaries, usually so scornful of wives. It is agreed that these religious women can be relied upon for hard work, and especially thankless troublesome work, and that religion in wartime probably pays a good dividend.

Irreverent clerks phone, "The old man is biting the carpets—for God's sake find Bertie and push her along." And he is never allowed to sleep away from her. For it is in the small hours that he is most restless, and most in need of support. Tabitha knows the answer to each special grievance, and can give it with the right tone of conviction.

To the everlasting complaint of red tape, she says, "But you must have clerks and files." To the cry that some equipment has failed, she remarks, as if discovering the point for the first time, "But these things have to be turned out so quickly there's no time to finish them properly."

"Finish—they're not even tested! It's awful. My poor old father would beat his head on his coffin, break out of his grave. But he was a real tradesman; he had a conscience."

"People don't understand."

"Of course they understand. They know as well as you do. But they're angry, they're cross. They hate this blinking war, it's getting on their nerves. It's beating them, and so they shout a lot of nonsense. But I'll resign—"

Now and then he does send in his resignation, but the Ministry at once appeal to him to withdraw it. It is hinted that while young men are dying for their country, old men should be prepared to work, even under abuse. A harried assistant secretary calls upon Tabitha with a bouquet and compliments. Will she use her valuable influence? Is there anything that could be done? Does the shoe pinch upon some private corn? Is the old man annoyed that old Billie has got a peerage? Would he like a peerage? Or another secretary? Would Tabitha like him to have a peerage? Would she like a D.B.E., or would she prefer a week end at Windsor? Can she make the old man understand that he is indispensable?

John, who is present at one of these interviews, asks the young assistant secretary, "But is he?" The other, quick, ambitious, college bred, instantly recognizes in John a related spirit, and answers with raised eyebrows, a shrug of the whole face, "How can you tell? If he went there would be a terrific row in Parliament, and all sorts of rumors in the factories; perhaps a first-class crisis."

"And if he doesn't go, there'll be a fine mess."

Again a shrug. "But there might be a worse one if somebody else had done the job. After all, there always is a mess, isn't there?"

"A bloody mess."

"You can hardly expect a game of skill when half the pack consists of jokers."

"And all the players carry guns."

The two young men smile at each other like members of some secret cult. For the whole evening John wears the relics of a smile, as if to say, "It's a funny world; and the more you know of it, the funnier it looks."

74 John is waiting for the results of his final examination, and meanwhile assisting in the office. In consultation with a young woman called Brett, who is Smyth's chief secretary at Hackstraw, he opens the mail and decides what is worth taking to Smyth. It amuses him to find how much power resides in this young woman's hands; she decides what shall have priority, that is to say, often, what shall be attended to, and what is trash to be thrown away, that is, circulars, letters from cranks, religious institutions. She uses her own judgment about what is a crank, and puts nearly all inventors in that category.

"Here's a suggestion for rocket guns," John says. "What about it?"

"Basket," says the young woman briefly. "We get those every week."

"It's been tried, has it?"

"No, but it's silly; you've only got to look at it."

And when John argues that it might be worth examining, she grows peevish, and says, "Oh well, if you know better, you'd better take over. But Smythy won't thank you for covering his desk with fancy notions; he hasn't time."

"I suppose that's the real trouble. There's no time to go into things."

"Well, look at the mail, and it gets worse every day."

"It's really a question of selectors, all the way up."

The young woman merely looks cross. John says no more, because he perceives already that what is called an office machine is more like a nervous ganglion. Brett's feelings mustn't be upset or Smyth will also suffer, and Gollan will be badly served and some army commander will be short of trucks or ammunition, and soldiers will die. He therefore discreetly plays his part as Brett's pupil, and follows his own thoughts. Gollan, indeed, is hardly aware of his presence. He breakfasts now, when he is at home, in Tabitha's room, and lunches in his office. He is seldom seen except when he hurries across the hall to some inspection, with his train of courtiers—Tabitha on the right; Smyth, pale, worried, resigned, a step to the rear; two anxious young experts ready to fly into statistics at a glance, behind Smyth; and two typists for a tail. When he catches sight of John he stops with an air of amazement and cries, "Hullo, Johnny, you here! It's the holidays, is it? And what next? Whitehall in a beetle bowler?"

"I suppose with this leg it will have to be an office."

"Or Parliament. Either the talking shop or the scribbling shop. Oh, Johnny, to think you might have been an engineer! And when are you going to do your Romans?"

"Do you mean the final examination? I've finished with that. I'm—"

But Gollan has not waited for an answer. He is already jerking out of the door at a speed which gives to the whole party the undignified appearance of beggars hastening after a tourist.

Nevertheless, John is part of the ganglion. He is a nerve center, valuable for special reactions. His mother wires to him for private papers. Smyth sends him down to the works to find out, with tact, why a certain manager wants to leave. Has he been tempted away or is he disgruntled? And in these missions he shows valuable sensitivity to atmosphere. He is also good, with long experience of essays, at a report. Thus, although he takes his first, he is advised to stay at Hackstraw in charge of a new department of industrial relations. He acquires a secretary of his own, but further offends his stepfather. "Hello, Johnny. So you've got a job!"

"Yes, sir, I'm running this new office for you—Industrial Relations."

"Industrial poppycock; it's not my office. They pushed it on me. Lots of scribble, scribble. And one scribble breeds another. How's the time, Smythy?"

"We're late, sir."

"What are we doing here then? Come along, man. I hate being late; tell 'em to step on it." Gollan, after two years of war, declares that hard work suits him—it makes him younger.

In fact he looks even older than his age. He is now completely bald; his face is sunken and wrinkled like a dried bladder, in which his little glittering eyes seem the only live thing; he has shrunk down a couple of inches in height, so that he appears all legs and arms; and he is very deaf. He knows of his deafness; he talks incessantly to avoid being talked to; and because of his weakness he throws himself into vigorous attitudes, and shouts, "Hurry up, I'm waiting. There's a war on, you know."

75

ONE day John is summoned by telephone to the London office of Gollan Industries. A mysterious voice tells him to come at once, and to tell no one where he is going. He will be met at the door. He leaves by fast car and is met by a clerk and led to a small office on the top floor where Gollan is lying on the carpet with his head in Tabitha's lap. His eyes are closed, he breathes heavily, and now and then utters strange grunts. His collar is open, and Tabitha is holding a glass of water. Smyth, a typist, and a clerk are standing round.

Tabitha, who has that air usual to her in a crisis, of being unnaturally calm because she is uncommonly moved, looks up and says, "We must have a doctor *at once*! Could you telephone, John?"

At this the sick man utters a louder grunt and raises one hand. It appears that he is protesting against doctors; he struggles as if trying to get up.

John stoops down. "But, Jim, you're ill; you must lie down for a moment. Don't you think you'd better have a doctor?"

A strange harsh voice whispers, "Who—?" and then, "John!" The claw-like hand moves feebly in the air and grasps at John's coat. "John—John—"

"Yes, Jim?"

"Not stroke—" The old man's hand falls away and he sinks back. "Saw ri'—awri'—in mint—fi' mint."

Tabitha shakes her head and looks frowning at John. She is commanding him to get a doctor.

John glances at Smyth, and the two go out into the corridor. "It's very like a stroke; oughtn't we to have some advice?"

The official makes a face. "But is it safe, up here in these offices? Stone is somewhere in the building; he'd leak at once."

"I see; you're afraid that the Press—"

"Any rumor of an illness would be very unfortunate just now, after this Russian collapse. It was a great piece of luck that the chief was up here when he fell. Luckily the typist had the sense to send for me first."

"If we could only get him to Hackstraw, we could send for Bain; you can trust Bain—a Scotch oyster."

Suddenly Tabitha appears beside them. She startles both the men by her look and voice. "Have you sent for a doctor yet? He may be dying. Where's the telephone?"

John and Smyth look at each other in alarm, as if to say, "Now what? She doesn't understand; women never do grasp a big issue." How are they to explain to her that Gollan's death is a risk that should be taken? The man's function is so important that, like one of those ancient kings whose sacred power set them apart from the touch even of a doctor, he is outside common humanity.

"That would be taking a very grave responsibility, Lady Gollan, and against the chief's express wish," Smyth says nervously.

"I think we ought to be careful, Mother."

"Careful." Tabitha brushes them aside. "But it's murder," and she insists on telephoning for a doctor.

Luckily, while she is telephoning, and before a doctor can be found, the typist runs in to say that she has brought the luggage lift to the top floor, and it is waiting.

Smyth, John, and the two clerks at once carry Gollan to the lift and prop him on a packing case. He himself is anxious only to help. He clings to John. "You stay with me, Johnny. Quite awri'. Not stroke. Keep it from papers."

"We'll keep it quiet."

"Yes, qui—keep qui—no fool taw—gemme home quick."

The clerk has already fetched a taxi to the yard. In less than an hour Gollan is at Hackstraw, where he insists on walking to bed to show the servants that he is in good health. And even now he will not have the doctor. He repeats as they put him to bed, "No doctor—people will talk if see doctor—don't want talk. Johnny, you stay." And watching Tabitha with a suspicious glint, he mutters, "Awri', Bertie, Johnny'll stay—I'm awri' now." Tabitha takes the hint and leaves the room.

And when next morning Gollan leaves for what is called an inspection tour in the north, but is really a week's holiday in an obscure seaside village on the North Wales coast, he takes John with him as well as Tabitha. He no longer trusts Tabitha. He is afraid, with a cunning desperation, that she will betray him to the doctors.

"Don't you fuss about me, Bertie. You women are a lot of fusspots; I'm all right."

In fact after the week's rest he appears as vigorous as ever. He is perhaps a little more erratic in movement—he is apt to trip over his own feet; and his stream of talk sometimes breaks off in the middle. But when this happens in public, Smyth or John, or both, are ready with some appropriate remark; and the old man moves on, as if he had finished.

All Smyth's precautions have not prevented gossip. As usual in such cases, the rumors seem to spring up of themselves, and take at once an extreme form. To Smyth's indignation. it is said that Gollan has had a stroke.

"Which is almost certainly true," John says.

"There's no evidence for it; that's the great danger of talk, it's so utterly irresponsible."

But the very rumor, hinted in one or two obscure papers, makes John more necessary to Gollan. The old man scarcely lets him out of his sight. He needs him not only to interpret his wishes, but to guard him from close observation.

He is now very affectionate again. He says to John, "Hard work.

I'm working you hard; but it'll all be yours. I'm leaving you the Halt and the foundry. You're looking after your own."

He must have John's devotion and does not care what it costs. Millions are nothing to him if he can keep his job, his field of action. He introduces John as the heir to Hackstraw and its works, even to the Stones, who receive the news with decent approval. For one thing, they are assured of two-thirds of the estate, invested in Gollan Industries; for another, they regard Gollan once more as a great genius. They tell how he has built up the Halt factories from nothing in less than ten years, and Hector quotes him to board meetings. "My father-in-law says so and so, and I think we may trust his judgment. He has practically won the war for us."

Gollan dreads and hates Stone, and does not like even to be too closely approached by his daughter. He is afraid that they will detect some change in his appearance. He grumbles to John, "Keep the flies off me, keep 'em off the old carcass, I've too much work to do; no time to waste."

And even the inner circle of the court—John, Tabitha, Smyth—cannot decide that he is not still doing useful work. For not only does he possess the magic power of his reputation, he is still full of nervous fire which, if it resembles more the working of some fever than the warmth of vitality, is effective. In some respects it is more effective. For the old man is more impatient, more suspicious. He is more dangerous to a defaulter and will not hear of difficulties. At the least criticism or opposition, he cries out like an angry child, "I know. I know all that; but just you do what I say, what I tell you. There's a war on. There's no time for talking; no time, anywhere."

And under this pressure of impatience and intolerance, extraordinary feats are performed; production rises in a steeper curve; the minister sends his compliments, and when John suggests that the old man needs a rest is much perturbed. "Not just now; you know what people will say. Those rumors did a lot of harm. No, I rely on you and what's his name—Smith—Smyth—to keep him going; at least till the present crisis is over."

76

But there is always a crisis. The Russian armies are broken; the Bolsheviks have made peace. The Passchendaele offensive has collapsed; bogged in mud, shot to pieces. The German armies released from the Russian front are gathering for a new, a greater attack.

There are prayers for victory in the churches; new agitations by pacifists; mysterious negotiations; wild rumors; an outcry against generals, bishops, the supply departments and the profiteers.

Tabitha is especially bitter against the profiteers. Although her approach to the Church has been so gradual, a slow breakdown of prejudice, less a discovery of her mind than a change in her soul brought about merely by the cruelty of experience, she has some of the narrowness of the convert. She is angry with the wicked who do not perceive the immense obvious truth which has changed her own life.

One night there is a scene. She has taken Gollan, after a long committee of Hackstraw Industries, to supper at a restaurant, where John is to meet them. It is late, and after the theaters close the place is filled by supper parties, of which one large party in a corner, six or seven young women being entertained by three much older men, is very noisy. Their laughter and giggles penetrate even Gollan's deafness, and he twists his head round to look. Tabitha exclaims in a furious voice, "Some of these profiteers."

She hates these people and their gaiety; she feels that they are like brawlers in a church: blasphemers whose wickedness may bring down a punishment on a whole people. "They ought to be turned out," she says loudly. And the supper party glance over their shoulders. They are laughing at her, and become even more noisy.

Suddenly John comes in and is immediately hailed by this very party. Tabitha recognizes, in a broad back and thick neck hitherto turned toward her, Dick Bonser; and next him, Millie Minter of the Comedy theater. Bonser, as everyone knows, is keeping this girl and financing her new piece.

Tabitha gets up quickly to go, and Gollan, interrupting his own monologue about the sins of the War Office, slowly rises with a confused air. The supper party, which is also on its feet, surrounding John with cries of acclamation, is barring the way to the door. But Tabitha, chin in air, walks through it, and meeting John in its midst, says to him loudly, meaning to be overheard, "How can you speak to such people, drinking and laughing here while men are being killed?"

John takes her arm and quickly guides her through the press. Gollan, not understanding what has happened, follows, still talking about the War Office.

"I'm sorry, Mother—" John, wrapping her in her cloak, wears an apologetic air—"but I can't cut my own father."

"Why not? He never cared for you."

"And then, you know, we have certain business relations with the Bilman group. Gollan Industries uses a lot of rubber."

And in the car he brings up the subject of war hysteria, criticizing the newspapers.

"I don't know what you think, Mother, but it seems to me rather a bad sign, as if people were losing their nerve."

He is trying, in a polite manner, to tell Tabitha that she is allowing her religion to carry her away, that she is in danger of hysteria; he is expressing also a certain disappointment in her.

In the last few years John has learnt to admire his mother as a woman of the world: narrow, autocratic, extravagant, and impatient, but charming in her poise, her frankness, her sense of dress, her ease of approach. He has been ashamed for her in that scene. He does not perceive that she, too, is changing, developing, every year.

"Of course the mob is always ready to believe any rubbish, but I always hoped we wouldn't get too mobby. Don't you think that all this stunt about night life is a bit cheap? After all, night life is the usual thing in wartime; there was a gallant colonel there tonight. And really one can't blame soldiers for wanting a little amusement."

And Tabitha listens, not to the arguments, but to the voice, so calm, so reasonable. For a long time she has been oppressed by a sense of guilt far deeper than her old shame in her safety. She thinks, "James warned me that Oxford would ruin him; and it has ruined him. It's made him heartless, shallow."

As they get out at last, she says with a sigh, "Don't you really feel how wrong it is?"

"What is wrong, Mother? Not to let the war get you down? No, I can't say I do."

"Oh, it's not that."

"What is it, then?"

But she does not answer. She can't describe her feeling that she has destroyed a human soul, and that of her only son.

And John has no intention of being cut off from any part of his experience. It seems to him that he has only just learnt how to enjoy life. He enjoys being an important person, who, as Gollan's right-hand man, sits in committee with other important persons; and it is a special pleasure, after such a conference with officials, with committee men like Stone and Smyth, essential string pullers, forever weighing their words and composing their expressions, forever diplomatic, purposeful, to go to some party of Bonser's, where everybody is bent only on enjoyment, and does not hide the fact; where there are no pretenses.

Of Bonser's old syndicate, one is dead, killed at the front, and one in jail. His new associates are all pirates of the same kind. Bonser himself, in fact, and all his circle, are what Tabitha calls profiteers, that is, adventurers who have seized a chance of fortune. That mysterious and complex being, the nation, which is fighting for its life, that mother country which they all profess to love, is, like all mothers, a prey. The Unions have picked her pockets, which she can't protect, of a thousand millions; and mill girls have fur coats which three years before would have looked well on a duchess. Skilled craftsmen earn more than vicars, and working-class households draw in a thousand a year. Small manufacturers, builders, tradesmen, dealers, men who were laborers and now own a shed, some shovels, ladders, and picks, are making more than a judge or a prime minister. The restaurants are full day and night of the new rich, the new successful, whose faces show the joy of triumph, whose every gesture is full of eagerness to seize on the delights of life. And these very new rich, rich in that joy of life which is called vulgar because it is triumphant, can be seen at the stations saying good-by to their sons, packed off to die in the mud: the women, in their new silks and furs, their new arrogance copied from some stage copy of what they take for a lady, weeping down their new paint tears as honest as their greed; the men, shiny cheeked with guzzling and self-satisfaction, calling out, "God bless you, God bless you," with the true fervor of prayer.

"I take off my hat to the boys," Bonser says to John, resting his hand, decorated with a large diamond ring, on his son's shoulder. "My God, to think what they go through. War is a terrible thing, John, but it's done one good thing. It's made us realize what a lot of nobility there is in the world; it's made us understand that what really matters is the heart, the soul. Look at the feeling even in the pubs, the getting together. I see that some parson has been going to the pub in his village. That's the spirit, Johnny. What the country needs is true Christian fellowship."

His flat at Jermyn Street is crowded day and night. Privates, still stiff with Flanders clay, plod from the train and sleep on the floor; officers, come to town for their last days of leave, bring their wives or their girls, and use the beds and the sofas; chorus girls and chorus boys give parties and discuss their theatrical affairs till midnight; it is a neutral ground, where all meet in a comradeship not of the war but of pleasure, of life. Young anxious wives spending their last hours with their husbands, young prostitutes giving some second lieutenant a good time at his own expense, drink together without resentment. And often when Bonser comes in, red, glistening, bursting out of his clothes with hospitable glory, and shouts, "How's everybody? Here, what about a spot of something; what about some fizz?" they ask each other, "Who's that bloody man?" Probably half his guests never know him. They bring each other, loot the cupboards, give their orders, and depart.

"Chaps tell me I'm a mug to be used as I am," he says to John; "and of course a lot of these chaps do take advantage. Why, I can't keep a cigar in the place. But damn it, Johnny, I'm not a hunks. And we've got a tradition, you and me; it's in the blood. We're Hapsburgs on the mother's side; we've got a certain standard." And as he waves his great red hand with its ring, he is, to his own feeling, royalty, possessing by nature grandeur of soul, a generosity which is as much his curse as his virtue.

"I don't expect thanks," he says, "because it's something I can't help; it's me, that's all."

77

JOHN is full of laughter, but not of derision. He almost loves his father at such moments, with a love compounded of a pure kindness and the delighted admiration given to a poet in the high flight of his invention. And in this delight he feels a liberation. He has the joy of one who watches a good play and also knows the actors. He can appreciate them twice over, as performers and as friends.

"How is Millie doing at the Comedy?" he asks Bonser.

"She's a marvel, Johnny; that's why the critics were down on the show. They're jealous because she's come to the top so quickly. Those notices were an outrage. She was crying afterwards—she just crept into my arms and sobbed like a child. I don't mind saying it brought the tears to my own eyes. It's a cruel world, John. Why should a dear little thing like Millie be made to suffer so fearfully?"

According to rumor, the production at the Comedy has cost twenty thousand pounds and is losing a thousand a week. Neither has he secured the young woman for himself. She treats him with great rudeness and is living with her leading man. Bonser, paying court to her, falling on his knees, weeping, fondling, and finally being permitted to take a modest kiss, is a celebrated turn which, her friends say, is by far her best performance.

John sometimes suggests the question, among Bonser's friends, whether Millie will not ruin him; and whether he ought not to be rescued from her. But the very suggestion is received with scorn. "Just you try it," a certain Rose answers him one evening, in the bedroom, "and see what you get."

Rose is an ex-chorus girl who has married a young guardsman and accepted a divorce by family arrangement. She is a great foolish creature of fifty, who drinks too much and mourns her weakness. She treats John with amused tolerance, as a child in the world, and he sleeps with her because she exacts no show of special affection, no hypocrisy. She gives him a friendly accommodation.

"But we could prove that she's unfaithful."

"He wouldn't believe you, and it would spoil his fun, too. All the fun he's getting, poor boy."

"How could it spoil his fun if he didn't believe it?"

"Oh, go on, little boy; you know what I mean. It's what they all say, you ought to be a teacher."

John is annoyed by a charge which seems to accuse him of interfering in another's business. "I'm sorry, Rose, but I'm sure I never tried to teach anybody anything; it wouldn't be any good, would it?"

"There you go again! You're not really sorry; you're laughing at me. You laugh at me even when you—but I'm too much of a lady."

"Why, Rose, I couldn't do without you. I'm awfully fond of you."

"Yes, but you laugh, you laugh at us all, that's what makes some of them cross. All right, I won't spoil it, since you've only got a short time. Go to it, little feller, and then you can pour me a snifter. Poor Tommy got his yesterday. That's the fourth of my boys. I want to cry. I can't stand all this killing." And afterwards, the big soft creature to whom the war is measured by the deaths of her lovers, drinks and weeps, gently mourning both the dead and her own drunkenness. "Oh, it's so bad for me."

Everyone at the flat drinks. Young brides, who have never touched spirits before, sip their whiskies and lose their shyness. Astonishing confessions are heard. Young officers talk treason; young whores describe their first longings; some stranger announces suddenly that he's been converted to religion. There are long discussions about God, and the meaning of the world. One night John, escaped twenty minutes before from a conference at the Ministry, but already a little drunk and full charged with the mood of Jermyn Street, describes how at school he has practiced secret exercises to make himself taller; and it pleases him to feel that he is braving public contempt. For that, too, is a breaking out, a gesture of willfulness.

78

IN FACT, some girl remarks that little Johnny may be little, but he's quite enough for her, and raises a laugh.

For John, as a civilian in wartime, and heir to millions, is fair game to the envious. Total strangers bawl at him, "Get me a whisky, will you, Johnny?" "I say, Johnny, you might fit my piece in somewhere; she's parked on the stairs."

One girl, Poppy, after long stares and much spiteful cogitation, has decided to call him the professor; to another, Ruth, he is Cuthbert. Subalterns, over many whiskies, consult him about their problems. They ask him if Bertrand Russell knows his stuff, if pacifism is the way out. The same men, in another mood, will try to make him look foolish.

But all this, which years before would have enraged the schoolboy, now gives a certain elation. His ready good humor defies spite. It seems that the mob intuition is right: he really does belong to a different world. Even in drink he has a certain independence, a private place of what Rose calls laughter, but which is more like a certain contemplative serenity. In Jermyn Street he is one of the crowd, irresponsible, at liberty, but because of the crowd he is also apart; because of his liberation he can be amused by insults.

"Look here, chaps," Poppy calls loudly, "teacher is tight." She is savage against John because he is not unhappy, because he is well off; and she knows that he hates the name of Teacher.

It is three of these girls, including Poppy, who one night, with John and two soldiers who appear to be of the most friendly kind, join a riot in the Circus, and in getting away manage to leave John in the hands of the police. He is tripped as he turns to fly and carried off to the cells. The police have no mercy for young civilians who make a nuisance of themselves; he is fined, and the magistrate makes some severe remarks about young men who if they are fit enough to break the law are also to be presumed fit to fight.

Unluckily, there are many attacks at that moment in the Press on what are called the Cuthberts, that is, civilians exempted from the army. "Stepson of Production Chief Arrested" is the headline; and John's case is made a text for articles.

The first effect at Hackstraw is, of course, alarm and contempt. Alarm, in case the indispensable John shall be removed; contempt of what is called a stunt. Gollan is furious at the threat to his beloved John, and asks once more if they want him to resign. They, in his elementary mind, means the nation, in which he no longer bothers to distinguish government and people, much less one newspaper from another or one magistrate from another. And the second effect, therefore, as usual when any bureaucratic ganglion suffers irritation from outside, is to inflame its natural reactions. From this time, and long after the scandal is forgotten, the Gollan office grows more self-sufficient. The very office boys go about with the air of saying "to hell with the public."

Tabitha is now regarded as a danger, as a specimen of those numerous people who are suffering from war hysteria, who are weakening. John, seeing that she is suffering, that her face has become thin and lined, and that her hair is gray at her temples, thinks,

"Poor thing, it's all getting a bit too much for her." He uses all his charm to soothe her.

"My dear mother, don't you think you take the papers too seriously?"

"Do you take anything seriously?"

"That's a very interesting question; it raises the whole problem, doesn't it, of what I'm for."

Tabitha's large eyes are fixed on him as if trying to understand him, and he thinks, "Yes, it's a regular obsession. Why do women of a certain age take religion so badly? Something to do with their nerves, I suppose, or the change of life."

"What you are for?" Tabitha murmurs, as if she can't understand the words.

"I mean, in my job. You see, it's largely summing up the evidence; and one has to avoid any kind of bias."

"I'm not blaming you; it's not your fault."

And he gives it up. "No, we are what we are, aren't we?" He kisses her tenderly, as if consoling a child. "What you really need is a rest, Mother; a long holiday. You're worn out," and he slips away quickly to the office.

Work is waiting for him, the kind of work he enjoys: conflicts between sub-departments, demands from the Ministry and the managers which are irreconcilable, expressed on quiet paper that lies to be judged and does not answer back or get obsessions.

He is concerned for Tabitha. He thinks, "Poor woman, she makes herself very unhappy"; and at the same time he is so deeply amused by something that, finding himself smiling at a long letter about the defects of a buckle, he stops to examine the reason of this pleasure. And it turns out to be the thought, "Probably she's quite right; I am a bit intolerable."

He knocks off his report on the buckle. It does not suggest conclusions; but if one were suggested, Gollan would be certain to decide against it.

79

There is plenty of such work, for plans for a breakthrough in the spring have brought new schedules. The army demands more guns, still larger masses of transport, shells, tanks. All the Gollan engineers are exceedingly busy. John is laying out a new factory site at the Halt which will carry off another twenty acres of the park.

But it is the Germans who break through. In March they reach Amiens and threaten to divide the British from the French. It seems that the war is lost; but no one despairs, because all are sunk in an apathy of endurance or lost in a mass of work.

Gollan, who has long ceased to read the papers, hears of this last disaster, shouted to him by a secretary, with a silent momentary turn of the eye which seems to say only, "another mess," and then instantly flourishes a sheaf of papers at John. "Here you are, report on billycan—more ballyhoo."

"Have you read them?" John shouts.

"Read 'em, no; give me another twelve hours a day and I might read 'em—or I mightn't."

"The cans do seem to have been a bit expensive; I can understand the Treasury complaints."

"Of course they're dear. Things made in a hurry by amateurs out of the wrong material are always dear, damned dear. The question is, are they better than nothing?"

"But there was the other pattern; the Ministry seem to think—"

"The Ministry has always got new patterns. It's always being pushed about by experts and cranks and crooks on the make. If I listened to the Ministry the army would have nothing to shoot, nothing to eat, and nothing to wear except a lot of bumf scribbled with bilge."

But John and Smyth are alarmed about the billycans, about Gollan's whole position. There have been questions in the House. The agitation against the government, that is, against every man in authority, grows every day. Tabitha every morning opens letters so charged with rage and hatred that they seem like physical acts.

"I've lost two Sons, all I had in the World, because of your war you're so proud of, and the Capitalists like you is making Millions out of the Poor."

"Why should I rot here in the mud at a bob a day and poor old Jenny the same while coppersmiths which is my trade gets fifteen quid a week and takes out girls."

"The communists for me. I'm a bit sick of being pushed about and so is everybody in this country. Englishmen don't stand for it. What we want is a United Soviet Socialist Republic of the World with Universal Peace and Freedom, and no more of your bloody snoopers round the factories. Capitalism is finished. Free India. Take the exploiters off the backs of the workers. Down with the Jews. No income tax for the workers. Double rations and proper beer, send the girls home and stop them cutting their hair and taking men's jobs. Send the Irish home where they belong."

"It is men like you who are responsible for this fearful war and the deaths of a million young men. It is your muddleheaded greed and saber rattling which brought this destruction on us. The Germans only wished for peace. But our naval policy directly supported by you, by the steel and armament manufacturers, made it impossible for them to trust us. The obvious and sensible policy, which alone can secure peace, that is, the Total and Instant abolition of armies and navies and air forces, was definitely rejected by you on three occasions. You are therefore condemned by God and men and shall be destroyed at last with hell fire."

When Tabitha shows this letter to John, he says cautiously, "Yes, the lunatic fringe; the war seems to have stimulated all the cranks."

But Tabitha has withdrawn into a reserve of her own, where she does her secretarial duties without comment. "It's on office paper from the Halt. I was wondering if he ought to know about it?"

"No, lots of our best men are cranks; the chief accountant is a Seventh-day Adventist. It doesn't affect their work, and we mustn't upset the chief while this billycan affair is on. If he tried to resign again, people would think that the Ministry was in the wrong, and it really has been rather stupid."

Gollan comes in from the car with two serious-looking men: General Score, a retired gunner who has a plan for ending the war in two months with certain complicated dispositions, and Papworth, the famous newspaper strategist who wants to build eighty-ton tanks.

John and Tabitha, without even a glance at each other, automatically close in upon the intruders, who, innocently supposing that they must be polite to Lady Gollan, do not find that their prey has vanished for another half minute.

For at this moment of crisis the Hackstraw defenses have been extended. It is not enough to protect Gollan from the papers and the Ministry, from anonymous letters and experts, but from any kind of advice which may complicate or delay his judgment. And of late he has been so heavily bombarded that he has to be guarded at all hours.

"Look at this!" An excited young officer, staying in the Hall for convalescence, breaks in upon him in the office just after breakfast. Gollan actually has the telephone in his hand; John and Smyth stand by with preoccupied faces.

The billycan affair has taken a bad turn. A question in the House on the previous day shows that there is a leakage; somebody has had an inkling of the truth.

"Look here—" the youth waves some obscure weekly which has just reached him by post—"they've done for themselves! See, they can't get out of the salient—and *The Times* says we've started a counterattack."

But Tabitha has already cut him off. "How interesting; yes, I see—"

"But do look, sir." The soldier waves his paper at Gollan across Tabitha's shoulder. "Look at this map. Ludendorff's done for himself; it's the end of the war."

Gollan, fortunately, can't hear. He is especially enraged by newspaper maps showing that the war can be won, as he says, in three moves. John glances at the map. "Yes, it always looks easy on paper, doesn't it?" and shouts to Gollan, "Is that the War House? Don't forget we must have the exact gauge of the American can."

The young officer, cast down and resentful, turns to Tabitha. "The war can't go on forever, can it?"

"Oh no, of course it won't!" And with an affectionate glance, "How is your leg this morning? I'm sure you ought to try the electrical treatment. You really mustn't go back to France while you have so much pain."

Gollan turns from the telephone. "I think that's settled the blinking billygoat and his silly question. All he wants is to get into the papers. I want to win the war."

The next day it appears that the Germans are in retreat. In four months the war is over.

80

THE young officer, whose mysterious grievance against his hosts has been put down to war nerves, has long been forgotten. The Hackstraw offices are busier than ever at the task of what Gollan calls "sorting out"; that is to say, breaking up the war organization and turning over the factories to peace work. There is immense confusion and waste. Demobilization is like the collapse of a dam. Whole regiments demobilize themselves and go on a spree. Officers are living on their gratuities at the rate of five thousand a year. The girls who have been rich and gay on their earnings have nothing left but silk underclothes and a pregnancy; but they are determined not to go back to their mothers. Every city street is full of deserters, crooks, prostitutes, of which the amateurs are more dangerous, more diseased than the professionals. Everyone is on holiday, everyone is full of excitement, and a kind of joyful rage. The government goes to the country on the policy "Hang the Kaiser," and wins. But the votes are given as much for hope as revenge. Right has triumphed. Universal peace and justice have arrived, together with the highest wages ever known, the greatest liberty, the shortest skirts, votes for women, and a dozen new nations. Above all, the secret of prosperity has been discovered: that the higher the wages, the richer the markets. And the money to pay the wages doesn't need to be gold or silver. It can be made of any wastepaper. The keen young men, having spent their gratuities on a round of joy, borrow capital to start workshops, garages. The motor age has arrived. Everyone is to make a fortune out of cars. In short, it is to be something new in worlds. Gollan has received a peerage for his services to the nation, and two more threats of murder. He is enlarging the Hackstraw factory, the iron company, his truck factory and his shipyard, to supply the world. The old Gollan Industries is once more placed under Hector's management; but in fact, since Gollan controls its raw materials and its markets, it remains part of the larger group. Hector Stone is a figurehead. But he is very well satisfied with this place under the great Lord Gollan. Hector, honest worthy citizen, is not mean in his admiration for genius, once it is brought to his notice. He repeats everywhere Gollan's inspiring words, "Go out and get it; that's the order. Expansion—expansion. And plenty of cheap power, electricity; we can't have too much electricity."

When Gollan opens in the spring of 1919 a new iron field, and buys a coal combine to supply a new battery of steel furnaces, he is offered his eight million pounds of capital ten times over.

He has never been so optimistic or seemed so well. "This is a bally rest cure," he declares; "handling my own job in my own way instead of cat's-cradle with the Ministry and blind-man's-buff with the government. Just in time, too. A big job in front of us; we've got to build up our trade again."

He is enraged by the suggestion, made by an economist, that prices may fall. "That chap ought to be locked up. What we want is a pull all together, confidence and faith."

One evening he has a violent quarrel with two of the directors about the prospectus for the ironworks; they object to the plan for a complete new town, housing the workers close to the factories. He comes home in a state of excitement and tries to explain the argument to John and Smyth. "So I said to them, 'The fact is, you're a couple of muddleheads. Goods, goods, ships, steel, trucks, rails—crying out for 'em! Yes, I know your damned professor has been talking about trouble with money, but that's his game, noughts and crosses; but if you'll excuse me, you don't understand.' "

The old man makes a gesture as if to enforce an argument and suddenly loses the thread. He stands with a look of confusion. Tabitha says anxiously, "Yes; but it's nearly one o'clock."

"The fact is, my dear—" Gollan with a fearful effort of will overcomes the obstacle, whatever it is, in his brain—"that professor is nothing but an expert of the lowest class. I told 'em so. I said, 'Economics are one thing, but bu-business is another—one is bumf and the other is human nature.' And you're quite pale, my dearest love. How stupid of me; how thoughtless. I am a blinking fool, and dashed old blockhead. You're worn out; you're done up. You need a holiday. Yes, don't tell me; you're completely exhausted, washed up."

"Don't you think that we both need a holiday?"

"Not me; can't be done just now."

Even John agrees that it would be dangerous for Gollan to go away at such a moment. "This is a very big scheme, and he'll need all he's got to put it through."

Tabitha, with her reserved manner, says, "But can it succeed? That professor seemed to think that it was the wrong time."

"Have you noticed that the professors always contradict each other?"

"And what will happen if James is wrong?"

"Well, in that case—" he hesitates.

"We'll lose everything—and I suppose he is wrong."

"That's just guessing, Mother. Very good judges think he's right." John smiles, enjoying, as usual, a dilemma of judgment. "After all, no one can tell what's going to happen. There is a large demand, and there's also a lot of nervousness. It's not only a question of how people feel, but of stocks and cash. And no one on earth knows exactly what stocks are stuffed away in dumps, and what cash is stuffed away in old stockings."

"I'm sure he's wrong."

"Why, Mother? What reason have you?"

"Things can't go on like this—but it doesn't matter. The great thing is that they've stopped killing." Her intonation is so like that of the fat Rose that the young man wants to laugh. And it seems to him once more that women are a race apart in a world of which the fantastic difference is hidden only by their logical inability to detect and describe it, or by their natural bent toward dissimulation.

81

A RUMOR that Gollan is about to retire, probably invented by a speculator, causes the market to hesitate. It sends one or two steel shares back half a point. But it is contradicted so decisively by Gollan himself, by John and Hector Stone, that public confidence returns. Shares rise, and there is a large increase of orders.

People again talk of a boom, a real boom. "I can smell it," Bonser says. "It's coming on like Christmas. Look at the prosperity everywhere. Look at the way people are dashing it down. Especially the kids. And they're setting the pace. I'm putting on a new show next week—biggest ever; it'll cost me fifty thousand before I'm done."

"For Millie?"

"Yes. And I'll tell you a secret: there's going to be a wedding in the family." Bonser looks grave, reverent, and grips John's shoulder. "She's going to marry me, Johnny. Oh, I know I don't deserve it. But she's the only woman in my life, and she knows it. Thank God for women's hearts; thank God I can appreciate what Millie has done for me. Love is a wonderful thing, John, a holy thing; we ought to go on our knees when we think of it."

He confesses also, or rather boasts—for every one of his confessions, indeed every action of his life, is at once an impulse and an attitude, like the prancing of a child—that he is settling fifty thousand pounds on Miss Minter for life.

"Is that safe?" John asks.

"My dear boy, if you knew that dear little soul as well as I did—"

"A slump wouldn't be good for the theater."

"Don't talk like that, John; someone might hear. You might start something."

"Start a slump?"

"You ask old Jim Gollan—he knows. Ask anyone who's got what it takes. You don't understand business, Johnny, it's an instinct. I don't mind telling you that me and some of my friends have made a pact to talk up the boom. And it's having its effect already. It's giving employment, it's bringing gladness into the homes of the people. And they deserve it. The British working man did a fine job in the war, and talk of a slump now is simply unpatriotic. It's a dirty low trick—treason."

And he asks for a special allotment in the new Gollan issue.

Gollan has again had an attack, and is shut up in his room. But because he is ill and impossible to advise or approach, he is an absolute dictator. He commands the new prospectus, the terms of the new issue, including the scheme for a new town, and only one voice opposes. The issue is a great success, but Gollan, by telephone, at once gets to work to prevent the election of this critical person to the new board. He is very much excited by this opposition, for though it is but one voice in eighteen, it casts doubts upon his judgment. And that is to attack his power to work, his life. "My God," he shouts at John, "that dirty little runt, that rat! I gave him his first job." On the next morning, and two days before the election to the board, he is found dead in bed.

His will leaves to the Stones Gollan Industries, but to John a majority holding in the foundry, the Hackstraw Halt Works, and to Tabitha the entire preference capital in the same combine, that is, two hundred thousand pounds, yielding, at six per cent, twelve thousand a year.

John's half-million ordinary shares, at two pounds five shillings, are paying twelve per cent, and give him an income of sixty thousand a year.

He at once calls a meeting of the general board, and proposes to put off the building scheme, to cut down production, in fact, to take up a defensive position. "We don't know what's going to happen in the international market; let's wait till we have better indications."

He is opposed by Hector Stone and the majority of the board. Stone's speech is most moving. He points out that any change in policy would be a disloyalty to "one of the greatest men of our time; the man to whom, more than to any other, we owe our victory in the great war. And what is more, one of the finest business intelligences of our generation."

The plan is rejected by a large majority. John at once brings it in again in a new form, proposing to break up the combine.

The board, after three meetings and a fortnight's delay, spent in consulting friends, experts, company lawyers, golf partners, the newspapers, their wives, and each other, vote exactly as before, against John.

The next day shares begin to fall. The slump has begun. Bonser telephones to John. "I warned you; and now you've done it. Three days before our opening. Poor little Millie is practically off her head. I tell you, young man, if things go much worse, you ought to be poleaxed; and a lot of people will be keen to do the job—a whole lot."

A week later his name is in the long list of bankrupts.

82

WITHIN a week Hackstraw shares are unsalable at sixpence, and before six months all the companies of the group are in liquidation. Hackstraw is put up for sale, but it has been spoilt by the factories, and in that year of forced sales it goes for a ridiculously small sum. Yet the estate is not quite bankrupt. Tabitha is left with a few thousand pounds, which, invested in consols, give her what is called a safe income of under three hundred a year.

John proposes that she should live in Frood Green, to be near her brother. But she chooses, to his surprise, a boarding house at Sancombe, saying that she will first take a holiday.

Everyone, even the Stones and the investors in the Gollan combine, sympathizes with Lady Gollan. Everyone can understand the misfortune of one who loses a fortune. No one is surprised to see her, at forty-eight, quite gray, with deep arches in her high narrow forehead. Her flight to Sancombe is thought natural but unwise. She is said to be broken down in health and mind, to be reclusive, melancholy.

John himself is alarmed by her isolation. "You can't stay here all the winter," he says in November, when he visits her at Sancombe, and looks about at the empty boarding houses, ugly in themselves, and doubly mean in the seasonal emptiness which exposes them not as homes but as commercial speculations; at the concrete esplanade, blown with sand; at the lead-colored sea whose every movement is dull and heavy as if oppressed by the cold weight of its mass; at a sky of over-all cloud like cotton wool soaked in some gray rinse; at the hills hidden by rain, and sand dunes whose coarse grass gives out a sound like a discreet restrained sigh.

He accompanies her to church on Sunday, and seeing her rapt attention, her air of refreshment afterwards, his forebodings return. He thinks, "So she's not getting over it so easily; there's still a lot of hysteria." And looking with disgust at her bare cold room in the cheap hotel, without books or even a comfortable chair, he thinks to find a clue. "I suppose she's still mortifying herself for James's death, or simply placating her juju because she has had so many knocks."

He insists on buying her a warm rug and a shelf of books, and visits her every week end.

But in fact Tabitha is full of a secret excited happiness. Even the bare box of her room delights her, because it does not hide a big house full of problems, because it is part of a new peace and security. As soon as she opens her eyes in the morning, to see the cold light on the ceiling, and to hear the lap of the sea which seems to echo in the vaster emptiness and bareness of outside, she thinks with exultation, "All this is finished"—meaning not only the war, but, though she does not allow herself to know it, the long years with the reckless and unmanageable Gollan. She feels such gratitude for this uneventful life about her that she marvels at a sulky face in the village. "How can anyone be unhappy here? How can they worry about trifles? The war is over."

And this her song, "The war is over, no one is being killed any more. John was not killed." When he is sorry for her, and she laughs at him, she no longer feels that he is remote from her, incomprehensible. For she perfectly understands his failure to understand her; and in that failure she draws him close again. He is a child, to be loved as a child.

She thinks once more, "He doesn't really know anything." And her first anxiety, in all this new secure happiness, is about his future. John has been offered half a dozen posts already in big business, and rejected them all. But she consoles herself, "He is alive, that's all that matters; and as for work, God will provide."

She is shaken only for a moment, when he says one evening, "How would you like me to be a don? That is a nice safe humble job that doesn't attract the envy of a jealous god."

"Yes, why not? Teaching is a *good* profession. I was only wondering if dons can afford to marry."

"Oh, we needn't worry about that."

Tabitha smiles at him. "You mustn't be prejudiced against marriage just because I hoped you would get married."

"Were you so happy in marriage?"

"It's not a question of happiness; people are meant to get married."

"I see, it's a matter for providence."

Tabitha is no longer ruffled by jokes against her religion. She is too secure in it. She looks at the boy with the same affectionate amusement, and says, "You at least ought to be glad to be alive."

John is impatient. "Yes, yes, Mother. But about a job: you won't be disappointed if I look for a donship?"

"I know you will do what you like."

83

IN FACT John has already made up his mind to take a fellowship, and is divided only between St. Mark's, which has a vacancy, and an offer to join a new foundation at a place called Urrsley in the Midlands.

This offer has come from a certain Gow, a creditor of Gollan's, whom John has met one day in the corner of a boardroom, after a long and boring creditors' meeting. And Gow has said, "I believe you were at St. Mark's?"

It turns out that Gow has also been a classical scholar of St. Mark's, and has even known, thirty years before, John's tutor. They talk of the college, the state of education; and Gow, in his gentle apologetic manner, says, "I am inclined to think the old-fashioned classical education gave one something of value, something one doesn't get elsewhere."

"I'm rather with you there; a little philosophy may be a dangerous thing, but none at all is likely to be worse."

After this careful and apologetic testing of the ground, this slow approach, they find themselves in warm and convinced agreement that there is in fact no education like a good classical education; that the only education to be called a real education is one that includes history, logic, ethics—one intended to give a certain power of judgment, a certain detachment. And one day Gow, who has made and kept, in addition to inherited millions, some millions in the war, discloses to John his intention of giving some of it away. "Do you think, Bonser, it would be better to found a university college in some spot without any such institutions, of, dare we say, real education, or to give it to one of the old establishments?"

John is at once for the college. He is surprised by his own force of conviction, for he has not known that he possessed any.

"Now, in my own native place, Urrsley—"

"I know it. Any amount of money and brains—and one would rather live in Central Africa. Urrsley is just the place."

"I have been approached, of course, by the hospitals."

"Oh, damn the hospitals! I know the story—a practical good work, something to show for your money—that's the whole idea, nowadays: look after the flesh and the mind can take care of itself. A thoroughly *mob* idea."

Gow still hesitates. He is a cautious man, and he has learnt from his classical studies to hear the other side. But after six months' reflection he resolves to found a university college at Urrsley and invites John to join the advisory committee and to organize the philosophy courses.

Thus while the young man, in Tabitha's imagination, is supposed to be working at the Hackstraw offices on the liquidation of the combine, he is really spending half of each week at Urrsley, quarreling with architects about the proper form of lecture rooms, and plotting with the new principal, a man called Keeler, and an experienced string-puller, to defeat the scheme of a local committee of business men, bent on turning the college into a technical institute.

On the other hand, John and Keeler are at loggerheads about the building. There are already three or four different cliques in the committee which, in the true democratic manner, fight each other even more vigorously than they fight the enemy outside. John, Keeler, and Keeler's secretary—a young woman called Lang—unite against a chapel but split on a hall. "A college," Keeler says, "without some central meeting place is not a college at all; it will never form an idea of itself." "A college," John says, "is first of all for teaching; and the first need of students nowadays is a modern library with access to the shelves and some quiet rooms for study." And in this he has the enthusiastic support of Miss Lang.

She is a tall, handsome girl, belonging to the group of young people, sons and daughters of Urrsley professional men, who keep in touch with every modern innovation. They are so anxious not to be provincial, not to fall behind in the march of progress, that they often run ahead of it. Some of their younger matrons are capable of startling London with fashions which will never become fashionable; and Kate Lang has been heard to say, "But how provincial Londoners are—they don't seem even to have heard of Freud."

She has taken a degree in science, but is much more interested in socialist politics and the new psychology, which seem to her parts of one forward movement toward a more civilized world.

John, like Keeler, learns to depend on her; and in the struggle with Keeler he is profoundly grateful for her help. "How loyal she is," he thinks. "Few women would set a principle above personal feelings; Kit really does put first things first."

And when he compliments Miss Lang upon her soundness of judgment, she answers, "Of course I agree with you; you're so obviously right."

The two plan a new campaign for the library. They call themselves the Federals, and Miss Lang draws up a manifesto for the local progressives. She makes the affair political, and writes to the paper denouncing the charity of millionaires. She will not allow even John to find excuses for Gow. "Oh, I know he's well-meaning," she explains, "but why is he so gutless? Why does he let himself be pushed about by everybody?" and her voice expresses despair and rage. "I know what will happen: he'll propose a compromise—men like that always get out on a compromise—and we'll get a bad library and a beastly hall."

Gow in fact does suggest a compromise. A small hall is designed which can be enlarged in future years; and a modest library is built in which some of the shelves are open and there are a few cubicles for research.

Kate is furious. But John is so delighted to see the plans passed and foundations laid that he finally agrees to take a teaching post in the new college. He writes to tell Tabitha, "I could have a job at my old college, but I really think I'm more needed at Urrsley. As Keeler says, it is really a frontier town in education, and we've got to keep the wild Indians on the run. I mean the technical college tribe."

Tabitha feels a quick profound moment of apprehension. She sees John not only crusty and rusty, a deprived bachelor, but doubly remote from life in some provincial cave. But she reminds herself, "All *that* is over, we have peace; and how mean of me to forget that blessing, to feel aggrieved because John has the whim to sacrifice his brains in some obscure post." And she writes her warm approval of the Urrsley scheme.

She is inexpressibly startled when, two days later, John brings to Sancombe, for his usual week end, a young woman. "This is one of my colleagues, Mother. Miss Lang, secretary to the college."

Tabitha gazes at the visitor with a bright anxious stare; this look, the stare, her slow handshake, all express an intensity of interest which makes John smile at Kit, who glances back at him with humorous sympathy. They are agreeing that mothers, Victorian mothers, are comical.

84

BUT Tabitha and Miss Lang have already come to another understanding. The first sharp glance has said to the young woman, "You've come all this way to see what John's mother thinks of you"; and the girl's quick handshake has answered, "I thought we'd better meet."

Thus Tabitha has every reason for the excitement with which she hastens to order lunch for the visitors. "Thank God," she thinks. "So John can fall in love; and what a nice-looking girl. A college girl, of course, and rather pleased with herself. She looks so clever, and rather hard. Oh dear, but I must like her. I must love her. I ought to be glad, glad that he even looks at a girl."

And the moment she is alone with John she congratulates him. "But why didn't you tell me? She is perfectly charming, and really tremendously pretty."

"My dear mother, I don't need to tell you about all my acquaintance—Miss Lang is just a friend."

"Yes, of course." Tabitha is full of laughter and a deep gratitude, a religious gratitude, but she looks all the more serious.

"I suppose you are imagining some romance," John says, in a suspicious tone.

"No, John; how could I?"

"My dear mother, I told you I'm not a marrying man."

"Of course you're only friends; but I must go and see about another room."

And she bustles through the house with that restless activity in which a woman reveals her sense of a family crisis. "Is there a front room available for Miss Lang? A nice front room with a view of the sea?" She hurries up to see the room and to make sure that there are enough blankets on the bed, clean linen on the dressing table. She apologizes to Kit for the absence of flowers; she will get some.

"Oh, but please, Lady Gollan; you make me feel a nuisance."

"My dear, how could you be a nuisance? It was so good of you to come."

"But I wanted to come; I've heard so much about you from John."

"It's so nice for John to have friends in Urrsley; and really, he's looking very well."

These statements mean respectively, "Now I see that you are going to be nice to me I like you very much. I am of course very fond of John"; and, "I have been longing for John to meet some girl that he can be fond of; it's just what he needs to make him human."

And now that this private understanding is established, that Tabitha is approved, provisionally, as a mother-in-law, that Kit is accepted as suitor, the friendship proceeds with wonderful speed. The two women begin at once, choosing the shortest route to intimacy, to confess themselves, their feelings, their pasts. They discover that they are both fond of a quiet life, and both of them hate the new fashions. Both are liberals; and what is still more satisfactory, though they have both supported votes for women, they have strongly disapproved of the militants.

"So unwomanly, and really rather vulgar," Tabitha says.

"Hysterical," Kit agrees; "giving just the wrong idea." And she regrets that her education has been unpractical and romantic; she has not learnt any economics. Tabitha cries that modern schools are all bad, the girls simply learn to be frivolous.

John is left to himself during the rest of the visit; but, seeing the two women going on so happily together, is content. He thinks, "Mother is absurd, but at least she has good manners. And she can still be charming when she likes. As for Kit, it's really awfully good of her to sacrifice her holiday in this way. She must be bored to death. I knew that she had brains and sincerity, but I'd no idea she could be so really sympathetic and tactful." And strolling by himself on the beach, while Tabitha is showing Kit an old photograph album, with pictures of John at all ages, he thinks, "That girl really has uncommon qualities. As a colleague she's as good as a man—better, because she's so loyal; and she agrees so completely with my ideas."

One afternoon about a fortnight later, at a rare moment of leisure in the college office, the friends are discussing various ethical questions, when John, with a smile, recalls his mother's assumption that Kit and he, since they go about together as friends, must be on the verge of marriage.

Kit laughs; but then, characteristically returning to the serious aspects of the question, remarks, "All the same, I don't agree with the communists there, do you? I think marriage still has a certain social value between friends. For instance, when two people are working together it saves time when they can discuss points as they arise—right away."

"There's something in that." John is both amused and charmed by this common sense. He thinks again, "She really is a girl in a thousand, or, anyhow, in a hundred."

Three weeks later the couple are engaged, and Tabitha is now devoted to Kit. She welcomes her to Sancombe with a flattered joy. She will not allow herself to find any fault in the girl except perhaps her love of swimming a long way out to sea and taking John to climb on high rocks. But she is assured that both sports are very good for John's leg.

Tabitha has only one alarm on the eve of the wedding, while staying with John in Urrsley. She has been urged by both the young people to live in Urrsley, but especially by Kit, who points out that there are many quiet squares in the old part of the town near the cathedral, where fine old eighteenth-century houses are being turned into flats. John and Kit themselves have taken such a flat near the college, and why should not Tabitha take another?

"Oh no; it wouldn't do." Tabitha shakes her head with a wise smile.

The young woman, slightly irritated, asks, "Do you think we should quarrel?"

"Oh, Kit, what an idea. If there's one person I really am determined not to be, it's the difficult mother-in-law. And that's just why I mustn't be too near."

"Aren't these ideas just a little absurd these days?"

And indeed Kit is so friendly, so good-natured, she is so anxious for Tabitha's advice, that Tabitha is soon persuaded to take a flat: a third floor with two rooms and a kitchen in a delightful old square near the cathedral. "After all," she thinks, "the situation is quite exceptional; I shall have to act almost as Kit's mother."

Kit, who, having no mother or father, is being married from the house of a spinster aunt, has not even begun to get a trousseau. She is surprised when Tabitha cries out at the idea of a girl being married in old clothes. But she submits with amused patience to being carried round the shops; she smiles affectionately on Tabitha while the latter, in some dressing room, agonizes between three evening frocks, of which one is too dowdy, one is too flimsy, and one a little too pink.

"Shopping nowadays is really *impossible*!" Tabitha says, revolving like a nervous insect round Kit, who, statuesque in a petticoat, stands with her two muscular arms crossed and waits patiently to be dressed and undressed, pinned and unpinned. "But really, Kit darling, I think the chiffon may turn out the best. It's *dear*, and it's not so *smart* as the blue, but it would let out rather well."

"Let out? Oh, you mean for maternity purposes."

"Well, you say you don't want to spend any more money."

"But there's not going to be any children."

Tabitha is alarmed. "Kit darling, there's nothing wrong, is there?"

"No, but we decided not to have children. Jack quite agrees with me."

"Decided! But that's absolutely—" Tabitha in her first shock of amazement is about to say wicked. She gazes at Kit as if that solid calm young woman had sprouted horns.

"It really seems quite wrong in our case," Kit says, answering Tabitha's unspoken judgment with her usual serious air. "Jack and I have gone into the whole thing pretty thoroughly. Did you hear Doctor Fuljamb's lecture last year to women students' associations? No, of course, you were at Sancombe. Well, Dorothy Fuljamb is after all a fairly big authority, and she's all against families."

"But what would happen if nobody had children?"

"Doctor Fuljamb's argument is that there are too many people already in the country, and too few educated women. She thinks college-trained women oughtn't to waste themselves on having families and doing domestic work."

And suddenly, appealing to Tabitha, as from woman to woman, "You were for the vote, weren't you? And I did so agree with what Doctor Fuljamb said about our special responsibility under the vote. Not to give way, I mean, to all that sort of thing."

"What thing?"

"Impulse and instinct and sex; all those things that were supposed to make us unfit to be responsible citizens."

Tabitha is so confused that she cannot answer; her fingers tremble as she handles the frock. And afterwards, as she goes home, she is filled with panic. She remembers now all the rumors of strange and new ideas about sex and the family. In Russia, it is said, marriage has been abolished, and abortions are legal. All over Europe young people are living together without marriage, and even apologizing for being married. Skirts are growing shorter and shorter and woman strive to make themselves look like little boys with cropped hair and thin flat bodies. And everyone is talking about sex, because some Viennese professor has declared that all the ideas in the world, all the religion, the arts, arise from sex or its perversions.

"But Kit is so sensible," Tabitha says to herself. "She can't *really* believe such rubbish. How could a woman not want children? How could she get married and refuse to have children?"

But she is pursued by fear. It is as though the ground of her belief has been shaken. She is like a person who builds joyfully on rock and at once suffers an earthquake.

She goes at last to John. Since his engagement John has grown more touchy. But she bursts out to him, "What is this about not having children, John?"

"Well, we thought it better not. The flat's rather small, and we'll both be fearfully busy. It's not only the college work, but Kit has promised to do a research job for the council on family budgets."

"But, John—" Once more Tabitha is about to exclaim that to plan a barren marriage is wicked, monstrous; but catching John's eye, and seeing that he is irritated, she says only, "It seems so strange—"

"Why, Mother? It seems to me very reasonable to have some sort of plan."

Tabitha does not say any more. But for some reason she is relieved. Perhaps because she is used to thinking of John as a child in these matters, she draws from her talk with him a feeling that the whole project is childish. She thinks, "These children make wonderful plans, but they're all nonsense."

Her faith returns. Indeed, during the honeymoon, spent, by Kit's choice, mountaineering in Switzerland, when Tabitha trembles at every ring of the bell, she is as anxious for her unborn grandchildren as for the young couple. She does not say to herself, "If they are killed I shall have no grandchildren, and life will have no sense," but that is her feeling.

When she prays for God's blessing on "My dear son and daughter," she is praying for a whole family.

And her faith is justified. Tabitha, when the bride and bridegroom return, blesses her nearness, for they are at once overwhelmed with work and she finds herself needed every day to shop, to mend, even to cook and wash. So that she is able to notice when Kit comes down pale in the morning and unable to drink her coffee. The young woman explains these symptoms as due to being overtired, but Tabitha, alone in the scullery, faced by a pile of dirty dishes, finds herself laughing in triumph. She feels more than a personal delight; she says to herself, "Of course it was quite ridiculous. I needn't have been so frightened. Poor darlings, how silly they were. And how lucky that people aren't allowed to decide these things for themselves."

And in her relief, her renewed confidence in the final stability of the world, she can forgive the young woman's childish whims. Kit indeed seems to feel her pregnancy like a shame, a treachery. As she grows large she becomes more impatient of notice. She hates to go in the street and hides herself like a leper.

Tabitha's only anxiety is that she will carry this nonsense so far as to neglect her baby. But lo, as soon as the baby is born, Kit treats the episode in a scientific spirit, and talks of it even grossly. She is also most scientific about the child's nursery, and attends strictly, even rigidly, to her duties.

But she is also resolved to prove that having babies need not prevent a young mother from more important duties. She goes back to her office and her meetings at the fortnight. John, too, is extremely busy; he has scarcely time to admire the daughter who keeps him awake at nights.

Thus it is Tabitha who, having no distractions, is called upon to do all the nursery work which, in Kit's view, quite reasonably, is waste of time for a better-educated person.

And Tabitha is obliged to remind herself that this grandchild, christened Nancy, a girl who, on the whole, is remarkably plain, is not the wonder of the world. "The darling," she says to herself. "Of course she's quite an ordinary baby. I mustn't be silly about her. I do so despise a silly grandmother."

But she is silly. She gazes on the child as at a miracle; she laughs; she tickles its unresponsive soles; she marvels at its feet, its fingers, like minute white carrots; she makes absurd noises. The very flat seems different to her. It has become a home, a place of important significance.

How joyfully now, with what profound sense of its meaning, she repeats the psalm, "Blessed be the Lord God of Israel, for he hath visited and redeemed his people."

"Yes," she thinks, "God is love." And she sees her world secured once more, renewed in love. John is happy in the work he loves, and in his wife. He has passed through the dangerous crisis of marriage to a safe harbor. Above all, he has been brought back from the clouds, from folly and perversity, into the real world—Tabitha's world. He is a family man.

85 JUST before baby Nancy's first summer holiday, when she is seven months old, Kit, who is busy with her important work on family budgets, engages a nurse. The nurse, a tall buxom young woman, with a bad complexion, has been trained in some institution. She is noisy but efficient. She smokes cigarettes as she sews, but is medically clean. She watches Tabitha closely but permits her to do the unskilled labor—pushing the pram along the sand, spreading out the rug for the baby to roll and kick, lifting her down from pram to rug. Tabitha is one afternoon enjoying the privilege, and has just given the baby a kiss before placing her on the rug, when the nurse takes out her cigarette and says gravely, "You mustn't do that; it's not allowed."

Tabitha does not even answer this rudeness. She reports the woman to Kit. But Kit answers, "As a matter of fact, I was going to say something about that myself. I was going to ask you not to make a fuss about Nan; kissing is so bad for children."

"At seven months?"

"It does seem odd, but they say the first months of a child's life are the most important. Its mind is fixed then; I mean in its essential character."

Tabitha bursts out laughing and cries, "Oh, but you don't believe such stuff?"

The young woman looks still more sweet, except for her eyes and mouth, and answers, "Yes, it is funny, isn't it? But it's quite well established all the same. It's founded on scientific investigation of hundreds of cases."

Tabitha says nothing more. She recalls her resolution to be a good and wise mother-in-law. She thinks, "This is another piece of nonsense; it will be forgotten like the rest." She continues to make much of Nan when Kit is not present. And since Kit, busier than ever with her social inquiries, is much occupied, since the nurse has got married, she has, for most of the time, all the opportunity she needs. It is indeed Tabitha who sees most of Nan, who sees her first steps, interprets her first words, and tells the world how clever, how remarkable she is.

Even when she is not pramming, feeding, or bathing the child, her expression has that preoccupation which means in a grandmother that she is enjoying the supreme happiness of a grandbaby left in her charge. Probably for this year, Tabitha is one of the happiest women in England.

She is immensely startled when one morning John stops in the doorway as he is rushing out to the college and ejaculates, "Oh, I forgot, Mother. Nancy is apparently not to be kissed or dandled or made noises to. I believe Kit said something before, and she's rather upset."

"But, John, how could it do harm to show a child that she is loved?"

John makes an impatient gesture, meaning, "Please don't argue the point, I've no time." In fact, at the moment, he has half a dozen separate worries: with household bills, with a new lecture which demands long and concentrated thought, with a pupil whose parents want to take him away from the class, and, above all, with the college council about the appointment of an ancient historian. For he must discover quickly a short and decisive answer to that old question of Gollan's, which seems to haunt the minds of self-made men everywhere, and which has now been asked by a benefactor and a great man in Urrsley: "What is the good of teaching lads about a lot of damn Greeks and Romans that fought each other with bows and arrows thousands of years ago?" He is impatient with domestic squabbles. He answers Tabitha impatiently, "The idea is that kissing does do children harm; it gives them what is called a complex." And he walks away quickly before Tabitha, whose angry and amazed face is a warning, can retort upon him.

"Poor boy," Tabitha thinks. "It's not him, it's Kit. John would never have such silly wicked ideas." And she resolves to cherish Nan only in her own flat, or in some remote shrubbery of the park where she takes her in the pram, and where she can console herself and the child by being a little more demonstrative.

But Tabitha does not know how closely she is watched, not only by Kit but by many of Kit's friends and their nurses. She has not realized that as a woman of the last generation no less than as Lady Gollan, reputed to have been a smart and fashionable hostess in the wicked reign of Edward VII, she is always under critical observation.

Within a week a young don's wife, also lately married and full of the new gospel about the complexes of babies, reports that she has caught Tabitha in the very act of kissing Nan.

Kit is outraged. "Just what I expected," she says. "You simply can't deal with these grannies. They've neither sense enough to understand a principle nor strength of mind to act upon it," and she goes to John's study.

"Your mother's been cooing at Nan again—in the park. Mrs. Jenkins saw her. She's hopeless, Jack. I really don't see how we can ask her for this year's summer holiday; I shall never be able to leave her alone with the child for one minute."

John, who has snatched half an hour to complete a review, already two months late, for the *Metaphysical Monthly*, turns a vague and irate eye toward his wife. "Leave Mother behind? But we couldn't do that."

"My dear Jack, are you going to ruin the child's life just to gratify a sentiment?"

John, it happens, is much irritated that week end by a defeat in the council, which has decided to spend a large donation on a new physics laboratory rather than an extension to the library. He throws down his pen. "Dash it all, Kit, you can't take all this new psychological stuff for the tables of the law. Most of it is just guesswork—shots in the dark, or plain quack-quack."

Kit turns pale. She dreads this kind of dispute as much as John himself. "Please, Jack, I know you're prejudiced against the scientists, but you really mustn't drag poor little Nan into it."

"My God! But don't you understand—?"

"Oh dear, must we start it all again, must we muddle up everything about Nan? Isn't it simple enough? Surely you admit at least that it would be wrong even to risk Nan's getting a complex."

John suddenly crumples up his review and throws it into the basket. "Damn it all, this is like a madhouse; how is a man to do any work?"

And there is another fierce hopeless quarrel, followed by a week's misery, while the girl walks about with a pale obstinate face, while John passes from rage to desperation and back again. For Kit does not even listen to him. By the word "muddle" she condemns everything that is not in her own mind, which is in perfect order because it contains only a few very simple notions arranged and ticketed like a shelf of patent medicines. And John, since he is tired after a term's very hard work and needs a peaceful holiday, since he loves Kit and feels for her unhappiness, knows he is already defeated.

Tabitha, after nearly two years, when she has been indispensable at the flat and at the seaside, is so confident of being needed that she does not notice the want of an invitation. She helps, as usual, to pack, and afterwards at tea remarks to John, "I can easily pack some of your books in my trunk."

John does not answer, and Kit turns red. Tabitha gradually feels a crisis, looks with wonder from one to the other. Then she also colors. She thinks, "I must be very tactful, and I must say something." And suddenly she exclaims, "I suppose you can't trust me with poor little Nan."

"Oh, but, Mother—" John speaks in an alarmed manner, very strange in him. "We hope you will run down and see us. The trouble really is getting room—"

"No, no, John; you don't want me. Why not be honest?" and she gets up.

"But, Mother," Kit cries, "you mustn't run away."

"Yes, I'd better; I'm sorry. I'm not angry with you." The poor woman sits down and then gets up again. All are in such distress that it is a great relief even to John when his mother at last makes up her mind to go.

86

TABITHA doesn't realize at once that her happiness is over. She cannot do so until the John Bonsers have gone, and she is left alone in Urrsley. And then she feels, in that solitude, her sentence. She knows that she has been driven out. And as she walks through the streets she is full of angry amazement. Her whole body and soul cry out, "But why should this happen to me? Why should I, so tactful, so broad-minded, be inflicted with such a daughter-in-law, such an impossible creature, so stupid and cruel?"

Alone in her flat she breaks into tears. "It's not fair, it's not fair."

The flat, which she has loved, with its relics from Hackstraw, and even West Street, some fine rugs, a nursing chair, a few good small pictures, seems to her more dreary and senseless than a hospital, because it has no purpose. It is merely a place to be lonely in. It is the center, the pressure point of a loneliness that fills the whole world, the universe.

When she opens her door to go out, she meets loneliness again on the pavement, only more dreary, more ugly. It looks at her from every face, even from those of her acquaintance. She cannot bear Urrsley, and flies to London, but is astonished to find there the same ugly streets. She is revolted by the new fashions, and cannot bring herself to buy even things she needs. For why does she need anything?

One day, upon a desperate impulse to seek a friend, she calls upon Manklow in his office.

They stare at each other. Each is startled by the degeneration of the other's flesh. Manklow sees a small gray-haired woman with a pinched pearl-white face and immense eyes, too prominent and too bright. The little pretty nose is also too prominent and too sharp, the short chin is shorter, and has lost its roundness. The expression is strained, neurotic, at once frightened and angry.

Tabitha sees a wizened, twisted body, with a strangely blotched face. A pair of crutches lean against the desk. She exclaims, "But you've been ill."

"Arthritis." He raises one twisted hand and smiles. "I'm done for, Tib." But his expression has not changed; it is full of a self-satisfaction that now, undisguised, seems naïve. He is still pleased with the success which no doubt is a perpetual surprise to him, in such a treacherous world. He is delighted to see Tabitha, who can measure that success, and admire.

When she offers her sympathy, he puts his head on one side, deprecating kindness. He does not want that from her. And as a riposte he says, "Sad about your Jim; but of course he died just in time. He wouldn't understand us nowadays."

Tabitha will not discuss her husband with Manklow. She asks after Griller.

"Old Griller? He's still trying to be young. But of course the young rather jeer at him. They laugh at me," and Manklow laughs at himself.

"Why should young people be so unkind nowadays—so unkind, and so silly?"

"I don't think they're so silly. It's a poor age, Tib, and they see it. That's one good thing education does for them, anyhow: makes 'em dissatisfied."

"And so everything goes on changing for the worse."

"Yes, I think it does. I think perhaps it was a shade better when we were young. But not much." The man leans back crookedly in his chair; his genial expression is full of relish, as if he has got the better of somebody. "After all, Tib, we've been lucky; our people died before they could nail our colors to any of their old coffin ships."

Tabitha gazes at Manklow, so happy in his victory that he accepts disease as a general accepts wounds upon a field of glory, and wonders as usual if she likes him or detests him more. She thinks, "He's very clever." And by clever she means something contemptible, something between cunning and cowardice—the cleverness of an animal. She says at last, "It's not people, it's all these new ideas; I can't imagine who invents them."

"You've changed a lot since the *Bankside* days, Tib. Well, we all get conservative as we get older, don't we? Older and wiser. I'm that way myself. One of the truest and bluest."

"Then why do you write those articles for the socialists?"

"Can't fight against the stream, Tib. I mean, it's just no good. The only way to put the clock back, you know, without breaking the works, is to put it eleven hours forward. That's why I'm backing labor."

"But what can labor do?"

"Do itself in, like every other party; like your conservative party. That is the advantage of democracy; it has such rotten governments that they fall to pieces before they can ruin everything."

"I'm not a conservative. I don't change my party. I'll always be a liberal."

"A true, faithful conservative liberal," Manklow says, smiling.

And Tabitha, as she climbs the stairs of her expensive and old-fashioned hotel to which, although it has no lift and few bathrooms, she comes still, because Gollan has always gone there and because it is visible in decline, says bitterly to herself, "No, I really don't like him; if he had any real feeling he would hate all these new ideas and try to stop them. He would not allow these silly girls like Kit to fly in God's face and spoil their own children's happiness."

She calls at the Wrinches' house, but leaves the step without ringing the bell. One day, rather than return to her bitterness at Urrsley, she rings up Harry at the Cedars. He answers in a surprised, worried voice, "Tibby! But what a stranger. Yes, do come; come and stay."

87

She and Harry have exchanged letters at Christmas, and sometimes at Easter, and they have met once or twice in London, but she has never visited the Cedars since Harry's second marriage. She has felt too strong a repugnance from Clara in her victory. But now it is Clara who welcomes her and asks her advice. She does not know what to do with Harry, who is ill and will not rest. He has quarreled, too, with both the daughter Ellice, who has married badly, and with Timothy, qualified two years before, who refuses to come into the practice. "And the work is too much since this Insurance Act."

Tabitha indeed is shocked by Harry's thinness, his nervous restlessness, his anger against Timothy; and she sees that Clara is also worn out. She goes to remonstrate with Timothy in his East End surgery. Timothy has grown into a tall plump young man. Horn rims give to his broad pale face an expression of owlish simplicity. He is flattered by this visit from an aunt who, in his imagination, has had a distinguished career, and kisses her with solemn affection. But he will not hear of joining his father's practice. "I should have to live at home, and I can't stand Clara; besides, she doesn't want me."

"But, Timothy, she's most anxious to have you—she's terribly worried about your father."

Timothy smiles and looks suddenly mature, with the premature cynicism of the young doctor. "She may think so, but she doesn't really want anyone. She's too jealous. She knows that she's stupid, and that makes her jealous. She drove out poor Ellice; she drove me out; and she got rid of two assistants in the same way."

"She's frightened now, and no wonder; your father can't go on like this."

"Of course he can't. He needs a partner. Since the new act everyone is taking a partner. I'm in a firm here; there are three of us, so that we can get an annual holiday. Of course we've got a big panel practice; and it's the panel that kills. It's certainly too much for Father by himself."

"I hate Lloyd George; he stirs up trouble everywhere."

"Oh, it's not a bad act. Father was all for the act himself. The trouble is that he won't see that it's brought in a new situation. He won't adapt himself."

"Why should he, at sixty-four? After slaving all these years." Tabitha is angry. "Why should he change his whole life just to suit a lot of nasty politicians?"

Timothy looks at the excited little woman and assumes a mask-like expression, such as young doctors acquire even in a month of practice to meet unreasonable demands and foolish complaints. "Well," he says, "it's a difficult question."

"Not at all difficult," Tabitha says. "It simply means you don't care."

She goes home in great indignation against Timothy; but when she suggests to Harry that he take a partner there is at once an outcry. Harry will not risk his patients with any of these young quacks or old crocks, and Clara warmly agrees with him.

But one evening, when Clara is called away to the bedside of some aged aunt, the man suddenly perceives his sister and he begins to talk of the old happy times, when life was not a nightmare of work and worry and there was time for love. He takes Tabitha's hand and says, "Why have we drifted apart? It's not really my fault; I haven't had time to think for the last ten years." Excited by this talk, taken out of his routine, he is astonished by his own existence. "What has happened to us, Tibby? I can't do half what I ought to do, even now."

"You should get an assistant, Harry; some young man who will get to know the patients and learn proper doctoring from you."

"An assistant." Harry is surprised by this suggestion. "But I've tried assistants. You don't realize the difficulties, Tibby. We've had assistants—two of 'em—and they were good for nothing but eating for six and burning holes in the furniture. Clara couldn't stand 'em; and I don't blame her."

"But, Harry, other doctors find good assistants. Timothy started as an assistant. And it's the only way to get yourself any peace."

"That's true; the fact is, I did mean to have another shot, but somehow it got passed over."

"Let me draw up an advertisement," and she goes to the writing table.

"What, now?"

"Why not now?"

"Well, why not, as you say." And he laughs. "You're still the same as ever—rushing into things."

They draw up the advertisement together, and Harry carries it off to his study for an envelope. He promises that it shall be posted next morning. But next morning he does not get up for breakfast and Clara apologizes for him in these words: "Poor Harry didn't sleep a wink; I can't think what's upset him so much. It couldn't have been anything that happened last night."

And before lunch, when Harry is still invisible, she comes with her agitated voice and sly frightened eyes. "Harry is talking of an assistant again; it's such a pity. We've had two, and both of them drove him mad; he simply couldn't bear them to do anything for him."

"But I thought you wanted him to have help, Clara."

The woman darts nervously about the room, dusting and looking at Tabitha from various angles. "Harry has been so difficult these last few days, I'm really afraid he may worry himself into a breakdown."

"Do you mean that I upset him?"

"Oh no, no; but of course one does have to be so careful what one says—he's so nervous."

Tabitha leaves next day, and Harry, by some contrivance of Clara's, doesn't even say good-by. He is out paying visits, and when she telephones to him at a patient's, expresses surprise that she is going that morning. But he does not ask her to stay longer, and as she drives away she says to herself, "He doesn't want me—so much the better!" And jerking up the window of the cab to cut off Clara's waving hand and affectionate smile, she says to herself, "I don't belong anywhere any more. And when I try to push in I'm simply in the way." Her heart swells as if it would burst, but she refuses to cry. She cherishes her pain, to feed her anger against a world without justice or mercy.

She goes back to Urrsley not because she wishes to see the place again but because she hates it. And when Kit and John return, she visits them only by invitation. She does not even inquire for Nancy.

She makes so obvious her hurt feelings that even John is impatient. He agrees with Kit, who says, "It's too silly, and we've no time. Besides, we'll be nice to her and she'll come round."

Both are very busy and worried. Kit has begun new research and is also working for the progressive party in the council. John has suffered a great defeat at the hands of his enemies, a defeat so surprising and so bitter that for the first time in his life he commits an injustice. He insults the patient Gow.

Gow has explained the position. "It seems that we simply can't afford an historian, Mr. Bonser. The fact is that there is a real emergency, scientists are very badly needed. The war has had a startling effect on science; it has pushed forward all kinds of research—and laboratories are of course extremely expensive. So I'm afraid you'll have to take the history as well as the philosophy, at least for the present."

And John answers rudely, "So, after all, Urrsley is going to be a cram shop for dyers and soap boilers. Wasn't I a fool to believe anything else?"

Gow refuses to quarrel with the angry young man, and when he threatens to resign, makes a personal appeal to him. Keeler also points out that if John goes he will be left almost alone to support the cause of true education. But in any case, John knows very well that he can't yet desert his young classes. For nearly all his pupils have made sacrifices to become his pupils. They have quarreled with their families, refused jobs, and excited the scorn of their girls, out of a belief in classical studies, a loyalty to humane learning, which, expressed at Oxford or Cambridge, would raise a smile.

And so he is more closely entangled, and more oppressed by the work which can never be done so well as he could choose. He must reread his ancient history, as well as teach it; and he can never catch up with research.

When the time comes for another summer holiday, he cries in despair, "But I can't waste a month at the sea. I haven't the time."

"Really, Jack, you must try to be with us; Nancy is growing up so fast, and she needs you to answer her questions."

John bargains for a fortnight in London to do some special reading. There is a week's battle to decide the question, and the young couple do not even ask themselves what is to be done about Tabitha. They are too harassed to consider the whims of a cranky grandmother. They accept her reserve, her aloofness, and have built about it a routine which preserves a decent appearance and avoids trouble. She comes to tea once a week, when there is always a new iced cake. Nancy is brought down after tea and sat upon her knee for five or ten minutes to look at a picture book selected by Kit. Animals are allowed, and alphabets, but not Bible stories, which are considered misleading. And once or twice a term she is asked with other matrons to dinner and bridge, which neither John nor Kit play. They have no time for such distractions.

88

TABITHA, once more left alone in Urrsley, understands that her whole protest, her dignified submission to a cruel fate, is quite ineffective. It is simply not noticed. And it is because of the monstrous injustice that has betrayed her that she cannot forget her despair. She goes to church even more regularly, more devotedly. Her strong faith is not broken. She sees God's love at work in the world; she imagines evil as the punishment of those who deny love. But she finds no happiness in her faith; it turns to anger in her primitive soul, too proud to use religion for escape. Even in the midst of the general confession, "We have offended against thy holy laws," she is reminded that it is not she but Kit and John who have offended. It is they who have no health; and yet they are so far from being penitent that they won't even recognize their folly.

Tabitha forgives, like a good Christian; but how can she overlook the crime that goes on every day—the crime of obstinate consistence in doing injury? The act of forgiveness itself only reminds her of a situation which forgiveness cannot cure, and brings back to her the bitterness of soul which makes her life wretched.

She forgives, but her whole life is a protest against evil. She is dowdy in dress because she despises the fashions; she avoids her friends in Urrsley because their attempts to amuse her, like jokes at a funeral, offend her sense of calamity. And when she looks in the glass at her hollow cheeks and eyes she feels a certain satisfaction, the sense of a mourner, that it is right and proper to suffer.

Now and then someone in Urrsley asks what has happened to Lady Gollan, and is answered that she has become reclusive and unapproachable.

"And how is that?"

"The usual middle-aged trouble, I suppose. She's got up against everyone and everything, including her daughter-in-law."

"She must be a tartar if she has managed to quarrel with that nice Mrs. Bonser; you couldn't find a better wife and mother. So conscientious about everything."

It seems to them that most of these survivors from the fabulous age before the war would be better dead. For they are not even pitiable; they are merely superannuated. And, in any case, people are too busy with important new tasks to entertain unadaptable and foolish middle-aged widows.

89

ONE afternoon in the spring of 1924, when Tabitha is putting on her hat for the weekly tea party at John's flat, she gets a phone call from him. "Don't come today or you may run into Father; he threatens to call."

"Why shouldn't I meet your father?"

"Of course if you like, we'll be delighted."

"Did you ask him to Urrsley?"

"Good heavens no. I fancy he's looking for a job. But I don't want you to be worried."

"So I'm not to come till next week."

"But, Mother, come when you like. Of course we're out tomorrow and on Wednesday—"

"Yes, next week. I don't want to be troublesome." And she takes off her hat not without a feeling that she has heaped up a little more grievance against Kit and John.

She does not even think of Bonser till she has put on her kettle. Then she reflects, "That brute, he'd only pester me for money. Thank goodness John warned me."

A few minutes later there is a knock on the door; and when she opens it, to gaze into the dark landing, she is immediately kissed. "Hullo, my Pops."

Tabitha is so shocked with amazement that she cannot speak. But already Bonser has pushed past her into the entry, where he stands grinning at her, and panting from the stairs. Tabitha's first thought, as she looks at the man, grown fat and coarse with a brick-colored face and pouched eyes, is, "Now he looks what he is—a vulgar cad."

"Why, Tib, did I make you jump? By Jove, pretty as a picture!"

Tabitha makes no answer. She thinks, "But what a bother." She would prefer to be brooding over her tea in calm anger.

Bonser's jovial grin suddenly disappears. "I see I'm not wanted. All right, all right, I'll go quietly. Just let me take my breath. I suppose you haven't got a drink? No? It's my heart, you know; it's never been the same since my war service."

"Would you like a cup of tea?"

"Tea? H'm! Well, let it be tea if there's nothing else." He goes into the sitting room and drops into Tabitha's armchair. "A nice little nest you've got here. Ah, you always fell on your feet—or somebody else's. I suppose Jim had tucked away a pile where the creditors couldn't find it. My God, Tibs, you and your Johnny made a nice fool of me between you."

"How did we do that?"

"By making me hold on when I wanted to sell. Not a hint that you were going to knock the market. I suppose you cleaned up half a million between you out of that slump."

"We lost almost everything."

"Tell me another. Well, I'm not blaming you. The one I blame is that pup of yours; and he practically showed me the door. He seems to forget that he owes everything to me. It was me that insisted on a proper Oxford education for him. Yes, I made a gentleman of him, and he practically called me a tout. He's a fool, too, because I could make a fortune for him if he liked; it's there for the taking."

Tabitha brings in the tea and pours out a cup for the man. He puts it to his lips, sighs, and says, "Funny you don't keep brandy—it ought to be in every medicine chest. I'm not too bright, Tibs; pretty near on my uppers." And he begins to talk about his misfortunes. Everyone, it seems, has cheated him, not only Tabitha herself and Jim Gollan, but his business partners, and especially Miss Millie Minter, who after promising to marry him and accepting jewelry worth ten thousand pounds has jilted him for an actor, a common chorus boy without even the manners of a gentleman.

"I thought you had a wife before."

It appears however that Bonser's wife was not, after all, a wife. "It was a Scotch marriage and it turned out that a Scotch marriage didn't hold water unless you're both Scotch or do it in Scotland. Just as well, too; that woman was diddling me for years on the household bills. If it hadn't been for that I might have married her properly. And then she deserted me in Canada. She thought I was finished. But she made a mistake there. I was pretty near a millionaire even before the war started. And I could be one again, Tibs, if only I had a spot of capital. That's all I want, capital."

Tabitha is silent. She notices the darned trousers and patched boots and thinks, "He really is poor." But the idea causes no reaction in her feelings. They are already fully occupied and, as it were, fixed in her anger against that world which includes this man also—this intruder.

"I'm not joking, Tibs; it's what I said to that young cub and I say it to you: this place is full of money asking to be picked up. Why, there's a pub there on the London road going for eight hundred pounds —eight hundred, and right on a crossroads. But you're not interested."

"I haven't any money to spare."

"You've got two hundred pounds of stuff in this room; that's all we want, Tibs. Give me a hundred jimmies and I'll make you rich. Damn it all, Tibs, you owe it to me. You've ruined me twice over; you wrecked my life. Well, I'm not complaining; I know I was always a fool about women—too soft-hearted. But it's for your own sake."

At last he goes; he must catch his train. But on the landing he makes a last effort. "Of course I know it's no good talking to you, you're prejudiced, but if you should change your mind, if you should want to make a pot, a real pot, just drop me a line. Here's the address: Colonel Bonser, Palace Hotel, Bilbury Road; and you needn't invest a hundred—fifty would do. In fact, I could double a fiver for you if you liked. And that reminds me, I suppose you haven't change for a pound note?"

"I'm afraid not."

"That's a pity; but look here, if you could lend me half a crown I'll send you an I O U as soon as I get home."

Tabitha lends him the half-crown and he thanks her warmly. "But not a word to Johnny; he had the cheek to say that I wasn't to see you —molest you, he called it. And we don't want any trouble with the little worm, or I might lose my temper and tell him what I think of him."

"No, I won't tell him."

"Good-by, Tibs. And remember: fifty quid—ten quid—anything you like, however small; it'll bring you in a hundred per cent—a thousand very likely."

"I'll remember." She shuts the door behind the man and goes back to her room, to her anger. The anger is only a little more active, exasperated. She is surprised by this new outrage. "Really, Dick is too much."

She is impatient in her indignation. It works within her like a passion. She is upset. She can't keep still when she thinks of the man's impudence, and walks about from sitting room to kitchen with a frown. "Really, to come to me like that with such lies. And such swindles. Colonel—and Scotch marriage—Scotch marriage! No, it's too much." And suddenly, unexpectedly, she is seized with laughter. "Scotch marriage—Scotch and Colonel!" She falls into a chair helpless with giggles. Tears are forced to her eyes. "He really is beyond everything. What a blessing I was so discouraging. He might be a complete plague."

Two days later she receives a letter beginning, "I send you a P.O.

for half a crown." There is no postal order in the envelope, but there is a description in the letter of some cottage that can be bought for two hundred pounds. "Right on the main road to Brighton; it would make a first-class tea house." A postscript asks for a loan of five pounds, urgently, to meet an unexpected debt. "It will be repaid within the week, on my honor."

Tabitha says, "I knew he would begin begging," but she sends a pound. And Bonser asks for a meeting in order that he can explain to her the wonderful chance offered by the tea room.

90

"No, NO," Tabitha says; "I'm not quite such a fool." But it is impossible to take Bonser seriously and she is still full of amusement, which seems to affect not only her mind but her body. She finds herself energetic, bored with inaction. She buys a new hat. She does not answer Bonser's letter, but she goes to London on the day appointed, and then, feeling guilty, foolish, hurries to the rendezvous. But the very guilt is somehow amusing. She is amused at herself in her folly. She excuses herself, "And he won't be there; he wouldn't expect me."

But Bonser, it seems, has expected her. With the confident air of an old beau, he is waiting for her. He has got himself up to kill, with a flower in his buttonhole, his hat over his ear. The effect is that of a seedy bounder. "Colonel," Tabitha thinks, laughing at first sight of the smeared hair, the gorgeous blue necktie thrust into a yellow waistcoat, the tight blue coat bursting out at the seams, the horsey trousers darned at the pockets, the worn tan boots half covered by old canvas spats. "How perfectly awful he looks."

But Bonser is delighted with himself. He greets Tabitha with easy condescension. "Hullo, Pops; you're looking very nice. You can still knock 'em. Dammitall, it only seems like yesterday since you threw your eye at me and put me in your bag. And it was well worth it, old girl, wasn't it? A good time was had by all. What will you have? Come, this is an occasion; we've got to celebrate." And he carries her off by the arm to a saloon bar. Tabitha protests; she will not drink, she laughs at the idea of buying a tea shop, and she goes home by an early train. But she is more amused, more excited than ever, and in the next week she meets Bonser again. She begins to see him every week, and every week he has a new scheme. With only a thousand pounds he will open a string of night clubs to produce five thousand a year, and he suggests that Tabitha shall invest a thousand pounds. "It's real property, you know; safe as the bank."

"But, Dick, I couldn't get fifty without asking my lawyer."

"Is it in trust?"

"No, I don't think so. It's war loan."

Bonser shakes his head at her childish ignorance of finance, and asks her what income she gets. He then cries out, "So you've got at least seven thousand pounds—probably eight—wasting away in war loan. It's a crime—"

And when Tabitha refuses to take her money from the lawyer and give it to him, he is insulted. "You don't trust me, Tibby, that's your trouble. That's what broke us up before when you walked off and left me flat. You don't care a damn for me really—never did."

"Oh yes, Dick."

"No, no; not you. Suppose I asked you to marry me, what would you say? Why, you're laughing at me now."

"Oh no, Dick." But she can't help smiling.

And suddenly Bonser jumps up. "It's my own fault," he says bitterly. "I'm an old fool. But you won't catch me again." He walks off; and, in fact, he makes no more appointments.

91

"AND a very good thing too," Tabitha says. "I was seeing much too much of the man. I was encouraging him to be troublesome."

But now her life in the flat in Urrsley is so utterly flat and wretched that she does not know what to do with herself. She cannot even brood. The dignity of despair, of protest, is gone from her, so that her very solitude has no meaning. It is an agonizing vacuum. After three weeks, exhausted, sleepless, affected with crying fits, she writes again to Bonser and proposes, under safeguards, a meeting for tea. "I shan't be able to stay long, and I hope you won't talk any more nonsense."

Bonser instantly proposes a week end at Brighton, "to look at a property there." They meet, and Tabitha laughs at this suggestion. Bonser cries, "Oh, very well, but what did you come for?" And when Tabitha goes home she is committed to spending the week end, not at Brighton, but Sancombe. "The landlady knows me there; I'll say I'm staying with her."

"Oh, if you're afraid of a scandal—"

Tabitha is afraid of Bonser. But of course John and Kit hear about

Bonser's presence at Sancombe. Two separate busybodies, old friends of Tabitha, write to John. He rushes round between a lecture and a committee to call on his mother. "Mother, it can't be true that you have been seeing that blackguard."

"But I thought you liked him; you used to like him very much."

"My dear mother, it's not what I may have thought ten years ago but what's going to happen to you now." The young man is quite furious at Tabitha's folly, which has brought him this new worry.

"Don't you think, John, I'm old enough to look after myself?"

"I certainly thought so; but now it seems rather an open question."

Tabitha, in angry dignity, retorts that it is at least a question for her herself. And that week she does not come to tea at the flat.

"She knows she's making a fool of herself," Kit says, "and so she's getting up a new quarrel as an excuse for not coming near us."

"What nonsense! Mother was never like that. You invent these subtleties."

But in fact Tabitha is glad to break with Kit and John in case they attempt to drive Bonser away from her. Especially she does not want them to know of Bonser's repeated proposals of marriage.

"I certainly shan't marry him," she says; "but I'm not going to have him insulted, poor man."

These proposals, however, are troublesome, because each time Bonser is refused he grows more disgusted and stays away longer. At last he stays away for a month, and Tabitha is obliged to seek him in his East End lodging in order to explain that she did not mean to hurt his feelings.

He proposes again; she accepts him. And on the way home she feels quite drunk between reckless despair and a kind of humorous self-pity. "Why did I do that?" And on her wedding day, as she comes out of the sordid little registry office in Bilbury Street, she is smiling in bewilderment. "How has this happened?" she asks herself. "Am I quite, quite mad?"

But she is full of a secret abounding delight. The very recklessness of the proceedings is a delight to her; and she goes upon her honeymoon, to a hotel at Pynemouth, with more than the excitement of a young bride. For her joy is unlooked for, like a reprieve from death.

"How funny it is," she says to Bonser, when she finds herself alone with him in the big double room.

"What's funny?"

"The bridal couple."

"Funny! I don't see that it's funny. If you think I'm an old man yet, you're mistaken." He stops to look in a glass and pass his hand across the bald patch which begins to show through the curls; then, satisfied, he draws her arm through his and pats her hand. "You and me could give some of these young couples ten yards start in the hundred. The thing is, Pops, we've got the style; we've got the tradition."

By this he means that he knows how to spend money. He drives Tabitha, by hired car, to lunch in famous beauty spots; he buys her chocolates and stockings; he takes her to dances, and tells her, "Never mind the expense; I've made three fortunes, and now I'll make you another one."

"But, Dick, we mustn't be rash, must we? We have so little."

These words mysteriously depress Bonser. "There you go again," he says, "knocking it." And he adds with gloomy disgust, "I suppose we're going to have another cheap dinner in that foul hole of ours."

Tabitha understands the hint and suggests dinner at the Grand Hotel, where Bonser at once orders champagne. And afterwards in their bedroom he takes her on his knee and jogs her up and down. "This is the way the ladies ride. You're still a fairy, Pops. It's the little ones are the worst. Oh, the little devil."

She is delighted to see him once more in high spirits, and says, "You're not cross with me any more?"

"I'm always cross with you, you tightwad," which makes her anxious again. For she knows very well how much her new and unexpected happiness depends on Bonser's temper. When cross he can make her wretched by a look, but when he is cheerful her heart dances with his smile.

After a week of honeymoon she wakes one morning early, to a battery of pig-like snores, and looking at the broad red face on the next pillow, shining against the sheet like grocer's apples, she reflects, "But I'm happy; at fifty-four, I'm fearfully happy. Dick may be an idiot and a bounder, and of course he's completely unreliable; heaven knows what's going to happen to me, but there's no doubt about the happiness. Yes, I suppose I love him; I've always loved him quite madly—that is to say, quite stupidly."

And realizing her love she greets him on waking with so tender a kiss that he looks at her out of one yellow and puffy eye, and grunts, "What's the little game?"

"Nothing; only I love you."

He opens the other eye and says, "You're a cunning little devil, aren't you, Pops? You always get what you want."

"Have you got a head this morning?"

"Here, that's rather rude, isn't it? I don't like rude girls."

92 He is usually short-tempered before breakfast and does not show his real animation till after eleven, when he takes his first drink. Then he begins to chatter, to bounce.

"Look at that, Pops." He points his chin at a large neglected building in a wilderness of grounds.

"It looks like a ruined hotel."

"It's a gold mine, Pops. And look at the glass in the garden. By Jove, there's half an acre of glass. I always wanted a garden with glass."

"Dick, you don't want a hotel?"

"That's just what we do want. I've had my eye on this place for some time."

"We've never been down this road before."

But this is a very unwise remark. Bonser looks at her with indignation and asks, "Do you mean I'm a liar?"

"Oh no, Dick; but really— Look at the plaster falling off the walls —and the nettles."

"Plaster, nettles! My God, listen to her! Did you ever hear of plasterers, or see a scythe?"

"But, Dick—"

"I'm going to ask about this."

He goes straight to the agents and comes back in triumph, to find Tabitha smiling on the pavement as at a good joke.

He demands, "What's the joke?" And before she can answer, exclaims, "Eight thousand, and two thousand on mortgage. And I bet they'll take six and leave a half. They're jumping to sell; I knew they would be."

"But, Dick—"

"Shall I tell you why?" He draws himself up with a grin of cunning importance, and suddenly stoops forward. "Because it's not on the front, because it's on a nasty noisy main road and two miles from the pier."

"Yes, Dick, that's what I think."

"Of course you do; but I tell you the main road is an advantage, never mind how noisy. And why?"

"Why?" says Tabitha obediently.

"Because of cars—cars, Pops; cars which go along the roads and stop whenever they fancy. And there's more of 'em every day."

"But, Dick, we couldn't take a hotel; we don't know one thing about hotels."

"Anyone can run a hotel; you hire a manager. Look here, Pops, how soon can you raise three thousand?"

"But, Dick, we can't—"

"Oh, very well, we can't; all right, we won't. Not a word," and he walks off in disgust.

Tabitha thinks, "No, I can't; it would mean ruin for us both."

But after Bonser has sulked for two days she gives way. She says to herself, "What is the good of money if we're both wretched?"

Her last hope is that the agents for the Beausite Hotel will refuse Bonser's offer. But they are delighted to get rid of the property on any terms, and Tabitha is obliged to command her lawyer to sell out five thousand pounds of war loan. She instructs him also to keep the transaction private, for she is terrified of John's anger. She feels he has a right to be angry, since if she loses everything she may become dependent upon him.

And then she is at once so busy and anxious that she has no time to look back. Bonser's notion, she finds, of running a hotel is to invite town councilors to dinner, and when Tabitha protests at the expense, he answers, "You don't understand business, old girl. One has to know people."

"But need you give them champagne?"

"It's an economy in the end."

"At least we needn't drink it by ourselves."

"That's an economy, too; it keeps one in fettle. And where would we be if I knocked up at a time like this? Who would do the thinking?"

He engages a manager, a certain Giuseppe Teri, who has been running a night club, and commands him to get a first-class staff and the most expensive wines. He hires a head gardener and tells him to make the gardens a show so that people will stop to look at them. He orders furniture, carpets, and pictures, which are mostly classical nudes—"No one can object to real Academy stuff, and everybody likes the figure when there's no objection to looking at it."

And it is Tabitha who must hang the pictures and arrange the furniture. She has never been so hard worked. Her attention when John arrives one morning is only half for what he will say; the other half is for the muddles that Giuseppe and the furniture men will accomplish as soon as her back is turned. And John's first cry is, "My dear mother, if only you'd waited a month till the examinations were over."

"But you needn't worry about me, John."

"I hear you've sold out your war loan—how can I help worrying? What are you going to live on when that's gone?"

"But it's all being reinvested in this hotel; a very good investment."

"Do you really believe that?"

Tabitha, since in her heart she does not believe it, and since she is a bad liar, blushes when she says, "It really seems a good opening."

Mother and son then stare at each other and something is confessed between them. John says, "You know it's perfectly crazy to go back to a man like that." But he says it in a doubtful anguished voice. He feels that life is difficult, much more so than he had expected; that the most ordinary lives contain profound and tragic experience. He is vaguely aware that Tabitha has been unhappy at Urrsley, and that the loneliness of a middle-aged widow can touch extremes of active misery. A thousand new impressions of sympathy and guilt rush upon him. And Tabitha says, "You mustn't feel responsible for me, dear; if I lose my money I shan't ask you to support me. That would be a wicked thing."

"But of course I must; how could I let you go in want?"

"That's not fair to me or to you; it's putting pressure on me."

"It's nothing to do with fairness. Heavens, Mother, don't you understand that? Justice is a reasonable thing; it's neither here nor there in family life." This phrase, going beyond the case, obviously expresses some personal grudge.

"How is Kit?" Tabitha asks; and again they look at each other with wondering eyes.

But just then Giuseppe appears to ask Tabitha what is to be done about the new awnings; how high must they be?

"But, Teri, I gave you the measurements—but wait, I'd better see the men." She hurries away to give instructions, and when she comes back, agitated with long complicated arguments, she finds John looking at his watch.

"I must fly—I simply daren't miss this train."

Tabitha takes him to the station. At the last minute, just as the train is going, she remembers that she has wanted to make clear this point about her dependence on John. She has wanted to contradict his view that justice has nothing to do with such a case. But when she hops up on the step to peep through the window, she sees that John has already put his writing case across his knees and spread out a sheaf of examination papers for correction. And what shocks her is to notice for the first time that he has a bald patch on the top of his head.

"Poor Johnny," she thinks, as she drives away, "he's getting old already; and what a life, what an awful life of rush and worry!" She feels such a pang of grief for John that she wants to cry. But the hotel is in sight, and she sees at once that the men are putting the awnings on the wrong side, where they can't be seen from the road. "Oh dear, oh dear, one has to do everything oneself, and there's no time even to think."

At Urrsley, when John gives his account to Kit, the young people agree that even if Tabitha ruins herself she is better away from Urrsley, where she only adds to the complications of a life already too agitated.

93

AND Tabitha is aware, day and night, that ruin is advancing upon her with a speed that increases by compound interest. For as the bills mount, Bonser grows more extravagant. One day he brings home an immense second-hand open Isotta Fraschini, painted bright scarlet. And when Tabitha protests against the cost, he answers, "A good car is always cheaper; it doesn't need so much repairs. And we need a car, Pops, to spy out the land. We'll want to extend. My idea is a chain of Beausites all round the coast—save overhead costs."

He spies out the land every day. And though when he returns he complains of this hard life, he is always in the best of humors, slightly drunk and very affectionate.

"Wonderful little Pops, how are things today?"

"A few more to lunch; but the bank manager telephoned about the overdraft. Really, Dick, I don't know how we can go on."

"Don't you worry, Pops. The great thing is to make a splash and hang the expense. We'll soon turn the corner now, thanks to my Popsy."

He takes her on his knee. "Just to get round me," Tabitha thinks. But she is laughing; she is full of happiness—a pleasure painful in its sharpness, because it is terrified of what may come. And it seems to her that as a young bride she was too silly, too inexperienced to know delight, and that only now, when she has been saved from wretchedness, from the deadlock of the soul, can she enjoy life.

"But, Dick," she implores Bonser, "we don't need three gardeners."

"Now that's just like you, spoiling the ship for a hap'orth of tar. Let it alone, let it alone."

But he is patient with her; and when she nags him he only gives her a slap behind and says, "The Pops on the warpath! Well, it's only her little way."

94 At the end of its first year the Beausite is losing an average of forty pounds a week and owes nearly two thousand pounds to the bank, which is threatening to put in a receiver. Bonser has given a bill of sale on the furniture, and Giuseppe, in true Italian gloom, walks about like a mummer at the funeral of civilization. Tabitha runs about like a hen in a hailstorm, checking the stores, the linen, seeking to find out some way of preventing the maids from stealing sugar and the charwomen from making away with dusters. She says, "This is the end"; but still, like the famous lady who was found in the midst of her burning house changing into an old frock because it was raining outside, tries to make economies.

Bonser, however, does not even acknowledge a crisis. When he is not half drunk, he is full of new ideas which make him even more excited than drunk. He buys fruit machines for the back corridors, a cinema for wet afternoons.

One day he comes back in great excitement about an arch which he has seen at a bankrupt exhibition. It is for sale at three hundred pounds. "Designed by a famous French architect—the finest thing I ever saw: five hundred lamps in blue and red and a sort of fountain of lights playing on top. It beats anything in Piccadilly Circus by all the way from Tattenham Corner to Champagne Charley."

"But, Dick, you know we can't even pay the rent."

"And what a bargain—cost a thousand new. All wrought iron with beaten copper—real art work; it would be a crime to let it be broken up."

"The bank says we must close down next month."

"There you go, bank, bank, bank! My God, Tibby, you don't help much, do you?"

Tabitha hears no more about the arch and thinks it has been forgotten with a dozen other projects, equally fantastic, until one morning she finds a gang of navvies tearing down the stone gate pillars of the hotel. Bonser has bought the arch. He walks up and down exulting in this triumph, telling even passers in the street that he has secured the famous arch of victory from the South Coast Peace Exhibition, that it is a real work of art and cost him a thousand pounds. On the second day, when the arch itself—an enormous trellis of metalwork forty feet high and fifteen wide—is being bolted together, he has raised the price. "Two thousand pounds and dirt cheap at that."

When it is finished he gives a lunch party to the mayor and select business men of Pynemouth, at which he makes a long speech about the duty of an Englishman to support art. He refers to the dead in the late war and this noble memorial of their victory and their sacrifices. He himself and several of the party shed tears which are perfectly sincere, and afterwards the photographer of the *Pynemouth Gazette* takes a picture of the whole group standing under the arch. The report in the paper fills a column and is headed, "Victory arch saved for Pynemouth. Patriotic action of Colonel Bonser at the Beausite. A memorial for all time." And it begins, "The proposal to cut down the famous arch to make an entrance for the marine gardens, a piece of vandalism disgraceful to our town, has been finally and decisively set at rest by the statement of Colonel Bonser that the artist's original conception shall remain unimpaired in every detail."

But no one is surprised to see, a week later, a sign erected on top of the arch, in letters three feet high, illuminated in red and blue, BEAUSITE HOTEL. GARAGE. DANCING. Even the chairman of the arts committee is pleased, for he is a creditor, and he sees that the courtyard of the hotel is already full of cars.

95

IT IS probably true that the arch and its notice, DANCING, saved the Beausite. In the last two years all Europe has begun to dance. Giant palais de danse have begun to spring up in every town; the same papers which tell of ruin and misery, of the falling franc and a bankrupt mark, describe a night life more gay and extravagant than ever before. It is as though the war, which has broken the old frame of things, has projected the masses, whether they like it or not, into a new and looser society, more primitive, more free. It has made the rich poor, and given to millions of those who were stinted the little more which can buy freedom and luxury, if only for a week end.

Tabitha is astonished by the stream of pleasure seekers, old and young, which now begins to pour through the Beausite: people who seem to have boundless leisure and cash, complete liberty, no morals, and always smart new clothes.

"But I thought everybody was ruined," Tabitha says. "Where do they come from?"

"Ruined my eye," Bonser says. "The bust-ups are howling, but look at Woolworths. Look at all the little shops and little factories. And they like spending, this new lot. Now they've got some loose paper they're going to make it float."

The Beausite is now giving three dances a week; and in summer every room is full. Tabitha is busy from six o'clock in the morning, and often she is up long after midnight; for one disadvantage of the new popularity of the Beausite is that it attracts what Tabitha calls these modern girls, who, as she says, have no conscience. "I never feel any peace till a dance is over and we have got rid of them."

She is horrified to see girls not yet out of their teens drive up twice a week to the Beausite with some young man, dance their slow lascivious Black Bottoms and tangos, get discreetly drunk, and drive away again into some dark byroad, where they can turn off the lights.

Often there are a dozen cars in a row, one behind the other, each in darkness and silence, except for an occasional laugh or faint scream.

Tabitha complains to Bonser, who, to her surprise, takes the matter very coolly. "That's all right, Pops. Let 'em alone. So long as they're happy, we're happy."

"But, Dick, what about our good name, our license? I don't think you realize how bad things are."

"Bless you, old lady, I'll look after that. Got a light?" He likes Tabitha to light his cigars, which grow longer and fatter every day. He is still spying out the land, and is often away for the night, examining some hotel property, even a hundred miles away.

Tabitha, left to take charge, warns the police about the cars in the lane. One evening she causes Teri to send a couple of young dancers off the dance floor.

And now Bonser is very angry. "Do you want to ruin us?"

"But, Dick, you should have seen them; it was really disgusting, quite horrible."

"Damn it all, Pops, keep off the dance floor if you don't like to see people enjoying themselves." And he continues to grumble for some days. He orders the lights once more to be dimmed in the alcoves, and some new arbors to be set up in the grounds. "What do you think they come for, Pops, sermons? Well, I don't mind your being religious, I am myself, but keep it in its place; keep it for Sundays."

Tabitha is alarmed. She perceives now that the Beausite, with its cocktail bars, its bronzes and nudes, its shaded sofas, its dances under dimmed lights, has been acquiring a very fast air, and that Bonser means to have it so. She does not say to herself, "Dick is a completely selfish man who has used my money to give himself a new start, and is only kind to me now because I manage the hotel for him," but she has a thorough grasp of the truth. Her whole happiness depends on her usefulness.

And faced with the loss of that usefulness, she says to herself, "But perhaps Dick is right. After all, middle-aged women do tend to be narrow; perhaps I am a little old-fashioned."

She avoids the dance floor; and though she can't always avoid the couples who lie about on sofas in the passages, or share one chair in the garden, she turns her eyes from them and urges herself not to be narrow and old-fashioned.

One evening, however, she is called by a maid to deal with a girl discovered half dressed with a young man in his bedroom.

Tabitha orders the girl to leave, and there is at once a great row. The young woman, who is drunk enough to be reckless, refuses to dress, and when, by the young man's intervention, she agrees to do so, comes out upon the stairs and shouts that she won't be turned out; no one is going to put her out of this rotten pub.

Tabitha, horrified by this vulgar disgraceful scene, and yet driven on by the need of vindicating decency, advances upon her with an expression which is really one of desperation, but seems like ferocity, so that the girl gives way and bolts through the lounge hall, full of interested guests, to the front door.

There she turns to scream her last defiance. "It's just you nasty-minded old cats that make all the trouble. Jealousy, that's what it is, because you can't get it for yourself. And what about your own pets? What about Miss Spring and the Colonel?"

She then takes flight and Tabitha walks away to her office, in great dignity but with shaking knees. She says to herself, "Dick will never forgive me; but how did I know that she'd be so violent, and that she'd say things about him, too?"

Miss Spring is the cashier at the reception desk. She is a short thick-set blonde, with a round doll-like face which wears, however, like many doll's faces, a look of impassible self-satisfaction. She is very efficient, reserved, and always very polite to Tabitha, who has never seen her speak with Bonser. His attention has been given to the receptionist, a plain but lively girl of whom Tabitha has sometimes been jealous.

She thinks now, "It was only spite; or could he be seeing Spring outside? It's certainly odd how he never goes near her in the hotel."

She is distraught when Bonser comes to her, and cries out at once, "Oh, Dick; but what could I do? She was actually in a bedroom."

"It's all right, my dear." Bonser, so far from being in a bad temper, is most sympathetic. "You had no choice with a dirty slut like that. I've given orders she's not to be admitted again; I don't mind for myself, but it's the limit when a decent girl like Spring is dragged in the mud."

He sends Tabitha to bed and shows her the most affectionate tenderness. "Poor old girl, you're quite shaky still. It's a damn shame. The fact is, you've got too much on you here. You shouldn't have to do the chucking out; the whole job at a place like this is too big for you. It's not really in your line, either."

Tabitha protests that she enjoys her work, but Bonser is firm. He will not allow her, he says, to ruin her health. And gradually, in the course of a week, he develops a plan for another hotel, a small country hotel, which she could manage for him. "And it would be a real home for us. That's what I've always wanted: a real home where we could have some peace together. Of course I'd have to keep an eye on the Beausite, but that shouldn't take more than a week end now and then."

Tabitha is delighted by this suggestion. She sees herself at peace from the moral problem of the Beausite, and secure from Spring. She is still more pleased when Bonser, after spying out the land for some days, says that nothing would be more suitable for the new venture than the old inn on the Urrsley Road, the Freemasons' Arms.

"It's rather far from Pynemouth, but it's near John; and I've always thought it a pity you didn't see more of John and dear little what's-her-name—Nancy."

Tabitha isn't sure that she wants to be nearer John's wife, but she agrees warmly that there are good possibilities in the Freemasons'.

The place is bought at once, at a high price, for already it has become a house of call for motorists, especially trucks. But Bonser, by adding a garage, a cocktail bar, a lounge and bedrooms, very soon doubles its trade. A back wing added to an old barn in a side road is rebuilt as a dwelling house, which, with its private garden, is settled on Tabitha as her own property. "Good idea for you to have a separate estate; it often helps with the banks."

And when this quiet house, secluded behind trees, is completed and furnished, he gives a special dinner to fourteen guests to celebrate his settling in. He proposes Tabitha's health and declares that he is at home at last, till he goes to his last home. And there, too, his hope is to lie beside his dear wife and pardner, faithful unto death. He works upon his own feelings to such an extent that he sheds tears of champagne, and Tabitha has to put him to bed.

But his affectionate mood continues for nearly a week. He is then obliged, by an urgent message, to hurry to the Beausite, where he stays for a month. Each day he telephones to explain why he cannot come: there is an important dinner, a gala dance. "And how is my

Pops? How I long to be with her all the time, in our own little house, the dear old Barn House."

When he comes at last he brings flowers; but once more, after two days, is called away for a week. And Tabitha has already heard from half a dozen friends in Pynemouth that he spends most of his time driving Miss Spring about the country in his red car.

"I suppose it's been happening all the time," Tabitha says to herself. "He just got rid of me up here; he hoped I'd be consoled by seeing more of John. Well, what did I expect? I'm getting old."

Bonser's presents grow more expensive with the length of his absences. When after two months away he brings a fur coat, Tabitha says, "You don't love me, Dick, you only use me."

But he is not even hurt. He cries, "My God, Pops, I don't know what I'd do without you!"

She is angry; but when he goes away she misses him, even his noise, his whims. She despises herself for missing him, and so he is present to her. She would like to hate him, but cannot remain in hatred because the Bonser she hates is never the same Bonser who comes back to her, full of talk, good nature, and totally indifferent to her mood. The only retort upon such a man would be sulks; and with such a man sulks would be wasted, a mere humiliation.

96

THE John Bonsers have been delighted by the success of the Beausite at Pynemouth. They write affectionately to Tabitha, and send her Christmas presents. They think of her as a busy woman, who has no time, thank goodness, to be a burden to them. They are alarmed, therefore, when they hear that Bonser has bought the Freemasons'; and Kit is in consternation when, a few days later, that is, in 1926, Tabitha calls unannounced and asks at once for Nancy, for she asks with an air of determination, as if to say, "I'm going to have my rights."

And it is plain at once to Kit, as she says afterwards, that Tabitha has changed for the worse. She has grown more forthright in eccentricity.

Kit would have denied her. But it happens that the child is in the bedroom and within earshot. Hearing a strange voice and full of curiosity and the wish for attention, she comes running.

Nancy at four is rosy and fat with an absurdly small nose. As she trots forward she looks sideways out of her little blue eyes with a greedy coquetry which is comic, and as she puts her short hands on Tabitha's lap and offers her thick soft lips, lips like Tabitha's own, she gives her mother a glance full of impudence. She knows that her mother is disapproving, and utters a loud smacking kiss out of mischief. It is delivered, however, into the air. She feels no pleasure in kissing, but is charmed by the forbidden.

Tabitha, seeing Kit's eye fixed upon her, does not return the kiss. But she catches up the child and presses her in her arms. She is ready to weep. She murmurs, "Darling, darling, do you love your Granny?"

"Yes, Granny. Did you bring any sweeties?"

Tabitha fumbles for a bottle of acid drops in her handbag, and murmurs, "But have you something for Granny?"

"Yes, Granny." The child's mouth is already open, and she gazes eagerly at the bottle.

"Will you say your hymn for me?"

Kit intervenes. "I'm afraid Nan doesn't know any hymns."

Tabitha looks defiantly at the young woman and says, "Not even 'Gentle Jesus'?"

"I'm afraid not."

"But with her prayers?"

"I'm afraid she doesn't say any prayers. We aren't teaching Nan anything like that." And with a little rush of speech, appealing for comprehension, "It seems so wrong, don't you think, to teach people things you don't believe yourself?"

Tabitha says in an alarmed voice, "But would it do any harm?" And on seeing Kit's cold expression mutters something about Jesus' love for children and how important it is for children to know about God's love.

Kit answers patiently that there are different opinions on this point, and picks up Nan. "It's your tea time."

The child at once begins to scream. "I don't want tea; I want a sweetie. Granny, Granny, give me a sweetie."

Kit, disgusted by this behavior, carries the girl off to the nursery; and Tabitha, even more agitated, takes her departure. She says no more about prayers and hymns, but it is obvious to Kit that she is thinking of nothing else.

Tabitha indeed is quite amazed. "But what can she mean?" she asks herself. "To teach a child no religion at all, it's horrible; she must be mad." And her horror is not only for Nan's loss of something so valuable and important to her, but for Kit's wickedness. "How can she be so wicked? Doesn't she see what happens to these girls without religion, these horrible creatures who drink and go with any man they meet?"

And now she does not behave tactfully, or retreat into a dignified anger. She is both older and less prudent, more desperate and energetic. She begins to haunt the John Bonsers' flat in Bright Square. She gives Nancy presents of picture books showing the Bible stories. She waylays her in the park with sweets, and tells her that Christmas is a happy time because Christ was born at Christmas to bring love to the world. She complains to John that the child is being brought up a pagan, and asks him to use his authority. "How can you let her ruin the poor child, body and soul?"

John, of course, knowing that he has no authority, is obliged to offer some shuffling answer and escape. He finds Tabitha almost as troublesome as Kit.

Both he and Kit have, of course, the full sympathy of their university friends in this quarrel. The younger college set, serious and thoughtful people, in the full tide of reaction against their own childhood, are most of them strongly opposed to religious teaching for children.

A break between Tabitha and the young couple is probably inevitable, but it comes about at last quite suddenly.

A great friend of Kit's is a young man called Rodwell, who has been defeated twice at the council elections but has a large following among the students. He is a demonstrator in chemistry, clever, quick, a good speaker, and an enthusiast for all schemes of improvement. Kit acts as his political secretary, and he spends much of his time in the flat. At the weekly parties, for John's pupils and for Kit's social workers, he is a great light.

He is a bachelor, large and dark, good-looking in the style of a collar advertisement, with an excellent temper; and Tabitha, seeing him deferred to by John's guests, in John's flat, at once takes a strong dislike to him.

And one day late in December, while about a dozen people are listening to his account of some Church property in Urrsley, Tabitha comes in with a parcel of Christmas presents for Nancy, and, as usual, ignoring Rodwell, begins to look for the child, going first through the nursery and then to the bedroom. And having, in this manner, disturbed the whole party, she suddenly exclaims to the air, "The Church does try to do some good at least, and doesn't try to get on by telling lies."

"I beg your pardon?"

"It's not true that the Church makes money out of slums. It only owns the ground; it cannot turn people out if they are dirty."

The woman is plainly in a rage. Rodwell, after a discreet pause, asks in the politest terms if he can find Nancy for her, and succeeds in producing the child from the flat below, where she is playing with a friend. But Tabitha does not forgive him. She disappears at once with Nancy into the park.

Kit cannot forgive an attack on a guest, especially on the idolized Rodwell. She writes to Tabitha and asks her not to give Bible stories to Nancy. "I know what you feel about religious teaching, but it confuses Nan to have different ideas from different people." And in a postscript she writes, "I don't think it is quite fair to Mr. Rodwell to accuse him of being a self-seeker. He could have been on the council long ago if he had not fought the landlords about the slums."

After this, Tabitha pays no more visits to the flat. She feels herself entitled to see her grandchild by stealth, and lies in wait for her in the park. And Nancy soon enters into understanding of this plan. She gleefully accepts sweets and stories, and says nothing about them at home.

As for Nancy going to the Freemasons', Kit and John are agreed that this is impossible. For the Freemasons' has already a bad reputation. As the first house in Urrsley to cater for the new class of pleasure seeker, young people in cars looking for any kind of distraction away from home, it attracts all the worst characters.

Bonser himself helps to make the place detestable to all the respectable householders of Urrsley. As at Pynemouth, he has set out to find allies among the chief citizens. He writes a letter to the *Urrsley Gazette* about the absence of rational and respectable amusement in the neighborhood, and proposes to give biweekly dances, and to hold also a beauty competition for the prize of a car and a month in Paris.

But the result is a strong protest from the local Antiquarians' Society, objecting to any addition or alteration at the famous inn, and some angry letters from magistrates, councilors, an Urrsley mother, two vicars and three ministers, declaring that the Freemasons' is a disgrace to the country and a danger to Urrsley youth. There is even a motion in the city council to take away Bonser's license, and someone interjects, "Don't say Colonel Bonser; he's no more a colonel than I am."

The proposal goes no further, because it is discovered that the Freemasons' is outside the city boundary.

But Bonser is disgusted. He is astonished to find that he has made enemies in Urrsley. He cannot understand it. And since he has been there, even more noisy and extravagant, more gaudily dressed than at Pynemouth; since he has driven every day at high speed through its various streets and got drunk in all its restaurants; since, in short, he has thoroughly enjoyed himself in Urrsley, he can blame only Urrsley for not appreciating him.

He threatens to close the Freemasons' and leave the town to its fate. On second thoughts, since the Freemasons' is already paying very well, he only retires to Pynemouth, where he can console himself with Miss Spring, and excuse himself from visiting Tabitha more than once a month.

In fact, he has made the grave mistake of treating Urrsley, a Midlands town full of solid people, manufacturers, craftsmen, in the same way as Pynemouth, a seaside resort for retired people and their tradesmen. Urrsley has a public opinion of some moral content; Pynemouth has only taste.

97

NANCY feels no resentment when she is forbidden to visit her grandmother at the Freemasons'. She has caught the idea that the old person is ridiculous, and she has a quick sense of the ridiculous. As she grows from a round baby into a short burly child, she begins to study her grandmother. When Tabitha lies in wait for her with sweets, and kisses her and talks of Jesus, she takes the sweets, offers a cool cheek to the kiss, giggles at the piety, and runs off in explosions of giggles.

And after she goes to school, at six, she grows quickly ashamed of her, and avoids her with such success that Tabitha at last gives up her ambushes.

Nancy delights in school and especially in the discovery that she is clever, and that her brains are admired. She works with enthusiasm, and goes to the top of the class. And when some of the naughty little girls who play in the streets, who do not work hard, abuse her for her own virtue, she scorns them in a voice and with a look exactly like her mother's. "That silly Nelly pulled my hair again, but I didn't care; it's because she's such a f-fool."

It appears, to John and Kit's great satisfaction, that the child has inherited a strong and decided character.

Thus in 1930, when she is nine, she is already in the first form of the junior school, and is expected to win the class prize for English. Unluckily, a new mistress, Miss Fisher, who perhaps does not like conceited children, makes one day some rude remarks about her grammar.

Nancy is much hurt in her scholastic pride, and after the lesson, in telling the story to a certain comrade and rival, a child in spectacles, even more serious than herself, she is taken by an impulse to mimic the woman. The serious friend is amazed and even alarmed to see Nancy's face twist into a ludicrous form and hear her utter, in a loud voice and affected accent, a caricature of Miss Fisher's cultured speech. She looks round in fear that this wild and rude conduct may attract attention. It does. It collects a crowd. The serious child discreetly slips away, while Nancy, in the grip of her demon, performs Miss Fisher much larger than life. The crowd, which has rushed together to jeer at this folly in the detested Nan Bonser, stares, half scornful and half surprised. For an instant Nancy, having exposed herself publicly, is on the edge of a public humiliation. But the force, the power, the malice of the art is irresistible. In spite of its moral feelings, the crowd laughs—it is carried away on shrieks of laughter; and Nancy finds herself, to her surprise, an immense success.

From that moment she is pursued by girls asking her "to do Miss Fisher." Even girls of twelve condescend to look on, from a distance that will not compromise their superiority.

And when the school is tired of this act, it finds that Nancy can mimic any of the mistresses. She can do even the music master, adored by older girls and despised by the young ones.

Such arts of the rebel are greatly appreciated in any school. Nancy becomes a star in daily request. And when she is not performing she is studying to improve her performance, so that her work goes gradually to pieces. At first she merely ceases to rise, and it is not for a year that John and Kit perceive that she is falling behind. And since the cause is mysterious to them, they tell each other that the child is going through some natural reaction, that it was time for her to be a little less precocious.

When reports begin to say, "Nancy takes no interest in her work," when she is punished, when at eleven it is seen that she is in the same form as before, but at the bottom, beaten by children of ten, they grow alarmed. They use threats, appeals, bribes, to which Nancy replies with promises that she does not mean to keep, or indifference. She has no habit of affection for either of her parents, and she has discovered their helplessness before mere passive resistance and steady lying.

Her very figure expresses a lazy animal cunning. She has lost her baby charm, and is a plain child, with a round impudent face, short nose, and wide soft lips, always half open—a coarsened edition of her grandmother, with a quite different expression. And to every reproof she has an answer. "But, Mum, I do work—it's only the silly old mistresses are against me."

Kit cries in despair, "Really, she won't do a stroke of work unless someone is at her every minute; and I've no time." John, as he rushes from seminar to committee, exclaims, "It's extraordinary what little interest that child takes in things; she seems completely silly."

And this is a general view among grown-ups who see Nancy on every day of the week, dawdling back from school with her arm round the neck of a friend, and a large sweet thrust into one bulging cheek. The girls giggle, roll across the pavement, cannon into some old person, stare with laughing contempt, and then rush off again and giggle for ten minutes, until they appear drunk and helpless with a laughter of which they have forgotten the reason or excuse. Yet they understand each other very well. And in their mysterious private life of jokes, looks, nudges, and confidences they are as much at ease as mice under a farmhouse floor. Life is delightful to them.

And indeed, when Kit and John deplore the extraordinary change in Nancy's character, they do not notice how consistent it is. Nancy, who once enjoyed the satisfaction of working to be top of her form, has now the more delightful occupation of being a popular success, adored and caressed by the girls, and detested by the mistresses. Nothing is so corrupting as popularity; and after two years of glory Nancy is an extremely tough child. She pulls the hair of proper little girls, and says rude words to them when they cry. She herself is impervious to any insult. "All right, Nan Bonser," shrieks an unhappy child, pinched and badgered into tears. "You nasty thing, your grandy keeps a public house."

To which Nancy, sticking out one hip, crooking one knee, looking over her shoulder in an attitude of which every line expresses a kind of vagabond scorn, answers, "And sucks to you, three times."

98

NANCY has been hearing a good deal in the last year about her grandfather. For Bonser is once more in the Urrsley news. A paragraph in the gossip column, a new feature in the *Urrsley Gazette*, has announced that Colonel Bonser, owner of that ancient historic inn, the Freemasons' Arms, at the London crossroads, proposes to restore it as far as possible to its original form, when, in the fifteenth century, it was a pilgrims' hostel under the protection of St. Christopher. "Colonel Bonser is to be congratulated on an enterprise which will bring back into full public use a monument renowned in the history of Urrsley."

In fact, Bonser's determination to reconstruct the Freemasons' is not due to enterprise on his part but to the pressure of demand. Trade has grown so fast with the increasing flood of cars, ever cheaper, faster, easier to drive, which pour along every road, that the old Freemasons' is crowded out. He sends for an architect who has already reconstructed several village pubs in the Olde Englyshe style, and within a very short time laborers are at work. In a month the ancient Freemasons' has disappeared, and within six there is to be seen an imitation Tudor mansion, with imitation oak beams on the gables, imitation bottle glass in casement windows, papier mâché oak wainscots, and floors of rubber tile. The coachyard is roofed in for a dance floor; the barns become garages; a swimming pool is dug in what was the orchard; and a great arch of electric lights, commanding two roads, startles the traveler among the quiet woods and fields.

Business men in Urrsley admire the art of this building, but declare that, like so many original works of art, it will be a dead loss to the inventor. How, they ask, can a dance hall and swimming pool, putting greens and roller-skating floor pay, four miles from a town? But they are wrong. They are looking, without knowing it, at their first roadhouse, for even the name is not yet known to them; and it begins at once to be successful.

Of course there are protests from Urrsley. As the months go by and the Freemasons' becomes more frequented, the protests grow louder. At last there is a petition, signed by over a thousand householders, supported by the Society of Urrsley Antiquarians, the Sunday School, the Sabbath Day Defense League, the Blue Ribbon Association, presented to the County Council, and asking for the closing of the place.

But long before this co-operative enterprise of the responsible Urrsleyites has gone through its stages of incubation, proposal, debate, consultation, organization, the very signers know that they are wasting their time.

Already there are a dozen roadhouses to be reached within thirty miles of Urrsley. It is obvious that closing the Freemasons' will simply drive the young people farther away for their amusement. Probably the majority, certainly the great majority of solid respectable persons in Urrsley, fear and hate the Freemasons'. But already they are aware of a feeling, something in the very air of opinion, that such places must come and cannot be stopped, a feeling much more powerful than churches and councils and parents, the sense of a universal force at work, the young imagination seeking a new field, creation itself.

99 EVEN letters to the *Gazette* attacking the Freemasons' are no longer printed, for the *Gazette* has an eye to its circulation, and Bonser is now growing popular with the younger business set in Urrsley—men of thirty, just rising into influence and impatient with old prejudices. It is among these that, since the success of the new Freemasons', he spends most of his time. He has, in fact, discovered the truth of his own intuition that there is plenty of loose money in the place, and becomes an Urrsley citizen, subscribes to local charities, and younger councilors are delighted to dine with him. His enemies can abuse him only to each other, in private. True, they do this with the more energy. And it is an eddy of this hatred which Nancy's victim has thrown at her.

Nancy has taken no interest in the Freemasons'; and as for Bonser, when she has seen sometimes a large vermilion car rushing through the town and heard people say, with mixed intonations, "The Colonel again," she has not given him, any more than Tabitha, a thought.

But now, for some reason, perhaps merely because the abuse of Bonser has had unusual spitefulness, she is curious. She asks if her grandfather keeps a public house; and when Kit tells her in ten words that he has actually two hotels, of which one is the Freemasons', to which she must not go, she at once resolves to see it.

She therefore plays truant, as often before, on the next games afternoon, goes out by bus to the crossroads, examines the roadhouse with great interest, and returns. She relates the adventure to a friend, who is charmed by the enterprise, and both together make a second expedition. This time they explore the yard and peep into the dining room. A waiter catches them. "Here, what do you want?" But they do not run off. Nancy, secure in the vast arrogance of her successes as a school incorrigible, is afraid of no one. She stares at the waiter and licks her lips, not quite putting out her tongue, but suggesting the act. And when he seizes hold of her to push her through the gate, she jerks herself free and says, "Don't you touch me, or I'll tell Colonel Bonser; he's my grandfather."

"Oh indeed, Missy; why don't you know him, then? There he is—in the bar."

Nancy, looking toward the bar, sees two fat men with faces glowing as if with port rather than blood, walks up to them, and says to the air between, "I'm Nan. That man wouldn't believe you were my grandfather."

Whereupon the one who is slightly the fatter and more radiant grins at her, showing brilliant teeth, and says, "And how did you come here?"

"I just took the bus."

"To see your granny?"

"No, to see you."

Bonser bursts out laughing, and says to his companion, a well-known Urrsley bookie, sitting with him, "She's got a nerve, hasn't she? A chip of the old brick."

And in two minutes Nancy, seated on her grandfather's broad knee, is stuffing herself with chocolate, to the approval of the whole party. Her friend, abashed, keeps in the background.

After this, Nancy's greatest delight is to visit the Freemasons'. She takes the bus or begs lifts in cars; she makes rendezvous with her grandfather, who picks her up in his huge Bentley and carries her off in triumph.

And when Kit and John, on being told that somebody very like Nancy has been seen at the Freemasons', challenge her, she tells such lies that they are ashamed. Indeed, they don't know what to do with a child so clever in deceit. She breaks every promise. While Kit is at one of Rodwell's meetings, a vital meeting about housing or the poor, and John is wrestling with some pupil's difficulties which may affect his whole career, she is slipping out to the Freemasons' and back again, ready to swear that she has never stirred from Urrsley.

Nothing, it appears, will keep her from the Freemasons'; and as the months pass, Kit and John grow resigned to her escapes. They are beaten by the superior force of obstinacy and deceit. And Kit says, "That child takes after the Bonser side of the family; she only thinks of enjoying herself."

100

YET Kit, with her usual lack of penetration into another's feelings, is already wrong about Nancy. She is no longer enjoying the Freemasons' as a pure delight. As she grows out of childishness, into a plain lumpy girl, she begins to suffer strange pangs. She loves the Freemasons' even more, but with an anxious and troubled affection. She seizes every moment to fly to it, to the cakes, the sweets, the petting of visitors, the bathing pool; but she cannot enjoy them unless she is with her grandfather. She has a passion for Bonser. One day, when she stalks him in the garden with a young woman, he is so enraged that he gives her a slap. And that night Nancy knows extremest misery and despair. She cries for hours, stuffing the pillow into her mouth to prevent her father or mother hearing her, and when she wakes feels herself still wretched. For a week she does not go to the Freemasons'. She is too guilty, too terrified that her grandfather will frown upon her.

Now even her celebrity at school as a bad character gives her no pleasure. She is rude to her admirers as well as to the mistresses. She seeks loneliness, and broods upon her fate. She takes a hatred to herself; and looking in the glass is disgusted by her big mouth and little eyes, her short neck and fat chest. She wants to die.

But the same afternoon, mooning along High Street in a trance of self-pity, she hears a voice cry, "Hullo, kid!" and sees Bonser's great sun face stooping down to her from his car. He turns to his companion, the chief Urrsley publican, on the front seat. "My granddaughter; we're great pals. See, she came along to pick me up. Oh, she's going to be hot stuff, aren't you, Nan? And what is it today, sly boots? A drive? Is that the idea? All right, hop in. Aren't you going to say how d'you do?"

"Oh, Grandy." She darts into the car and throws her arms round his neck. In a moment she is nestled down beside him, being whirled away from hateful Urrsley. She is full of such love, such gratitude, that she cannot express it except by thrusting her elbow into Bonser's ribs.

For it appears that she is forgiven, that the divine man, having slapped her face, is prepared to let bygones be bygones.

It is an act of forgiveness like this which endears Bonser to her, for it proves to her that she is wanted at the Freemasons'. She trails after him like a puppy, contented if he notices her every half hour with a smile, in heaven on his knee. She would be a pest if Bonser did not in fact enjoy her sympathy, if he did not have common interests with the girl, an understanding of the flesh deeper than speech. Both love fast driving, sweet cakes, gossip and jazz. It is bliss for each to fly along at seventy miles an hour, and to know that they are in accord. They both love novelty, the latest thing. When Bonser has an idea for a fountain illuminated by colored spotlights, hateful to Tabitha, Nancy dances with joy. When in 1934 he has a wireless set built, they spend hours creeping about on the floor of the lounge, peering among the valves and wires. Bonser, with a screwdriver, promises Nancy to improve the sound, and at once produces silence. He curses the manufacturer who, he says, does not know his job, and sends for a mechanic. At last when the machine is working again, he stands beside it in triumphant self-satisfaction, turning the knobs and saying, "There's Moscow—no, Berlin; there's New York." And Nancy's expression, as she looks round at the visitors, seems to say, "Isn't he wonderful?"

"There you are, the Scala, Milan; that man is singing three thousand miles away. Can you beat it?"

In his face, which, with every year of prosperity, grows plumper, more crimson, until it is as round as the child's beside him, and even in those of the smart young people who have been called in for a drink and now crowd round to gather a new story about old Dick Bonser, one sees an expression of wonder which makes the most hard-boiled seem for a moment innocent and foolish.

He turns a knob and a screaming hysterical voice startles the room. "Hitler!"—with a smile of triumph. It is as though he has commanded the demagogue to do his will. "I suppose that chap is talking to about a hundred million people—and they used to say we'd invented everything."

To Nancy, Bonser is the greatest man she has ever met. She watches him giving his orders to gardeners and waiters, commanding a new greenhouse, a bigger swimming pool. She sees him in the lounge surrounded by groups of laughing girls and important-looking men, just descended from expensive cars, who crowd in to hear his jokes, or merely to claim acquaintance.

They laugh at Bonser, but they like to know him. They even boast of knowing him. For he has become a character, with all the privileges and charms of a character. Even Free Churchmen smile now at his loud suits, and point out his gaudy car as a local sight, honorable to Urrsley. His words on any subject are quoted, because they come from the "Colonel."

He is a character also with the special attractiveness of what is called the sport. He drinks, he gambles, he kisses girls. The fact, very well known, that he is behind several drinking clubs in Urrsley does him no harm with the mass of people, for nine-tenths of them gamble. A police raid on a club, when the proprietor, an old offender, is given six months in jail, is praised in the newspapers but derided in the streets. It is felt that the magistrates are out of date and vindictive; strangers, in buses and bars, agree that there was "some dirty work somewhere."

"Somebody did him down."

"He didn't keep in with the right people on the council."

"He should have taken a tip from Dick Bonser. He's the chap that knows how; he'll never be raided."

And this opinion is received with smiles of gratification. It is delightful to the poorest that Dick Bonser knows how to dodge the law and keep in with the police. He enjoys the glamour of a pirate, a highwayman, a man set free.

To Nancy, with this great man's kiss on her lips, stealing back home at nightfall seems like a descent from sunlight into a squalid prison. She finds her mother a bore, forever busy with papers, and forever pestering her to work; for her father she has a mixture of contempt and pity, in which the contempt is the larger part. She sees him as a futile little man, in shabby clothes, with a bald forehead and stooping shoulders, who can never make up his mind about anything. She knows also, she feels with all her nerves, that he is laughed at, that her mother is sorry for him and thinks him a failure, and that Councilor Rodwell, her mother's friend, is a much more important person, both in the house and in the town.

But Rodwell she really hates. For one thing, he tries to pet her. Once he has even pulled her down on his knee—detestable familiarity. She resents his superiority in the flat; and with it all, he is as big a bore as her father and quite as poor. He has no car, and his clothes are just as shabby. She can tolerate her father, who is at least not aggressive or conceited; but coming from the Freemasons', from her wonderful grandfather, she feels such disgust at the sight of Rodwell that she is ready to put out her tongue at him.

Should any of them ask her where she has been, she has no more hesitation in lying to them than a civilized person who, forced to live among petty and envious proletarians in a slum, hides his visits in the great world.

101

One deep bond between Nancy and Bonser is their attitude to Tabitha. It is understood between them that Tabitha is to be treated with respect, but avoided. At the sound of her step the girl looks at her grandfather, and, without a word, both remove themselves to a distance or escape into the hotel. For Tabitha is rarely seen in the hotel except at a very early hour when no visitors are about. She has a reliable manager, Gladys Hope, a large powerful woman, once a barmaid, handsome, big-bosomed, who has coped with the rowdies in the worst days of the Freemasons', and keeps better order than a man, with exactly the right mixture of rallying insult and genial violence.

Tabitha keeps the Barn House, with the faithful old maid, Dorothy, inviolate; she watches closely the hotel servants, she pays her regular quick private visits of inspection, but she ignores the visitors. She cannot bear them; but she is perfectly aware by this time that she will find no sympathy in protesting against the Eton crop, short skirts, cocktails, and casual embraces. They are universal.

And the Freemasons' itself, even while growing more lively, has become ordinary. It is not only tolerated, it is necessary. Young people accept it as a matter of course. Politicians remark that in Russia workers are given opportunities to dance and enjoy themselves. Respectable citizens rely on it for a holiday supper; business men need it to entertain business guests. And it has appeared, at first to the surprise, then to the resignation of all those old-fashioned persons in Urrsley who fought against Bonser and his ideas, that their notion of what is safe and proper for their families is already so out of date that it has no force at all. Even the fact that young girls, using their new freedom, run about the country, get drunk, are seduced or raped, seems to have no great importance or effect. The cheap motor has produced a whole new social order, apparently by itself and without any regard to logic, or politics, or morals, or security. It simply exists; and it has brought with it thousands of dance halls and roadhouses, and the absolute necessity, for young people, of a car or at least a motor bicycle, by which they can escape not only from their parents but their very towns and neighbors, by which they can be as free as wild Indians in a desert.

So that Tabitha, in her long skirts, is regarded in Urrsley as an eccentric; and Nancy herself, with the contagion of an idea which soaks into the very soul of a child, despises her. What in Bonser is tolerant indifference is in Nancy disgust.

Nancy has lately been very unhappy, for she has begun to understand Bonser's relations with women. She has seen him kissing Gladys Hope, the manageress, and felt a pain so sharp that it changes in that moment her whole feeling. She does not recognize it as jealousy, but she is never again free from it.

One day at the Freemasons', when Bonser has actually asked her to tea, he forgets about it and does not come back to the hotel. And Nancy, knowing that Gladys Hope is also out, and suspecting that the couple have met, cannot bring herself to go home. At seven o'clock she is wandering among the cinder heaps behind the garage, keeping out of sight and trying not to weep, when she hears Tabitha's surprised voice asking her what she is doing. "*Darling!* I thought you had gone home."

The child shrugs her shoulders and mutters, "Do let me alone."

"But, Nan, dearest, do you know how late it is? And your hair ribbon is all undone."

Nancy, cornered between the garage wall and a thorn hedge, turns and scowls. "Oh, do go away."

Tabitha, accustomed to find Nancy a quiet, very reserved child, can hardly believe her ears. "What did you say?"

"Go away, I said."

"That's not the way to talk to your grandmother."

"I don't care. I hate you; you spoil everything."

Tabitha sees in the child's furious stare a real hatred. Then suddenly Nancy dives under her arm and rushes away across the fields.

Tabitha is amazed by such unexpected depravity and cruelty in a child, and frightened by the hysterical tone. She feels that the child is suffering. After half an hour, when it is growing dark, and nothing more has been seen of Nancy, she begins to imagine disasters. She telephones to the flat to ask if Nancy has arrived home. Rodwell's voice answers that she does not seem to be at home. "But I'm sure there's no cause for alarm, Mrs. Bonser; that kid is pretty independent."

"Could I please speak to Mr. John Bonser?" Tabitha says in her most freezing tone.

"I'm afraid he's out; can I do anything?"

Tabitha rings off. But half an hour later John arrives by the bus. He has been alarmed by this latest freak of Nancy's.

Mother and son hunt the fields and a wood beyond. Tabitha calls in a shrill urgent voice, and John in a polite tenor which, by its very sound, seems to despair of any effect.

At last they are themselves rescued by a maid from the hotel. There has been a call from Urrsley. Nancy has arrived home, having walked all the way.

"I knew she'd be all right," John says, sighing for the waste of his time.

"But she's not all right, John." Tabitha, after her panic, is very angry. "It's all wrong for a child to behave like that at her age. She's like a little savage. Of course I know she hasn't been taught to consider others. Mr. Rodwell seems quite to approve of her running wild."

"It's not Rodwell's fault." John sighs. "And of course she has a passion for this place."

"This place is certainly much better for her than the Urrsley streets."

Tabitha will never admit that the Freemasons' is bad for Nancy. To her the alliance between Nancy and her grandfather is honorable to both, a kindly affection. She belongs to that old simple age where all love, even the most demonstrative, all friendship, was by itself good until it was proved evil.

"I mustn't deny it," John says, rather as if discussing a situation too dark for judgment than reflecting upon it.

He has refused a meal, even a drink, possibly from a desire to avoid his father, and is waiting for Tabitha's car and chauffeur to take him home.

A cold winter drizzle has begun to fall, and they are standing under the porch of the Barn House, a porch of lattice, lighted incongruously by a single electric bulb in a ground-glass cylinder.

"No," John says, "there are too many unknown factors in that problem."

Tabitha, impatient at the man's lack of decision, looks at him, and seeing him under this novel light, which illuminates his spreading bald patch, brings out his high prominent forehead like a dome, and casts his eyes into deep hollows, is struck with urgent pity. She thinks, "But he's already an old tired man."

And it seems to her that John needs rescue even more than Nancy. She exclaims, "At least we know Urrsley is bad. It's ruined you; I can't imagine why you stay in such a place. It's not as though they knew how to appreciate you. They don't know enough to know who is good."

And John, who in his forties grows once more affectionate with his mother, in the uncritical manner of his childhood, answers with a rueful candor, "But, Mother, I've tried to move out. I tried last year at London; but I didn't get the job."

He smiles at her as if to say, "Your mistake is to think me a great man." And Tabitha is startled. She had not thought that John could be refused a post. There is a pause. The veil of rain drizzling past the white light of the lamp, its hiss and drip, seems to shut them into their private place of suspense, where there is nothing to do but reflect upon the world, at once remote and therefore extended.

"That's because of Urrsley," Tabitha exclaims. "They think no one can be any good who comes from Urrsley."

"No." He is still smiling, now at the rain where it makes an opal necklace along the lintel. "The fact is, Mother, that I'm a bit behind. My philosophy is rather out of fashion. The real selling line just now is a patent called logical positivism, and I don't stock it."

"But, John, you don't tell me there are fashions in philosophy?"

"Yes, indeed there are; and you may be sure there always will be, just as with shoes—or cars." He nods toward the ten-year-old Rolls which has just appeared in the lane beyond the narrow iron gate. "The material is always the same, and the old solid first-class jobs go on forever and stand up to all weathers, but if you want to make a popular hit you've got to have a new style—the more startling the better. And I've been too busy teaching to have time for stunts. Good night, Mother dear; don't come out in the rain."

But Tabitha follows him to the car. She is excited and angry. "You know that's not true. You're just being clever. The real truth is, you've no push, you don't try."

"That's what I was saying, Mother. As a salesman, I'm a failure; and perhaps Urrsley does put rather too much weight on salesmanship."

And as he leans back in the deep seat to be driven away he seems to be already resigned to frustration.

But Tabitha is enraged. She feels that the case is desperate. She takes hope only from the discovery that John has at least tried to leave Urrsley.

She revives old acquaintances. Manklow is dead; but she writes to Lord Ducat, to Griller, who now, close on ninety, has lately been acclaimed as one of the giants of literature. Neither can help. But some months later she hears through Ducat's secretary of a vacancy at St. Mark's. She telephones at once to John, whose voice, for some reason always young and gay on the telephone, answers, "Yes, it's been offered to me."

"Oh, John, how wonderful; at last you can get away, and get rid of that horrible Rodwell, too."

"Get rid of him?"

"Leave him behind."

The voice sings back, "But Rodwell is not such a bad chap, you know."

"John, he makes a fool of you; you know he does—in your own house, in front of everybody. I never know why you will argue with him."

"That must be my own fault, mustn't it?" and the telephone is cut off.

Tabitha, calling down to a blank wall, says to herself, "Now he's cross; but it's true, true. And someone must tell him."

102

JOHN is well aware that he does not cut an imposing figure in Urrsley, or even in his own house, and that he has acquired a bad habit, the tutor's habit, of questioning any brash statement merely because it is brash.

He will interrupt some business man who has thrown out the remark, "There's no danger of nationalization in England; the workers wouldn't stand it," by the murmured suggestion, "On the other hand, it seems to work in France. What kind of nationalization were you thinking of?" And the question is merely intended to make a blow-hard examine his own nonsense and discover what, if anything, it means.

In the same way, he will irritate Kit in the midst of some hurried scheme for a political canvass by asking what she means exactly by the profit motive; and he can never resist baiting Rodwell. Yet in the resulting argument, which occurs almost every week on party afternoons, when students are asked to tea, he is always defeated.

"Hullo, John," Rodwell will say, "how's the philosophy?" And John will smile and go past. But a moment later his voice will be heard questioning one of Rodwell's confident speeches.

"What plan is this?"

"I was talking of the Brock scheme."

In the last seven years the Urrsley Progressives have won a large majority, and Rodwell himself, after four years in the Council, is one of their leaders. He has already the special air of a political boss, a certain bland assumption, something between the policeman's self-confidence and the actor's sang-froid, a certain self-satisfaction which does not sit badly on his good-humored face and solid figure, already growing portly.

As chairman of the housing committee, Rodwell has drawn up a plan of slum clearance, to demolish five streets of houses and move five thousand people to a new suburb at a cost of half a million pounds.

The very size and expense of the plan has given Rodwell a new prestige in Urrsley. The students admire him as a hero; the tories detest him as an extravagant demagogue.

"On the other hand," John says, with the air of turning over a proffered object to see what it is really made of, "I see that there's a meeting of protest actually in the Brock."

"That's a ramp by the landlords," says one of Rodwell's pupils, a young woman. Two-thirds of the crowd surrounding Rodwell are enthusiastic young women.

"Why do you stand for it?" says another. "Why don't we go and break it up?"

"They've taken care of that; you can't get in without a ticket. They've got a liberal M.P. coming."

"It *would* be a liberal," a young medical student cries. "Let's put a stink bomb through the window and smoke 'em out. After all, they've asked for it." His voice is furious with moral indignation. He is moved not only by the new fashion, which is to imitate the violence of revolution, but by a genuine anger and disgust. He really believes that liberals are wicked people who ought to be eliminated. Like nearly all the young Urrsley students, like the youth of Russia, Germany, Italy, he hates the liberals, and can offer plenty of reasons for his hatred. But the real reason is probably that liberalism has been succeeding for a hundred years; that his parents have talked it at the breakfast table; that it is a peaceful, honest creed which bores him and, above all, is boring to others. Nobody can cut a dash by being a liberal. So he spits upon liberalism.

He is startled when John, whom he knows to be a lecturer at the college, remarks, "But do the Brock people themselves want the plan? I'm told that at least half of the tenants are quite happy where they are."

"And what would you do?"

"Well, it's rather complicated. You'd have to clear out some of the bad houses, rebuild some of the others—"

"But that's the liberal plan," say shocked voices.

"And it would take five years," Rodwell says, smiling.

"On the other hand," John says, "it would be fairer, so why all the hurry?"

Kit, passing through the crowd with a plate of cakes in one hand and a lock of hair falling over her eyes, as usual overworked and enjoying it, exclaims, "But, John dear, can you imagine the mess, patching up here and rebuilding there? We must clear the whole Brock or we can't begin to have a comprehensive scheme."

"That's the real point." Rodwell, hearing himself quoted, becomes very serious. "We need to plan the whole area to make a good job."

"I don't see why." And John begins to argue that the real motive behind this plan is not the welfare of the people or even the beauty of the town, but only a desire for a large showy operation. "A lot of planning is simply a stunt, the latest hocus pocus."

"Didn't I say you were really a liberal?" Rodwell is amused. And all at once John, to his own surprise, finds himself in the middle of an angry speech. "What if I am; what does the label matter? It isn't an argument any more than the word 'plan,' or any other of your slogans for the half-baked. And your real idea is to push people about. All you great statesmen are the same; you simply go all out to make your power felt."

Rodwell, who never loses his temper, smiles and gives the usual answer that all governments have to interfere sometimes with private lives. The students, who are mostly his own pupils, stare at John, laugh, or exclaim contemptuously, "The old stuff." One very young boy is demanding with an angry amazement if Mr. Bonser wants to stop planning. John tries to explain that he is not against planning, only against unnecessary regimentation. But of course he is involved at once in qualifications. The audience is bored as well as irritated. Rodwell smiles; some student interjects a phrase, a favorite of John's, "on the other hand," and everyone laughs.

The philosopher, taken aback, feels himself confused, and tries not to look foolish. He says, "Of course the truth is seldom very easy to get at." Then he tries to cover his discomfiture by drinking his tea. But he spills it in his saucer.

103

SUDDENLY he sees Tabitha in the room, pushing toward him. She has come in during the argument and he is struck by something wild in her look. She is neatly dressed in her customary black, which makes her seem thin and small as a child, but her walk has an uneven movement, she is frowning and moving her lips, and two patches of color high on her cheeks give her a feverish appearance.

"Mother!" he kisses her. "How nice to see you here."

"Why do you let them?" she says in a shrill angry voice. "They were laughing at you; and that horrible fat man."

John smiles. "There's a lot to be said for the planners, you know; it was ony that I wanted to make them see—However—and how are you?"

"But why are they so cruel, wanting to hurt people, those poor old women in the Brock who are going to lose their homes?"

John, seeing that Tabitha is attracting attention, proposes to go into the square where they may walk in the gardens. He himself is suddenly eager to escape. "It will be cooler there." But Tabitha, who is more excited than he has seen her before, looks angrily about her. "No religion, no kindness, that's what's wrong. They've forgotten Christ; brought up like savages."

There is now a silence in which these last words are audible through the room. "Worse than savages," the shrill voice cries, trembling with its own temerity. "Savages do have some kind of God."

"Come, Mother, let's go," and he draws her, almost by force, out of the door. He is relieved to find that Tabitha's excitement has calmed his own nerves. He feels only a mild dejection as they walk arm in arm across the pavement into the gardens.

It is a warm but cloudy spring evening, and under the trees which surround the gardens the shade on the gravel walk is like a green twilight. The cries and laughter of children playing on the central lawn make this shade between the rows of tree trunks which flank it, like the pillars of a nave, seem more withdrawn and peaceful. John presses his mother's arm with a feeling of mutual sympathy as from one refugee to another. "You mustn't mind those children, they'll grow up; before they're forty most of them will be fossilized conservatives."

But Tabitha is quivering with impatient wrath. "Why do you talk to them? Oh, how I long for this term to be over."

"Why this term especially?"

"Because it's your last in this horrible place."

"Oh yes, St. Mark's."

"That's what I came about. Have you written? You oughtn't to wait a single day."

There is a short pause while they walk slowly on, startling at every pace the sparrows who are mating and fighting almost at their feet. Tabitha, suddenly uneasy, exclaims, "You haven't written. I knew you would put it off."

"Yes, I've written."

"Thank goodness for that."

"But I haven't posted the letter yet."

"What do you mean? Why not?"

"I don't really know; I suppose when it came to the point, I didn't want to leave Urrsley."

"How can you suppose such nonsense? No, no, it's because you've no ambition. Where is the letter? We'll post it now."

But John strolls slowly on, reflecting: "Yes, it seems after all that I don't want to go away. I rather hate it here, of course, but—it seems that I don't fancy a move. The fact is, I suppose, that I've really been enjoying the job—in a way." He examines this suggestion and says with approval, "You see, Mother, I mayn't have many pupils, but they're rather a special kind, probably the pick, and really keen. They have to be keen in Urrsley, because they're always told that philosophy is a dead loss. There's a special feeling in a place like this; it's completely different from Oxford or Cambridge. Keeler calls it a frontier; and there really is a kind of frontier atmosphere, a terrific seriousness and tremendous loyalties." He smiles at some recollection. "Yes, really rather heroic. It may be a bit simple-minded, of course, but—wouldn't I find anywhere else rather flat and complacent? Wouldn't I go flat myself without my young enthusiasts? I know Keeler feels just the same with his crowd. And they go and sit at Mrs. Keeler's feet, and she talks art to them. It's almost religious; it *is* religious—" And warming to his idea, he turns toward Tabitha, giving her his confidence. "Yes, you may say, of course, that what all this amounts to is that I'm stuck in Urrsley—*spiritually* stuck. But that may really be my advantage, too; I might hate to be unstuck—I might even fall apart."

But he sees in Tabitha's face a look of despair. And he understands that she can never understand him, or the battle of his life, the tension, the faith, the exciting enterprise of rescuing some young mind, still interested, still curious and sincere, from the enemy, the vast darkness of nihilism, mechanism. He sighs to himself and presses her arm. "You musn't worry about me, Mother."

"How can I help it? To see you wasting yourself, and so stupidly." Tears pour down her cheeks. "It's so stupid; just because you are—so obstinate. Why, why are you so blind? How can you like it here? Everything is wrong. Kit—you know how weak she is, she is completely under Rodwell's thumb. And Nan, poor little Nan, without anyone to care for her."

"Darling mother, Kit is as loyal as any wife could be."

"No, no, she despises you; she thinks you're no good for anything and it's my fault. Oh, why didn't I believe Jim! Oxford ruined you."

He tries to console her. He assures her of his happiness. He tells her that he is everlastingly grateful for his education. "Heavens, without that I might have been like—" and he is going to say Rodwell, but swallows the name for fear of provoking more anger. But she grows hysterical with misery, and he is glad to persuade her at last into her car. She kisses him then, long and earnestly. It is a kiss of pity and appeal. "You forgive me, Johnny?"

"But, my dear mother, you've given me all the happiness I could have."

She shakes her head and sinks back into her seat with her handkerchief to her face. And as the car drives away, John turns with relief toward the house. But he changes his mind. He does not want to see Rodwell again, or Rodwell's students, that evening; and strolling once more beneath the trees, he thinks with surprise, "It is true; she gave me everything that matters, but how can she understand that? You could not get it into her head by an operation."

104

"It's Kit," Tabitha decides, when she finds herself once more at the Barn House. "That's why he won't go. She persuaded him. And he can't tell me the truth because he can't admit how weak he is with that creature. Yes, Kit has ruined him and Nan too." And her hatred against Kit rises every day.

When at Easter Nan is sent to stay with the spinster aunt at Cheltenham, a usual arrangement, Tabitha says, "That woman does not care how miserable the child is so long as she is kept away from me."

When, as usual at Easter, Kit and John go rock climbing with a party in Wales, she says as usual, "She knows John is terrified of heights, but what does she care if she kills him? Then she can have Rodwell."

So that when a wire comes from Wales, "All safe here. Pay no attention to papers. Love," her terror is full of an angry triumph. "I knew there would be an accident; I knew she'd kill John in the end."

And in spite of Bonser's protests—who has indigestion and wants to be nursed—she leaves at once for Wales. She finds John in bed with a chill. But there has in fact been an accident: one of the party has fallen and broken a leg; the rest, in going to his help, have been benighted in fog and wet.

Kit is annoyed by Tabitha's arrival. She says that there is no necessity for the journey, John is already on the mend; the doctor is quite happy about him.

"He doesn't know Johnny's chest," Tabitha says.

"But I do; and it's five years since he had any trouble—even asthma."

Both women are tense and irritable. They are afraid of each other's weapons. On the next night John's temperature begins to rise. The doctor is hastily sent for and shakes his head. "Pneumonia; it's what I was afraid of."

Tabitha demands a specialist, nurses, oxygen.

For Kit will not admit that her husband is dying; and even when he is dead insists for some minutes that he is in a coma and can be revived. Then she breaks out in anger against the local doctor, "You don't realize perhaps that this was an important case; my husband was a distinguished man, and now his life has been muddled away."

She is angry all day, while Tabitha is making inquiries, arranging for the funeral. Then she insists that the funeral shall be in a local graveyard, where there are already memorials to climbers killed on the mountains. "John would like to lie there; he loved the mountains."

Tabitha is silent, not from sympathy with Kit but politeness to the widow.

"Some people think I made him come," Kit says coldly; "but it isn't true. He loved climbing; he said it took him out of his books and gave him ideas—"

"John always had plenty of ideas, but he was never really strong."

"Do you mean that I killed him?"

"Of course not; but he was looking so tired these last years. I don't think Urrsley really suited him."

"But you know how he loved the place; there is always so much going on—such interesting developments."

"It was a pity he saw so little of his own friends. Of course he was never much interested in party politics."

"You can't mean I kept his friends away?"

Tabitha, for all her good resolutions, is silent. She feels that Kit should acknowledge so glaring a fact. But the other retorts, "Really, you know, it was a problem to get John to see anybody. I had to beg him to come in even to our own parties. I always felt that if John had gone to Oxford or Cambridge he would have sunk right away from life."

Tabitha sees that Kit is already drawing a picture for herself of a wise forthright wife in charge of a difficult scholar, whose gifts, such as they were, would have been wasted without her management; and the cunning of this scheme, however unconscious, enrages her. Her pulses quicken. She wants to say, "You wretched woman! You never understood or valued a man far too good for you." But she perceives that it is a hopeless enterprise to make Kit believe a truth so damaging to a delicate conscience, and, by a great effort, remains silent. Her very silence, however, makes the younger woman almost as pale with anger as she is red. They part suddenly as by electric revulsion.

The funeral is attended not only by Bonser and Nancy, a deputation of students, of local climbers, of college representatives, but an immense crowd, attracted by the report of the accident.

Many of these are visitors, who have come by bus from inland towns or seaside places, of whom the large proportion belong to the species of holiday-maker which, when it is not being amused by something in motion, by a cinema, by a bus ride, is utterly bored and even wretched. To these the funeral is a God-sent distraction. They swarm over the graves of the little cemetery, break down part of the wall, trample down grass and flowers, and carry on a loud chatter of talk throughout the service. Shouts are heard.

"Come up here, Jimmy."

"Ere, I can't see anything."

"Wot's 'e doing now?"

"Oo is it?"

"I dunno."

One large bus, carrying an advertisement "Holiday Trips," stops in the road within ten yards of the grave in order that the passengers may look on; the humming of its impatient engine obliges the little old vicar to raise his voice. But it accords with the service better than the clamor of the mob. It has a formal and regular note. It seems to repeat, "Hurry up, hurry up; there's no time to wait."

Kit, with red swollen eyes, stands at the head of the grave and visibly holds herself rigid. She throws back her head and defies the ceremony to make her waste another tear. Nancy looks down with a sullen air, as if offended by this new assault upon her feelings, and clings to Bonser in a group which arouses popular sympathy. Indeed, Bonser, carrying his tall hat at the graveside in one hand and resting the other on the child's shoulder, which he caresses with a sympathy worthy of any stage, touches all the trippers who are near enough to admire.

"See the gentleman with the kid? He'd be the grandfather; you can see how he's holding himself up."

Tabitha, standing on Bonser's other side, gazes into the grave and feels an angry desperation. Now and then she raises her head and looks angrily at the bus, a gesture which amuses and also annoys some of the passengers.

"Why shouldn't we look on? What 'arm are we doing?" They put her down as a silly old lady, full of class prejudice.

Tabitha's anger is directed not only against the mob, against the bus and Kit, but against something much larger and more indefinite: against a fundamental injustice which puts the good, the wise, the gentle, simply because of their goodness, forever at the mercy of the malignant, or simply stupid. "It's not fair," she feels; and the feeling is so intense that she can hardly bear it.

She finds some comfort only in Nancy's grief. "After all," she thinks, "the child appreciated her father, even if she doesn't realize that he threw himself away at Urrsley." And she asks that Nancy shall come and stay with her after the funeral.

But Kit has disapproved of that same grief, so morbid and un-child-like. She dislikes all Nancy's recent moods, and tells herself that the girl has reached the awkward age. She refuses Tabitha's invitation, and takes Nancy first to Cheltenham and then to London. The flat at Urrsley is broken up, and Kit herself moves to London, where, as Tabitha now discovers, Rodwell intends to fight a constituency at the next election.

In the winter Nancy is sent to a boarding school far in the north, and when Tabitha asks that she shall spend part of her holiday with her grandparents, she is told by letter that, "I don't think the Free-masons' is a good place for Nan. She is far too inclined already to look on life as one lark after another; and you'll excuse my saying that her grandfather is not the person to discourage her in this view."

And Tabitha's letters to her granddaughter are not answered.

105 Now Tabitha, seized with a new restlessness, begins to appear more often in the hotel. She leaves to the capable Gladys the catering and the bar but she watches over the cleaning and the servants. She will discharge a charwoman for leaving scrub marks on a floor, or a maid for failing to dust the top of a wardrobe.

And gradually, in the nature of the case, like a vigorous empire with ideals of order, of conduct, of justice, set among barbarians, she extends her dominion. Visitors are startled by the sudden appearance of a very small thin woman with high-dressed white hair, a pug face, much wrinkled, and wearing a fierce expression, who passes quickly through the rooms, and who suddenly descends upon some young couple. "You mustn't dance in this writing room."

"Who on earth is that?" one asks. "Mrs. Grundy in the flesh."

"That's Mrs. Bonser herself; she's a bit of a terror."

Tabitha reappears as if in pursuit and beckons a waiter. His expression as he runs up is eloquent of her prestige. She says in a soft but penetrating voice, "The writing room is only for residents; don't let those people in again."

The waiters grin at each other—but only when Tabitha is safely out of the way. A young woman says, "What a survival! The complete Victorian."

In fact, Tabitha's new severity is not Victorian. It is that of a woman in her sixties who hates the world but is not yet defeated by it, who has still the courage of anger. All her thoughts and acts are full of this contempt, this anger. When in the next year Rodwell is elected to parliament, when within three months later she sees that he has married Kit, she says to herself, "Of course; just what I expected. Rodwell is one of the clever ones who swim with the stream, and so of course he gets everything he wants, while poor John is wasted and dies of a broken heart."

When she goes to church, she attends with critical ears. She says of a preacher who talks of God's mercy on sinners, "Yes, that's all very well, but why doesn't he tell the truth?" And the truth for her is that sinners don't want to repent, that the world is given to evil.

It gives her a bitter pleasure to read in the paper of children all over the world fed with party propaganda and taught to hate; of young boys drilled to fight for some nationalist cause; to see Germany, Russia, Italy, Spain, ruled by thugs. And as she walks in her black dress through her garden, looking sharply for snails, she says to herself, "What do you expect in a world where Rodwells are great men? But wait till it all goes smash. Then they'll see. They'll know what a judgment means. They'll find out that God is not mocked."

One day she reproves Gladys for painting her face. The good-tempered Gladys, who has endured Tabitha's despotism for eight years, answers mildly that everyone is using lipstick now. "You feel funny without it."

"I don't care what you do outside, but I won't allow it in the hotel."

Gladys's pale broad face, with its strong bones and black eyes, wears the expression of a cow that is kicked. But she continues to use lipstick. She is a complaisant woman so long as she can amuse herself in private, but she cannot bear not to look attractive. Tabitha gives her notice, and suddenly she becomes impudent. "Excuse me, Mrs. Bonser, but I'm not your servant; the Colonel is my boss."

"I engaged you."

"You go and see what the Colonel's going to say about it." And the woman, furious with her injuries, cries, "You go and ask him. I should think he's as sick of your temper as I am."

Tabitha goes to Bonser in his favorite corner of the lounge. Fortunately it is the morning and he is alone.

"I've given Gladys Hope notice, but she says she will only take it from you."

"Given Gladys notice? Not on your life."

"If she doesn't go, I will."

"What d'you mean? Threatening me? My God, Tibby, you're asking for it."

"And she'll go today. I won't have her in the place another hour."

Bonser jumps up. "All right; don't stay for me." He flings out of the room. But in twenty minutes he is back again; and now he does not suggest that Tabitha shall go. His very selfishness, his cunning, assure him that he can't do without Tabitha. For years he has done no work, nor given a thought to management. Even at the Beausite, where his visits are rare, he leaves everything to Teri, and only grumbles at his peculations. He is rich, and takes no more interest in making money. His pleasure is to spend it, on gambling and women. He appeals to Tabitha. "But, Pops, what's it all about? What's the row? What's the poor girl done? I'm sure she's always been nice to you."

"I'm not going to have another Spring at the Freemasons'."

"What do you mean?"

"You know very well you've been to her room; it's been going on for years. I don't care what you do at the Beausite, but I won't have it at the Freemasons'."

Bonser begins to bellow. "It's a lie, it's your infernal jealousy. You never did trust me. All right, Gladys'll go. But so shall I. Yes, I'll clear out. I shan't stay where I'm not wanted."

"Very well, Dick; but Hope will go now."

Gladys Hope, to her surprise, is then turned out. She goes, however, with dignity, informing the staff that "the old bitch thinks she's the boss, but she'll learn different. We'll see who gets the last laugh."

When Bonser leaves the same afternoon for a hotel in Urrsley, and is seen in the streets with Gladys; when it is known that he has put her in an expensive flat, people think that she has indeed had the last laugh. But within a fortnight the man is back at the Freemasons'. He comes to Tabitha groaning, complaining of his indigestion. "I've been poisoned by some filth."

This is his usual cry after a debauch. He is deteriorating fast, not only in his flesh but his spirit. He cannot bear the smallest pain or discomfort, and will sulk because he has a hangover.

"You've been drinking too much," Tabitha says, "and seeing too much of that woman."

"What woman? What are you driving at? You've always got some jealous maggot in your brain, haven't you? I was stopping with old Councilor Brown; and it's his blasted cook that's poisoned me. But a lot you care—"

"You do look rather yellow. I'll get you some calomel; that always suits you—that is, if you're staying tonight."

"Damn it all! Staying! Can't a man stay in his own house?"

"Very well, I'll tell Dorothy to make up your bed in the dressing room."

"What d'you mean, the dressing room? Are you being funny? Look here, Pops, come off it. It doesn't do." And then he grows pathetic; he falls on a couch. "A chap comes home practically dying, and all you think of is to work off your spite."

"But, Dick, I thought you might prefer the dressing room."

"What do you think I came back for? Why, Pops, how long have we been married? We're too old to play these silly games."

And at night he takes her in his arms, kisses her fondly, assures her that he forgives her. "You're difficult, Pops; you know yourself that you're not everyone's woman. But there's something about you that gets me every time; yes, you've got me." And then he complains again of his heart and sends her for a tot of brandy. "By God, Tibby, I must say you're a good little nurse."

Both perceive that a shift has taken place in their relations, that now

Tabitha, by mere force of moral character, is the master in the home. But for Tabitha this means only more work. She takes Bonser to her bed, she nurses him, as a duty, and she is too proud to take advantage of her power even to remonstrate with him when he makes a nuisance of himself. And he is a great nuisance, not only in drink, but often in spite. For he does not like to be dependent, and will assert himself by some brutality.

Husband and wife are bound by ties which, like creepers on old walls, as they grow stronger also make deeper wounds and a greater weight.

106

ONE night in the spring of 1938 a party of young people from London, who have had several drinks in the bar, are playing a game of tig in the bedroom corridor. They defy a young chambermaid who tries to quiet them. Bonser, who has come back drunk from Urrsley, is deep in sulks and won't interfere. He waves the girl away. "Let 'em alone—the dirt! What's the good of talking to 'em?"

Tabitha, called from her sitting room in the Barn House, goes through the private door into the hotel and finds a young man in evening dress wrestling with a girl. She is shrieking with laughter but also accusing him of tearing her frock.

"The corridor," Tabitha says. "Excuse me, it's not allowed."

The young man, amazed by this reproof, is going to utter a rude answer when Tabitha murmurs, "You must go; I'm sorry. Yes, I'm afraid you must all go."

All at once another of the party, a young woman, comes up to her and exclaims, "Granny!" Then, smiling broadly, she holds out her hand. "You don't even know me. Nan."

Tabitha is flustered. She stares with an incredulous expression. She sees a small plump girl with a broad cat face, a snub nose, a big mouth, small blue eyes, and dark brown hair. She is powdered, rouged, and painted, her eyes are made up, her mouth is like a wound, her hair, which is at least rich and glossy, is elaborately curled like that of a hairdresser's dummy. She resembles perfectly any of those young prostitutes who, at sixteen or seventeen, hang about the main London road waiting to be picked up by some man with a car.

"Nancy!" Tabitha says at last. She allows her hand to be taken and receives a warm kiss. The girl is laughing at her confusion, and her laughter, showing good teeth, wrinkles her nose and makes her eyes almost disappear. It is a hearty delighted laugh, and it causes in Tabitha a strange emotion of pain and excitement.

"I've come to see you," the girl says, "only we were rather late and the men are such idiots."

The rest of the party, including the wrestler, are now surrounding Tabitha and Nancy with looks of great interest, like scientists watching a daring experiment. No doubt they have discussed with Nancy this project of bearding the tartar.

Tabitha, suddenly aware of this curiosity, recovers her anger and herself, and says tartly, "Yes, come in. But I'm afraid your friends must go downstairs."

Nancy at once waves imperiously, "Go away, you idiots; off with you!" and chases the party to the stairs. She then follows Tabitha into her room, smiling, exuberant with self-confidence, and takes Tabitha's hand. "Darling Granny, how marvelous—and you didn't know me! And there's Grandy. Good Lord!"

She has caught sight of Bonser slumped in his chair and gazing at her with stupid amazement. She runs up to him, kisses him on the forehead, and exclaims, "Just the same as I remembered." Then she looks at Tabitha and smiles with that sidelong glance which, in a woman, is like a wink, and, like a wink, offers a private understanding. It declares, "What a joke he is; what a great baby!"

Tabitha does not accept this offer, so disrespectful to Bonser. She asks in a sardonic tone, "And where have you come from?"

"Oh, town; home, you know. We have a flat in Westminster."

"And does your mother know of this visit?"

"Oh, Mother—" the girl wrinkles her nose—"she's in America on her committee or whatever it is. And Tom is rather a friend of mine—he doesn't interfere. He knows it's no good, anyhow."

"How old are you?" Bonser growls. "You can't be more than seventeen." He climbs to his feet and stands swaying over the women. He puts out a thick finger. "And painting your face like that; it's disgusting."

"Well, you see, Grandy, the trouble is that I've got such a queer face I have to do something to it."

"Getting yourself up like a tart."

Nancy again smiles at Tabitha. She says, "I'm sorry, Grandy. Are you frightfully shocked?"

It can be seen that she is utterly indifferent to his criticism. She looks upon him as an old fool, a back number.

And suddenly she hears the music. "Lordy, what will Billy say? I must go and dance."

"Are you engaged to Billy?"

"Billy? Lordy, no. I use him, that's all, for his car." And she flies away. They hear her say in the passage, as she opens the private door to the hotel, "Good God, have you been waiting? Well, if you must be such an idiot!"

"I always said she'd grow up a tart," Bonser says.

Tabitha agrees with him. Yet she is confused, like someone who, having foretold some disaster—a fire or a train smash—suddenly comes upon it, and is startled by its actuality, its crude living energy. She is glad when the girl goes away without saying good-by. And three months later, when old Dorothy tells her that Miss Nancy is in the bar, her first reaction is annoyance as to an interruption. She says shortly, "If she wants me she can come and see me."

But Nancy hastens to see her, and to introduce a young man, tall, serious, and pale, called Godfrey Fraser, who has driven her to the Freemasons' in a small ancient car. Having introduced him, she sends him away at once to fetch her bag, and apologizes for him. "Don't mind him, Granny, he can't talk. He's terribly slow, but really quite intelligent; and he's just had T.B., poor freak. He needs country air. I suppose you couldn't possibly find us a shelf somewhere for the week end."

"Who is the young man? Are you engaged to him?"

"Good heavens no! But I use his car a good deal—if you can call it a car. The wretch is too too poor. Don't mind where you put him, Granny; he'll gladly sleep on the bar or under the sink."

Even in three months the girl has changed. She is less exuberant, more simply dressed, more self-conscious. She looks older and has assumed the manner of one slightly bored by life. At tea in Tabitha's sitting room she talks about herself for two hours, as one disillusioned. She has, she says, been bored at school, which was stupid, and she is bored at home, where her mother quarrels with her, but she turns Tom Rodwell round her finger; she is especially bored by all the London dance bands and all her young men, summed up in a word as idiots.

The young Mr. Fraser has been sent on various errands, to clean the plugs, to find a safety pin, which, Nancy says, must be in the car. She says to Tabitha, "That will keep him happy for half an hour; we don't want him here, do we?"

"He seems a nice young man to be treated so badly."

"Godfrey doesn't mind; the poor mutt likes to be used."

"And you take advantage of his unselfishness."

The girl looks at Tabitha in amused surprise that the old lady should dare to be so old-lady-like. Then she says, "I know Godfrey is a lamb; I might even marry him some day. He'd be a safe bet, wouldn't he? But I'm not going to settle down into a frow until I've had some fun."

And when she goes, half an hour later, she embraces Tabitha warmly, looks into her eyes and says, "Are you too frightfully shocked at me? Yes, you are. Oh dear, I suppose I'm awful."

"You don't care in the least whether I'm shocked or not."

"Oh yes, I do, cross my heart. I suppose you couldn't possibly lend me a couple of quid till next week. You see, I'm afraid we were rather relying on stopping here. Of course, it was perfectly stupid of me not to write and say we were coming."

Tabitha lends her two pounds, and says, "Don't call it a loan unless you mean to pay me back."

Nancy cries, "But of course, darling, of course I'll pay you. I'll send you a P. O. on Monday."

Again Tabitha is relieved to see the last of this creature. It makes her angry to think that any young girl can be so cool in her selfishness, so corrupt. She thinks, "Of course she is preparing misery for herself." Yet she is disturbed, oppressed. And when no postal order arrives, she says, "That means she's not coming again—and just as well. She only upsets Dick."

In fact, Nancy is not seen again at the Freemasons' for five months. Then, late one summer evening, she walks in with a tall young man, fair, stooping, with a languid but attentive manner, as if much accustomed to society but always ready to enjoy it. His name is Scott. Nancy calls him Louis or Lu, and commands him as she has commanded the others, but with more conscious authority. She is now very smartly dressed, and the lofty manner has become less affected. She is perhaps more pleased with herself, and her airs have become true.

She explains to Tabitha that Lu Scott is an officer in the air force. "I'm afraid he's rather conceited; I only keep him for dancing." She does not mention the two pounds, but asks for rooms.

Tabitha says, "At eleven o'clock!" and she thinks, "What blackmail."

"Oh, I knew it was hopeless, Granny. But we've been asking all down the road, and everywhere seems to be full."

"I was the last resort."

"I didn't want to bother you. Never mind, we can doss down in the car, can't we, Louis?"

"You could sleep in the dressing room," Tabitha says, "if Louis could manage in an attic. We have a maid's room empty."

"Oh, but that would be marvelous." And the couple are taken to their rooms.

Tabitha, lying in her own bed, hears Nancy next door humming to herself, rattling a drawer, getting into bed. About an hour later the bed jingles again, and the door to the passage is opened, very carefully.

Tabitha, still drowsily awake, is surprised by this carefulness, and more surprised to hear a creak on the attic stairs. Now she is intensely wakeful; and it seems to her that someone is treading softly through the attic corridor, that there is a door opened and closed.

"I'm just imagining things." But after twenty minutes she slips out of bed. Bonser's sulky voice asks, "What are you playing at? Why can't you lie still? Now you've waked me up."

"I was wondering; I thought I heard Nancy go upstairs to the attic."

"What of it? I told you she was a tart."

"Oh, Dick, I can't believe it. In our house."

"What's biting you tonight? You know what she is as well as I do. Look how she was brought up; no religion, no standards, no home, that female public meeting for a mother, and no proper respect for anybody. Well, you saw how she treated me that first day; just laughing at me, her own grandfather. And she laughs at you, too, make no mistake. Forget her, for God's sake, and come to bed. We'll kick her out tomorrow."

Tabitha lies down at last to satisfy Bonser, but she is so far from sleep that even to lie still is agony. Her whole senses are in a tumult; her brain is saying, "It's stupid to care, the girl is worthless." But her ears are straining to catch the least sound from the dressing room.

An hour later she creeps again from the bed and goes into the passage; the dressing room door is ajar and she pushes it inwards. There is no one in the bed. But Bonser is already stirring, and growling. He misses her warmth and hastily she flies back to slide down beside him.

"Damn it all, what's up now? Keeping me awake all night. How do you expect me to carry on?"

Tabitha has suddenly an urge to laugh. The tension inside her, confused, agonizing, seeks to break out; and it seems to her all at once that there is something comic in the whole situation, something for which laughter is the only adequate refuge. But she is shocked by her own impulse. She drives it back wrathfully. "No, it's too abominable; it's too wicked. Dick is right, we must tell her that we can't have her here at all."

In the morning, when she goes to breakfast, she is dismayed by

Nancy's kiss, her high spirits, by the young man's gentle politeness, while he leans thoughtfully over his coffee and discusses the ethics of bombing. Is it right to bomb civilians? "If it f-finishes a war quickly," he murmurs, with his hesitating stammer, "it would s-save lives; but it s-seems all wrong to kill women and children." He is much perplexed by this question. And Tabitha stares at Nancy with indignant wonder. "I can't believe it—she couldn't do such a thing."

The couple drive off with many thanks, and as Nancy waves from the window of the car, her scarlet lips parted in a smile of content, Tabitha is convinced. "Of course she went to him; she wouldn't know any better. And not yet eighteen—a child."

107

AND now she is obsessed with Nancy. That stealthy movement in the dark, that daring visit of the girl boldly going to her lover, has made the girl live in her very nerves. She can't forget her for a moment.

"But what can I do? She laughs at my ideas."

Yet she feels such anxiety, such guilt in her own inaction, that after two days she goes to find Nancy at her home.

But the girl is not at home, and Kit Rodwell, just about to take out her young daughter in the perambulator, receives her with impatience.

"I haven't seen Nan for three days; we thought she was going to you."

"She left us on Sunday night. She had a young man with her called Louis, and I was rather worried."

"You mustn't ask me about Nan's young men; she seems to have dozens, and each is more utterly useless than the last."

"But, Kitty, she's only a child; is it safe?"

"I really can't be responsible for Nan; she seems to have no feeling for her home or me or Tom." Kit speaks with angry disgust. She has grown thinner, and is already gray. In appearance she is much older than her age, in manner less assured but more impatient. She never looks at the person she speaks to; her eyes are always fixed just beside or above, as if examining some distant prospect.

Suddenly she leaves Tabitha, opens a door into the next room, Rodwell's study, and calls out, "Don't forget to let me see the speech."

"There's no time now." The man comes out with his secretary, a young woman with a cloud of fair hair and large blue eyes, to whom he is talking rapidly about the arrangements of the day. Both look vaguely at Kit when she begins to talk about the political situation. "How can they expect Germany to disarm while this wretched government goes on building more planes?" And it can be seen that this argument seems to her so clear, so unanswerable, that she imagines the government, in ignoring it, to be moved by some deep and evil motive. "It's abominable. I suppose the armament manufacturers are behind it."

The young secretary turns her large eyes upon Rodwell with a look of sympathy. In fact Rodwell is plainly bored. As an M.P. of five years' standing, he has grown both fatter and more important. His good-natured air is now that of the statesman, who, secure in private knowledge and special experience, can condescend to the rubbish talked by amateurs.

He has just made a speech to his constituency, assuring them that there is no danger of war, provided nothing is done to alarm Hitler. "The Germans are frightened; they feel encircled by enemies, and we have to reassure them. That is why the rearmament policy is so wrong and dangerous." But the same argument in his wife's mouth makes him impatient. "Yes, yes." He has had too much politics from Kit.

To Tabitha he is very friendly and cheerful. "Nan? You needn't worry about Nan; these young women nowadays know how to take care of themselves." He speaks as for a public, the public with votes; and followed by the sympathetic and devoted secretary, he walks out with the smile of one who makes a good exit.

Tabitha turns again to Kit. "But, Kit, I do think that someone ought to speak to Nan; she's so young."

Kit is still more exasperated. "It's no good speaking to Nan. She's never had any idea but amusing herself, and I really can't feel responsible for that."

"You don't blame me?"

"It's certainly not my fault." And the woman, unable to bear another moment of this foolish discussion, picks up the child, a small fat girl, comically like her father, and carries her off to some inner room.

Tabitha comes away in a rage. "She's not fit to be a mother—and blaming me for Nan's wildness! But she would never admit anything."

Exhausted, desperate, she returns to the Freemasons', to find a wire from Nancy, "Can you lend me five pounds? Urgent," and giving an address at a small hotel in Sussex.

"I suppose she has that man there," Tabitha says; and wires, "Please explain."

But there is no answer for two days; and then a note from a private hotel in South Wales. "Dearest Gran, I'm in a frightful hole and I don't know what I shall do unless I can get twenty pounds at once. I wouldn't ask you if I knew anyone else who had any money. Only don't think of sending it unless you really have it to spare. I'll pay you as soon as I get my next allowance. All love from Nan."

Tabitha is outraged. "Isn't that typical? What can one do with such a creature? And she carefully guards against any sense of obligation by telling me not to send anything unless sending it means nothing to me. And what is she doing in Wales?"

She writes a severe note, asking for some explanation. What is Nancy doing? Is she with Louis? What does she want the money for?

Three days later there is a telegram, "Can you wire ten pounds? Very urgent. Strictly on loan. Reply at once. Desperate. Nan."

This telegram arrives when Tabitha is shopping in Urrsley. She does not get it till the evening, and finds that the money cannot be wired that night. She is now in a panic. The word desperate terrifies her. She imagines Nancy turned into the street, or in prison. She can't sleep; and Bonser abuses her. "Do keep still for a moment. What's wrong with you tonight?"

"Nothing."

But Bonser, though he disregards Tabitha's feelings, has an acute knowledge of them. "I suppose you're worrying about that little bitch again."

"I am certainly not going to worry about Nan after the way she's behaved."

"What are you doing now, then? My God, you grandmothers beat the band. Meat for monkeys."

Tabitha says to herself with bitterness, "If only she were worth worrying about."

In the morning she wires ten pounds. And again there is no acknowledgment, no news for a month; until one afternoon, coming in late from the town, she finds the girl in her sitting room, stretched out on the most comfortable chair and smoking a cigarette.

"So there you are," she says coldly. "Did you ever get that ten pounds?"

Nancy slowly recoils herself, kisses Tabitha, and says in an absent-minded voice, "Oh yes, I told you."

"You did not tell me. Don't you know you ought to acknowledge money? It might have been stolen. I'm not speaking of ordinary good manners."

"Oh, but I'm sure I did." The girl plainly does not care if she did or not. She has forgotten the money. She is as indifferent to that old benefaction as to Tabitha's rudeness. She accepts both as proper from a grandmother. She falls back into her chair and says to the air, "The fact is, I've had a bit of a knock."

"What does that mean in English?"

"Louis has chucked me. Of course I always expected it. But no, that's not true. It's given me rather a shock. I feel rather a fool."

"If you go about with young men you must expect shocks."

"But I really thought he was smitten; why, I can't imagine. My looks are not exactly a strongpoint, are they; and I'm not particularly clever, either."

"It's a pity, certainly, that you didn't work harder at school."

"You're telling me. I suppose I couldn't stop here for tonight, could I?"

"If you'd only written to say you were coming." This is to teach Nancy consideration, and to write. But before the girl can change her mind she says, "I'll go and see," and orders a bed to be made up.

On the next day Nancy asks if she can stay for the week end. And she continues to stay. She is very depressed; and nothing is left of the young exuberance of a year before but its frankness. She moons, smokes fifty cigarettes a day, and grows thin. She is very untidy.

Tabitha abuses her, "All that smoking is very bad for you; it will ruin your complexion."

And she answers with absent-minded patience, "Yes, I look awful, don't I?"

She does not eat, and Tabitha says, "If you don't eat you'll be ill, and that won't help."

And the girl answers, "Oh, I'm never ill; I'm fearfully tough."

Bonser has gone away to Pynemouth. Of late, it is said, he has been having trouble with Miss Spring, who is demanding more money than he likes to pay now that he is also supporting Gladys Hope. What with letters from Pynemouth and the continued stay of Nancy at the Freemasons', he goes away in a very bad temper.

Tabitha and Nancy, left alone, take supper together in Tabitha's dark little drawing room, and afterwards sit on the veranda looking on the garden. The girl, having dined on a plate of soup, is chain-smoking. Tabitha, sewing household linen, looks at her now and then over her spectacles with an impatient frown. "You're brooding," she says at last. "You can't go on like this."

"Oh, I'm not really pipped, Granny; I'm only fed up with myself. I've been such an idiot." And she begins to talk about her home and how much she has disappointed her mother. "She never could forgive me for being stupid, and hating Tom; but I don't really hate Tom, I only rather despise him—he's really too pleased with himself."

It is warm but not drowsy. The air is thin, and the greenish light of sunset gives the young grass and leaves a tint so vivid that it seems unnatural and crude. The birds are chattering in that sudden liveliness before their sleep. A blackbird beginning to sing high up in the immense elm at the foot of the garden abruptly breaks off and dives away under a crooked branch. There is the feeling of intimacy and peace which belongs to a quiet evening, probably because of the dusk shutting out distance, and a certain premonition of bed.

Tabitha feels this intimacy as between herself and Nancy and it makes her heart beat quicker. It seems to her that this is a special evening when something important has happened. She is full of sympathy for the girl, still so young, who has suffered such a wounding blow, and she wants to express this sympathy. At the same time she wishes to use the opportunity of teaching the girl a valuable lesson which will perhaps save her from such another blow.

"Of course, I suppose Tom is a good man, and I oughtn't to despise anybody, really; I'm pretty useless, goodness knows."

"It's very wrong to say such things," Tabitha exclaims. "You've had a disappointment; but life is full of disappointments." And she gives the girl a little sermon on the value of misfortune. "It was when I began to be unhappy that I found out what religion can mean."

The girl answers gloomily, "Oh, it's not as bad as that!" As if Tabitha were offering her a drug. And she adds, "I'll get over it. I only want time."

"All that smoking doesn't help your nerves."

"No, I suppose not." She reaches out her still childish red hand for another cigarette, and says, "You know, Granny, what I really want is a job; something to take my mind off. The only thing is, what can I do? I thought of being a secretary to an author, or something like that, but I can't type."

"A secretary has to know how to spell," Tabitha says, "and to have some method." She bites her thread as if biting an enemy. She is furious with Nancy for so calmly putting aside religion as a cure for her unhappiness.

"But what I thought I could do—only you wouldn't allow me, would you—?"

"What is this proposal?"

"I thought I might help here in the Barn House. You seem so busy. Of course I shouldn't want any pay."

This is a solution so delightful to Tabitha that she has not dared to hope for it. And in case, by accepting it too joyfully, she may offend fate, she says, "Oh, the Barn House would be much too quiet for you."

"But I love it for being quiet, Granny. That's just what I do love, peace. You can't even hear the people in the hotel."

"Very well, my dear, certainly stay if you like; there's always the shopping."

"And I could help sometimes in the hotel, too, I suppose, when somebody has a day out?"

"I'm afraid Miss Frew wouldn't like that; she's rather touchy. No, you mustn't interfere in the hotel."

"Good heavens, I shouldn't interfere. Miss Frew terrifies me; and I don't know anything about managing hotels. There's only one thing, Granny, if you don't mind my saying so: I do know something about dancing, and the Freemasons' could do with a new dance floor, and new music, too, just as a matter of business."

"Perhaps, but you mustn't say so to Miss Frew. The dance floor is Miss Frew's department. Dance by all means—but as a guest."

"Heavens, Granny, I wouldn't dance if you paid me. I'm past all that."

108

IN FACT, Nancy does not recover her exuberance, nor go dancing. When old flames, Billy, Godfrey Fraser, come to see her and to take her out, she answers, with her new air of disillusionment, that she has no time, she is too busy. And she goes shopping or tries to keep accounts. Tabitha hears again the old note of impatience when the young woman exclaims, "Those idiots have sent the wrong cigarettes," or "Fortlings are really too stupid." She so firmly refuses all distractions that Tabitha herself begins to be anxious. She urges the girl to go to the cinema in Urrsley, or the play. But Nancy answers, "I can't be bothered; I'd much rather have a peaceful evening with you, and get my feet up." And, putting her feet up, she will smoke and discuss the bad behavior of the hot-water system, the imbecility of boilermakers, the incompetence of maids, and say fretfully, "Why can't people do a proper job?"

And apparently from mere restlessness and superfluous vigor, she ascends to the lofts to examine the water tanks and goes to the cellars to see why the pipes make a noise.

One evening, when she is at the shops in Urrsley, Miss Frew and the hotel chef give Tabitha notice. It appears that on the afternoon before, during the cook's absence, Nancy has examined the kitchens and condemned them, to the kitchen maids, as a disgrace.

Tabitha apologizes for the girl, but the manageress is firm. She can't, she says, stand disloyalty; she feels undermined.

Tabitha is highly indignant. She says to herself, "Why must these children meddle? Why can they never leave well alone?" And as soon as Nancy returns from her shopping, she meets her with the news. "I thought you were not to interfere in the hotel."

"But, darling, I only said the kitchen was a mess. And really, you know, it's a stroke of luck if the Frew does go."

"The chef has been here ten years."

"That's what I mean, darling. I didn't want to worry you, but really the Freemasons' is a bit antediluvian."

"Nonsense, we only opened it in 1925."

"But, Granny dear, that *is* antediluvian. That's *why* the lounge is a morgue. If you only saw what other places are doing. The Three Feathers at Barworth has a complete sun-ray roof. You know, Granny, it's none of my business, but this poor old Freemasons' is beginning to smell. People take one look and go on. You can see them."

"It's quite good enough for me," Tabitha says tartly. "You mayn't know, perhaps, that it was designed by a London architect, and has been admired all through the country."

"All right, Granny, I'm not going to bother you."

But on an afternoon of the next week she is discovered in the lounge with a young man called Humphrey Roger, a fat, pale young man with long fair hair falling into his eyes, a loose tie which flops on his round stomach, and an ingratiating manner. He is, however, quite without tact. He proposes to pull down the lounge, throw it into the dining room, and build a new dining room, in pink concrete, over the swimming pool.

"It's a wonderful opportunity you have here, Mrs. Bonser, for something really modern, quite unique."

"It would really be rather beautiful," Nancy says.

But the young man does not like the word beautiful. It is out of fashion. He bends politely toward Nancy. "It would be perfectly adapted to its functions." And he goes away and draws up a sketch plan of new buildings to cost eight thousand pounds. He also demands fifty guineas for this preliminary work.

"And really, it's worth it, Granny. Though you needn't pay him if you don't like. After all, it's his first job; he ought to be glad of the advertisement."

Tabitha loses her temper. For suddenly it has been revealed to her how much she loves the Barn House and even the hotel, how little she can bear the idea of any change in either of them. They are the only secure and dependable elements of a world in turmoil. They are not only a home to her but they have insensibly grown to be an essential part of her being, her activity.

"I won't have *any* changes," she says. "Do you want to spoil the place?"

And Nancy, with her mother's good temper, says no more. But she begins to talk of looking for work in London. "Something with a little more scope." And as she says it she reveals in the lift of her chin a trait of Tabitha herself. She has obstinacy as well as energy.

Both women understand the crisis. Tabitha says to herself, "Let her go if she must. I'm not going to have everything turned upside down." But she is embittered against the young, who are never satisfied to be at peace.

The struggle is not made up, but rather intensified by Bonser's return. He comes back from three weeks' debauch in a very bad temper. He complains of being cheated by some bookmaker, and ill used by a friend. Probably he has had a quarrel with Gladys Hope. And in a moment of dejection, when he is three parts drunk, he complains, "No one can say I'm mean, Tibby. And then they kick me around—turn me into the street." Weeping, he says, "I'm done for, Tibby. They've broken my heart at last. I'm not long for this world."

Actually he spends weeks in bed; and though he does not stop drinking, drink no longer enlivens him. When he is drunk he grows merely more violent against his enemies, and he cries, "I know you want me dead, Tib. All right, it won't be long now."

He won't hear of any alterations or even repairs. He can't bear noise. He says, "Let me alone; let me die in peace."

He has taken such a bitterness against women, on account of the mysterious insults put upon him in his last debauch, that he no longer comes to the lounge, and never sees Nancy. But it is understood that men visitors will always find whisky in his bedroom; he welcomes anyone to whom he can tell the story of his wrongs.

He is delighted especially with Godfrey Fraser, who comes at this time to spend his Easter holiday, and who listens to him with the serious and respectful air which he shows to all life. "You keep away from the girls, Godfrey," he tells him; "they're like sharks, their teeth go backwards: once they get a hold of you they never let go until they've chewed you down and turned you into cat's meat. Look what they've done to me! Look how my wife runs me around, and that granddaughter of mine. Sitting here like a couple of crows, and waiting for me to die. Waiting for the pickings."

It is Tabitha who has asked Fraser to spend his Easter holiday at the Barn House. He has been ill and is threatened with a sanatorium, and Tabitha says, "The poor boy needs looking after."

Nancy laughs at her. "Really, Granny, you're too transparent; as if I were going to fall for that dumb dub again." But when she hears Godfrey's cough she gets to work, with bustling impatience, to cosset the man. She rubs his chest with oil, she doses him with tonics. She is like a vigorous small child with a new doll who puts it to bed with a fire of admonition. "Going to drill in this weather? It's perfectly imbecile! And just because you fancy yourself in khaki!"

Both Tabitha and Nancy are agreed that Fraser, who has lately joined the Territorials, has no business to go drilling. To his solemn argument that in view of Hitler's threats it is a duty to prepare for war, Tabitha answers that war is none of his business, with a weak chest. And Nancy cries, "War? Hitler is not such a fool. He's just a bluffer. Good lordy, wasn't last time enough?"

And in these words she repeats the feeling which is expressed every day and all day in the lounges of the Freemasons' by the young: a feeling that war would really be an abominable interruption to their amusing and crowded lives. For in the twenty years since the last war life for the young has grown much more amusing. They have more money, more education, much more freedom. And those who are not militant Pacifists, or Communists or Fascists, or the mystics described by Nancy, with warm contempt, as Peace Pledgers, sweep away the very idea of war with a sentence, "There can't be a war; the Maginot Line is impregnable, and the French army is the best in the world. If Hitler is fool enough to go to war, he'll be beaten in a month."

Both the unorganized natural pacifism of ignorance and militant pacifism are strong in Urrsley, and Godfrey, coming home in uniform, is scowled at by women and jeered at by small boys from the poorer quarters. The *Gazette* writes of those who want a larger air force as warmongers, and an election is won on the cry, "Cut down armaments."

But though Nancy laughs at Godfrey and calls him the chocolate soldier, she misses him when he goes back to his office, and makes him promise to return the next week end. She cannot perhaps do without a young man, and it becomes the rule that Godfrey should spend all his week ends at the Freemasons'. Nancy perceives, as if she had not before noticed these qualities, his intelligence, his reliability, and says, "That office will kill him; he ought to be in the open air. We ought to buy a farm down here, and then he could run it for us."

"When you have the Freemasons' you can make a farm."

"Will I have the Freemasons'?"

"I suppose so."

Nancy is thoughtful for a whole day after this news, and then remarks only that if she does inherit the hotel she will get rid of the genuine oak beams in the dining room. "They really are a bit too bygone."

When Godfrey comes for his next visit she takes him over the place and points out to him what must be done to bring it up to date. "Godfrey agrees with me," she tells Tabitha, "that the dance floor is a disgrace. And you know, he'd be good at a job like this. His legal knowledge would be useful if we had trouble about the license."

A week later she announces her engagement. "I told Godfrey we might as well be married, then he could chuck that beastly office."

And in her new role, which she is playing with such enjoyment, of the sensible young woman who knows how to manage life, she explains to Tabitha how glad she is that Louis Scott refused her. "He was all right to play with, but marriage is quite a different thing—a different pair of shoes. It's more of a partnership. The important thing is for husband and wife to respect each other." She describes Godfrey Fraser as "solid gold all through; you couldn't *not* respect him," and concludes very seriously, "I don't say we're *bound* to be happy together—nobody can count on that—but at least we'll have a damn sight better chance than people who rush into it with their eyes closed."

"How much are you thinking of Godfrey in all this?" Tabitha demands, as a lesson to the girl's egotism.

"Oh, I know I'm rather selfish, Granny, but Godfrey will be good for me there. He's got such ridiculous principles."

The engagement is announced, the Rodwells send congratulations; and to everyone's surprise, Bonser agrees that Godfrey shall leave the office and become assistant at the Freemasons'. "I'm sick of all these women buzzing round; give me a man for a change—a real man, and a soldier. Ah, it takes an old soldier like myself to appreciate a man like Godfrey—a fellow you can trust. He's too good for Nancy by a long chalk. But damn it, these modern girls are all the same—a lot of floozies, jeering at everything decent. Yes, I shan't be sorry to die now; at least I can feel the old Freemasons' will be in good hands."

109

NANCY wants to be married at once. "Let's get it over," she says. "I hate only being engaged; it's so fidgety." And the date of the wedding has actually been fixed when Chamberlain goes to Munich; whereupon Fraser insists on a postponement "until the situation is a bit clearer."

Fraser's view is that, in case of war, bombers will cause great destruction in England, and that no one has the right to leave a young wife, perhaps pregnant, to face confusion, panic, and probably starvation and revolution, which, as he imagines, must follow such a disaster. But this idea, even hinted, angers both the women. Tabitha is angry because she has set her heart on this marriage, which will, as she says to herself, settle Nancy. The word "settle" represents to her a whole world of security, of housewifely prudence: all that she desires for Nancy and for the mistress of the Barn House. And she desires it all the more because she is secretly convinced that the war will come and, like the last war, send all the young people who are not securely fixed in marriage and family affairs rushing about the world and getting thoroughly unsettled; while Nancy is irritated because she is sure that war will not come, and because Fraser takes Hitler seriously. "I should have thought Chamberlain's word is good enough even for Godfrey; after all, Chamberlain *knows*. He's got all the inside information." And she tells everybody that she has heard from the most reliable sources, from a German "who knows Goebbels quite well—really a frightfully nice boy" whom she has met at a friend's house, that the Germans love the English and have never had any intention of making war on them—information easily believed, because thousands of others are hearing the same news from the nice German visitors, who this year are seen everywhere in England, at schools, country houses, London dinners, youth conferences; all attractive-looking young men, full of enthusiasm for ideals, and explanations of Nazi plans, all perfectly sincere, since they have been chosen for their sincerity, their idealism.

Often they deplore certain events in Germany: the Jew-baitings, the attack on the churches, saying, "But it is revolution, you know; and there are far more cruelties in Russia. In revolution there are always bad things as well as good; fools and brutes take their opportunity." And they speak the word "revolution" with a naïve joy, as if to mean, "We are on the right road, with the brave and the noble who make new worlds."

One of them is staying at the Rodwells' to study English politics. His interview with Rodwell is published, with the phrase, "You must not forget that we are socialists in Germany." He is taken to meet a group of Rodwell's friends in the House of Commons.

A party of twenty who have been playing hockey at schools and colleges come to Urrsley and spend an afternoon at the Freemasons'. Urrsley students come out to meet them in the afternoon, and the two parties bathe together in the hot July sun. First there is a discreet unacknowledged competition in swimming and diving. The self-chosen champions of each nation show their tricks and their speed. In these the Germans, probably athletes chosen by the party, have an easy superiority; and afterwards the young men, stretched on the grass or walking slowly on the lawn in twos and threes, talk together. One sees everywhere the earnest looks, the sudden gestures: those movements in a young man which remind at once of the child's skip, the pure exuberance of life, and the man's force.

"See," Nancy says to Tabitha at an upper window, "they're not murdering each other." And afterwards, when the whole student party is at tea in the lounge, talking and arguing with such animation that they can be heard throughout the hotel, she goes into them to make sure, as she says, that they have enough to eat, but probably, as Tabitha feels, simply to be with them, to enjoy their young company. While Tabitha herself, wandering restless in the upper corridor, is full of terror. She is afraid that at any minute there will be a fight, or that the whole mass of young creatures will suddenly rise up and break the windows, wreck the hotel. She feels the mass of youth as a dangerous explosive force; even its charm, the crude charm of Nancy multiplied by forty, has become overwhelming and frightening. "I suppose they are all in some movement," she thinks; and it seems to her that the world is full of youth movements. Every day she has read in the papers of strikes, riots, marches, rebellions, by students, or some resolution passed at Oxford or Rome, or Bombay, or Pekin, demanding revolution, the suppression of armies, or the destruction of empires, freedom for the world, the union of all the religious or the abolition of all the religions, the wiping out of the Nazis or the Fascists, the Communists, the Jews, the Moslems, the Hindus, the Europeans in Asia, the Asiatics in Europe; and feeling as if the air itself is full of electric youth, she says, "But of course there must be war, with all this egotism and recklessness. If Hitler doesn't make war someone else will, or it will simply start by itself."

Nancy comes back through the corridor whistling to herself. She is flushed with excitement; her pursed-up mouth seems to kiss the air of a larger world.

"Aren't they nearly finished?" Tabitha asks fretfully.

"I've sent for the bus. They really are rather nice, Granny; and it's rather wonderful what they're doing in Germany."

"Murdering and blowing trumpets—egotism."

"But, Granny, they're not thinking of themselves—they're devoted to Hitler. It's quite extraordinary."

"Yes, because they've no sense. And then there'll be this war; and Godfrey will be killed, and we'll all be ruined."

Nancy makes a face, meaning "Granny in one of her moods," and goes discreetly away. She begins to whistle again only when she is round the corner. Tabitha goes to ask the head waiter why the bus has not come. She is impatient to get rid of all these young people with their dangerous enthusiasm, their love of revolution and Hitler.

She loathes Hitler so much that the very name makes her grow hot. When Bonser, to show off his third new wireless, turns on a Hitler speech, she goes out of the house. She can't bear even to hear the voice which has such power over millions. And when she reads in a paper of "that genius among demagogues," she says angrily, "I don't call it genius to be a liar and a cheat."

Yet this is exactly why she trembles with hatred and fear at the name of Hitler, because he has this genius in lying and cheating, and because she feels the immense power of lies and fraud, especially with the innocent. She thinks, "Everyone is telling lies—the Communists, the Nazis, all the nationalists—and the young swallow them. They like to swallow them; they'd rather have lies than truth, because lies are more exciting. But it can't go on; it's impossible. If I talked about a judgment they'd laugh at me, but that's what they will get."

110

BONSER, like Tabitha, is convinced that there will be a war, and that it will ruin him. He has an immense admiration for Hitler, listens to all his speeches which he cannot understand, reads three or four newspapers a day, and tells everyone, "It's coming all right. He'll beat the lot of 'em, that artist. And he actually wrote in his books that the people are a lot of sheep; and they kiss his arse for it. That's the stuff, that's pretty smart, that's artful. I take off my hat to that bugger; he's spoofed the world, and serve it right for a lot of mugs."

But his excitement is full of bitterness. He is drinking more heavily than ever and begins to have symptoms of delirium. "Yes, we're done for; he's done for us. And he might have let an old man die in peace." He weeps, imagining that he has cancer, that Tabitha is robbing him. He staggers at night, half drunk, into some startled visitor's room and says, "It's all right, don't be frightened. I'm dy-ing, that's all. I've been poisoned. But it doesn't matter. We'll all be dead soon, when Hitler sets about us."

One evening he has a kind of fit, very like epilepsy, and is put to bed. He greets the doctor with the words, "I'm dying, doctor. I don't care. I've had enough of this damn world. But don't leave me with these women, or they'll finish me off. I know their tricks, the bitches."

He is taken into an Urrsley nursing home, from which he writes despairing notes to Tabitha. "Take me out of this."

Tabitha sends her local doctor, who reports, "He's well enough to be moved, but of course there is considerable risk. A stroke, however slight in effect, is a serious matter at the age of seventy-one. On the other hand, the patient's depression is an adverse factor."

Tabitha orders an ambulance, and prepares to fetch the Colonel home again. On the day before, however, startled by the invasion of Poland, she telephones to know if the ambulance will be available.

A surprised voice answers, "Yes, ma'am, all correct."

"You saw that the war had started?"

"Oh yes, ma'am."

"I thought you might be needed if there was bombing."

"Yes, ma'am." The voice accepts the suggestion as it has accepted the war, with brisk attention to the matter in hand. "We're on the emergency list. Very well, ma'am, the nursing home at five-thirty."

But before lunchtime Bonser is at the town hall offering his services, as an old soldier, to the country. "At a moment like this," he declares to the committee, "a man has no right to be ill; and, dammit, the Bonsers always died with their boots on." And he is at once appointed to take temporary charge of a local depot for recruits.

The committee, in fact, is not at all surprised by the Colonel's patriotic excitement. It has already had applications from men much older and much more crippled. It would have said, if it had leisure for reflection, if it had not seen the morning's news, that the whole nation had taken a dose of some reviving drug to quicken all its faculties, to enlarge its imagination, to make it more active, friendly, and enterprising.

In the next weeks, when thousands of young men are going into uniform, thousands of girls are joining war factories, their talk makes trains and buses gay, as if war were a holiday occasion; for all have new jobs, more money, more friends, and, above all, a change which feels like freedom.

Bonser, having visited his camp, consisting at first of one half-ruinous barn in a stubble field, inspected the staff—one quartermaster sergeant of seventy-two with a wooden leg, and two N.C.O.'s almost as decrepit—received their salutes and ordered them a case of beer, gives the general instruction, "Carry on," and disappears into London, as he says, "to pick up my old kit."

And three days later, having procured from some store in London, or possibly, as some suggest, a theatrical costumier's, a colonel's outfit and two rows of medal ribbons, he is in the bar of the Urrsley

Grand Hotel, telling a group of attentive and respectful young people that the Bonsers are an old military family, that his great-grandfather fell at Waterloo in the last charge of the old Guards, and that, dammit-all, he knows he is a fool to volunteer again, he knows what he's in for. "England always does the dirt on the gentleman, especially the old soldier; chucks 'em on the scrapheap as soon as a war's over. And why? Because she knows she's got 'em on a string. She knows they'll always be there, loyal and true. Once a king's officer, always a king's officer—it's in the blood."

And those who one month before would have jeered at the mildest word of patriotic sentiment now look round cautiously to see if they may venture as much as a smile, and decide not to risk it. The atmosphere is changed.

Thus the Colonel, from the first days of the war, takes up a position in Urrsley which, though it carries very little responsibility, has a fine appearance, very satisfactory not only to himself, but to the town. And if, as people notice, he sometimes drags one foot, droops an eyelid, shakes in the hands, and is forgetful of names, these small disabilities are regarded with sympathy and respect as the consequences of his old war service and hardships on many fronts.

There are of course many people who suspect something of the truth. They say that he is not a real colonel, perhaps only a major; that if he really fought in South Africa, he was probably a trooper; they notice that at his daily visits to his camp he confines himself to the order, given with a genial wave of the hand, which is not very like a military salute, "Carry on, sergeant-major." But these very people delight in joining his circle at the Grand Hotel bar, and hearing him explain how Hitler will be beaten.

"It's a motorized war, the tank and plane have changed everything. They call Hitler clever, but he's only had the sense to see the facts. That's all this blitz is—speed. Everyone who knew anything about tactics knew that the motor would change war; it's changed everything. But we have the answer: first the Maginot Line, and then the fighter."

All this, of course, is directly from the morning paper, often from *The Times* or *Telegraph* of that very day. But still it is convincing. It has power from the lips of the Colonel; it confirms the papers, which, after all, have no more authority in this matter than belongs to writers, journalists—persons who are dealing in ideas every day and may be totally irresponsible.

For Bonser, after twelve years, during which he has been talked about, hated, laughed at, and applauded, has made a deep impression in Urrsley. He is more than a character, with that mysterious power which belongs to all characters, of touching upon some nerve of common life; he is a personage. He has a moral standpoint; he believes in roadhouses, in fun for the young, in the Church and the Empire; he is highly successful in business; he has an immense self-confidence. And when he assures a tableful of the shrewdest men in town that the war will be over in six months, they are relieved from doubts and anxiety caused by the sudden fall of Poland.

"That's what we expected. The experts knew Poland couldn't hold out. A poor country like Poland can't afford a mechanized army. The little countries will all be washed up in a year or two. They can't stand the pace."

111

AT THE Freemasons,' where, at the first raid warning, Tabitha and Nancy have driven the whole staff into shelter beneath the stairs, there is now a party of workmen extending the lounge and laying down a new dance floor. For the young officers appointed on construction and training at two new airdromes in the neighborhood have explained to Bonser that the old floor is too small and too rigid, and that the lounge is too crowded.

"Is that so? I'll take your word for it." The genial Colonel is now very friendly with all young officers, as a modern colonel should be. "Dammitall, I used to like a hop myself when I first joined the regiment. I'll see about a floor for you. I'll put it up to the War House. As for the lounge, I know that's out of date. In fact, we had a plan to modernize it some time ago, by a real modern architect. But the women—my wife and granddaughter, they were against it. Well, you know what women are, conservative; they hate any change."

Roger's plan is brought out, and the young man sent for to enlarge the lounge. He points out that to enlarge the lounge by itself would be a pity; that already the dining room is too small. And he spreads out his magnificent sketches for the new Freemasons'.

"I see," Bonser says; and his air is that of the genial Colonel, a father of the regiment, who is also, in spite of ripe age, thoroughly up-to-date, the very reverse of a Blimp. "The modern idea—steel, reinforced concrete. And what about the kitchens? What I always say is, mechanization."

"Quite, sir. What I've tried to remember is first of all the function, the use. Now in a living machine—"

"Ha, very good idea there for the windows—they'll catch the eye all right. There's only one thing, the bar. Is it big enough? I should like a couple of yards at least on the bar."

Roger promises a satisfactory bar, and the Colonel waves his hand. "I like your stuff, laddie; carry on."

He has probably very little idea of what he means by these words. He feels simply that, together with a certain careless gesture, they go with the uniform. And when a fortnight later a gang of navvies sets about the demolition of the old Freemasons', he is gratified by the sense that he, too, like Hitler, is bringing about a revolution.

And indeed it is this same sense in reverse: the feeling that since there is war there must be violent change, which makes Tabitha submit without a word to the destruction of the old Freemasons'. Only for the Barn House she fights; and even then must see one whole wall pulled down and her drawing room cut in half to fit in with Roger's plan.

But this, too, pleases Bonser. He delights to sleep, during six weeks, in a bedroom of which one wall is canvas, because he can make light of it. "We old bushwhackers are used to roughing it a bit." And coming out from breakfast, not to neat lawns and rolled walks, carefully maintained for twelve years, but to heaps of earth and scaffold poles, to trucks breaking through the hedge, to a cement mixer next Tabitha's sacred garden, to deep mud tracks among broken roses, metaled with fragments of composition paneling from the old lounge, he loves to stand as on a battlefield, and tell the foreman that it is necessary to be up-to-date.

"Can't say I like this new style, but there's no doubt it's the stuff for the troops—functional; that's what we want. Tudor is more artistic, it's a lot cozier and it's real English; more natural, too. But—" with the gesture of a man who makes a sacrifice for his country—"what we've all got to do is to keep up-to-date. The war is going to make a lot of changes, and I shouldn't be surprised if it put Tudor right down the drain—at least for the hotel business."

And he pats the clerk of works on the shoulder. "Over the top—that's the word. If you want more men you've only got to ask. This is a war job."

112

THE airdromes, which within three months fill the new Freemasons' with customers, even before walls are plastered or the windows painted, are already found too small. Thousands of laborers are constructing, within thirty miles, two larger ones. Planes scream and dive over the Freemasons' night and day; and Tabitha lies awake expecting every moment that one of them will fall upon the roof. But she is too busy to feel the tension, the weariness.

She is still her own manager. Bonser no longer condescends even to order the cigars, and Nancy is away for days at a time. She now drives for an air marshal on his tours of inspection; and when she comes for a few days' leave to the Barn House, she is preoccupied. She either pays no attention to the new buildings, or, being asked her opinion of the restaurant, now nearly finished, a glittering structure of steel and glass like a ship's bridge, she says coldly, "It's all right, I suppose; a bit sissy, but that's Roger."

"I don't know why your friend Roger hasn't been called up," Tabitha says.

"It would be a pity to get him killed; and he wouldn't be any good as a soldier."

Nancy seems to have little indignation against scrimshankers and conscientious objectors. Like most of her friends, she takes the war coolly and speaks of it with detachment. When the Germans begin their attack on the west and bomb Holland, to the horror and indignation of Tabitha, Nancy says thoughtfully, "Hitler said he'd do it, and he's done it. Us next; and it's our own funeral if we were such fools."

And when the Germans have overrun Holland and Belgium in a few days, and the older people, the government men, are asking, "But what can they do against the Maginot Line—what's the idea?" she remarks with the same somber air, "I shouldn't be too sure of anything with Hitler; he's got something."

In fact, behind all the confident statements about the strength of the frontier, the excellence of the French army and the British fighters, the spirit of the British army in France and the quality of the 75 gun, there is uneasiness. There's always the feeling that Hitler is an extraordinary man, a character on an immense scale, and that to such men miracles are possible. When a week later the newspapers show in their maps a slight bend southwards on the northern frontier and describe it as the bulge at Sedan, everyone at once is fascinated by this bulge.

"That's nothing," Bonser says, as he is hoisted into his official car to go to Newbury races. "The important thing is our development on the left; Gamelin and Weygand know what they're doing. The more the Huns press down on the right the worse for them." But the young are skeptical. Their mood is no longer that of the cocktail party, but the morning after.

The bulge has grown no larger, but Nancy, who arrives one afternoon bringing her marshal for a three days' tour of inspection, declares, on the strength of a letter from Godfrey, that the Germans will probably break through.

"What about our tanks?"

"We haven't got any."

This creates an astonished silence in the bar. A councilor from Urrsley says loudly, "That's the sort of talk that helps the enemy."

But a flying officer called Parkin, a friend of Nancy's who is standing by, turns round and declares, "That's right—not a tank! We haven't anything!" He speaks with cheerful relish, and it is plain that he likes to shock the councilor. "It's the war at last. The Hun is really started this time."

"But what about the Maginot Line, Mr. Parkin?"

"There isn't any Maginot Line there. He's going round the end. Trust him. Hitler's always got a new one, hasn't he?"

"But how—round it?" Everyone, including the barman, everyone except Nancy, Parkin, and two air cadets is astonished to hear that the Maginot Line does not cover the whole frontier of France but only the eastern edge.

"Well, that beats all," the barman exclaims. "Why didn't they tell us?"

Parkin spreads his chest and utters a laugh which is at once gay and decisive. "You'd better ask 'em"—in which can be heard the complement of Nancy's remark, "If we're such fools."

Parkin has just been promoted to wings, which seem to glitter even in his small blue eyes. He is a small fair man with a ginger mustache, a long broken nose, and broad shoulders, who greets Tabitha with the most impressive politeness. He bows from the waist, presses her hand, and then springs upright again with the air of one who has done the handsome thing in a smart way. Parkin is tremendously smart: his new uniform has that miraculous neatness which is smart; he has a smart swagger; his expression is alert—which is the smart expression; his talk is rapid, smart, cynical. His little mustache, curled slightly upwards, achieves a smartness which is too neat to be human. It is probably dressed with some hair fixative. Although Tabitha recoils from Parkin at sight because of his swagger, above all, because Nancy plainly likes him, she is obliged to smile at his talk. He stays to dinner, drinks much but remains sober—that is to say, not more high-strung than before—and goes off at last, with a noise like a battle, on a powerful motor bicycle with a defective silencer.

"Isn't he neat?" Nancy says. "Did you notice his nails? I never knew anyone so clean. Of course he's rather a cad, but they say he's good at his job. Did you hate him frightfully? Of course, he's not your type at all."

"He's very amusing." And after a moment, Tabitha asks, "Did you hear from Godfrey this morning?"

"Yesterday. He's quite well; the billet seems to suit him. Don't be afraid I'd ever ditch Godfrey for young Parkin. I'm not such an idiot."

But this statement throws them both into dejection. They look at each other and understand that Nancy has made a confession. Tabitha says, "I suppose it's very dangerous in these new fighting planes."

"Yes, and Joey is quite reckless; he's bound to get killed one day. Probably quite soon. I think that's one reason why he's so on wires. It must be an extraordinary feeling."

"All the same, that's no excuse for the way some of these boys behave; there's that poor girl who came here in the kitchen only last Easter, going into hospital with a baby. And she's not sixteen."

"I can't be sorry for her if she's such an idiot."

"You're very hard, Nancy. How could that child look after herself?"

"They get warning enough. Joey tries to sleep with every girl he meets—it's routine. He doesn't mind if you say no—not unless you're rude."

"I wonder how you can have anything to do with such a person."

"Wasn't Grandy rather on the loose at that age?"

"I suppose that's your mother. Of course it's quite untrue. He was rather wild at one time, and he had difficulties, but he always kept his standards; he was even rather religious. You know what he thinks of your upbringing."

And Tabitha is not even aware that she is inventing this noble Bonser. Her mind is not concerned with the past, but with Nancy, who seems to her on the edge of a final disaster. She invents the past to instruct Nancy, to warn her, to make her ashamed, and also to express her contempt of the present.

In a week the bulge has broken, the French front has collapsed, and the British are in retreat. The old world has fallen in pieces, and people are walking about with an air not of consternation but of awakening. They say, "Did you see the latest? They're south of Paris!" and smile as if there was something comic in such startling news, or perhaps in their own unpreparedness. They are like sleepers roused to extraordinary possibilities; and when one asks, "What next?" another answers, "Oh, anything may happen—absolutely anything."

"I don't see what we've got to be surprised at," Nancy says, on one of her flying visits. "We simply shouted for it."

She has brought Parkin with her, who is at the moment fighting the war news with Bonser. She looks at them with a deeply thoughtful air, and says, "Look at the warriors impressing each other. All the same, Joey is good in the air."

And in the evening the couple dance together, slowly, intensely. Tabitha, looking through the glass door, as if from an ambush, sees the girl's face turn slowly past, on the man's shoulder, with an absorbed frown.

"People will tell me it's the war," Tabitha says to herself as she climbs to her sitting room, her retreat. "They'll say I'm an old fool to be disgusted. But it *is* disgusting, it's horrible."

And when Nancy, exhausted, with red eyes and puffy cheeks, comes to say good night before driving Parkin back to camp, she says to her, "You have no right to encourage that man; you're engaged to Godfrey."

"Does it matter at a time like this?"

"This is just the time when it does matter—at least we can keep faith."

"Godfrey knows I see Joey."

"Godfrey is too good to you. But you know very well it's a disgrace the way you treat him, and I won't have it going on here. If you must flirt with Mr. Parkin you will have to do it somewhere else."

Nancy disappears then for six weeks, but she writes now and then a card. "Here for two nights; awful billet. All love" or "No news from Godfrey. Joey has had a crash, but no harm done. The new commandant is an idiot. She sheds tears when the girls break leave." No address is given, but Tabitha says, "Just as well, for I wouldn't answer. She's not going to get round me this time."

113

ONE hot afternoon in June, when the swimming pool is full of cadets and their girls from Urrsley, there is news of Dunkirk, and before Tabitha has begun to grasp the fact that the British army is being carried across the Channel in tugs, yachts, she sees a tall thin officer gazing about him in the lounge.

"Godfrey! How delightful!"

"What a change, Mrs. Bonser; the old place is quite up-to-date."

"You'll stay?"

"I should love to. Any news of Nan?"

"I haven't seen her for weeks; she is behaving very badly to all her friends."

There is a pause. Tabitha feels the man's eye fixed upon her with that curious inquiry of the young to which she is growing accustomed.

"Did she tell you our engagement is broken off?"

"No. How disgraceful! It's all wrong."

The young man looks at her again, and after a pause answers that, of course, it has been a blow to him, but on the other hand he's sorry for Nancy. "I never knew her so upset."

"Then why did she do it? All because that odious little man likes to dance with her."

"Well, you see, she's fallen for him. It's what you may call a case."

"That's no excuse. No decent girl would be in love unless she wants to; and Nancy has no right." And seeing on the young man's long lean face, prematurely worn and old, a look of tolerant patience as with a foolish old lady, she exclaims, "Oh, I know you young people think that everything is allowed, that everyone ought to do what they like, but what is going to happen if there is no truth anywhere, if no one is faithful?"

"I think Nancy is faithful by nature; she's a very true kind of person."

"And she treats you like this."

"Oh, she told me all about it from the beginning."

The young man says these words as if they excused everything, and he refuses to pity himself. Gradually he lets it be known that Nancy would like to return to the Freemasons' and to bring Parkin with her.

"No, no; I won't. Don't ask it, or I shall be angry with you. You've been too weak with Nancy as it is. It's not right to let her behave so selfishly. How can you be surprised at all these wars when people behave like savages?"

Godfrey, like Nancy, accepts the old lady's prejudice with polite calm, and says no more of asking Nancy to the Freemasons'.

114

TABITHA has used the word "savages" with meaning, for the bombing of London has begun and refugees are pouring along the railways. Two families of refugees have been allotted to the Barn House. She has given them five rooms, between four women, two old men, and seven children. But they have brought in two more families, amounting to nine persons of all ages, and the whole twenty-two are in a continual tumult. The parents squabble all day; the children, wild and destructive as foxes or monkeys, rush about in droves, making war on all the world; yet at the least reproof, or even advice, the whole mass join together in a screaming attack upon the common enemy.

Indeed, they reject all Tabitha's arrangements, even for their comfort. Beds have been made up in four rooms and two attics for the small children, but they insist on dragging together blankets and mattresses into the two largest rooms with a communicating door, and here they sleep as in a camp of nomads, heaped together and always with a light burning as if the night were full of demons. They say, "We got to be together in case of bombs." And the destruction of the bedding dragged about the floors, trampled upon with muddy boots, is no more to them than to primitive savages the dirtying of grass or leaves gathered for a night's bivouac.

Like savages, too, they are strangely particular about food. They are full of taboos based on obscure fears. The women have never heard of porridge, and cannot make a pudding. They live chiefly, young and old, on white bread, strong tea, and tinned salmon. None of them can knit or even sew. A torn dress is mended with a safety pin, a hole in a child's stocking is left to devour the whole foot. Yet Tabitha's offer to mend is rejected with indignation, like an encroachment. Indeed, they direct toward Tabitha a special hatred and suspicion, perhaps because she is their benefactor, or more probably because she feels responsible for them, and her visits irritate their touchiness. They shriek at each other, meaning to be overheard, "Why can't she keep out; snooping around."

But Tabitha can't bear to see babies with sore noses and rickety legs. And if from fear she avoids her visits, her daily battles with the mothers, she is attacked by such shame that she cannot sleep. She feels that barbarism is advancing, and she herself is responsible.

The billeting officer, an old sapper long retired, Major Wakelin, is called in three times a week by one party or another to make a peace. He is a little wraith of a man whose huge white mustache seems to have drawn into itself all the richness that should have nourished his meager body and small dried-up countenance which quivers with nervous anxiety. He is so used to being run off his feet that his only pace is a trot. He trots now among the turmoil, squeaking, "Yes, yes, that's quite all right; a little misunderstanding. Yes, we're settling down very nicely here. It's a tribute."

And to Tabitha in parting, he cries, "Wonderful work, wonderful job you're doing here, Mrs. Bonser. Very difficult crowd here. You've got a slum lot. But they'll settle, they'll settle; just let 'em alone to settle themselves."

He praises Tabitha as the most devoted of his aides, but complains privately that it is just these devoted and public-spirited old ladies who are most difficult. The higher their standards of duty, the more trouble they make.

The railway platforms are crowded day and night with that residue of fugitives who, usually the most helpless, oppose all attempts at sorting them into billets. Some refuse to go into the country; they must be near shops. Others won't go anywhere unless they can be together, that is, in a group of twenty. This woman won't enter a car; and the other will not walk two hundred yards—she's used, she says, to a proper place with trams.

Tabitha explains that this is an emergency, when everyone has to adapt himself, and they glare at her with resentment, or grow abusive. "Oo are you to push us about?"

The little Wakelin runs between, rubbing his bony hands together in high satisfaction. "It's all right, everything's all right; we're getting along like a house on fire. And now, Mrs. Bonser, what about another party for the Corn Exchange?"

"The Corn Exchange?" Tabitha is indignant. "The Corn Exchange is a disgrace."

"Yes, yes, the Corn Exchange." Wakelin pretends not to hear. "Plenty of room now. That's all right, ma'am—" to a ferocious old woman who has opposed every effort to move her brood—"I quite agree, I'm with you, you want to be with your friends. Yes, thirty-seven persons in all. I've got just the place for you."

And half an hour later the thirty-seven persons are descended from a bus into the Corn Exchange, which is, to Tabitha's eyes, even worse than the railway platform. For though it has a roof and walls, these serve to keep in the smell; and the mass of people it contains camp upon the floor in the same squalor and promiscuity.

"Let 'em settle down, settle down," Wakelin says to Tabitha. "Get 'em fixed and they'll soon settle down." And he points out with glee how the old inhabitants of the Corn Exchange, that is, old in twenty-four hours, have already devised for themselves a scheme of things, primitive but workable. A rug gives privacy to some new-married couple; a bucket behind a chair is a common latrine; a chalk mark on the boards is the boundary between two private properties; there are boys on guard over family provisions, and even a local self-appointed magistrate who, amid cries of rage, still manages to take evidence and give a judgment. There are even standards of dress and decorum. Children can sit almost naked while their clothes are being dried or cleaned, but grown-ups cover themselves at least with a hand or turn their faces to the wall when they strip. Modesty exists still as in the African tribe, and begins again from the first instinct.

"Wonderful, wonderful how they shake down. Get 'em settled, and they'll start at once. It's a tribute, a tribute, Mrs. Bonser," and he rushes away.

But to Tabitha, Wakelin is a renegade who runs away from his duty. "He knows the Corn Exchange is a disgrace, but he thinks he can talk his way out of anything. He's just like all the rest of them." By them she means not only Hitler, Stalin, politicians generally, but all the modern world, and with redoubled indignation she goes back to fight with her own barbarians.

She is busy all day, for when she is not pursuing wild children, or disinfecting the corridors, she is at work in the four rooms still reserved for her own use. She has now no help but old Dorothy, and they use every spare moment to dust and to polish. They are, if anything, more particular than ever before: the linen is brighter in its sharp folds, the curtains more often washed, the furniture and silver more glittering; the very frames on the walls, light gold surrounding impressionist landscapes, seem to have a special weight and brilliance; the Turkey carpets in the parlor and dining room seem to glow with a special richness and depth, seem to declare, "We are good honest stuff from an honest age when people went to church, and even rulers respected the truth."

To Tabitha, the Barn House is like a fortress of civilization, of truth, of cleanness, of human dignity and faith among the rising flood of wickedness. She is like the captain of the last tower, who fights to the end, and her every glance is war-like. At sixty-eight she is shrunk to a very little old woman, thin and light as a famine child. Her white hair, still long and piled on the top of her head in the style of the old Empire, is too heavy for her small face beneath, full of surprising wrinkles, as if its fine white skin were tissue paper crumpled at random. In this whiteness the black eyes seem preternaturally large and bright, like those of some nervous lemur, just caught and caged; the mouth, with dark bluish lips, stands out sharply and shows by its quick and subtle changes the play of the woman's mood. Now it is compressed in anger; now it quivers with nervous resolution; now it is pursed in scorn; now it grows broad and soft in recollection. And behind every one of its emotions, of all the woman's activities, her exasperation, her defiance, is her wrath against her granddaughter. Nancy is present to her feelings even when she is lost to her mind, like the disease whose ache, because it is everlasting, is forgotten in the pressure of work, but whose existence, because it is chronic, prompts that very passion of energy.

When she beats up a pillow, half the vigor of her hand is indignant against this child. When she picks a crumb off the carpet, she thinks, "Nancy would let it lie; what does she care for keeping things nice?"

It is at night especially, when she can't escape into work, that she feels the pain of Nancy's worthlessness. When Bonser, indignant with her for lying awake, growls, "Still worrying about that little bitch? I told you long ago she'd come to a bad end, and that's that. So forget her," she feels at once a misery so deep, a sense of frustration so cruel that she can hardly breathe in case she shall weep, and at the same time an angry satisfaction. "Yes," she thinks, "yes, to a bad end. Nobody can behave like that and not be punished for it." And she has a vision of Nancy chastened, even more chastened than before, after her jilting by Scott, coming back, a prodigal returned, to the Barn House.

"Perhaps she won't be so contemptuous then of her old grandmother's ideas; perhaps she will find the need of God."

115

THEREFORE she is startled, but not surprised, when one day a note comes from Nancy at an address in Urrsley itself. "Could I possibly meet you somewhere without Grandy knowing? I'm afraid I'm in rather a jam."

Tabitha wrinkles her nose at the word "jam," but flies to the address given. She imagines Nancy deserted, broken, in debt.

"So you've written at last. I suppose that means you want something." And she looks round at the shabby lodging. It is in a back street not much above the level of a slum. Then she gazes keenly at Nancy for the signs of remorse.

The girl is in plain clothes, which are shabby and creased. She seems much older than her age, matured, heavy, at once coarsened in feature and bolder of eye. She has lost all charm of youth. But she is plump and rosy, her expression is cheerful, and the bold eyes look at Tabitha with an expression which seems to invite her to share a joke.

"What is it, Nancy? Has that man, too, thrown you over? You can't expect me to be surprised."

"Well, Granny, for one thing, I've been sacked—turned out of the service."

"What for?"

"Oh, the usual."

"What is the usual?"

"Well, look at me, darling; I'm four months gone."

"Gone." For the moment Tabitha is bewildered. Then she flames into rage. "Aren't you even ashamed?"

"I'm sorry, Granny. I can't pretend to feel very wicked, only rather silly."

"Do you even know who the father is?"

"Oh, Granny!" Nancy bursts out laughing. "You *do* have a low opinion of me."

"I haven't heard from you for nearly a year. Is it still Mr. Parkin?"

"Yes, it's poor Joey."

"Poor Joey?"

"Well, you see, it was me who undertook to make all safe because Joey rather hated to be bothered with the arrangements."

"Safe, safe!" Tabitha groans. "And does the man propose to marry you?"

"No, he's furious with me; he thinks I've let him down. He probably thinks I've done it on purpose to catch him. But don't worry about all that—it will work itself out, somehow. The only real problem is financial. You see, I can't go home because Mother would be even more upset than you are—she doesn't really approve even of matrimony; and I can't go to the Freemasons' because Grandy would have a fit. On the other hand, I'm absolutely broke."

"And can you blame your mother and your grandfather for having fits, as you elegantly express it? Are you surprised that they may feel badly treated?"

"I'm sorry, Granny; I know how awful all this seems to you. But things really have changed since you and Grandy were young. I mean you had to be more proper, hadn't you?"

This remark, though spoken in a placating tone, startles Tabitha with the idea that the girl knows something of her elopement, and is hinting at it. For a moment she is silenced with indignation; for she feels how mean, how unfair it would be to make such a reprisal upon her, as if the circumstances of her flight, as an innocent girl of high moral character, with Bonser, so handsome and seductive, so full of good sentiments, and this vulgar escapade, of pure egotism and sensuality, with the ugly and cynical Parkin, were to be judged in the same light.

"What do you mean?" she asks with a furious glance and trembling lips. "What about me and your grandfather?"

"Only that things have changed; that I can't feel so terribly wicked; that you mustn't be too upset."

And Tabitha, reassured, seeing that the girl is not attempting some impudent counterattack, takes a deep breath and says severely, "You mean that you'll be completely happy if only someone will pay for your board and lodging?"

"Well, Granny, if I can lie low somewhere, I won't be a nuisance to anybody—which I do rather hate. My idea is to have the baby without any fuss, somewhere in Wales, and afterwards, of course, I can set up as a war widow. Mrs. Something. One doesn't even need black nowadays."

Tabitha listens with horror and thinks, "But she has no moral feelings at all."

"And you don't think of marrying the poor child's father?"

"Marry Joey. It's an alarming idea—when you know Joey. But I suppose I would—yes, of course I would. I'd jump at him. You see, Granny—" and again Nancy's bold eyes seem to ask for the appreciation of a joke, a private female joke—"that's the real trouble: I'm so fearfully in love with the wretch."

Tabitha, frowning still at the girl, refusing to accept this joke, complains to the air, "In love! In love! As if that excused everything. What about Godfrey? What about your family? What about your work, your duty? But what's the good of talking to you? You simply laugh at me. You don't care twopence for the simplest rules of decency. I don't know why I don't walk out and leave you—no, I don't." This last crescendo is due to an appearance on Nancy's lips of a smile. But the girl, with unexpected tact, casts down her eyes and assumes a modest air.

"Don't pretend you care, because you don't," Tabitha ejaculates. But she is appeased by the attitude. It shows at least the primitive instinct of good manners.

"And where is this man?" she demands.

"Darling, what's the good? It's a dream. Even if Joey did sign on, in some fit of lunacy, he'd walk out in a week. And I really can't have him pestered. It will only make him hate me worse than ever. It's not his fault I'm like this; and you mustn't ask me to blackmail him. I really can't sink to that level."

"I'm very glad to hear you have a level."

And Nancy, suddenly breaking into laughter, kisses her warmly. "Darling Granny, how lovely to hear your insults again."

"That's all very well, if they did you any good. And now I suppose I'll have to pay for your lodgings and Mr. Parkin's baby. And as soon as you are up again you will run after more men."

Nancy surveys this possibility with the current detachment. Her expression is almost like Godfrey's when she says, "I don't feel like that, Granny; but, of course, I do seem to be an idiot about men."

Tabitha springs up as if pricked. "And so you're quite prepared for the streets. And when you're there, you'll say you couldn't help it. It is all because things are different."

Tabitha leaves ten pounds and goes away in a rage of energy. "It's incredible," she breathes. "I don't believe she's even sorry for herself." Tabitha's prodigal has somehow glided through her fingers and she feels the more anxious for a creature so elusive of penitence; she is the more determined to bring her into a steadying relationship with society. She goes at once to the squadron leader who has for six months past lived at the Freemasons', and before the next morning she has Parkin's address.

He is at a remote airdrome for interceptor fighters, in the south-east. But by that afternoon she is waiting for him in the anteroom of the mess. It is a bare hut of wood, just completed, and carpeted with new matting. Walls, floors, tables, curtains, all are new and skimpy, and have that look which belongs to all barracks, especially temporary barracks, of the barest utility. They seem to say, "All are conveniences for the use, the temporary use, of men under orders to go here and there, to fight, to risk their lives, to die; men so essentially homeless that homes are a curse and a danger to them." Tabitha, looking about her, feels the presence of that male idea of service life, which is an intense maleness, at once hateful to an old woman, the wife, the mother, and fascinating to the young girl.

Parkin has been sent for. He comes swaggering, with a look of impudence on his long crooked face, and greets Tabitha with nonchalance. "How do, Mrs. Bonser. You'll have tea?"

His manners have changed. He no longer bows or flourishes his hand. He is perhaps less excited by his uniform.

"I came about Nancy, Mr. Parkin."

"Nan? Oh yes." The young man strokes his mustache. "How is she?"

"You know very well how she is, and whose fault it is."

"Did she say it was mine?"

"No. She doesn't even know I've come to you, Mr. Parkin. What do you propose to do about this very serious matter?"

"I don't propose to do anything, Mrs. Bonser. You see, I don't accept responsibility."

"You can't get out of it like that." Tabitha's voice and hat shake with indignation.

"You think I ought to marry her?"

"Certainly you ought."

Parkin frowns and suddenly becomes eloquent. He points out that Nancy and he have never thought of marriage, and would probably make a failure of it. "I suppose you and Nan are betting on me getting outed, which is pretty likely, of course. But suppose it didn't work, Mrs. Bonser. And suppose the ruddy war does stop some time. Where are we then? I haven't a bean, neither has Nan, at least as far as I know; and married men don't get the first cut at the jobs, do they? I'm not thinking only of myself, you see. Even if I did marry Nan, she couldn't live on a wedding ring."

Tabitha looks keenly at the young man, who looks boldly at her and adds for full explanation, "It's the financial end that worries me."

"Mr. Parkin, if Nancy had money of her own would you marry her?"

"It would make a difference. At least we could split up again without me feeling that Nan was getting left."

"Split up again?"

"If the thing didn't work out. Yes, it's a proposition. I'll think it over."

Tabitha is about to explode, when she catches the young man's eye fixed upon her with a certain cool sharpness, at once cautious and aloof, which checks her. She thinks, "I must be careful, for Nancy's sake. These young people are so incalculable."

Nancy's view, indeed, when she hears of this transaction, is that "Joey has more sense than I expected."

"Do you have any respect for each other?" Tabitha asks in exasperation.

"I don't know about respect, but I admire Joey, he's a terrific person. He doesn't care for anybody or anything."

Tabitha has about five thousand pounds of her own—the remnant of the Gollan settlement, added to the accumulations of twenty years. She is able to settle three thousand upon Nancy; and for this amount Parkin agrees to be married. But he does so in a very cool manner; and at the wedding, in a registry office, behaves so carelessly that even Nancy is disturbed. Moreover, he has only twenty-four hours' leave, and returns directly to his unit from the door.

Tabitha exclaims that the man is a brute as well as a cad. But Nancy defends her husband from this criticism from another age, as Godfrey has defended her, and in almost the same words. "Joey hates being made to do things, and he never puts on an act. He's terribly honest."

116

WITH this practical judgment there is also a new sentiment. Apparently the wedding, even in a registry office, to Tabitha so cheap and mean, a mere legal preliminary to copulation, is for Nancy an important event. It is a marriage. It has given her a new name and changed her conscious being. She says, "Nan Parkin; it looks queer, doesn't it? My capital P's are wrong, somehow." She talks to strangers of "my husband" in a tone which strikes in Tabitha a nerve long forgotten, the nerve which makes women slightly hysterical at all weddings. She says, "Yes, my husband is a night pilot; I'm rather worried about him all the time." She wonders when and where she and Parkin will set up house together, and remarks, "Joey says he prefers the country, but I believe he'd be bored without his pubs, and Joey bored is rather alarming." She seems to have forgotten her intuition that if Parkin were made to marry her he would walk out. She writes to him every week, and when he does not answer says with resignation, "Joey was never much of a writer; he wasn't brought up to it." She calculates his leaves, and each time expects him, and when he does not come finds a new excuse. "It's the new blitz, I should think," or, "Pilots are always getting moved round."

Even reports that Parkin has been spending his leaves with an old flame called Phyllis do not seem to shake her confidence. She says only, "Joey can't be expected to cut all his girls just at once."

And she continues to live in her double room at the Barn House, a room which she has repainted, recurtained, and refurnished to her own taste. She is exceedingly busy, with the energy of a girl who never reads and seldom reflects, and this energy seizes upon any pretext. In the eighth month of her pregnancy she insists on digging in the garden (grow more food) and going to market by bus (save tires). When the baby is born, a son called John, or Jacky, she wants at once to bathe him, to dress him, to be active about him. She is highly indignant with the monthly nurse, who keeps her in bed. And Tabitha smiles at this impatience and says, "You mustn't be silly."

"But she needn't be so bossy."

"That's what all you girls think when you're having your first baby. You must be reasonable. All in good time."

Nancy, lawless as usual, slips out of bed; and after a week achieves her liberty. But it is liberty to govern her nursery, to devote herself to her baby. And in these tasks she is anxious and concentrated. The eternal mother has arisen in the flibbertigibbet, to bound and direct that sensuous force. All her views assume rapidly a new relation and coherence, of which the nursery is the magnetic center. She now complains of Parkin, when he does not write and does not even acknowledge a photograph of the child. "He might at least say he's heard of Jacky. He's really a bit too selfish." When she finds an excuse for him, it is, "But of course he does hate babies, especially small ones."

And when, after the first excitement of this important and absorbing role, she begins once more to be busy in the household, she enters upon the task with a new responsibility. Apparently the maternal form in Nancy, which is strongly marked in a new solidity of figure, has for her mind not only an inward turning coherence, but an outward polarity. She has now a new attitude to Tabitha and the housekeeping. As she rules with absolute power over her nursery and Jacky, so she displays a certain confident authority in the world that turns about that nursery. She demands regularity, efficiency; she is indignant when the water is not hot for John's bath, or the milk is not delivered in time. She is furious with some officer visitors who wake the baby one evening by blowing a horn in the road. She says of Bonser, who, in the last months, requiring more and more drink to keep up his military vigor, has several times been brought home very drunk and very quarrelsome, "Really, Granny, he's not fit to be out; he's giving us a bad name." And to Tabitha herself she is the managing daughter. She commands her to rest. "Now, Granny, don't worry about those accounts, hand them over." And she adds up columns of figures, getting the results never right, but, as she says, when Tabitha complains, "Quite near enough." Indeed, she values herself on her accountancy, because she can add up at speed, and get results that are near enough. Or she urges Tabitha into a chair. "Now, darling, remember what the doctor said about the old heart; no more stairs today. I'll go round for you." And she makes the round of the house, not dashing along in her old style, but with the dignified bustle of a matron, aware of her position.

Tabitha, delighted with the girl's new thoughtfulness and industry, is yet caused much new suffering by both. She hates being coddled, and she knows that Nancy's housework is more dashing than effective. She sits in agony hearing her rapid progress overhead, and at last springs up to pursue. And when she catches her it is with a frown; she holds up a dusty forefinger and exclaims, "Off your own mantelpiece. And do you ever look under a bed?"

To these reproaches Nancy only makes a face meaning, "I'm a busy young wife and mother and not an old fusspot in love with a lot of old tables and chairs. I've got a bigger idea of a woman's job."

But she is eager to exploit every part of this new job. She wants to knit, to make the baby's clothes, to sew. She throws contempt on the school that failed to teach her to sew or to cook. She abuses her mistresses—"A lot of old suffragettes."

"But I was a suffragette," Tabitha says; "and you've no right to despise suffragettes. Some of them were killed to get you the vote."

"You weren't a real suffragette," Nancy answers, for she has formed her own idea of suffragettes to suit her prejudice. And in her enthusiasm for this art, new to her, of a woman's life, for babies, sewing, cooking, she is eager to blacken the names of all those who decried it—her mother's generation. She says of them with scorn, "The oners! One vote, one hat, one kid, and all spoilt!" She herself is going to be the mother of what she calls "a proper family—at least six."

"I suppose," Tabitha says dryly, "Joey will have some views on that matter."

"Of course I'll have to keep them out of Joey's way, but that's only a question of method, a properly organized nursery."

117

TABITHA is always ready to disparage Parkin, for, according to Godfrey, his affair with Phyllis continues and he appears strongly attached to her. "It looks like a case," Godfrey says. The young man, who is still Nancy's devoted friend, plans with Tabitha to put off for the young wife a discovery for which she seems as yet unprepared. "Keep her away from town," Godfrey says, "when Joey's on leave; I'll give you warning."

But one week end Parkin brings his Phyllis to Urrsley. They stay at the Grand Hotel and make themselves conspicuous in the streets. Bonser has a report of them at once from his Urrsley gossips, and willing to hurt Nancy, whom he detests even more since she has become daughterly to Tabitha, tells her, "That precious husband of yours has got his girl at the Grand. I always said he was a four-letter man—no traditions."

Nancy, who does not hide her contempt for Bonser, makes no answer. But she slips away to Urrsley; and when she returns she is extremely frank about her reactions. "It really is a bit of a knock. Well, if you saw the girl! She's not even a peach, but just a great silly lump of blonde dough. I thought at least Joey had some taste."

She asks suddenly at breakfast, "Do you think Joey brought that creature to Urrsley just to teach me where I get off? Do you think he hates me?"

The problem gives her pain as well as surprise. It preoccupies her for a long time, and she refers to it often. "But he can't hate me all that much—what a lot of trouble!" Or she remarks, "Joey is rather a fiend, but he's not vindictive."

She is deeply thoughtful, and even absent-minded. She has, it appears, this question on her mind, where it causes as much disturbance as those parasites which in oysters exasperate the creatures to the slow composition of pearls.

"I don't see why he should actually hate me," Nancy suggests after a week's concentration, which extends even to her forehead, where two fine wrinkles show between her thickened brows, and to her voice, which scolds.

But at the end of a month she declares one day to Tabitha, during a peaceful evening when Bonser is away drinking with his Urrsley friends, "After all, I don't see why Joey shouldn't hate me; I'm his wife and I've given him a baby—two things that Joey loathes even more than being grounded." And she becomes once more busy and active. She has disposed of that irritant problem. She has made her pearl hard and smooth.

She is only a little impatient and severe. The wrinkles and the scolding voice do not quite vanish. Some bitterness of mind, like the rheumatism of an athlete, has been stored up by that effort of thought. She scolds Tabitha. She is at times so severe against the maids, young girls who are maids only because they are too young or too unreliable for the factory, that Tabitha has to intervene for them. "We mustn't be too particular in wartime."

But Nancy, thrusting out her large bosom, answers with severity, "I can put up with their slacking, Granny, but they're not going to bring their men in. That simply means the end of all discipline."

She seems to welcome new responsibilities. She has fought the dirt of the refugees with even more vigor than Tabitha, but when in 1944 they at last succeed in having themselves moved to town she misses them. She is delighted to welcome a visitor who has alarmed Tabitha—old Harry, driven out of a solitary lodging in an East Coast hotel by some secret military operation.

Harry, a widower for five years and retired for three, has preferred solitude to living with Timothy's young wife, whom he paints as a tyrant, at once mean and fussy, who allows neither peace nor even warmth to her household. And he laments his Clara, so devoted. Without her, in fact, he has been unable to carry on the practice, and scarcely to form any other relation with life. She has cut him off too long from any other society. He is at once perplexed and impatient, a shrunk old man, not much heavier than Tabitha. Nothing is left of his old energy and concentration but the gestures. Breakfast makes him impatient to go out, but in half an hour he returns from the gardens or the fields, tired and confused, as if he does not know why he went there. He sits for hours apparently in deep meditation, until a drop of rain on the window makes him jump and say, "It's raining," or the whisk of Tabitha's skirt rouses him, and he cries irritably, "Sit down, Tibby. Nan's quite right, you are a regular fidget. But you never could settle to anything from a child."

Tabitha means to him, as always, a shiftless person, whose irresponsibility may still be dangerous. His imagination, having run all its life into a deep tunnel which has come abruptly to a dead end with his work, has turned from the darkness ahead to the nearest light, which is at the other end of the tunnel. He gazes out on childhood and sees a troublesome insubordinate Tabitha. "You were a great anxiety to us all; and, by Jove, we were right! Running off with that blackguard!" And seeing Tabitha shake her head, he exclaims, "I don't care, that's what he was, a blackguard. To carry off a girl of eighteen, even if she was a bit headstrong. He ruined your life for you."

"But, Harry, my life hasn't been a failure."

"H'm. That wretched fellow with his magazine, and that old company promoter who went broke, and now this. It doesn't come to anything, does it?" Obviously he thinks of his own life as a model. He speaks with calm satisfaction of Timothy now in a large practice, and even of Timothy's wife, although she has refused him house room. "She's a good wife for a doctor. A good manager."

For him Nancy is the pillar of the Barn House. It is for her that he rises from his chair in the evening, and says, "Come, my dear, make yourself comfortable; you've had a hard day, and what would we do without you?"

Nancy accepts a comfortable chair, cushions, and her work basket. She is growing matronly even in her habits, and already she looks ten years older than her twenty-four. She knits and sews with the concentrated frown of one doing necessary work, and sometimes, turning a row, or rethreading a needle, speaks gravely to Tabitha of some important question like the state of the linen in the hotel, or the need of a new housemaid on the top floor.

The war news interrupts with a tale of hard fighting in Italy, a slow advance against strong positions.

There is a deep sense of peace, of security. The fire crackles and sparkles on bright fire irons. The old man smokes a cold pipe and gazes at the fire with wrinkled brows; he is drowsy with warmth, the flickering wrinkles are habitual like those of an old hound; he hears probably nothing. Tabitha, with her spectacles falling off her nose, knits with rhythmic speed. Nancy picks up her sewing again, says briskly, "So that's that!" and thrusts in her needles.

Tabitha feels her happiness like a presence, the emanation from all the house about, of which Nancy is the center. She thinks, "How lucky I have been; how wonderful that the girl should turn out so well after that bad beginning; that she should be content with this quiet life, and so affectionate. She has really a good heart; that has saved her." And because her mind is occupied as usual with Nancy, because she is always thinking of her, studying her, because, that is, of her absorbed tenderness for the girl, she frowns and catches her breath. "My dear child, you can't cut buttonholes with those enormous scissors."

"But I can't find my others."

"You lose everything; really, you are too feckless. I don't know what will happen to you."

And when it is bedtime, her voice is a challenge and reproach combined when she says, "You'll wait for prayers?" She is alert to prevent a defection.

Nancy smiles. "Oh yes." For now she consents to prayers. As a mature woman dealing with the old, she puts up with whims. She says, even, "I'm going to begin Jacky on a prayer. Mother would be horrified, but I think a bit of religion keeps kids out of mischief."

"That's not a reason."

"Why do you pray, Granny? What do you hope to get?"

But Tabitha, not having a ready answer to this surprising question, answers severely, "Because it is right."

Nancy, amused, goes to get the books. Her smile means obviously, "The old thing follows a routine."

In fact, Tabitha has never prayed with such intensity. But her prayer is not a request, it is a challenge, an affirmation. And when she leads the Lord's Prayer, and begins, "Our Father, which *art* in heaven, *Hallowed* be thy Name. Thy *kingdom* come. Thy will be *done*, in earth—" she looks over her spectacles at Nancy, and raises her voice in the manner of a lecturer, as if to say, "Listen to this, my girl, and take a lesson which you will need. Learn the truth before it is too late. You may forget God, but He won't forget you."

118

ONE morning Harry's exile is explained. His seaside town has been an invasion base. Europe is invaded, and it is suddenly perceived that Germany will be beaten. Peace descends upon Europe with the acceleration of a falling rocket, and with the same effect of disintegration. An enormous close-knit pattern of effort and idea, locking together nations, classes, the whole world in a significant relation of ally or enemy, sags apart, like a web when a gust of wind blows out its center. And millions who have longed for the war to end find themselves lost, disjointed.

Even Hitler's death brings confusion. Many refuse to believe it. It is held that such a demonic character is still capable of new tricks.

On Victory day bonfires are lit in Urrsley, students and factory girls dance round them hand in hand, but afterwards the young people are as preoccupied as the old. They are asking, "What next? What is going to happen to us?" This demobilization is not like the last, simply because the last, by fathers and mothers, by everyone over forty, is remembered. In the factories men say, "There may be a shortage, but so there was last time, and still they had a slump, unemployment." Those in war jobs want different jobs, and everyone is looking both in hope and fear for something unexpected, unpredictable.

The armies disband, not like schoolboys going for the holidays, but like refugees. The trains are full no longer of patient soldiers, being looked after by authority, but anxious and irritable young people hunting for work, homes, and obliged to look after themselves. And like refugees they are apt to panic. They seize on huts, cellars; they buy shops at enormous prices. Families that have split up rush together and find that they have grown apart and cannot understand each other; young couples that have cheerfully borne with each other in war lodgings are suddenly resolute to be free. There are ten thousand divorces in the courts. Louis is divorcing his wife after two years; Nancy suddenly perceives that she must divorce Parkin, who declares, by return of post, that he has had the same idea for the last fourteen months—ever since Jacky's birth.

"He would say that," Nancy exclaims, "just to be nasty. Thank goodness I can get rid of him. It's not fair to any child to have such a father."

Parkin, it seems, out of hospital after being shot down in North Africa, and released with a small pension, is hesitating between a business appointment and a university course. Meanwhile he is back with Phyllis in a London flat, and offers all necessary evidence for the divorce court.

But Tabitha, who has urged the divorce, regrets it as soon as it is arranged. For it increases in Nancy the restlessness which has suddenly loosened all war ties. She says, "How lovely to be free again; I can't imagine how I stood Joey so long." And she goes to a cocktail party in Urrsley, where she meets several old dancing partners.

But Nancy's unsettlement is only a detail in Tabitha's new weight of anxiety. She sees the Freemasons' ruined by high wages and high prices. She and Harry are tormented by a vague alarm, like animals at a threat of storm, a change of air pressure. Old Harry snaps at Tabitha, "Coal is up again. Why didn't you order a truck? But you never think." Tabitha does not know where to look for that special fate which, among the earthquakes of the settlement, will swallow her up or crush her. Bonser's extravagance is a standing worry. He is spending at the rate of a hundred pounds a week. But when one day he is picked up unconscious in Urrsley High Street, she is horrified by the idea that he will die.

As soon as Bonser has put off his uniform he has been perceived to be an old worn-out sot. His little court of temporary clerks at the

Grand Hotel is demobilized, and he falls back upon touts and harpies in the pubs. But even they will not listen to his war stories, stale twice over.

He is living with a woman called Irene, or Ireen Grapper, who, at nineteen, is already a known whore. She is very plain, with the face of a bird, a narrow flat body and crooked legs; and her make-up, with enormous magenta lips painted over the small tight mouth, her immense tower of coarse tow hair, standing up like a Ramillies wig, makes her bad features more striking. She has no taste, no imagination, a small greedy mind, the effrontery of a shoplifter. But with her special skill she quickly makes herself indispensable to the old lecher. And she commands him with the arrogance of that power. She takes his glass away from him and says, "You've had enough for tonight." She will cut him off in the middle of some long speech about the Potsdam meeting with the phrase, "Shut up, you old fool, you're gaga." And the man will answer only by grinning foolishly round the table, and wagging his head as if to say, "Ladies are privileged."

And she robs him openly. She will take out his pocketbook to pay a bill, and put it in her bag with the remark, "Here, I'll look after this."

One day she brings him actually to the door of the Barn House. But Nancy, fetched by Dorothy, interrupts him in the passage. "Excuse me, this is private."

Bonser begins to bluster, "This is my secretary, Miss Grapper."

"I'm afraid she can't come in just now; Granny is resting."

"What d'you mean, can't come in?" He pushes up to Nancy.

But Nancy makes herself broad. "I thought this was Granny's house."

And Miss Grapper seizes Bonser by the sleeve. "Oh, come away, you old cuckoo! What's the good of arguing?"

"You're quite right, my dear. I'm going, and they won't see me here again. You hear, Mrs. Parkin? I hope you're satisfied with your day's work. Why, do you know I could bust up the whole caboodle here? Where would you be then?"

"You're busting it up as it is, Grandy. Have you any idea what you're spending?"

Bonser now begins shouting that the money is his, isn't it? What business is it of any blank tart where and how he spends it? And even from the car, as Grapper drives him away, he thrusts out his great swollen face and bellows defiance.

But when a month later he is carried to hospital, his only demand is for Tabitha, and he welcomes her with excited joy. "Take me home, Pops; take me away from these bitches."

And at the Barn House, while Dorothy and Tabitha, like two intelligent ants grappling with some vast stupid helpless prey, struggle to undress him and put him to bed, he waves his arms and cries, "Keep her out; keep them off me."

What saves him from being a disgusting object, as usual without any help on his part, is the beautiful skin, smooth, soft, elastic, and pink, which encloses this mass of fat; a baby's skin, upon which no amount of debauchery has had any effect, which has survived to join his second childhood to his first, and seems to apologize even for his infantile terrors now, his silly deceits.

"Don't call me Dick; she might be listening. You don't know her. It was just a bit of luck they didn't let her into the hospital."

He has bolts put on the doors of the bedroom, and at the sound of a car stopping in the side road he will scream, "There they are! Keep 'em out!"

He is full of distrust. For him the world consists mostly of crooks trying to take advantage of him. He implores all his visitors to save him, sometimes by watching the door and sometimes by hiding him elsewhere. He clings to Godfrey Fraser's hand for an hour, begging to be taken away. "You're a gentleman; you're not on the grab. Get me away from here. I'll make it worth your while. I'm not broke yet."

And Godfrey soothes him, holding his hand and telling him that he's safe, till Tabitha can persuade him to take his sleeping draught.

Fraser has just been demobilized and is spending his first days at the Barn House until he can find a job. Nancy has given him a warm welcome, and spends long hours deep in serious talk with him. He is plainly still in love with her, but just when Tabitha is in hopes that this old affair, so suitable, so sensible, will be revived, she comes upon the girl in the arms of an excited bald major who has just arrived in a jeep.

And when, to remind the couple of her presence, she gives a loud cough, both, still holding hands, turn and smile upon her, as if to say, "What a joke they are, these old women."

"It's all right," Nancy says. "This is Pop-eye. Don't you remember Pop-eye? He's just back from Burma."

Almost every day some of Nancy's old friends pay a call. And all are full of anxiety, plans, a kind of nervous excitement. It is as though, conscious of a break-up, they value every old relation.

Tabitha is no sooner used to seeing Nancy arm in arm with the major when one morning she sees the girl rush across the gravel to embrace a tall brown-faced officer who has just screwed his way out of a very long low car.

"Granny, you remember Louis." Nancy drags the newcomer across the gravel to be presented. "Lu Scott, just out of a prison camp in Italy. I didn't even know he was alive."

Tabitha gives her hand to Scott, whose eyes, however, are fixed on Nancy. "It's go-good to see you again, Nan; you look w-wonderful."

In fact Nancy's eyes sparkle; her thick lips, half parted in delight at Louis' escape, have, since they express so candid a delight, the shape of beauty.

And all that day she is with Louis, talking of his plans. He is demobilized, and intends to start a plane-hire company with an engineer called MacHenry. After lunch, in the lounge, he describes their scheme. They've paid a deposit on a field next to Dunfield airdrome, and bought an option on two Dakotas coming over from France next week. "The g-great thing is, they s-say, to get s-started first, to build up goodwill."

Scott, in spite of his bronze and his look of the veteran, speaks with a dreamy thoughtfulness. His hesitation has grown even worse, and it seems to go with a hesitation in his mind. "We were wondering if you'd come in, Nan. But n-no."

Nancy, much surprised, says, "What, me? Investing in a plane company?"

And Tabitha interjects, "Nancy's money is settled on her; she can't gamble with it."

And Louis, not at all put out by Tabitha's opposition, murmurs, "Yes, I s-suppose it is a bit r-risky. What did you think of the B-brains Trust last night, Nan?"

"Me, Louis? I didn't listen. I've no time."

"That question about the e-go." Louis has been reading philosophy, psychology, and theology in his prison camp. His mind is bemused by vast dim notions. "Whether there is really a self?"

"I wouldn't know. But do tell me about the company."

Nancy pays an affectionate good-by to Louis and speaks of him tenderly. "Poor old boy, I'm sure he'll be cheated all round. I only hope this Scotsman has some idea of business."

119

THREE weeks later, when Tabitha has forgotten about Louis in other alarms, especially Godfrey, who proposes, with Nancy's warm approval, to join the Church and go as a missionary to Africa, Nancy comes in from a drive and is full of a visit to Dunfield.

"They've actually started. But you never saw such a mess! Three wooden huts in a field, and two planes tied together with string. And just to make things quite hopeless they've brought Joey in as a pilot; he's already smashed up one of the planes."

"Joey? Have you been seeing Joey?"

"Oh, Granny, for heaven's sake! As if I would dream of Joey. If you'd heard the way he spoke to me, and seen how he looked at me. I really think that crash affected his brain as well as his face—and that's bad enough."

"I never knew what you saw in that man."

"Neither do I. It was the war, I suppose. But poor Joey, he's going to have some shocks now. Do you know they hadn't even got a ledger; they weren't even making an allowance for depreciation." And during two more days the girl exclaims, out of some deep meditation, "Really, those boys! Throwing away their gratuities—it's pathetic!"

One morning Tabitha, as usual aware by the sixth sense of an anxious old woman of all Nancy's movements in the house, surprises her at the telephone. "No, no, Louis; you want at least three books. No, I can't come over; but any clerk can show you. Don't you realize that you may be losing money all the time?"

And she explains to Tabitha, "Louis wants me to go over and start their books. I told him I couldn't get away."

But two days later she goes to Dunfield, twenty-five miles by car, in half an hour, and returns the same evening. "Did you ever hear such cheek? They want me to go again every Saturday and do their books."

"You can't possibly agree to that."

"Of course not."

But, in fact, she goes every week, rushing to and fro with even louder complaints. "I've no patience with the idiots; they can't even get their buttons sewn on."

"And what about Phyllis: is she too busy?"

"Good heavens, Phyllis walked off on the first day. She's not the sort to cope." Nancy's tone, dividing women into copers and non-copers, expresses utter scorn for the latter.

There is a pause. Then Tabitha says, "You realize how dangerous it is to see Parkin. It might cost you everything: your divorce, your only chance of peace and happiness."

"You're telling me, Granny."

But she suddenly utters a deep sigh which makes her look, for the moment, haggard.

And the next week she does not come back from Dunfield. She telephones that she must stay the week end. "I simply must get them straight before Monday. It's quite respectable, as we're still stopping at the hotel; the huts aren't ready yet. Nothing's ready."

On the Monday morning a letter comes, asking if it is possible for her to invest some of her settlement fund in the company. "I don't want to risk much, but it really seems as if a few hundred might make all the difference."

This letter frightens Tabitha so much that she has a palpitation, a sudden pain in her breast. She says to herself, "You are a silly old woman frightened of shadows." Then in a fit of desperation she telephones to Dunfield that she will come to see the airdrome and to bring Nancy back with her. She sends for her car, and leaves at once.

She is directed to the Dunfield Hotel, which proves to be a converted golf club: a long wooden structure, whose cracked planks and paintless window frames remind one of the illustrations in Bret Harte. It is like a hotel in some new Wild West; and to add to this effect the long bare lounge is occupied chiefly by the bar, which passes within two yards of the main door. This bare echoing hall, with its scrubbed tables, and the bar itself are crowded with young men and girls, some in uniform, from camps, others in half uniform or full equipment on leave or in transit. All are moving restlessly about, and talking incessantly in a dozen accents. The noise of heavy nailed boots on the hollow floor, the shouts of greeting, are prodigious, and bewilder the old woman as she stands within the swinging doors.

Suddenly Parkin appears before her. For a moment she does not recognize him. She sees only a small thin man in a yellow polo jersey and blue denim trousers sharply creased. His big head seems out of proportion with the wizened body, the long face absurdly long. And one side of it is distorted out of human shape. It is darkened and seamed like the bark of a tree; the right eye, a small fragment of hard blue like a piece of bottle glass, trembles and wanders from point to point. On this ruined countenance the ginger mustache, neat as ever, the yellow hair oiled and brushed as if for a hairdresser's advertisement, seem out of place, like the gestures of a dandy on a battlefield. And the man has abandoned his smart manners. He does not even offer his hand to Tabitha, but ejaculates with disgust, "Come over to have a look at us? You won't see much. We haven't a plane to fly. No spare parts, not even tires. Government won't release 'em, though they've millions rotting in store."

Nancy, just behind, smiles at Tabitha as if to say, "Humor him, he's worried." She cries, "Come on, Granny, I'll get you a chair; we'll have lunch in a minute."

Tabitha finds herself compelled through the crowd milling about her. She is sat down next the bar, and a glass is put in her hand. "Sherry, Granny?"

"But, Nancy, are you quite mad?"

"Just a minute, darling." Nancy has gone and does not reappear.

Tabitha thinks, "She's avoiding me; she knows what fearful risks she's running. But that only shows how careful I must be. Above all, I must be nice to Parkin."

The crowd at the bar are leaning over her as she sits below the counter, though they pay no attention to this old woman, this foreign body which has been lodged amongst them. Louis' voice, somewhere from above her head, is murmuring that for his part he'd like to see a new government; "this one can't even an-swer letters."

A pale, thick-set man with very black hair and thick eyebrows, whom everyone calls Mac, declares that what the country wants is a change of government, but it won't get it. "In my opeenion the people will vote in the old gang, because they didn't lose the war."

The barman declares that the old government is no good because it hasn't used science.

"It's the psychology is all wrong," Louis suggests.

But a young major, with his shirt collar undone and no tie, remarks that psychology is bunk. What is wanted is a real philosophy of production. And this rouses up at once a vigorous argument by a dozen voices. It appears that most of the young men have been going to lectures, or reading pamphlets. They are full of large phrases and important names: Keynes, Marx, even Plato, Kant, and Einstein. Tabitha is thrust almost under the counter; a knee knocks her hand and spills half the sherry which she has not touched. She has forgotten it in her bewilderment, her sense of being not only pushed aside but of being shut out. She is surrounded by creatures of a world so restless and unsettled that no one seems even to have an address. One shouts to another, "Hullo, Bill, where are you for?" And the answer is, "Dunno. Waiting for orders."

"Got a bit of leaf?" another asks.

"No, I'm in a draft. India."

And a worn little man from some Eastern prison camp confesses, "Ah ain't been home for five years."

"What's home?"

"Ah'm not rightly sure; the old woman's been on the move a good bit."

All the time, below the volleys of greetings and inquiries, the discussion rolls like a ground bass. Words like planning, scientific management, which Tabitha has heard for a quarter of a century, are thrown to and fro with a new enthusiasm. She perceives that to these young men they are new, exciting. The barman's handle flies with a bang. "That's what we want, a plan. Winston was all right as a war minister, but he's got no policy. What we need is a bit of policy for a change."

And two girls in uniform, who have stood bewildered by the slogans of economics and psychology, pounce on the word.

"I should think we do want a change. All our girls are sick of this job. Why can't we go home?" They are full of resentment against the servitude which three or four years before has seemed like liberty. They want a change. Everybody wants a change. Parkin, whose voice has been heard throughout, dominating by its bitterness, shouts, "I should bloody well think so; and we've had enough of being pushed about. Englishmen won't stand for it. What's the good of the war if it leaves us all tied up? I tell you what: if this government does come in again and goes on mucking around, we won't have a single air line in Europe, nor a single airdrome fit for modern traffic." He pushes his way from the group.

Someone shouts, "Nan, Nan! Where's that Nan?" Tabitha suddenly finds Nancy's face close to her own.

"Poor Granny, you're quite lost. I got swept away; someone I hadn't seen for years."

She leads Tabitha to a table where Parkin and Louis are already seated. They do not get up because they do not notice her; they are arguing about communism, and Parkin receives Mac, who has now arrived, with an angry speech. "I tell you what your bloody Russia is: a lot of mugs bossed by a lot of thugs."

"I tell you why all you m-echanics are communists," Louis says. "It's because you think in terms of m-achinery."

But the engineer is not to be moved from his faith. He remarks in a lively pleased tone, "We've heard that beforre; it's only worrds. But I'm talking of a real process, the economic process." And it is obvious that he thinks of this process with pleasure as something other than words, something real, powerful, and easily grasped. "It's the process that makes us tick, Joey—the dialectic; and you can't argue with the dialectic. It just pooshes you over, like a tank."

120

SUDDENLY Parkin grows furious. "How long are we going to sit here? Where's the bloody card?"

Nancy runs for a menu. Her look as she hands it to Parkin is that of a tactful nurse or mother who does not allow herself to smile while she humors the child. She notices that Louis is fumbling for a pencil, and brings one from her bag. He wants to write down the name, given to him by the disheveled major, of a new guide to philosophy.

Louis, pencil in hand, has noticed Tabitha, and stares at her with dreamy amazement; but before he can speak to her, MacHenry is arguing once more with Parkin, and again the three men, ignoring the women, discuss planning, the coming election. Tabitha is eager for lunch to be over. She thinks, "The girl is drifting; it's all this restlessness." As the men get up, still talking, she turns to Nancy. "When will you be ready to go?"

Nancy looks confused. "Just one moment, Granny."

Parkin pushes between them to take his cigarettes from the table and struts away calling to Louis.

"How can you let him be so rude?" Tabitha's anger swells upon her like a wave of blood, a fit.

Nancy smiles at her. "Well, Granny, poor Joey's rather down the drain; we have to be a little diplomatic." And Tabitha thinks, "Her smile's quite different. I must be careful." But her anger carries her away. "Do you call that diplomatic, to make yourself so cheap?"

"Let me bring your coat."

She brings the coat, and Tabitha waits for her. "Are you ready? I must be back before your Uncle Harry's tea."

"I can't come just now"—with a slight darkening of color. "I phoned to ask you if you would bring Jacky over."

"Bring Jacky here? But it's impossible. No, I won't. I won't let you ruin yourself for a silly whim. Do you want to lose your divorce? Do you want that man back?"

"But, Granny, I am back. That's what I was going to say. Don't look so horrified. You see, poor Joey really does need—"

"Need, need! And what about your needs, and that poor baby's needs? How are you going to live? You know this company is hopeless."

Suddenly Parkin puts his head between them. "If you wouldn't mind minding your own business, Mrs. Bonser—"

But Tabitha now forgets all precaution. She is carried away by rage and despair. Her face becomes red and her voice shrill. "It is my business, Mr. Parkin. Nancy is my only granddaughter."

"She's my wife; you seem to forget that."

"And how did you treat her? How will you treat her? You're not fit to have a wife. You simply want to make use of her, rob her."

The man has taken her by the arm and is pushing her down the steps toward the car. Her very excitement makes her unable to resist; she loses her breath and can't speak.

Nancy, with a nervous supplicating glance, appears on her other side and helps her into the car. She murmurs apologies, encouragement. But Tabitha summons her strength for a last sally. "You wicked girl! It's wicked—to be so weak. And poor Jacky—but you shan't have him."

Then she falls, half fainting, among the cushions. Parkin shuts the door and his voice sounds outside the window. "Damned old hag. Don't you bring her here again or there'll be trouble."

As the car moves forward she seems to detect an answering voice, which is at once familiar and strange, like someone long remembered, in a new dress. It is murmuring an apology. And it recalls to her Nancy's bridal tones, full of that conciliation which, to an austere outsider, seems almost indecent, like a flaunting of honeymoon sheets, and also that maternal glance. It is, she feels sure, spoken through lips that only do not laugh because they must be tactful. And when Nancy comes next morning to fetch the boy and her heavy luggage, she can barely bring herself to speak to the girl.

Nancy, well aware of her unpopularity, has a humble and supplicating air. Her tones and looks are those of a little girl who has stolen jam, her very face and figure seem softer, rounder; she does not thrust herself out in front, but, on the contrary, leans modestly forward and turns up her eyes. She cries, "I know you're angry with me, Granny. Perhaps I am being silly."

Tabitha cuts her short. "You are being worse than silly, and you know it. All I say is: don't expect me to take that man in here when he's spent all your money as well as his own."

"Darling Granny, don't worry about us, we don't deserve it."

"No, you don't."

121

BONSER is full of consolation. "The silly slut," he says; "you're well rid of her. We only want ourselves, Pops; just you and me. Yes, we can trust each other." And he looks at Tabitha with a sly anxiety. As he gains strength he grows more suspicious. He refuses his medicine and tells Tabitha, "These doctors, running up a bill and keeping you sick. There's nothing wrong with me, Pops, and you know it. All I need is to get out of this hole and have a bit of fun."

Tabitha answers that he is not fit to be out. But at once he has a new suspicion. "I'm up to that spoof, Pops. I've got friends you see, friends outside. If anything happened to me they'd put the coroner on, pronto."

"No one's trying to poison you."

"And I haven't made my will yet, either. No, I'm not so green."

He weaves cunning on cunning. "Poor little Popsy. I know I've been a bit naughty these last six months, but it's because you were unkind to poor old Dick. You looked down your little nose at him, and he couldn't bear it. But she's going to be nice to the old boyo, and give him another little tot."

"Dick, do be reasonable. How could I let you kill yourself?"

"Popsy, you'll break my heart at last. But you always were cruel to me."

"Don't talk nonsense, Dick; you don't care a penny for what I say. Why do you want to go out? Is it whisky or Irene?"

"Irene, that bitch? My God, she was murdering me."

"You're quite right there."

"Of course I'm right, and so are you." He stretches out his big arm and pulls her down on the bed.

"Just two fingers, two and a half, and I'll be good, I'll go to sleep, and I won't say any more about going out tomorrow."

Tabitha sits still and angry in his grip. She thinks, "He's up to some trick," but suddenly she catches his eyes fixed upon her, from between the thickened lids, with a look of such naïve childish cunning that to her own surprise she begins to laugh. "Dick, you know it's no good; you've had enough."

And he also laughs. "Ah, the clever Popsy, you can't get round her; she's a little devil."

"You see, Dick darling, if only you'd have a little patience."

"Say it again, Pops," and he kisses her. "Pops, you make me cry." And in fact he is tearful; but at the same time his voice grows more cajoling. "There's only us left, Pops. And we've got to stick together, haven't we? Nobody else gives a damn for us. Look at Nancy. She's only waiting for us to die and leave her the dibs. Forget her, Pops; forget the whole rotten bunch of 'em. We've got each other, haven't we? We've got the dear old Barn, thanks to you; and where could we have a better home?"

Tabitha laughs at him. "And just now you wanted to get away from the dear old Barn." But she is softened with laughter, and she cannot quarrel with his lies. The very warmth of the big hand covering half her thin chest penetrates her with the kindness of the flesh. It remembers her happiness with the man. She says, "You always made a fool of me, Dick." But as he compliments, fondles her, she is moved by a feeling that expands as if by itself, as if old dry roots were swelling in the flesh that laughter has softened, quickened, with a pressure, with keen sudden pangs that cause her at last, do what she will, to burst into tears. She does not want to cry; she hates this pain of love which is so despicable, which has no grain of respect, but yet she rests her aching head against the man's chest. She sighs, "We were happy, Dick; you did make me happy, fearfully happy. I know I had no right, I behaved badly to everybody."

"Don't you believe it, Pops." He kisses her, and though she can't see his face she knows he is grinning with enormous self-satisfaction, the joy of the amorist, the conqueror, the beguiler, the salesman, the look she has seen on his face a thousand times while he has flirted with some woman. "Don't you believe a word of it, honey. You were a sweet little dear; and so you are now, every little bit of you. And you never did anyone any harm except when you made me mad for you, and that was nice, too. Nice, nice—very nice."

She goes to sleep in his arms, thinking, "I must be careful or he'll make a fool of me again."

And the next day, Thursday, when Bonser demands the car for that afternoon, she pleads with him and says, "Not today. I couldn't come with you today; and not to Urrsley."

"Saturday, then, that's a promise."

"Very well, we might have a little run on Saturday if you're really better."

"Oh, I'll be better, I'll be good." And he lies down contented.

Tabitha, seeing Dorothy on guard at the door, knowing that the garage is locked and the key in her own secretaire, goes for her daily inspection of the hotel. But when she is at the end of the furthest wing a maid comes running. "Please, mum, there's a car at the door, and the master's downstairs in his dressing gown."

Tabitha runs to the door, but the car is disappearing into the main road. And in the upper corridor Dorothy's chair is empty, the bedroom door is open, and Bonser's clothes have been taken from the chair.

Dorothy comes hobbling with a scared face. "Oh, mum, I was called to the phone. They said it was my nephew back from Germany; and then they couldn't find him—they kept on asking me to wait."

"Meanwhile the master's gone. Don't you see it was just a trick?"

"But I thought master wasn't going out till Saturday."

The old servant is bewildered. She begins long confused explanations. It appears suddenly that she, too, has her terrors. The grumbling devoted old woman is afraid of being thrown upon the world. For her, too, the Barn House is a refuge as well as a fortress.

But Tabitha, with a calm and resolute face, assures her, "It can't be helped; it's not your fault. He's gone, and that's all about it."

For it is specially important in such a crisis to preserve discipline and a proper demeanor in face of the enemy.

"Don't forget, Dorothy, that this is Friday; you've got all the Barn laundry."

"Good gracious, mum, so I have!" and she hurries back to duty.

There is no clue to Bonser's whereabouts, and old Harry is in terror of some final disaster. He wants to go to the police. Nancy comes one afternoon to support him. "We must find Grandy; these creatures will simply loot him."

Nancy is living in the huts, and her woman has left her. She is showing traces already of a hard life: she is untidy, her hair is greasy, her hands gray. And she is anxious about money. "Joey had a crash landing with our only good plane, and the hangar doors were damaged in that gale. I don't know how we're going to carry on."

Tabitha makes no comment on this expected news.

"I was hoping you might be able to make us an advance."

"My dear, the Barn House is all I have; and I think I'd better keep that clear of debt in case you and Jacky need a home."

"But we can't allow Grandy simply to throw away the Freemasons'. He ought to be shut up."

"What do you mean, shut up?"

"You know he's not fit to be about, Granny; he's mad. Our own doctor here would give a certificate. For his own sake. It would be quite easy; it's done every day."

"It might be easy for you," says Tabitha, "but I don't think he would like it; and I don't propose to put my husband into an asylum on any account." And speaking with that severe air of a shocked person who firmly changes a subject, she says, "That coat of yours is really a disgrace. You should at least have it cleaned."

"It's the only one I have, and there's no room to keep anything; you've no idea what a frightful pigsty we're living in."

"I've a very good idea."

The girl, having borrowed five pounds, goes away with an anxious preoccupied expression. It is obvious that she has relied on an inheritance. And Tabitha thinks, "Yes, my girl, you're beginning to find out that those who indulge themselves in every whim cannot expect to be spoilt. Life is hard and cruel; it has to be taken seriously." And she returns to her work in the hotel, watchful of the dust, battling with a careless expensive staff who have made so much money in the war that they hate the very idea of work, who have lived in billets and despise anything that aspires to more dignity.

122

Two days later Fraser is on the telephone. He has found Bonser, with the help of a young officer friend who has joined a detective agency, and who, he assures Tabitha, has acted with great discretion. But he gives a bad report. Bonser is at a Paddington lodging house of the worst class. He is described as very ill, very confused in mind, but quite determined to stay where he is. "I really think, Mrs. Bonser, it is pretty urgent to take him away at once and put him under proper care. The people who've got hold of him can't keep him if you get a doctor's order, that is a certificate, that he isn't responsible."

Tabitha perceives at once that there has been activity behind the scenes; she asks if that proposal came from Nancy. And the cautious voice answers, "Nan did telephone, but I haven't seen her; it was Scott who called. But Nan is very worried, of course."

And now Tabitha sees a regular conspiracy. Nancy, Fraser, Scott, the young detective, and no doubt half a dozen more, planning, rushing about in cars, making stealthy inquiries, closing in on Bonser at his hiding place. "And so she went to the police?"

"Not the police, Mrs. Bonser. It's all quite private. I don't think perhaps you realize how dangerous the situation is. The Colonel is being robbed, and he's obviously been set against his family, with the idea, I gather, of complete control. He might leave everything away from you."

"And how long has this plot been going on?"

"Plot, Mrs. Bonser?"

"I'm surprised at you, Godfrey, wanting to put the Colonel into an asylum; he was always very kind to you."

"But, Mrs. Bonser, for your own sake, as well as his."

"You're not thinking of him at all. You're only thinking of Nancy; and Nancy is thinking of herself—or at least of that husband of hers. What is the address?"

Fraser, in his resigned and precise voice, gives the address, and begins once more to explain himself. He is very sorry to seem unkind, but in view of the urgency of the case—

Tabitha hangs up with a decisive gesture, which expresses her wrath, not only to Fraser at the receiver's end, but against all these conspirators. As she hurries to catch the next train to town, it seems to her that she is flying to Bonser's rescue, not only from the young harpy Irene and the police, but from all the young, heartless, self-absorbed, eager only to thrust their elders out of the way, into a lunatic's cell or into the ground.

"And they really thought that they could put him away; and that I would agree to it, after fifty years. They thought they could do what they liked with my husband!"

And now, as she hurries from Paddington station through dirty streets, she is full of protective tenderness toward this victim of youth.

The lodging house proves to be a tall slice of dung-colored brick in a street like a sewer gully, but the knocker is bright, and there are bright yellow curtains at the windows. Tabitha's ring is answered, after long delay, by a woman with a singularly yellow face and a black silk dress much too tight for her. She peers at Tabitha with bird-like eyes, at once sharp, suspicious, and foolish, and mutters, "Colonel Bonser? Never heard of him!" And she begins to shut the door.

"I'm Mrs. Bonser, and I want to see him."

"I don't care who you are."

"I know he's here; and you can't keep me out."

The woman mutters furiously and holds the door. Then suddenly, as Tabitha glares at her and presses forward with her puny weight, gives ground and, chattering like a frightened parrot, retreats into the darkness of the back stairs. Probably she is intimidated merely by Tabitha's excitement, as dangerous and unpredictable in the old as in children. She shrieks back from the dark, "Third floor front, I suppose you mean. It's nothing to do with me." And the shriek dies away again into chattering, which seems to mean that the woman washes her hands of the whole affair.

And this scream has the effect of a whistle in some rabbit warren, or the sudden flash of a light among rubbish dumps; suddenly the place is rustling with life. Doors open; there are thumps as of feet dropped suddenly upon rickety floors; a startled voice from overhead calls out something; a frowsy girl in a wrapper striped like a bed tick stares from the landing and then slips into a room. The house is obviously a brothel of the cheaper sort. It recalls to Tabitha some of the places in which Bonser has lodged her, still too innocent to comprehend her surroundings, more than fifty years before. Then she has enjoyed the squalor as an adventure, but now she is revolted. She feels ill and faint. Evil has become terrifying to her as well as horrible.

On the third floor, three doors out of four stand ajar, and at each there is a watcher: one betrayed by half a pink face, another by a hand on the jamb, the third by a faint exclamation of surprise.

Tabitha turns to the fourth at the front, and goes in quickly without waiting for an answer. She is surprised by a room heavily furnished, in an old-fashioned style, with a chimney glass, a felt on the boards, thick rugs, an armchair in plush, and in the darkest corner a high mahogany bed. On the bed there is a great heap of tumbled clothes, from which at the head projects a dark purple lump.

"Dick?" Tabitha is asking a question.

There is a hissing noise from the lump; she goes to the bedside and peers into the face. It is almost unrecognizable: all the features seem to be softened, bulged, swollen with blood. The mouth hangs open and dribbles, the eyes are slits. But there is still a flash of life in their cunning brightness.

Tabitha utters a cry and takes the man's hand. "But, Dick, you know who I am?"

His hand closes on hers. "Tibby." He grins crookedly. "It's little old Pops. Thought herself so clever; lock the old man up, collect his dibs. But I gave you a surprise, Popsy, didn't I? I got away from Popsy. Worked it with Ireen—diddled the old devil with the young bitch!"

"You needn't have plotted against me, Dick; I didn't want to shut you away."

But he does not listen. He is full of his recent triumphs. "Ireen, too, silly bitch. Thought she'd go-t me. Thought I—too weak to go out by myself. But I got porter, gave him fi' pounds—help me lift, put me taxi. And here I am, at old Moll's. Good ole Moll. I knew she wouldn't tell—do what I want."

"If she gives you drink, Dick, she'll kill you."

Bonser is already growing drowsy again. His eyes fall together; he grins lazily. "Sly lil Pops, telling the tale."

"But, Dick, you really are very ill; you must have a doctor. Do let me go for a moment."

"No-o, you stop there." He takes a firmer grip. "You stop there where I can see you."

"I won't go away; I only want to telephone."

He shakes his head slowly to and fro and his eyes close. He seems to be asleep, his hand relaxes. After half an hour Tabitha, with the most cautious gradual movement, releases her fingers. Her hand is free when suddenly he grabs her by the wrist. His whole face is triumphant with joy. "Aha, thought you'd got away with it—clever Pops." He chokes with laughter and grows a terrifying color—dark as a bruised plum. "Ole Dick's not so easy—he's not so gre-en. D'you remember those bookies and the Watling Estate—what a game it was!"

And he wanders into a long history of old glories; tells again how he has cheated the world, and especially the crooks. "They thought—Dicky Bonser, he's a gentleman—fair game—honorable family—got to put up with anything. But they didn't think of this one—Dicky diddled 'em—as a gentleman—gelmanly—and didn't care a blast—for anybody—because you see—he *was* a gentleman—good family—" And as his eyes close again, he murmurs something about his imperial ancestors.

Ten minutes later he wakes up again with a cry, stares suspiciously at Tabitha, but seeing her still there takes a firmer grip and begins again his chant, "It's the breeding, the blood—never say die," until once more he dozes off and lies with an expression of peaceful confidence.

123

And so hours pass. Bonser wakes at the smallest movement on Tabitha's part; then, satisfied with her presence, talks, boasts, until he sleeps again. Tabitha, aching in her constrained position, looks about her, and counts the empty bottles which peep at her from every corner. A half-empty bottle of brandy stands on the bedside table with two dirty glasses, of which one is marked with purple lipstick. "The old woman downstairs drinks with him," Tabitha thinks. "He always hated to be alone; that made him kind to me sometimes—and now it has killed him." She has a confused sense of some tragic relation in fate; her tired brain proposes the word judgment. She pushes the brandy bottle across the table, out of Bonser's reach, and then she dozes.

And when she wakes, stiff in every joint, it is growing dark. Bonser is speaking to her with a lively, a refreshed voice. "The old Pops, here we are again. On the loose. Got away from old Harry and old Dorothy, from that damned old Barn. Have a drink, Pops, it's up to us to celebrate."

"But, Dick, I'm sure you've had enough for today. I'm sure the doctor would say that you've had enough."

"The doctor?" He seems to meditate. "You want a doctor?"

"We must have a doctor."

"Oh well, if you must—ring the bell—old Moll—she'll get your doctor." He lets go Tabitha's hand and she goes across the room and pulls at the old-fashioned bell rope. Suddenly she hears a crash, and sees Bonser with the brandy bottle at his lips. He has pulled the whole table against the bed so that the glasses have shot down upon the floor, and the bottle has nodded into his hand. She rushes to snatch it from him. But such is his delight at the trick he has played that he chokes, brandy runs from mouth and nose, while Tabitha slaps his back. And he crows, "Oh, Pops, you didn't think of that one; not so clever! Where's your hand? You stay put." He takes her hand again and then suddenly falls into a deep sleep, snoring and groaning.

There is whispering at the door which is cautiously opened. Tabitha sees the face of the woman on the stairs, flabby as a bladder full of liquid. "Did you ring the bell?"

Tabitha holds up her finger for caution, and murmurs that she must have a doctor as soon as possible. The flabby one answers with a surprising energy of indignation, "That's what I said; he shouldn't be here at all—the state he's in."

"Yes, if you would fetch a doctor."

The woman comes further into the room, pulling her wrapper about her with a gesture of a moral Roman. She wants to discuss this interesting situation. But suddenly Bonser starts up with a shout, and the female Cato, instantly dissolved into limp flesh and fluttering drapery, lumbers from the room.

"Who's that?" Bonser grasps Tabitha so hard that her bones crack. "I don't want doctor—don't you bring that crook here—worse than Ireen, worse than any of you. None of your tricks, Pops. Don't you try frighten me—I'm all right—getting better every day."

He glares into the air and breathes hard as if struggling against some enemy. "Better and better—it was the doctors—killing me—that damned old Barn—no fun—nothing, giving me the blues. You, Pops, it was you killing me."

"Dick, how can you say such a thing? You know that the drink—"

But Bonser wags his head. "Not so clever, Pops; I got away—you couldn't play me up—not ole Dick—" A convulsion takes him, his face and lips grow dark, his eyes stare with defiance. "I'm all right—not going to die yet—not by a long chalk—not for all the bloody crooks and bitches in the world." He rolls against Tabitha, almost thrusting her off her chair, his voice fades and wavers, but he grins with triumph. "Can't frighten me, Pops. I know all the tricks. I got away from you, got away from Gladys, got away from Ireen—" His song of triumph rises in a chant. "Got away every time—spoofed 'em, spoofed the whole—"

His great soft weight slumping against Tabitha forces itself through her arms and spreads on the floor. The corrupted body seems already to be dissolving. But the face twisted sideways and upwards against the bed leg still wears a grin; and the fat lips babble still the joyful refrain "Spoo-fed 'em—spoooofed 'em—the whole—" which sinks away into a murmur, like a child crooning itself to sleep. Before the doctor arrives he is dead.

Fortunately there is no need of an inquest. The Urrsley doctor can explain the case very well: dropsy, alcoholism, hobnailed liver and ruined kidneys, arteries like iron pipes and a worn-out heart. "The wonder is that the old rake has lived to seventy-six."

Tabitha is astonished by the obituaries in the Urrsley papers which draw the picture of a valuable citizen, a man of foresight and business ability, hospitable, generous, independent of judgment; they write of his war services, his devotion to duty.

Tabitha thinks, "Of course they never knew Dick, they hadn't an idea of the real Dick." But now, when her mind, revolving continually upon Bonser, opens up every day half-forgotten scenes and speeches, she is presented with such a mass of confused detail, such inconsistencies, that she loses herself in mere recollection. She remembers her honeymoon and laughs, then grits her teeth in pain. She wonders at the man's impudence; at the frankness which hid nothing but never told the truth; at the romance which the old liar created for himself as if by a natural faculty—like those little spiders which spin themselves a sail on which to float along the breeze—by which he was able, even in a squalid death, to draw himself out of despair and project himself into a happy illusion.

She remembers his robbery of some poor old widow in his Watling fraud, and says, "He was a wicked man; really capable of anything." But the very judgment throws her into the memory of some tenderness to herself, some charming piece of flattery devised to please her. She sees him again coming into her Urrsley flat, no doubt already bent on getting her money, and at once she thinks, "But where would I be if he had not come: an embittered old woman these last twenty-three years, a miserable useless old woman, and probably dead long ago. He brought me to life again; it was like a resurrection from the dead." And lost in this confusion of good and evil, as in a world, she gives up trying to form a judgment; she returns upon her loss, her solitude, and says to herself like thousands of widows, simply from the depth of their own feeling of loss, "The papers are right; there was something special about him."

For Bonser, that danger and burden, has also been the ground and the sky of her life. The loss of him seems to her, therefore, what the loss of a cover is to a book. What has appeared like a mere external addition, an expensive and heavy ornament, is suddenly perceived to be not only the chief support and protection of the whole, but the form of its existence. In fact, from this time, Tabitha begins to have a certain unsettlement in her looks and even in her dress, so neat before; that air of disorganization which leads people to say sometimes of an old person that he or she is "going to pieces." And this is due to her sense of having too much to think of, too many responsibilities in different places, and a boundless realm of decision; she must remember all and decide everything.

124

BONSER, moreover, has left his affairs not only confused, but obscure. He has burnt his only will, drawn up twenty years before, in Tabitha's favor, and told the lawyer of his intention to rescind it, but he has made no new one. Four women, including Irene Jonson, have letters promising large legacies, but no legacies have been made. There is a mortgage on the Freemasons', and an overdraft at the bank. The letter box is stuffed with bills not only from wine merchants, but drapers, dressmakers, and furriers, for clothes ordered by half a dozen different women. The bookmakers' claims, between them, amount to more than three thousand pounds. It appears doubtful if the estate is solvent.

Tabitha is not much surprised by this state of affairs, but she is shocked. She has the same feelings as any officer of a besieged garrison when the enemy finally blows up the gates and advances to the attack. Thus there is a certain wildness in her actions. All in a day she discharges the chauffeur, sends the cars to be sold, and orders the Beausite for sale. With a look of furious and concentrated resolution, but a hat slightly crooked and some wisps of hair escaping at the back, she hastens to the bank. She is not of course unaware that she is being noticed; she is even conscious that there is something wrong with her dress, but she is too agitated by more important impressions to trace this uneasiness to the hat, even to stop to look at herself in a shop window. And the passers-by, for their part, say to themselves, "Another poor old thing in a fluster about nothing," and pass over a distraction which in anyone younger would cause them to stop and stare, and even to feel alarm for public security.

Tabitha's purpose is to persuade the manager of the bank that if he will continue the overdraft she will make the Freemasons' pay. And she is thinking at the same moment of five other things, such as, "I must save the Freemasons' because when Nancy is ruined she will be dependent on me. Will Dorothy remember to turn off the gas stove? Was I right to advertise the Beausite for sale so soon? Why hasn't Nancy written? She didn't even come to the funeral. What is happening to her?"

The bank manager is always delighted to see Tabitha. Like many of those who, not being rich, deal in wealth, he is a philosopher, a reader, a man of culture, and some ten years ago he has discovered with some amazement that the tiny ugly old woman whom he knows as a hotel keeper is the very Mrs. Bonser of so many memoirs, the mistress of the *Bankside* circle, the dear friend of poets and artists so deep in literary history that scholars are paid to excavate them.

He has accosted her with reverent excitement. "I see, Mrs. Bonser, that there is a portrait of you in the new life of Boole."

"Of me?"

"After the drawing by Dobey; one of his finest, if I may say so."

"Oh yes, Dobey. Poor boy, he died. Excuse me, Mr. Bacon, but I'm rather rushed, and I wanted to know—" and she pulls out a notebook—"about the loan account."

It appears that she has never read Boole's life, or looked at Dobey's collected works. She does not even know of Griller's autobiography, the *Pullen Diary*, Hodsell's *Bankside Days*, or the recent *Glories of the Decadence*. She is apparently interested only in business, and the manager shakes his head once more at the injustice of life which herds discriminating and sensitive souls into country bank offices, and allots to a woman, so limited in imagination that she does not even recognize her luck, a central position in a famous epoch of English letters, the devotion of Boole, the happiness of knowing in the flesh that almost mythical genius, the fascinating Dobey.

He has not again spoken to Tabitha of her past, but he still has a special deference as he hastens to meet her at the door, and to hand her a chair. And as he reseats himself behind his desk, his eyes, fixed respectfully, regretfully, upon her, are observing not the dry cheeks, the feverish eye, the crooked hat and nervously twitching fingers of an agitated old woman, but trying to find therein some trace of the muse whom Boole has worshiped, whom Dobey has immortalized.

"I came about the overdraft, Mr. Bacon. You understand that things are rather difficult just now, until—"

"Oh, quite, Mrs. Bonser; you have all my sympathy."

"I'll probably have to draw on you for the next few weeks."

The manager lowers his eyes and gently strokes the paperweight, made from a shell case of the Kaiser war, in which he had been a young mortar gunner; and he explains with an equally delicate touch that the policy of the bank in the matter of overdrafts is under review until the political situation is a little more defined.

"In fact, Mrs. Bonser, till we see what the so surprising results of this election exactly portend."

Tabitha has forgotten the election, two days before. She has not even noticed the labor socialist victory and their great majority; and her confused expression is not lost on the observer. "Of course," he says, rather to console himself than her, "it is only a small percentage that have changed sides, and those are chiefly the young people."

"Yes, yes—" Tabitha catches at the word—"the young—they don't —they don't know—" She pauses with open lips, unable to decide among all the reasons which cause young people to be rash: cocksure, belligerent, and impatient of advice. The manager, after a short pause, politely continues, "And we must remember, Mrs. Bonser, that at least four million new voters have come on the register in the last six years; and, as you understand, in wartime young people are unsettled. They get away from home influence, they lose touch with balanced opinions." He lifts his paperweight, and one can see that it represents for him now an opinion which he is weighing, as a man of experience, for the benefit perhaps of his own children. "But there you are, Mrs. Bonser," and he plants the weight gently and carefully on the bare table as if storing on one side an article of value not needed at the moment. "It creates a difficulty; we don't quite know where we are. These schemes of nationalization may seem fantastic, but we must not, on that account, fail to realize that they may be tried. Mr. Attlee is, they say, a sensible man, but he is in a very difficult position. His majority includes some very wild and reckless elements; it is, I believe, the youngest house in history. We may be on the eve of great changes—very great changes."

Tabitha, her head still tingling from the manager's respectful farewell clasp, finds herself in the street. She thinks angrily, "I suppose he bows and scrapes like that because he doesn't mean to do anything," and she goes home with a still more resolute and feverish air. Her hat, now quite forgotten, flaps over her ear. "The election," she says. "But why, why should that matter? Everyone knows that everyone is mad."

She finds old Harry waiting anxiously, in great distress. "So that finishes it," he says. "I thought so. And, anyhow, how could you manage a hotel?"

He tries to console himself with this idea: that in any case a foolish spoilt creature like Tabitha could never have managed a hotel.

"Don't be absurd, Harry; of course I'll keep on the Freemasons'."

"My dear Tibby," he instructs her, "hotel keeping needs method and money. You can't go on without capital."

"We're going on, all the same. Why haven't you a fire?"

"I thought it wasn't so cold, we could save."

Tabitha rings the bell and orders old Dorothy to light the fire. It is a reaction like the defiance of the veteran who shakes his fist at cannonballs.

And when it appears, at the end of a week's cursory examination, that Bonser's debts have swallowed up the Freemasons', and that even the Barn House will be needed as security against the overdraft, she will not listen to the lawyer's advice, or look at the accounts. She declares that she will carry on; she will raise capital elsewhere.

But she takes no step to do so. She continues her daily routine, with a little more severity, a little more restlessness. She is wandering all day from room to room, in search of dust, or, more probably, merely to see once more those possessions which, because they threaten to disappear in bankruptcy, are seen with a new, a penetrating affection.

She runs from room to room; and hurrying upstairs brings on a heart pain which obliges her to sit on the first chair in the upper corridor.

And as, with hand at her heart, she feels the pain diminish by jerks which are like the retreat of some vicious creature, a weasel or polecat, driven backwards in angry leaps, her eyes gaze through the low window at Roger's new buildings, sparkling glass and bright concrete in the morning sun; she notices that the willows about the swimming pool are already higher than the roofs, and she feels a sense of triumph and desperation which seems to tear her apart.

Roger, whom she detested so much, has been killed in some air raid, but his buildings are now her pride. She can never forget the day when a polite young woman came to photograph them for the *Architectural Review*. A copy of the review, containing the photographs, lies on Tabitha's work table. She has learnt from it that her restaurant is remarkable for its clean lines, its classical dignity, combined with a total absence of pretension.

But the very delight in this masterpiece brings on anxiety that makes her forget pain. She springs up again. "What is that wretched lawyer doing? I must write and explain."

And at night she double bars the doors, bolts the windows, as if to keep enemies out—not only bankers, creditors, lawyers, bailiffs, but the whole world which has plotted against her faith and her creation.

She is veering toward that madness of the aged which causes some respectable old couples to lock themselves in from the world and take their food through the letter box until they die, and are found by a policeman, mummifying among heaps of old newspapers and furniture black with the flue of years.

125

SUDDENLY the whole position is changed. Dorothy, going through Bonser's old suits before giving them to the refugees' committee, finds a key with a numbered label. The key belongs to a safe deposit box held in London under the name of Bromley; and the box yields jewelry worth two thousand pounds, a bag of souvenirs, three gold watches, bundles of love letters from various women, and some pornographic toys. It holds also papers in the name of Bromley which prove that Bonser, under that name, has accounts in three different banks, amounting altogether to more than four thousand pounds. The whole is more than enough to pay all the personal debts and to leave Tabitha a few hundred clear. True, these few hundred are not enough to pay off the overdraft, but it turns out now that the bank during the five weeks since the election, by some mysterious process which has operated in spite of government speeches that seem to confirm the worst fears of universal state ownership and reckless economic experiment, has recovered its nerve. Probably it has simply become reconciled to a situation. It agrees to continue Tabitha's overdraft, so that she can maintain the Freemasons'.

The old woman is congratulated on all sides, but she appears less gratified by her escape than overwhelmed with new worries. She has ordered for both the Barn House and the hotel new fittings, repairs, upholstery, carpets; and complains all day of the burden of workmen, the cost of materials.

Only old Harry has the full benefit of renewed security and comfort. He praises. "It's really very cozy here, Tibby; old Dorothy looks after us very well. I don't know what we should do without Dorothy."

He grows sentimental about the past. "We had a happy childhood, Tibby. It was good in those days."

He shows his relief, his delight, in small pleasures, with that candor which is called childish because it forgets to be self-conscious. He twitters to himself, laughs suddenly at nothing, and coming to the fire in the evening rubs his bony rheumatic knees. "What a nice fire. Ah, you're lucky in Dorothy; you always were a lucky girl, you always fell on your feet."

He has forgotten Nancy with the rest of the last half century. His past breaks off behind him so that he drifts like a leaf, carried through the air by a breeze and lightened by casual rays of warmth.

And Tabitha is glad not to hear Nancy's name. Fraser, coming to lunch one day, has brought the news that the Dunfield company is moribund. "I'm glad to think Nan will still have the Barn House to fall back on." But Tabitha makes no answer. She is too exasperated against Nancy for sending no news, for not even coming to her grandfather's funeral. "If the girl can't show common good feeling why should I trouble about her? I'll hear soon enough when that ridiculous company is wound up."

This bitterness grows when the Barn House repairs are finished; for she has nothing else to occupy her mind. "Really, that girl is extraordinary. A Hottentot couldn't be more utterly irresponsible. What on earth can she be up to? What is really happening at Dunfield?"

The papers are full of the difficulties of returned soldiers. One has robbed a shop to pay his wife's war debts; another has committed suicide because his old employer is dead and his job no longer exists.

"But that man will never kill himself; he's too conceited. I mustn't have such bad thoughts. And Nancy will never admit that he's ruined her life. I suppose she voted for the socialists because *he* was against the government which wouldn't give him everything he wanted."

Every day she is more indignant with the ingratitude and folly of the girl. "If she won't write to me, I certainly won't write to her. I won't even *think* of her."

But she sleeps even worse than usual; and even her sleep is oppressed, full of apprehension, so that she wakes in a fright, and wonders if the house is on fire. She says to Dorothy bringing in her tea, "No letters, of course. Oh, those aren't letters. I don't call bills and circulars letters."

One morning, very early, she finds herself wide awake in the dark, crying aloud, "Don't, don't"; and it seems to her that some tragedy has happened, that Nancy is lost to her, and she will never see her again.

She gets up trembling, faint, and asks herself if she has been dreaming. She has seen nothing in her dream, but only felt the action, like something recorded in the nerves, and for a moment she cannot distinguish it from memory. Then she is angry with herself. "You are simply a foolish old woman, always afraid of something." But she cannot stay in bed. She is still in terror; no reasoning can drive it away.

She is afraid not because she is old but because she has suffered. She dresses hastily as for some urgent call, only to move about the room, from one chair to another, and then to the window, looking out impatiently at the slow dawn, in which the hedges and trees and her own yard buildings are still like shapes only half formed in some brooding imagination.

She would like to go out into the dark garden, but she fears to disturb Dorothy, sleeping overhead, or the hotel. She is held within her cage by the long habit of consideration for others' comfort, a deep sense of justice.

But at half-past six when Dorothy is sleepily creaking down the attic stairs, she is startled to find her mistress, dressed and impatient, waiting for her in the corridor. "I'll have my tea as soon as you can get it, Dorothy. I've a lot to do today." And she begins at once to elaborate tasks: counting silver and checking the linen. She argues with herself. "It was a nightmare, and nightmares don't happen." But at once she perceives from all her experience that nightmares do happen. It is with a sense of one still under the compulsion of a dream that late in the morning she finds herself at the telephone, calling up Dunfield Hotel. She is told that Mrs. Parkin is no longer at the hotel. She is living in the huts by the airdrome. Shall they send a message?

But Tabitha, having allowed her fear so much expression, is now in a panic. She dare not provoke news. She says that the matter is of no consequence. Half an hour later she is on the way to Dunfield in a hired car. And the driver, hearing his passenger mutter aloud, "Foolish, foolish old woman," says to himself, "Poor old ma, she's dotty as a dart board. Well, they ought to be dead."

Tabitha is directed from the hotel to a side road, where she finds, hanging askew among some rusty wire at the edge of a field, a sun-cracked signboard, reading "Dunfield Planes. European Service at All Hours."

Across the field there is a small hangar, a plane fuselage without the wings, and a long smart two-seater; close to the road, behind the ragged hedge, three huts among a choppy lake of mud mixed with cabbage stumps and dead bean stalks—the rubbish of the abandoned kitchen garden.

Tabitha thinks, "This can't be the place; it's deserted." But at once the very squalor and silence, the calmness of the pools in the broken path, appear horrible. She cries, "Stop, stop!" and gets out of the car before it has quite stopped, almost stumbling to her knees.

Her fear is now a certainty. She thinks, as she hurries along the path, trying even in her panic to avoid splashing her shoes, "I knew there would be some disaster. Yes, even when the Freemasons' was saved."

But suddenly the door of the right-hand hut is opened; a small boy in a dirty frock comes staggering out, and gazes with heavy wonder at the strange woman.

Tabitha turns abruptly to catch him up and kisses him. She is ready to cry with relief. At least the boy is safe. She says in a trembling voice which at once startles the child, "Jacky, don't you know me? But of course you don't!" and she laughs with an even more terrifying effect. The boy gives a loud cry of fright and indignation.

Nancy is heard calling out reproof, and she appears in the doorway of the hut, wiping her hands on a sack apron. The gesture is that of a char, suddenly called from the tub. The figure, presented to Tabitha's startled gaze, goes with it. She sees a short fat woman with a pug face shining and red with steam, and tousled hair, of which dark greasy wisps stick to her forehead.

Nancy gives a cry of surprise and hastens to embrace Tabitha. "Granny, how nice to see you. But what a day to come. I'm in a state. Why didn't you warn me?"

Tabitha goes into the hut and sees piles of dirty plates and saucepans, washing hung from the ceiling, and in the next compartment a table still covered with a crumpled cloth stained with tea and gravy.

"Isn't it perfectly beastly!" Nancy says, smiling at Tabitha's expression. "But, you know, we can't get help even if we could afford it."

"You've got fatter. You're not—"

"Yes, I'm afraid so. Poor Joey is furious; it seems I can't look at him without catching a baby."

"Didn't you think? How are you going to manage?"

"I don't know." The girl moves her thick shoulders, not in discouragement but resignation. "I don't suppose we can go on here much longer." She starts. "Good heavens, here's Joey; I thought he wasn't coming till lunchtime."

A small figure in rubber boots is seen toiling through the mud of the field. Its every movement, as it kicks its way, is full of exasperated bitterness.

Tabitha turns hastily to Nancy. "Are you happy?"

"Well, there's hardly time to worry."

"You said yourself he only wanted a servant."

"He's got a wife, poor Joey."

"Poor Joey, poor Joey!" Tabitha ejaculates in wrath. "Why is it always poor Joey?" But in spite of her indignation she sinks her voice as Parkin is heard outside, kicking the wall with his boots.

Nancy runs to drag off his boots. He walks into the kitchen in his socks, holed at the toes, stops short, and glares at Tabitha. She is startled by the man's thinness, the deep wrinkles in his long narrow face, and above all by this stare, at once furious and uncertain, the look of a fugitive in a strange country.

He ejaculates at last, "You, Mrs. Bonser? I didn't know I was to have the privilege."

Tabitha catches Nancy's eye beseeching her to be wise, infinitely forbearing, but Tabitha does not need to speak. She is frightened of something unexpected. She feels a danger.

She hastens to apologize, to lie. She had been passing that way, she explains, and she noticed the signboard of the company.

"The company!" Parkin sings out the word with a drawl of disgust. "A nice company—without a plane to fly. What have you done with my raincoat, Nan? Why can't you leave my things alone? That's all I ask, leave 'em alone."

Tabitha interposes quickly, "But I hear the government—"

"The government won't give us a screw or a bolt, and so we're turning away charters at a hundred pounds a week. But of course we're nobody. We only count four votes between us; we can rot for all the government cares. And as for hook-ups, we haven't the cash. It's not under the table, Nan; I can see that even with my game eye."

Nancy, who has been creeping under the table, emerges to poke into a corner. "Nor in the corner," Parkin says; and suddenly he kicks at a saucepan on the floor, sending it flying against the wall. Nancy turns her head from a cupboard. "My poor milk saucepan! Don't break the poor thing. Jacky was playing with it."

"What's it doing on the floor, then?" The man jerks his neck upwards with a nervous movement. "Why can't you put a single thing in its place?"

"There isn't a place, Joey."

"What are you laughing at?"

He takes a step toward the girl, and for an instant both women are afraid that he is going to strike her. Tabitha gives a faint exclamation. It catches his ears. He turns away from Nancy, glares at Tabitha, and says, "Excuse me, Mrs. Bonser, I don't like these domestic scenes any more than you do."

The two women are silent; Nancy, breathing hard, looks round with a desperate expression, as if praying for the coat to fall from the air. Lu Scott comes lounging in and says, "What about a spot of lunch, Nan?—if I could have it early. I've got to go to the village."

"Is that Joey's coat?"

The tall boy takes off the coat and looks at the collar. "Yes, so it is; but Joey left mine at the pub. I say, Joey, what about this letter from Central?"

The two men begin talking together about company affairs. Parkin's rage has vanished; his very expression has changed; only his shaking hand, as he lights his pipe, shows that he is under stress. Scott, having made his retort about the coat, is equally easy, aloof. They are tolerant of each other, or perhaps merely aware of each other's independent power of offense. Parkin is reckless, but Scott is big, obstinate, and aloof from common prudence. He is a gentle egotist, but a determined one.

Nancy and Tabitha lay the table for lunch; and when Tabitha asks where to find forks, plates, she whispers like a slave. But this is not from humility or fear, but simply from dread of a scene which will do irretrievable damage to feelings, to the family relationship, which surrounds and holds all their lives.

So far from being humble, Tabitha, while she tiptoes past the lordly and aloof masters of the house with glasses, and indicates to Nancy by a movement of the eyebrows that she has left the jug on the dresser, is full of angry scorn. She is like a trainer in a den of stupid beasts, ready to tear her at a sign, but contemptible in their very brutality. As her sleeve touches Nancy's round red arm, still wet from the tub, she glances at her to convey this private and scornful understanding, and receives that peculiar movement of the eye, upwards and sidelong, which is Nancy's wink.

But Tabitha doesn't find any humor in the situation. Nancy's cheerfulness irritates her. "These girls don't respect themselves or anything else, and so of course the men are brutes."

MacHenry has come in with the paper, and some news about the conference with Russia. The men sit down arguing, Parkin abusing the new government, Scott mildly suggesting that it is new and ignorant, that it needs rope.

"Yes, to hang itself."

And MacHenry, laughing in his triumph of the man with an answer to everything, says, "Trouble with you, Joey, you've got no pheelosophic background. Centralization requires what you call red tape."

"Too bloody red."

"All the s-ame, Joey, nationalization—" Scott gets up and looks vaguely round. Nancy puts his pipe in his hand and he lights it thoughtfully. The men, still talking, light up, and fall into armchairs. Nancy and Tabitha clear the table and retire into the scullery, which is a small lean-to shed at the back. But here they can talk about their own affairs.

"What is going to happen?" Tabitha asks. "What will you do?"

"Well, there is one hope—it's rather small, but Joey clings to it."

"Oh! What does Joey cling to?"

"Central Air Lines might take us over. I suspect they really want Mac, he's a genius with engines. In fact, a lot of people are after Mac. But he won't leave us, he's very loyal."

"Central. Will you go to London?"

"The office is in London, and they'd only take Joey for the office.

Of course he loathes the very idea, but if we're really bust he may have to come round."

"Doesn't Phyllis live in London?"

"I've thought of that; but there's a bigger snag than Phyllis. We'll have to put up some cash as well as our planes. And then we're to take on a flat, rather a nice flat near Kensington Gardens. But being nice, there's a pretty big premium. It all adds up to rather a lot."

"And what about your money—?"

Nancy moves her shoulders. "It's not enough—in fact, I don't seem to have much left." And suddenly, before Tabitha can say "So you've lost it as I warned you," she lifts her head from the sink and says, "But, Granny, you couldn't walk out on a man who's had such awful knocks."

And at these words the different points of a situation which have appeared by themselves merely separate exasperations fall together into a shape so large and dark that Tabitha, in seeing it rise and in feeling its shadow, can feel and see nothing else. There is a long silence, while Nancy continues to wash.

Tabitha dries; and from the door comes the sound of the men's political discussion, as remote as some noise in nature, perpetual and indifferent, like wind in trees or a stream among rocks. Both women, as they dry the plates, understand that their lives are at a crisis.

"How much does the company want?" Tabitha asks at last.

"Oh, too much—nine or ten thousand."

There is another pause. Tabitha gives a long sigh. "Nine thousand? But that's impossible."

The men rise with a scraping of chairs, and Parkin shouts, "Are you ready, Nancy? For God's sake get a move on."

"Oh Lord, I forgot we are going to town." She runs into the little cluttered bedroom to pull off her apron and stuff her untidy hair into a beret. Tabitha, seeing the girl's swollen figure, made hideous by the tight jean of overalls cut for a man, finds herself ready to cry. She says angrily, "But it's impossible—nine thousand pounds!"

"My coat, Granny, I must fly. Joey will have a fit."

She shakes Nancy into the man's coat, too tight in the sleeves, too long in the skirt; and as Parkin begins to swear, the girl hastily touches her cheek with daubed lips. "Thanks for coming, but you see how it is. I have to be frightfully tactful." She rushes out crying apologies.

Joey pokes in his head. "I'm shutting up here, Mrs. B."

Tabitha finds herself in the yard. Nancy, weighed down by Jacky, has gone off toward the hangar; Scott and Mac are already driving their smart two-seater across the muddy ridges to the road.

126

"NINE thousand pounds!" Tabitha says, bewildered. "But what did she mean? I haven't got half." She toils along the broken path toward her own hired car. "Nine thousand pounds! She might as well have said a million." She gets indignantly into the car and is driven away. Already she longs for the Barn House, its cleanness and order, above all, its peace, its security.

But two hours later, at the tea table with old Harry, chirruping over a toasted muffin, with her bright silver reflecting a scene of familiar possession as clean and polished as itself, she is oppressed by a fit of rage. "Nine thousand pounds! What is she thinking of? She's no right; and all because that wretched Joey Parkin is good for nothing."

Harry looks up in surprise. "What's that, Tibby?"

"Nothing. I didn't speak."

"And how was Nancy?"

"Quite as well as she deserves to be."

A fortnight later the party at Dunfield is surprised by another visit from the old lady. She appears suddenly one afternoon in a state of excitement, which leads Parkin to suggest that she is either drunk or mad, protests against the mud, asks two or three times why the planes can't fly, abuses Nancy for not resting every afternoon, rejects tea, and drives away again.

Parkin is enraged. "I won't have the old cat spying on me." And he curses Nancy for being untidy. "My God, you look like a dog's breakfast."

But Nancy is thoughtful. "She wasn't spying, she's worried."

"Let her worry and leave us alone."

"I dropped a hint about the money; I fancy it's working."

In fact, Tabitha is, as they say, distracted. What shall she do? There is no answer in prayer. She sits in church with wide eyes and wrinkled brow while a mass of images and impressions sport through her brain. She hears the preacher describe the moral confusion of the world as a consequence of materialism, and suddenly she wants to laugh and cry at once. She steps out into the churchyard only just in time, and there, sitting on a grave, she dabs her nose and admonishes herself. "What are you laughing at, you stupid old woman? You're hysterical."

As the door opens for the congregation to come out, she jumps up and darts toward home, with her nose in the air and an expression of great firmness and resolution.

But she has no firmness. In that sudden turmoil of feeling something has been broken and dissolved. She is cast loose; and now she is aware only of opposing forces, which drag her here and there. She perceives that she is attached to Nancy by sympathy more powerful than love. She is furious with that slapdash and sensual creature, but she is joined with her in a profound community of life. So that even as she rushes down the road, attempting, with her hat over one eye and a long coil of white hair bouncing on her coat collar, to make the world believe that she is a perfectly collected, respectable, and moral old lady, she is living Nancy's life. She is toiling with her, plotting to keep her Joey in a good temper, carrying her baby, worrying about bills, fighting for her marriage.

And when she escapes into the Barn House, it seems, for all the new embellishment that she has conferred upon it, like an old faithful servant, like Dorothy herself, to threaten her. The very chairs and tables seem to say, "You can't desert us; you have a duty to us."

Harry, even in his withdrawn reverie of old age, perceives her new restlessness. He complains, "What's wrong with you, Tibby? You can't sit still. You'll have another heart attack unless you're careful."

"I'm worried, Harry—it's about the Freemasons'. Suppose—"

"What—?" And all the old man's forebodings spring up. "I thought you'd have trouble. You never had a head for management." He mutters angrily to himself, "It's a pity I didn't take that room at Brighton."

"But, Harry, you couldn't live alone."

"Better that than Mrs. Timmy."

"Perhaps you could come with me," Tabitha murmurs.

"With you? Where?"

"If I had to move."

"Move? What on earth for? Can you never be satisfied?"

Tabitha says no more. She knows that what she has said is a yielding to force, to one of the forces that drag her apart. But by saying it she has given it form. It is an idea, no longer an impulse. And it stands up at once to do battle with her, to impose itself upon a confused and exhausted will.

127

THREE weeks later, when Nancy is within a month of her time, Urrsley is surprised to see the Barn House and the Freemasons', and almost all their contents, advertised for sale. But it is considered, after very little reflection, that this is what might have been expected. Mrs. Bonser is getting old. "Yes, there's been a change in the last few months. It's no wonder she wants to retire and have some peace for her last days."

At Dunfield, however, Tabitha appears in a new light—as a woman of business. She herself has bought a six-thousand-pound share in Central Air Lines, secured by trust, after her death, to Nancy; and Central Air Lines, on their part, have taken over the Dunfield Fly-Hire, with its three partners and two planes.

They are glad to secure MacHenry, and willing to employ Scott as pilot. Parkin is their difficulty, for he is neither a safe pilot, a good mechanic, nor a trained clerk; but they agree with Tabitha's lawyer to find him a place and pay him a salary.

Tabitha herself, having set these tremendous movements in action, is in the state of one attacked by a critical disease, who, having decided upon a major operation, lies half anaesthetized in the theater, while her mind revolves through terrors, despairs, vague hopes and sharp pains, back to the thought, "It had to be done," which seeks the resignation of one compelled by fate.

Everything at the Barn House cries to her, "Murderess, traitor." She cannot look at her garden any more than her chairs. She is humble before Dorothy, who, after a first unexpected explosion of wrath, declares that she has been badly used, that she has no place to lay her head, that she will go to the Union and die, and finds herself, to her own great surprise, head housemaid at the Grand Hotel at three times her former pay.

As for Harry, before whom Tabitha feels a guilt so deep that she can barely face him, he discovers, in his confused misery, the idea that Tabitha is ruined and needs consolation.

"Poor little Tib," he mutters. "You mustn't blame yourself; you weren't up to it. We can't change our natures." It is obvious that, in this new degeneration of mind, he can't live alone; and though Nancy has made it plain that she is anxious for Tabitha to lodge near her, neither she nor Parkin are prepared to welcome a bewildered old man of eighty.

But when Mrs. Timothy comes for him, he seems at once to recognize and accept his fate. He is obedient as a child. He is anxious not to offend in any way.

Mrs. Timothy is not the shrew that Tabitha has fancied. She is a harried young woman, thin and nervous, who bemoans to Tabitha the difficulty of running a doctor's house without maids. "And Timmy is so upset if a single call is missed." She is resigned to this bad luck of having old Harry, after all, thrown back upon her hands. "Of course we must have him; but goodness knows how we shall manage."

Brother and sister are weighed down by an equal guilt before Mrs.

Timothy. Under her patient and suffering eyes they say good-by. "You do understand, Harry," Tabitha implores the old man. And he, now little taller than she, gazes vaguely at the air and mutters, "Don't worry—your luck." He is probably trying to console her with the idea that luck will again save her, in spite of herself.

"I'll come and see you, Harry."

But he answers by a hasty shake of the head. "Mustn't be a nuisance. Mrs. Timmy, it's very hard for her."

He has to be lifted into the car; and Mrs. Timothy, in saying good-by to Tabitha, seems to draw more depression from his weakness. "He's feebler than I thought. He'll need a lot of waiting on." And again a voice seems to accuse Tabitha.

She can't bring herself to attend the sale. Her retreat from Urrsley is like the flight of a criminal from the screams of his victim, and when she arrives at the Dunfield Hotel she is so exhausted that she spends the first week in bed. The major operation is over, but the patient is still suffering from shock, from exhaustion in every vein and fiber.

128

YET when she is allowed up again she seems five years younger, brisker. She shops with precision and energy. Her smile to a tradesman's good morning is full of youthful zest.

And, indeed, Tabitha, though still light-headed, feels that lightness elsewhere in her soul, as if kindness has been renewed. An operation is like a death, but convalescence is a resurrection. The enormous effort of Tabitha's revolution has projected her into a new career, new responsibility. She fusses as Nancy comes close to her lying-in. Her fuss is the measure of her concern, her obsession, and makes Nancy laugh. "Heavens, Granny, I'm hideously well."

Confidence which, to Tabitha, seems foolish. For she has known too many rash young mothers who crippled themselves for life by some folly.

In fact the baby, a daughter, is born unexpectedly and too quickly, three weeks before its time, in the hotel, when Parkin has already moved to the flat in London. But Nancy is less troubled by the absence of a nurse and doctor, and the want of an anaesthetic which has allowed her to be torn, than Parkin's absence in London. "He'll be lonely."

"If he goes to Phyllis now, I hope you'll have nothing more to do with him." The emancipated Tabitha speaks with new force.

"Oh, but it wouldn't be just foulness, Granny. And it's not that

Joey is so much of a womanizer, either. I think he rather hates women, really. It's simply that he gets wild to forget himself for a minute and let off the pressure. He's so awfully steamed up."

"I never heard such nonsense; you've no right to find excuses for such conduct."

Parkin, calling in a smart new car, in a smart new suit, as he darts about the country on some business of Central Air Lines, forgets even to ask for his daughter. He gives Tabitha a careless wave, as one acknowledging a member of the mess; kisses Nancy and says, "Hullo! You look fatter than ever. Well, I've got to be off." Then he curses the government which has refused his new company a permit to enlarge its offices. "And it's no good writing; the bloody bureaucrats know when they've got you—they just laugh." And he makes gestures with his arms as if to break a cage. His look, his voice, is full of astonished rage. Parkin has been master of huge dominions of air, the king in every company, night fighter, surrounded by deference and gratitude. Now he is the same man, but the world treats him as a nobody, crowds him out of its way.

"I tell you what," he says. "Something's going to break soon; this bloody lot of Stalins are going to get a surprise!" and he struts away.

"Thank God they've given him a car," Nancy says. "He's always better when he can rush about."

But she is impatient to be in town; and when the doctor and Tabitha point out that getting up too soon may do her an injury, she answers, "If Joey gets up to mischief, that will be a worse injury; and he's always hated to be alone in a room."

She frets so much that, after a week, even the old-fashioned country doctor urges a surrender. And all the way to town in the car Nancy talks of her husband. "He's rather insane, of course, but that goes with Joey. No, I couldn't bear a dull man after Joey."

Her whole mind is concerned with this man, whom she has studied with such unexpected penetration, because he's the first subject which has engaged her imagination; to whom she is at once mother, nurse, wife, and mistress, judging without rancor, managing with humor, enjoying with a sensuality that takes a double delight to please the man with herself, and herself not only with him but with his pleasure.

The flat of four rooms has been neatly furnished and is surprisingly clean and tidy. It appears that Parkin has a military idea of decoration. The pictures hang in pairs; each chair has its ashtray on a weighted strap; a small Turkish table opposite the fireplace has an ashtray, cigarette box, and matches, neatly arranged on a polished surface. And Parkin's first deed, as he comes in and finds the two women, is not to greet Nancy but to flick some dust off this table and ask the two women to admire it. "That came from the Sultan's palace in Constantinople; ebony and mother-of-pearl. Absolutely unique. Look at the workmanship."

"It's lovely, Joey."

"It makes the carpets look pretty sick. Why can't we get a decent rug anywhere?"

Indeed, Parkin turns out, in this new setting, to be an attentive husband, or rather, householder. He has views on curtains, cushions, even flowers. And almost every day he brings home with him from the office ex-pilots, who are now at work in London, to be entertained, and, at the right moment, to admire the Sultan's table.

Nancy and Tabitha often cook supper for ten, and wash up afterwards. But on Tabitha's face, as well as Nancy's, when, exhausted, the women are still before the sink at midnight, there is the consciousness of success. The home is established; its mechanism works. Nancy, wiping a saucepan, sighs to Tabitha, "It's time I gave Sukey her feed—how those boys stay and stay."

"And talk! I never heard such talk."

"Well, I suppose they like it or they wouldn't come; and as for Joey, he loves a crowd."

She brings the baby into the kitchen, squats down, with her steam-damp hair falling round her shining face, and unbuttons her overall, so that her great breast springs out from it like a fruit miraculously bursting from its flower to maturity in one instant. And as she leans over the baby she says with a drawl compounded of weariness and the pleasure of the child's biting gums, "Oh Lordy, it's the politics and the cheerio business—how I should loathe to be a duchess."

"You wouldn't be a good one."

"I envied you upstairs."

Tabitha, polishing spoons as she sits with a watchful eye on the nursing, makes a face which means, "I was better employed"; and, "I wasn't wanted."

Voices are heard at the door, the handle rattles. Nancy gets up, still holding the baby to her breast, in the position of a young monkey who hangs to its mother crouching on a branch, and opens the door a few inches. A young man's voice says, "We wanted to help."

"No, Timmy, you can't come in; you're not wanted; you go on amusing yourselves."

"But, Nan," says another, "I'm quite a good washer-up."

"No, no, Bill. Run away, little boys."

The little boys, who are as old and older than Nancy, withdraw, protesting. She shuts the door and returns to her seat. "We don't want anyone, do we, Granny?" And with a prodigious yawn, "I've had enough of them for one day."

"Yes, indeed, quite enough."

Cars are still passing; a late bus, stopped at the lights, starts with a roar. There is a burst of laughter from the sitting room, and heavy boots thump downstairs. Someone, having made his most effective jape, is going to his lodging. But these sounds seem to give to the quietness of the kitchen a special quality, as if it hung remote and aloof from the world of anxiously caught buses and smoking room jokes. Nothing can be heard but the soft smacking of the child's lips, whose greediness has an arrogant sound.

"They're going at last; thank God for that!" Nancy says.

"One of mine." Tabitha fondly gazes at a spoon from West Street. "Silver; a good solid pattern. You can't get spoons like that nowadays."

"Joey and his table, it's pathetic."

"How much did the ridiculous thing cost—and has he paid?"

"It was worth it, whatever it cost; it's kept him happy for weeks. The real trouble is that there's its twin in Barker's window. I'm terrified he'll see it."

"He ought to be satisfied—he's been lucky enough."

There is another long pause. And then Nancy, with an unusual effort of reflection, asks, "Are men ever satisfied, except with themselves?"

"It's not only men; don't you ever think why we pray 'forgive us our trespasses'?"

"Do you know, Granny, Suke is really getting human features. She's going to be rather like Grandy."

"I hope she has his eyes."

"Go on, Sue. How maddening babies can be when they stop and look at you as if you were a leaky barrel."

"Yes, you let her suck too fast," Tabitha says severely. "You ought to get up her wind. Let me have her."

"Well, don't make her sick. Heavens, what a little pig—just a bag of milk."

The baby, propped on Tabitha's shoulder, wags its head, too heavy for its slender neck, and turns about its round blue eyes, staring into space with an expression of indignant wonder. Suddenly, without the smallest change of expression, it gives vent to an enormous belch, and the two women burst out laughing, as if they have enjoyed some private and joyous triumph.

"Oh, how rude," Nancy says. "I suppose she'd better have the other side now."

"Have you washed the nipple?"

"Oh, it's all right."

"All right! What are you thinking of?" Tabitha, shocked, red with indignation, goes to the basket for wool and boracic. "You really are incurable, Nancy; you don't deserve a baby. No, it's a serious matter."

"Well, don't be cross; I'm so sleepy."

And such a scene is repeated every night, so that Tabitha has never gone to bed so late or so tired, and yet so deeply content. She rests, as it were, upon the peace of Nancy's spirit; and lying awake, she thinks, "What a piece of luck that Parkin should be house proud—it's his only virtue; but what a good one in Nan's husband, when she is so careless, so slapdash."

129

SHE goes to bed late, but she must get up early. For it is her prized duty to shop; and that means to be out before the shops open. She stands in queues forty yards long, until her ankles swell over her shoes, and her heart flutters. But she has no time or mind to reflect on these warnings. She is full of the most anxious problems. Shall she stay in this queue for offals, needed for Parkin's supper, at the risk of missing, in the next street, stockings badly needed by Nancy, or hasten at once to the grocer's where it is said there are oranges available for children? She is in agony between the vision of Nancy's face when Parkin scowls at her thick legs and says, "More ladders? What a slut you are, Nancy!" and that of Jacky or Susan with rickety joints.

As the queue shuffles and sways, this tension of worry and exasperation breaks out of her in a protest, "Oh these queues."

"You've said it," a young woman beside her bursts out in rage; "and my kids locked up in the back room till I get home. But what's the government care?"

Exasperated voices break out on all sides, from the same tension of anxiety and impatience. "They don't have to queue."

"They don't care for women, a lot of men like that."

"Ah, and the government women are the worst."

A mild old gentleman in gold spectacles points out with a deprecating air that the government cannot help the shortages; but an angry voice shouts, "We've heard all that before."

And this phrase, uttered with bitter indignation, apparently has the force of a clinching argument. Half a dozen women eagerly take it up. "That's enough. Tell us another."

The old gentleman grows nervous, and hastily blows his nose. But he has attracted hatred and suspicion. A young woman cries, "I bet that's a government chap himself."

"Yes, a snooper. The government put 'em in the queues."

The old gentleman smiles feebly, then looks earnestly at the sky. This instinct is wise, because he is now in danger. The queue jostles him.

"Ought to have their necks wrung out."

"Dirty nark."

Luckily there is a sudden movement of the queue forwards, in which one woman especially, a battered old creature in a man's cap, quickly improves her position. There is a murmur from several objectors, when she thrusts out a prominent chin, and exclaims, "A lot of grabbers, that's what they are."

But she in her turn has raised up enemies for herself, who therefore support the government. A shrill voice asks, "And what about old Chamberlain that made the bloody war?"

"Or the one before that made the unemployed?"

Faced with the inadequacy of all governments, the queue is silent for a moment. But the tension is not relaxed; and as again there is a surge forward and the queue jumper makes another yard, voices break out again. "Look at 'er; she was behind me just now."

"What d'you expect when they don't have a proper queue—why isn't there a proper queue?"

"Ask the government."

And a dozen voices demand together, "Yes, why don't they do something about the queues? What are they paid for? Why can't they do their job?"

This is the note that sounds through all the bitterness, impatience, the demand for some new better arrangement, the most ancient and continuous demand of all humanity, aimed century after century at sun and moon, to magicians and spirits, to gods and kings; and now, since the government has taken over the responsibility of all these powers, at government alone, with concentrated intensity of desperation and anger.

The woman in the cap, having made her purchase, passes down the line, and all eyes are turned upon her. "There she is. I bet that's the last of the liver." To which she replies with a look which says plainly, "You can all go to hell. I've got my man's meat and ten minutes' start on the shopping"; a look of triumph mixed with desperation.

And Tabitha, having obtained kidneys, two pairs of stockings, instantly forgets her waiting and her indignation against queues. She has much more important things to think of; and they instantly possess her mind. "Will Nancy have remembered to order more bread? Has Jacky been allowed to escape into the street? Will Parkin come home in a good temper? Or has he had another quarrel with his directors?"

For Parkin abuses his new directors almost as much as the government—all governments in turn. Both Nancy and Tabitha live in terror that he will be sacked.

"I cross my thumbs," Nancy says, "when I think of Joey and the board. He does so hate brasshats; I suppose it's because he's not one himself. Today he's been asking for more pay and a new car."

And Tabitha lies awake, thinking, "Of course, that's what will happen. He'll lose his job—and what then? What will happen to us all?"

And she feels already all the disasters that can follow the loss of a job: new quarters, new inconvenience, new insecurity.

"But, whatever happens, I'm not going to have him treat Nancy as he treated her at Dunfield—never again. That was impossible." And the old woman sets her jaw for battle. "Never again."

But Parkin receives an increase of pay and triumphantly brings home a new carpet. He grows, week by week, more indignant with all ruling powers, but also more manageable in the house. He even compliments Nancy upon her cooking, "Supper tonight was almost eatable"; and he acknowledges Tabitha's services in bringing home a chicken in the words, "You ought to be in the black market, Mrs. Bee."

Tabitha has, in fact, by sheer energy of need, discovered the black market. For in the Parkin household a chicken, a few eggs are at once translated into the spiritual values of peace and goodwill.

She defeats a very dangerous mood, one evening, due to some rude exchange with a director, by a bottle of real olive oil. One morning, when Nancy has been bidden to the wedding of an air marshal's daughter, she cannot wait for the lift and reaches the third story with panting lungs and blue lips.

"Oh, I was so afraid you'd gone."

Nancy is running about in knickers and bare legs. "My dear Granny, it's not till twelve; I have a million things to do first."

"Look at these!"

"But, Granny, not nylons! Oh, not nylons! Where did you find them?"

"It was that little man in the parade."

"How absolutely marvelous. I'll put them on for the wedding—if I ever get there."

"Why shouldn't you get there? I'll look after Jacky and Sue."

"But of course you haven't heard the great news. Joey's resigned. He says he can't take any more. He's fed up. Fed up with the company and with the government. Fed up with everything in this country."

To Tabitha, in her exhausted state, these words are like a blow on the chest. She sits down slowly, carefully, and the room swims. She murmurs, "But, Nancy, what are you going to do now? Where will you go?"

"Joey's got a fancy for Canada. Heavens, look at that milk." She runs to the stove, where milk is boiling over. "Really, you'd think it just waited for you to turn your back. Milk has a jinx."

"But has he a job in Canada to go to?"

"Good heavens no; that's not like Joey. He only decided this morning, like that. All I've had is six words over the phone."

"Nancy, how can he, with you and the children?"

"It's a bit chancy, isn't it?"

And now, hearing the tone of this remark, looking at Nancy as she darts suddenly from stove to shelf, Tabitha sees that the girl is changed. She is tense; her voice has the tone of those who in wartime said to each other, "We can only die once." Her movements are quick, and perhaps a little dramatic. She exclaims a louder damn when she spills the milk.

"Canada." Tabitha is trying to imagine the journey to Canada. "That takes a week."

"And the wonderful thing is, Granny," Nancy's voice exults and also mocks at the exultation, "Joey really does want me with him—he's very much impressed by the news that you can't get servants in Canada. Joey's always missed his batman."

"Canada!"

"Yes, I'm not so sure—"

"It can't be decided like that—all in a minute."

"I meant about the place. I'm rather keen on New Zealand. They say it's good for children; and it's not really so far by air."

"By air! But, Nancy, you know I'm not allowed to fly."

This cry makes the girl flush. Parkin has already made it plain that Tabitha can't be one of the party. She is too old and ill; and, besides, she is an enemy. "Why should we put up with her?" he has said. "She always thought I was a tout. And she's such a damned old mummy, panting and fussing round as if we couldn't look after ourselves."

There is a short silence. Nancy gives Tabitha a stealthy glance full of pity, remorse, and alarm. She wants to avoid a scene. She has no time just then for scenes.

Tabitha's desolation slowly gathers moment. She mutters, "But I could be useful; I can still work."

And this crude utterance forces Nancy into the open. "I'm most frightfully sorry, Granny. We'd love to have you, but of course it's quite impossible at the start. We'll be so uncertain; we don't even know where we'll have to go, or if we'll have room for ourselves. We may be in some hut—" She pauses, looking for words to assuage the misery in front of her, words which don't exist. Both are glad when the bell rings. Tabitha, who is nearest the door, goes to open it, and a young man in air force uniform brushes past her. "Hullo, Nan. Aren't you dressed yet? I thought you were coming to the church." And Nancy's answer, which seems to make little of weddings, "Church! I doubt if I'll make the reception. Something's happened, Timmy."

And from that hour, till the day of departure, Tabitha does not see the old Nancy, intimate, frank. The girl is already far from her. She is preoccupied, and she never has time to explain the matter of preoccupation. She appears before breakfast, "For God's sake, Granny, take Sue a minute, I've got to rush round to—" and she vanishes for the rest of the morning.

She telephones from some unknown address, "Tell Joey I can't get the— No, tell him he'd better call me at Harvey's. It's about the— But I'll explain when he calls. Tell him it's frightfully urgent."

Even her affection is different. It is both more effusive and more guarded.

She is immensely grateful when Tabitha offers to pay for the journey to New Zealand, to give the young couple an allowance out of her investment in the air lines. But the very warmth of her thanks, rushing forward, is like a defensive action against some plea, some intimacy of grief.

Tabitha is still permitted to shop for the house, but she is no longer reliable. She forgets things, she misses her turn. One day she faints in a queue and is sent home in a taxi. The doctor is disturbed by her condition. He accuses her of doing too much. "Rest, rest, Mrs. Bonser. In some ways it's a good thing that the young people are going off. You'll be able to take it easy."

Tabitha does not even want to laugh at him. She is too tired to laugh.

130

It is the last morning. Parkin is strapping a suitcase. Nancy is answering a telephone call. Tabitha lies in an armchair. Her heart has been troublesome since that accident in the queue, and she is not allowed to go to the air station. She is listening to Nancy's voice. "Yes, it is sudden; but Joey couldn't stand being bottled up. . . . Yes, quite new to us both, but— No, not yet, but they say there are openings. . . . Oh yes, a terrific uprooting. . . . No, I'm absolutely terrified."

Tabitha hears the elation in the girl's voice as she glories to her unseen friend in the desperate act; and the word runs in her head like a passing bell. "New, new. Why should that make her so excited? Neither of them know what they are doing—they have simply got a vague idea that over there everything will be better because it is new. And I am to be left alone because of a whim in the head of a man like Joey, who never stops to think."

"Good-by, Mrs. Bonser; take care of yourself. No, don't get up." Parkin, with no expression on his ugly candid face but one of urgency, shakes Tabitha's hand. He picks up the baby from a chair, and he says to Nancy at the phone, "I'm taking Sue to the taxi; you've got about two minutes." He goes out. Nancy utters a cry like a parakeet. "No, no, I must. . . . Yes, Joey's waiting. . . . Heaven knows; probably years. Good-by, darling."

She lays down the receiver and turns to Tabitha. "Oh, these last words!" Tabitha has lifted herself by the arms of her chair. The two women look at each other and Nancy assumes a false bonhomie. But the look has already acknowledged the moment; it is one of those glances which admit, "We shall never meet again."

Nancy's face puckers, tears run down her cheeks; she smiles at Tabitha and says, "But I couldn't help it, Granny, could I? I couldn't say no."

What Tabitha hears still is the word "new" singing in the girl's voice. And she feels that Nancy's exhilaration is even increased by her grief of parting, as the joy of flight is sharpened by danger. She answers bitterly, "If only he really cared for you—it's such waste."

"Don't worry about me, Granny, I'm fearfully tough."

An angry shout comes from far down the stairs. Nancy jumps, an expression of alarm and amusement comes into her face, and she hastily kisses Tabitha. "Good-by, darling, darling Granny. I must fly or he'll have a fit. Joey's bad at traveling."

But Tabitha cannot say good-by. She hears Nancy rushing downstairs and calling with a gay voice, like an elder sister late for a party, "Coming—coming. Don't get too excited, everything's under control."

The old woman sinks down in her chair. She has a pain in her chest, and thinks, "I'm fainting; I must take that medicine."

But she does not reach out her hand to the table beside the chair; she has not the energy or the will. Living is not worth while any more, it is nonsense.

She does not faint; but gradually, in the course of a month, she becomes very ill. The doctor sends her back to hospital.

Meanwhile, there is no news of the Parkins. The nurse is apologetic when she reports that no cable has arrived. But Tabitha appears indifferent to the fact. "I didn't expect news at once; my granddaughter is very bad at sending news."

She is not merely apathetic, but she uses the apathy of her sickness as a barrier against useless suffering. She thinks, "Nancy is gone from me; she doesn't even think of me. Even if she did trouble to write, it would only be to ask for something. It would mean more worry, more pain."

She is surprised, resentful, when after three weeks of calm despair in the ward she is found well enough to get up. Apparently her body has a life of its own and has pursued its own private ambitions. It has used apathy to accumulate force. And now it is strong enough, in its turn, to act upon her mind.

For when, in the next week, on a fine afternoon, she is first allowed to go out, into Kensington Gardens, the warmth of the sun on her skin gives her a faint pleasure. She looks about her. She is close to the round pond. It is August. The grass is faded, the elms are dusty; there is dust even in the sky, whose blue is a powder blue, and on the water, where the toy boats, languidly flapping in the hot puffs of air, make bright marks like the touches of a polishing cloth on half-cleaned silver. Only the children, dressed in rompers, with burnt shoulders and peeling noses, are lively. They prance and yell at the boats, "Come on—come on!" They are furious; they leap with sudden hope, or, seized with despair, rush wildly round the cement path of the margin, shouting for some nurse or parent to bring a stick, somehow to make a wind.

Others, after long agony and only by some miracle, having recovered their precious boats, are, with anxious frowns, putting them out again. What is a boat for, if not to sail?

And some mysterious warmth rises in Tabitha to meet the warmth of the sun. It is like a sap, which diffuses through her nerves a sensitivity, so that they respond not only to the sun warmth, but to all the life about in its complex of feeling; to the middle-aged leaves, still strong under sentence of death; the parched grass; the flowers in the beds, watered that morning, but already running to seed and soon for the rubbish heap; the children in their absorbed animal existence, their passionate ambitions and fears, their brutal angers, only not dangerous because of their weakness; and she tries to protest, "No, no, I'm too old, too lonely." She is frightened by this agitation of sympathy. She turns to go home, seeking the peace of despair.

But right in her path there stands a small square girl, a child so square that Tabitha's eyes are instantly caught by the spectacles. She is very fair, and her hair, clipped round, makes square edges upon her projecting scarlet ears. Her body is square, her arms are square, her plump hands are square, her thick, absurdly short legs are two oblongs, her freckled eyebrowless face, with its insignificant nose and two large dirty tears hung mysteriously upon its square brick-red cheeks, is completely square, and she has in the middle of it a square hole, astonishingly large and square, for a mouth. And now from this hole issues a tremendous ear-splitting yell of misery and protest against the whole world, the very universe; a yell so powerful that it causes the child itself to reel sideways, in one block.

Tabitha is seized with laughter. She can't help laughing, an irresistible passion of laughter shakes her whole body, and at once a tearing pain shoots through to her heart. She thinks, "Stop—stop—it's killing me—I'm dying," and sinks breathless upon a seat.

She is protesting with all her might against this laughter, this life which has taken hold of her, which is threatening to kill her, but still she is full of laughter. Her very agony is amused at itself. She presses her hand to her heart as if to grasp that frightful pain in her fingers and squeeze it back, crush it out of existence. She is terrified that it will kill her, and never has she wished so ardently to live. Her whole being prays to be reprieved this once—for a month, a week, till that letter comes from Nancy.

And the prayer that is torn from her is not to the father or the son or the spirit. It is the primitive cry of the living soul to the master of life, the creator, the eternal. "Oh, God," her blue lips murmur, "not quite now."

Gradually the pain becomes less, the terror falls away before the longing, the prayer. She perceives that she is not going to die that afternoon. And as, cautiously straightening her back, she looks again at the sky, the trees, the noisy quarreling children, at a world remade, she gives a long deep sigh of gratitude, of happiness.